... an international forum for innovative research and applications

THE JOURNAL OF

Visualization AND Computer Animation

Editors

Nadia Magnenat Thalmann, *University of Geneva, Switzerland*
Daniel Thalmann, *Swiss Federal Institute of Technology, Switzerland*
E. Catmull, *Pixar, USA*
T. L. Kunii, *University of Tokyo, Japan*

Aims & Scope

Information conveyed graphically helps fix difficult concepts in the mind but animation is an important additional dimension enabling an understanding of data that is virtually impossible to obtain viewing still images. The advent of faster and cheaper machines has accelerated the growth of scientific visualization whereby scientists can turn mountains of numbers into movies and display measurements of physical variables in space and time.

The range of topics covered in the journal includes scenario-making right through to the post-production stage. The aim is not only to publish research papers on the technological developments (both hardware and software) that will make animation tools more accessible to end-users. It also seeks to publish material on new application areas for animation films, and will commission and encourage submissions of case studies to demonstrate to film-makers what techniques have previously been drawn on and their results. Critiques of films and book reviews will also appear in the journal.

ISSN 1049-8907   Published Quarterly

Further details and subscription information available from:

Dept AC, John Wiley & Sons Ltd, Baffins Lane, Chichester, West Sussex PO19 1UD, UK

Subscription Dept C, John Wiley & Sons Inc, 605 Third Avenue, New York, NY 10158, USA

New Trends in
Animation and Visualization

New Trends in Animation and Visualization

Edited by

Nadia Maganenat Thalmann
University of Geneva, Switzerland

and

Daniel Thalmann
Swiss Federal Institute of Technology, Switzerland

JOHN WILEY & SONS
Chichester · New York · Brisbane · Toronto · Singapore

Other Wiley Editorial Offices

John Wiley & Sons, Inc., 605 Third Avenue,
New York, NY 10158-0012, USA

Jacaranda Wiley Ltd, G.P.O. Box 859, Brisbane,
Queensland 4001, Australia

John Wiley & Sons (Canada) Ltd, 22 Worcester Road,
Rexdale, Ontario M9W 1L1, Canada

John Wiley & Sons (SEA) Pte Ltd, 37 Jalan Pemimpin 05-04,
Block B, Union Industrial Building, Singapore 2057

Library of Congress Cataloging-in-Publication Data:
New trends in animation and visualization / edited by Nadia Magnenat
  Thalmann, Daniel Thalmann.
       p. cm.
    Includes bibliographical references.
    ISBN 0 471 93020 2
    1. Computer animation. 2. Visualization. I. Magnenat Thalmann,
Nadia, 1946 – II. Thalmann, Daniel.
TR897.5.N49 1991
006.6—dc20   91-19182
                                                                CIP

A catalogue record for this book is available from the British Library

Printed in Great Britain by Courier International, East Kilbride,
Lanarkshire

Contents

7. Tool and Techniques for Scientific Visualization

Part 2.   Visualization Problems and Applications

8. Visualization Modeling: Making Visualization a Creative Discipline

11. A New Concept for Visual Analysis of Three Dimensional Tracks

Part 3. Rendering of Natural Phenomena

12. The Simulation of Natural Phenomena

13. Techniques for Rendering Filiform Objects

14. Fractals and Their Applications

Part 4.   Advances in Computer Animation

16. Techniques for Facial Animation

17. Techniques for Cloth Animation

18. Dynamic Simulation as a Tool for Three-dimensional Animation

D. Thalmann   257

Preface

This book contains a selection of research chapters on advanced computer graphics techniques in animation and visualization.

For the second consecutive year, a program on Scientific Visualization and Animation has been offered to postgraduate students at the Swiss Federal Institute of Technology in Lausanne.

This year, a few invited professors at the MIRAlab research group of the University of Geneva have also contributed to this program. The result of this collaboration has made it possible to put together various top contributions on scientific visualization and animation. The interest of these chapters presented here is to combine basic foundations of computer Graphics techniques with applications in all areas of visualization.

This book is divided into 4 main parts. Part 1 is dedicated to the foundations of Computer Graphics for Visualization and Animation, including the 2D and 3D aspects. Specific topics are filling and clipping of shapes, shape interrogation and hypermedia. For dynamic applications, latest research developments in object-oriented graphics, 3D hierarchy and virtual environments are emphasized. There is also an introduction to tools for Scientific Visualization.

Part 2 offers a wide view on the visualization problems and its applications. More specifically, chapters on visualization modelling, interactive scientific visualization and visualization in architecture and in high energy physics have been presented.

Part 3 deals with the rendering of natural phenomena. Difficult topics like fur, water and hair are discussed and applications using fractals are also introduced.

Finally, part 4 is devoted to advances in Computer Animation. This part deals mainly with the visualization and animation of human bodies. In particular, chapters are dedicated to human modelling, facial animation, cloth animation and dynamic simulation.

We would like to thank Professor Liebling and Professor Nicoud from the Swiss Federal Institute of Technology in Lausanne for their collaboration in the organization of the postgraduate course in Scientific Visualization. We express our gratitude to Gaynor Redvers-Mutton, Computer Science Editor at John Wiley, for her support.

Nadia Magnenat Thalmann
Daniel Thalmann

Part 1

Advanced Computer Graphics Techniques for Animation and Visualization

Part 7

1

Fill and Clip of Arbitrary Shapes

Roger D. Hersch
Laboratoire de Systèmes Périphériques, Ecole Polytechnique Fédérale de Lausanne

A didactic introduction to advanced fill and clip algorithms is presented. The algorithms are required to be able to fill arbitrary shapes given by spline and straight line segments. Processing complexity should be linear to the perimeter of the shape outlines and to the number of contour intersections, $n \cdot \log_2 n$ to the number of local minimas and square to the surface actually filled. The rasterization of the intersection between filled and clipped shape does not require any contour intersection computation. Original clip and fill contours are segmented along local minima and maxima (walls). At initialization time, an ordered list of active walls is associated to each local minimum. For shapes without contour intersections, the ordered list of active walls can be used directly to produce successive contour scanline intersections on each scanline and generate the horizontal spans representing the interior of the shape. For shapes with contour intersections, coherence is checked at each scanline. The detection of a non-increasing intersection location at a given scanline leads to the reinsertion of the corresponding wall into the current list of ordered walls. Results show that the overhead for construction, maintenance and access to the sorted data structure is important for small and simple shapes. It becomes relatively small for complex and large shapes.

1.1. Introduction

Filling of clipped shapes is a necessary operation for software emulating the overlay approach dominant in traditional graphic arts. This software emulation approach was initially described by Warnock (1982) and became dominant with the widespread use of the PostScript language (Adobe 1985).

Many filling and clipping algorithms are known (Rogers 1985). None of the standard filling algorithms suits the needs of a general-purpose efficient winding-number fill and clip algorithm. Recently, an algorithm (Wallis 1990) has been published which comes closer to the needs of Fill and Clip. However, it requires a large x-transition table and the sorting of contour scanline intersections on each scanline.

There is a need for an efficient and robust general-purpose fill and clip algorithm working in raster memory. Applications generating output for PostScript compatible devices need to show the result of graphic operations interactively. Window managers are required to clip text and graphics to the exposed part of a window which may become quite complex if non-rectangular windows are to be supported, as is the case on the NEWS windowing system for Sun Workstations (Gosling et al. 1989). Furthermore, high-resolution output devices (color and film plotters) require the development of new effective graphic algorithms capable of working with data distributed on networks of parallel processors.

The algorithms described in this chapter are based on previous work and experience (Hersch 1986,1988,1990). They fulfil the following requirements.

(1) The fill and clip shapes are arbitrary complex shapes given for example by Bezier splines and straight line segments having any number of contour intersections and self-intersections.

(2) Algorithm execution time is linear to the perimeter of the filling and clipping shapes, linear to the number of filling and clipping contour intersections, $n \cdot \log_2 n$ to the number of local minimas and square to the surface of intersection between filling and clipping shapes

(3) Filling any partition of the original shape separately generates discrete partitions which can be assembled to form exactly the same discrete shape as the one that would have been generated by filling the original continuous shape (partitioning criterion).

These requirements are essential for a general-purpose filling algorithm. Shape complexity (1) shall only be limited by available memory space. By requiring execution time to be linear (2) to the number of shape-scanline intersections, one ensures acceptable filling performances for complex shapes. The last requirement (3) is essential for the manipulation of continuous shapes. Segmenting continuous shapes into pieces and filling each one separately shall have no effect on the resulting discrete shape. This also implies that continuous shapes of arbitrary small dimensions may be filled in exactly the same way as large shapes. The vertical scan-conversion and filling algorithms developed in (Hersch 1988) ensure the correct filling of segmented shapes (Figure 1.1).

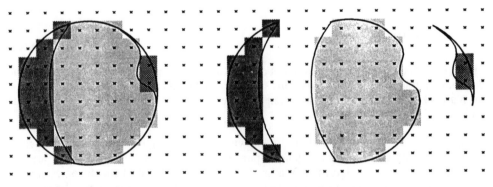

a) boundaries of continuous shape
   and corresponding discrete shape

b) segmented shape and
   separately filled shape parts

Figure 1.1. Filling segmented original shape

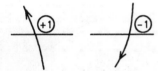

a) Intersection with ;   Intersection with ;
   positive contour part: negative contour part:
   increment   decrement
   winding number   winding number

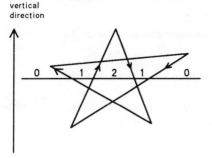

b) Winding numbers associated to
   the straight line segments

Non-zero winding number rule : consider a horizontal straight line intersecting an arbitrary shape given by oriented boundaries.

Start at the left–hand infinity of the straight line and mark the corresponding segment bounded by the first intersection with the winding number zero.

The winding number of the next line segment to the right will be the winding–number of the preceding segment incremented or decremented by one, depending whether the shape contour line intersecting the straight line has a positive or a negative vertical direction.

By repeating this procedure, every horizontal line segment will have a winding–number attached to it. All segments with non–zero winding numbers are interior segments.

Figure 1.2. The non-zero winding number rule

Like other algorithms of this kind, the definition of interior and exterior shape parts of the filling and clipping shapes must conform to the non-zero winding number rule (Newell and Sequin 1980) (Figure 1.2).

For didactic purposes, a parity interior fill algorithm based on contour tracking will first be presented in Section 1.2. This algorithm is then extended to winding number fill in Section 1.3. Finally, winding number fill and clip is introduced as a further extension of the two previous algorithms.

1.2. Parity Interior Fill

In this section, we consider the problem of filling a simple shape given by a single contour without self-intersections. Parity fill incorporates elements of the well known flag fill algorithm (Ackland and Weste 1981) and of descriptive contour fill (Hersch 1986).

Each filling algorithm implies a paradigm defining the nature of the discrete representation of a continuous shape. From this paradigm, one can ascertain whether a pixel is an interior pixel or not. Generally, a pixel coverage higher than 50% is required for interior pixels. In order to fulfil the partitioning criterion, it should be possible to create the same discrete shapes either by parity interior fill or by the complement of exterior fill (Figure 1.3).

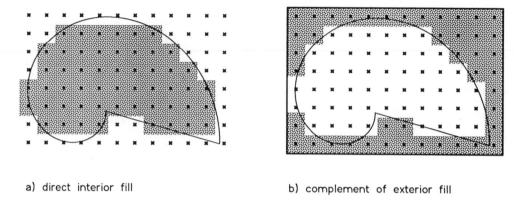

a) direct interior fill   b) complement of exterior fill

Figure 1.3. Discrete shapes generated by interior fill and exterior fill

The following filling paradigm removes any ambiguity and produces the same shapes independently whether interior fill or complemented exterior fill are used.

Basic filling paradigm (interior fill):

The set of discrete pixels representing a closed continuous shape contains all pixels whose pixel centers lie within the shape boundary.

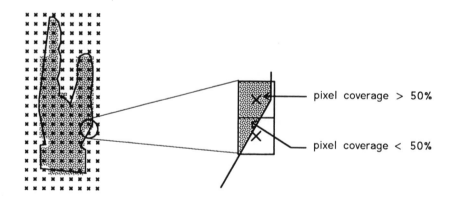

Figure 1.4. Interior of a filled shape

Consequently, exterior pixels are those pixels whose pixel centers lie outside the continuous shape boundary. The filling paradigm is derived from the fact that shape boundaries are relatively smooth. The shape boundary part which intersects a pixel can generally be approximated by a straight line segment. Therefore pixels selected as interior pixels have a surface coverage of more than 50% (Figure 1.4).

Each filled shape is composed of discrete horizontal spans bounded by a left and right continuous contour boundary. The interior span's starting pixel lies immediatelely to the right of the left continuous contour boundary. The interior span is followed by an exterior span whose starting pixel lies immediately to the right of the right continuous contour boundary. The last pixel of the interior span is the pixel immediately preceeding the starting pixel of the exterior span (Figure 1.5). Starting pixels have their centers to the right of contour–scanline intersections.

The set of all starting pixels (or flags) is sufficient to fill simple, non-intersecting shapes. This set can be obtained directly from the set of all scanline–contour intersections.

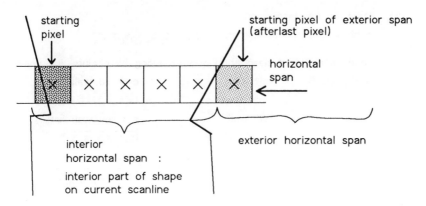

Figure 1.5. Interior horizontal span defined by starting pixels of interior and exterior spans

$$x_s = \text{roundup}(x_i) \qquad \text{where } P_i(x_i, y_i): \text{scanline–contour intersection}$$

$$y_s = y_i \qquad \text{and } P_s(x_s, y_s| : \text{starting pixel}$$

For a one pass interior fill, we need to cross all scanlines, from the lowest to the highest and at each scanline compute incrementally (Hersch 1988,1990) the intersection with all shape contour parts (complexity: linear to the shape perimeter projected on the y-axis). In order to avoid sorting intersection points along the x-direction on each scanline, contour parts shall be segmented along local extrema in the y-direction and ordered along their relative position on the x-axis (Figure 1.6).

Definition: *A wall is a contour segment starting at a local minimum (birth point) and ending at a local maximum (death point).*

The segmented shape description provides for each local minimum (birth point) an *ordered list of active walls*. Walls are ordered along their intersection with scanlines (x-sort). For shapes without self-intersections, the ordered list of active walls does not change on scanlines between two successive birth points. The ordered wall lists associated with each birth point are built by inserting on each new birth point the new corresponding pair of walls into the ordered wall list belonging to the previous birth point (complexity for binary insertion of a new pair of walls: $\log_2 n$). When constructing a new list of ordered walls, one must verify that the superior extremity (death point) of each wall is higher than the ordinate of the current birth point. Walls with death points $y_{\text{WallDeath}} < y_{\text{ListBirth}}$ are eliminated from the current list of ordered walls.

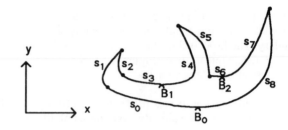

(a)   Initial figure description :

contour 0 : spline segments $s_0, s_1, s_2, s_3, s_4, s_5, s_6, s_7, s_8$

(b)   Topological figure description ordered along birthpoints and walls :

Birthpoint B_0:	left wall:	$\overline{s_0 s_1}$	ordered wall list:
	right wall:	$\overline{s_8}$	$(\overline{s_0 s_1}, \overline{s_8})$
Birthpoint B_1:	left wall:	$\overline{s_3 s_2}$	ordered wall list:
	right wall:	$\overline{s_4}$	$(\overline{s_0 s_1}, \overline{s_3 s_2}, \overline{s_4}, \overline{s_8})$
Birthpoint B_2:	left wall:	$\overline{s_6 s_5}$	ordered wall list:
	right wall:	$\overline{s_7}$	$(\overline{s_0 s_1}, \overline{s_3 s_2}, \overline{s_4}, \overline{s_6 s_5}, \overline{s_7}, \overline{s_8})$

Figure 1.6. Shape described (a) by a continuous contour description and (b) by a segmented description along local minima and maxima

Let us now formulate the complete filling algorithm for the generation of single contour shapes without self-intersections.

(1) Generate from the continuous contour description a segmented ordered description containing a list of birth points and for each birth point, a list of ordered active walls.

(2) Initialize the current scanline y_{scan} to be the first scanline above the lowest birthpoint.

(3) Take as the current ordered active wall list the list associated to the lowest birthpoint.

(4) For each wall belonging to this active list: compute its actual real intersection with current scanline y_{scan}. Incrementally compute its intersection with all remaining scanlines intersecting that wall and store them in a special, dynamically allocated buffer.

(5) REPEAT

(5.1) For the current scanline, fetch the intersections of the first pair of walls. Compute the coordinates of the pair of corresponding span starting pixels. Fill the associated interior horizontal discrete span.

Apply the same procedure for each pair of remaining walls in the current ordered list of active walls. Walls having their superior extremity below the current scanline are removed from the current ordered list of active walls.

(5.2) Increment the current scanline $y_{scan} := y_{scan}+1$
Test in the birth point list if one or several new birth points with ordinates

$$(y_{scan}-1) \leq y_{Birth} < y_{scan}$$

become active. If yes, take as active list of ordered walls the list belonging to the new birth point with the highest ordinate $y_{Birth} < y_{scan}$. As in point 4, scan-convert the corresponding new walls incrementally.

UNTIL the last current ordered list of active walls becomes empty.

For the discussion of apparently ambiguous cases, like contour parts including horizontal straight line segments, the reader is referred to Hersch (1988). How to obtain starting pixels incrementally, by recursive subdivision of Bezier spline segments is discussed in great detail by Hersch (1990).

Interior fill can be extended, without creating problems, to shapes having several non-intersecting contours. All contours are considered as belonging to the same shape. They are segmented into ordered lists of walls.

1.3. Winding Number Fill

The previously described interior fill algorithm is limited to contour shapes without intersections or self-intersections. In this section, we consider shapes having any number of contours without any limitations on intersections or self-intersections.

The interior fill algorithm presented in Section 1.2 implicitly assumes a parity fill rule : each contour–scanline intersection is the boundary between an interior and an exterior span.

By associating to each scanline segment a winding-number instead of the exterior/interior label, the interior fill may be converted into a winding number fill algorithm. The previous shape description is maintained after having been segmented into ordered lists of walls. These ordered lists of walls are valid exactly at the associated birth point ordinate. Above, they may become invalid due to intersections or self-intersections. At intialization time, the contour orientation (positive or negative intersection of wall and scanline) of each wall is recorded together with the wall descriptor. At filling time, the winding number of each successive horizontal span can be easily computed by simple incrementation and decrementation.

The filling algorithm is similar to the one in the previous section. Three additional processing steps are necessary.

(1) In point 1, add to each wall its intersection direction (positive or negative) with horizontal scanlines

(2) In point 5.1, maintain for each horizontal scanline segment its winding number. Horizontal scanline segments are only filled if their winding-number is non-zero. A continuous interior horizontal scanline segment starts at the starting pixel of the first

non-zero winding number span and ends at the pixel before the starting pixel of the next zero winding number span.

(3) After point 5.2, a further processing step is needed in the main loop in order to check the current ordered list of walls. Successive walls should have increasing x-ordinates for their intersection with the current scanline. Walls i whose intersections with the current scanline do not meet $x_{i-1} \le x_i$ are reinserted at the correct place in the current ordered list of walls. This leads to one reinsertion step per intersection between two walls.

1.4. Fill and Clip

Intersecting arbitrary filling and clipping shapes is difficult and requires a large amount of processing power if one would like to compute all intersections between both shapes and generate the clipped original outline shape description.

Nevertheless, the rasterized discrete representation of an original shape can easily be intersected with the discrete representation of the clipping shape by applying simple *AND* operations between bitmaps (Figure 1.7). Such a solution is feasible, but requires a bitmap having twice as much more memory as the bitmap of the resulting filled and clipped shape.

Voici un texte qui
sera découpé selon
une surface donnée
(forme de coeur)

.ci un texte
ˉa découpé sʻ
ˋ surface d
˒ de ⌐

a) text and clip bitmaps   b) enlarged bitmap clipped text

Figure 1.7. Intersection of a discrete text representation and a discrete clipping shape

A computationally cheaper solution is to consider the fill and clip shapes as belonging to the same shape, but with walls characterized as fill or clip walls. A slighty modified version of the winding number fill algorithm presented in the previous sections can be used for clip and fill. Instead of a single winding number, one has to associate to each horizontal span a *fill winding number* and a *clip winding number*. The intersection of a filled and clipped shape is a shape where both the *fill winding number* and the *clip winding number* are non-zero. Such a condition can easily be verified for each scanline segment to be filled.

The following modifications are applied to the previous interior and winding number fill algorithms.

(1) In point 1, add to each wall its intersection direction (positive or negative) and its characterization as a fill wall or as a clip wall.

(2) In point 5.1, maintain for each horizontal scanline segment its fill and its clip winding number. Horizontal scanline segments are only filled if their fill *and* clip winding-number are non-zero. A continuous interior horizontal scanline segment starts at the starting pixel of the first non-zero fill *and* clip winding number span and ends at the pixel before the starting pixel of the next zero fill *or* zero clip winding number span.

(3) After point 5.2, as for simple winding number fill, add a further processing step in the main loop in order to check and maintain the current ordered list of walls. Successive walls should have increasing x-ordinates for their intersection with the current scanline. Walls i which do not meet $x_{i-1} \leq x_i$ are reinserted at the correct place in the current ordered list of walls.

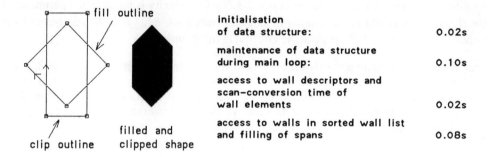

initialisation of data structure:	0.02s
maintenance of data structure during main loop:	0.10s
access to wall descriptors and scan-conversion time of wall elements	0.02s
access to walls in sorted wall list and filling of spans	0.08s

Figure 1.8. Clip and fill applied to a simple shape

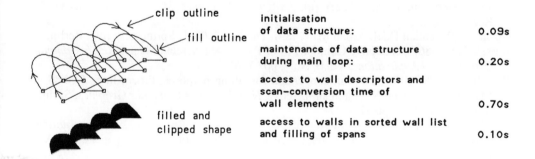

initialisation of data structure:	0.09s
maintenance of data structure during main loop:	0.20s
access to wall descriptors and scan-conversion time of wall elements	0.70s
access to walls in sorted wall list and filling of spans	0.10s

Figure 1.9. Clip and fill applied to a complex shape

The fill and clip algorithm has been applied to the following simple and complex figures. The following processing times have been measured on a 16MHz 68'020 μP. Separate measurements show the time required for the initialization of the birth points and walls data structure, for maintaining the data structure during the main loop, for scan-conversion and for filling.

The analysis of the different processing times clearly shows that a certain overhead is required for constructing, maintaining and accessing the birth point and wall data structure. This overhead is important for simple and little shapes but becomes relatively small for complex and larger shapes.

1.5. Conclusion

A general-purpose algorithm for filling and clipping arbitrary planar shapes is presented. Sorting operations are reduced to a minimum. The algorithm does not require the computation of intersections between the fill and clip shape contours. Due to the partitioning criterion, large shapes can be subdivided into several parts and filled separately, for example by different processors of a multi-processor system. Complexity is linear to the perimeter of the shape contours and to the number of shape intersections, $n \cdot \log_2 n$ to the number of local minimas (birth points) and square to the effectively filled surface.

This filling and clipping algorithm leaves room for further improvement. At present, every wall is completely scan-converted, even if some wall elements are not boundaries of the resultant discrete shape. A prediction of wall intersection locations would enable scan-conversion to be restricted to those shape parts which delimit interior and exterior parts of the final clipped shape.

References

Ackland BD, Weste NH (1981) The Edge Flag Algorithm - A Fill Method for Raster Scan Displays, *IEEE Trans. on Computers*, Vol 30, No 1, pp.41-48.

Adobe Systems Inc (1985), *Postscript Language Reference Manual*, Addison-Wesley, Reading, MA.

Gosling J, Rosenthal DSH, Arden MJ (1989), *The NeWS Book*, Springer Verlag, Berlin.

Hersch RD (1986) Descriptive Contour Fill of Partly Degenerated Shapes, *IEEE Computer Graphics and Applications*, Vol 6, No 7, pp.61-70.

Hersch RD (1988), Vertical scan-conversion for filling purposes, Proceedings CGI'88, in: Magnenat-Thalmann N, Thalmann D (eds.), *New Trends in Computer Graphics*, Springer Verlag, Heidelberg, pp.318-327.

Hersch RD (1990), Efficient Rendering of Outline Characters, *Proceedings SID International Symposium*, Las Vegas, May, published in SID Digest of technical papers, Vol XXI, pp.392-394.

Newell M, C.H. Sequin CH (1980), The inside story on self-intersecting polygons, Lambda, second quarter 1980, pp.20-24.

Rogers DF (1985), *Procedural Elements for Computer Graphics*, McGraw-Hill, New York.

Wallis B (1990), Fast Scan Conversion of Arbitrary Polygons, in: Glassner A (ed.) *Graphic Gems*, Academic Press, New York, pp.92-97.

Warnock J (1982), A Device Independent Graphics Imaging Model for Use with Raster Devices, *Proc. SIGGRAPH '82, Computer Graphics*, Vol 16, No 3, pp.313-319.

2

Research Topics in Shape Interrogation

Nicholas M. Patrikalakis
*Massachusetts Institute of
Technology, Cambridge,
MA, USA*

P.V. Prakash
*Prime Computer, Inc., Bedford,
MA, USA*

H. Nebi Gursoy
*Intergraph Corp., Huntsville,
AL, USA*

George A. Kriezis
*Parametric Technology Corp.,
Waltham, MA, USA*

This chapter focuses on two important problems in shape interrogation. First, we address the problem of surface to surface intersection. In particular, after briefly reviewing the principal features of extant techniques, we will summarize our research on two basic intersection problems. First, the computation of intersections of an algebraic (implicit polynomial) surface with a rational polynomial parametric surface patch. Second, the computation of intersections of two rational polynomial parametric surface patches. Some outstanding issues in the surface intersection area are also identified. Second, we address the application of medial axis transform in shape interrogation. This technique reduces a shape to its medial axis (or skeleton) and associated radius function, and is an effective tool for the extraction of important geometric features of a shape such as constrictions, maximum thickness points, and the associated length scales. It also contributes to the systematic solution of various design and manufacture problems such as decomposition of complex regions to simpler subregions, finite element mesh generation, design of arrangements of complex systems, clearance problems and NC tool path planning. Representative examples are given to illustrate the effectiveness of the technique. We conclude with identification of some outstanding research problems in this area.

2.1. Introduction and Outline

Intersection is a fundamental process in geometry needed in building and interrogating models of complex shapes in a computer environment. Intersection computation is needed primarily in the evaluation of set operations on primitive volumes necessary in the creation of Boundary Representations of complex artifacts. Such capability is useful in the representation of the design of complex objects, such as, for example, the internal subdivision and structural reinforcement of marine and aerospace vehicles, in numerous analysis tasks, such as finite element discretizations of three-dimensional solids, in feature recognition and in simulation and control of manufacturing processes (Chryssostomidis and Patrikalakis 1988). Intersection is also useful in computer animation allowing discovery of interference of two moving objects. Similarly, intersection is useful in scientific visualization providing methods for visualizing implicitly defined objects and for contouring multivariate functions that represent some property of a system. Once the geometric model of an object is available in a computer representation, there is frequently the need for idealizing and discretizing its shape in terms of finite elements for analysis and scientific visualization of relevant properties of the object (e.g. stress tensor, velocity field etc.). The medial axis transform (MAT) promises to provide an automated method for idealization and discretization of structures or, more generally, of objects to be subjected to computer simulation or animation. Such a method would permit designers to concentrate their efforts on the creative and intellectual aspects of design and analysis rather than on their tedious aspects as frequently true in today's engineering practice.

This chapter is structured as follows. Section 2.2 provides a brief review of the principal characteristics of extant surface intersection computation techniques. The chapter next focuses on methods, recently developed by the Design Laboratory, which promise to provide reliable processing of surface intersections in an efficient manner. Specifically, Section 2.3 outlines our technique for the computation of intersections of algebraic (implicit polynomial) surfaces with piecewise rational polynomial parametric surface patches (such as rational B-spline patches). Our method exploits the convex hull and stability properties of the analytic representation of the algebraic curve of intersection in the Bernstein basis within a rectangular parametric domain. Section 2.4 summarizes the methods we developed allowing computation of intersections of two piecewise rational polynomial parametric surface patches, such as two rational B-splines. These are based on convex hull properties of rational B-splines and a combination of subdivision, vector field, topological and differential equation techniques. Section 2.5 describes some outstanding problems in the area of surface intersections. Section 2.6 provides some motivation for our work on medial axis transforms as a method of shape interrogation. Section 2.7 provides a brief overview of medial axis transforms, summarizes a method for computing such transforms for planar domains and for decomposing shapes into simpler subdomains once their MAT is known. Section 2.8 outlines several applications of the MAT, and, finally, Section 2.9 concludes the chapter with an identification of some outstanding research problems in the shape interrogation area.

2.2. Review of Intersection Computation Methods

The fundamental issue in intersection problems is the efficient discovery and description of all features of the solution with high precision commensurate with the tasks required from the underlying geometric modeler (Patrikalakis 1990). Reliability of intersection algorithms is a basic prerequisite for their effective use in any geometric modeling system and is closely associated with the way features of the solution such as constrictions (near singular or singular situations), small loops and partial surface overlap are handled. The solutions resulting from most present techniques are further complicated by imprecisions introduced by numerical errors present in all finite precision computations. Surface intersection methods can be classified in four main categories: analytic, lattice evaluation, marching and subdivision. Most of the methods have been developed in the context of polynomial surfaces, and, apart from some recent articles (Barnhill et al. 1987; Barnhill and Kersey 1989), relatively little has been published on the intersection of more general classes of surfaces. A brief review of intersection techniques updating the exposition of (Patrikalakis 1991) is attempted below. A more detailed review of the extant literature may be found in Kriezis (1990).

Analytic Methods rely on the derivation of a governing equation describing the intersection of two surfaces. For polynomial surfaces, the resulting equation is an algebraic curve described in terms of implicit polynomials. This equation can, for example, be obtained by elimination of three Cartesian coordinates for the case of an implicit algebraic surface intersecting a rational polynomial parametric surface (Farouki 1986), or by elimination techniques for two algebraic surfaces, see, for example, Canny (1990) and references therein. The intersection between two algebraic surfaces can be also handled as an algebraic rational polynomial parametric surface intersection when a rational polynomial parametrization of one algebraic surface is possible or another polynomial parametric surface which contains the curve of intersection can be found. The second approach has been used in the intersection of two quadrics (Levin 1979; Sarraga 1983) where a third parametric polynomial ruled surface, is found which also contains the intersection between the quadrics. The intersection between two rational polynomial parametric surfaces can be handled, in theory, by obtaining an algebraic (implicit polynomial) representation for one of the surfaces (Hoffmann 1989; Canny 1990). The relatively high degree of this algebraic representation and the subsequent substitution of the second rational polynomial parametric surface into this high degree equation leads to an algebraic curve of even higher degree. Detecting the topological configuration of a real high degree algebraic curve with integer coefficients is a very complex problem, see for example Sakkalis (1991). Extension of such methods to extract the topological configuration of algebraic curves, to curves with coefficients involving radicals of integers or with coefficients drawn from the class of algebraic numbers (i.e. from roots of polynomials with integer coefficients) appears to be possible within current theory, but at significant increase in the computational cost and the processing memory requirements. However, no such statement can be made for algebraic curves with transcendental coefficients. Curves from this class arise frequently in geometric modeling applications.

Once the algebraic intersection curve is obtained as above, it must be traced. For special cases, the resulting implicit equations can be solved in terms of explicit expressions involving radicals (Levin 1979) or in terms of rational parametric polynomials for algebraic curves with known singularities and whose genus is zero (Abhyankar and Bajaj 1988).Once the range of the independent variable in such cases is determined, the above explicit equations can be used to trace the intersection curve. The local extrema and singular points of the curve can also be used to advantage (Sarraga 1983; Sakkalis and Farouki 1990). However, for general cases explicit representation of algebraic curves in terms of elementary functions is impossible (Sederberg et al. 1984). The class of algebraic curves with integer coefficients can be analyzed using the cylindrical algebraic decomposition algorithm (Arnon 1983). This method, as implemented in rational arithmetic, although providing a guarantee that the solution is topologically reliable, is impractical, because of its very large memory requirements and poor efficiency. A more efficient approach motivated by Morse theory has recently been proposed by Sakkalis (1991) and exhibits computational complexity of $O[n^{12}(d + logn)^2 logn]$,where n, d are the degree and maximum (integer) coefficient size of the algebraic curve representation. The processing memory requirements for this method are unknown.

Lattice Evaluation Methods reduce the dimensionality of surface intersection problems by computing intersections of a number of isoparametric curves of one surface with the other surface followed by connection of the resulting discrete intersection points to form different solution branches (Varady 1983; Rossignac and Requicha 1987). For intersections of parametric patches, the method reduces to the solution of a large number of independent systems of three non-linear equations in three unknowns. The reduction of problem dimensionality in lattice methods involves an initial choice of grid resolution,which, in turn, may lead the method to miss important features of the solution, such as small loops and isolated points which reflect near tangency or tangency of intersecting surfaces. The connection of discrete solution points to form intersection curve branches requires determining adjacency on the basis of minimum mutual distance which may lead to incorrect connectivity particularly at singular points or for near singular situations.

Marching Methods involve generation of sequences of points of an intersection curve branch by stepping from a given point on the required curve in a direction prescribed by the local differential geometry. However, such methods are by themselves *incomplete* in that they require starting points for every branch of the solution. Starting points are usually obtained using lattice and subdivision methods (Barnhill et al. 1987). They also require a variable stepping size appropriate for the local length scales of the problem. Incorrect step size may lead to erroneous connectivity of solution branches or even to endless looping in the presence of closely spaced features (Geisow 1983). Reliability of marching as well as lattice evaluation methods can be substantially improved by the determination of all *border, turning and singular* points (collectively referred to as *significant points*) of the curve (Sarraga 1983; Farouki 1986; Sakkalis and Farouki 1990). Curvature analysis or power series expansions about each point of the solution to control the step size along the tangent also improve the reliability of marching methods (de Montaudouin et al. 1986). For algebraic curves, the desingularization method based on birational transformations (Bajaj et al. 1988) allows marching through singularities. Knowledge of all significant points within a domain and the multiplicity of singular points also provides an independent count of the number of monotonic branches between significant points. This count is usually able to confirm the number of branches obtained using lattice and marching methods and provides added confidence in the solution (Farouki 1986).

Subdivision Methods involve recursive decomposition of the problem into simpler similar problems until a level of simplicity is reached, which allows simple direct solution, (e.g. plane–plane intersection). This is followed by a connection phase of the individual solutions to form the complete solution. Initially conceived in the context of intersections of polynomial parametric surfaces (Lane and Riesenfeld 1980; Thomas 1984; Chen and Ravani 1987), they can be extended to the computation of algebraic–rational polynomial parametric and algebraic–algebraic surface intersections (Geisow 1983; Sederberg 1984; Patrikalakis and Prakash 1987). Section 2.3 is devoted to our work on intersections of algebraic and rational polynomial parametric surfaces. Subdivision techniques do not require starting points as marching methods, an important advantage from the reliability point of view. Many elements of subdivision techniques are also parallelizable, which is an important advantage for future large-scale real-time applications. General non-uniform subdivision allows selective refinement of the solution providing the basis for an adaptive intersection technique. Subdivision methods have been used in diverse ways to address intersection problems

(Petersen 1984; Solomon 1985). A disadvantage of subdivision techniques is that, in actual implementations with finite subdivision steps, correct connectivity of solution branches in the vicinity of singular or near-singular points is difficult to guarantee, small loops may be missed or extraneous loops may be present in the approximation of the solution. Furthermore, if subdivision methods are used for high precision they lead to data proliferation and are consequently slow.

As can be seen from the above review, common problems of state-of-the-art techniques include the difficulty in handling singularities, surface overlap and efficiently identifying closely spaced features and small loops. Recently, there is strong interest in developing techniques to detect the existence of loops in an intersection curve (Sinha et al. 1985; Patrikalakis and Prakash 1987; Prakash 1988; Prakash and Patrikalakis 1988; Cheng 1988; Sederberg and Meyers 1988; Sederberg et al. 1989; Patrikalakis and Prakash 1990; Kriezis et al. 1990a; Kriezis 1990; Kriezis et al. 1990b; Kriezis and Patrikalakis 1991; Wang et al. 1991). The loop detection literature and our work in this area is summarized in Sections 2.3 and 2.4 of this chapter.

2.3. Algebraic Surface and Rational Polynomial Surface Patch Intersection

The representation of planar algebraic curves within a rectangular domain in the Bernstein basis coupled with *a priori* computation of the significant points of the curve is employed in recent work by the Design Laboratory (Patrikalakis and Prakash 1987; Prakash 1988; Prakash and Patrikalakis 1988; Patrikalakis and Prakash 1990) to compute intersections of algebraic (implicit polynomial) surfaces and rational polynomial parametric surface patches conveniently expressed in the Bernstein basis (rational Bezier patches defined over rectangular parametric domains). Our method combines the advantageous convex hull and stability features of representation of the algebraic intersection curve in the Bernstein basis; the *a priori* computation of border, turning and singular points (*significant points*); and, adaptive subdivision techniques to provide the basis for a reliable and efficient solution procedure. Using elimination techniques, our method could be also extended to handle intersection of two algebraic surfaces for which rational polynomial parametrizations are not available. Our method relies on accurate computation of an analytic representation of the curve which provides the capability to transform the problem at hand to the intersection of an auxiliary integral Bernstein–Bezier surface patch (*control surface*) and an (auxiliary) *control plane*. This transformation allows the use of subdivision methods in the solution of algebraic surface–rational polynomial patch or algebraic surface–algebraic surface intersection problems and provides an efficient method of obtaining points on every segment of the curve.

We investigated the use of symbolic substitution of the rational polynomial patch equation into the algebraic (implicit polynomial) surface equation (Patrikalakis and Prakash 1987, 1990) and obtained explicit expressions for the coefficients of the algebraic curve of intersection expressed in the Bernstein basis. These expressions are compact when the primary data for the patch and the algebraic curve were expressed in the Bernstein basis, and are the net result of any cancellations that might occur. Further use of sophisticated summation techniques (Prakash 1988) improved the accuracy on these coefficients. This method was used in case of intersections between planes and quadrics with up to rational bicubic surface patches. A numerical evaluation of these coefficients was required for higher order cases as there was an explosion of time and space required to derive them symbolically. This approach required repeated multiplication of Bernstein polynomials and summation of the appropriate coefficients and was used in cases involving up to degree four algebraic surfaces and bicubic patches (Kriezis et al. 1990).

The second part involved the computation of significant points on the intersection curve. The significant points consisted of border points (ends of the curve on the boundaries of the domain), turning points (at which tangents of the curve are parallel to the parametric axes) and singular points (where first derivatives vanish) on the curve. The border points were isolated reliably using subdivision and the variation diminishing property of the Bernstein basis and computed accurately and efficiently using a modified Newton method. The turning and singular points were computed together as, singular points may be regarded as points where the turning point equations in both parametric directions are valid. The basic idea here was to use a quadratically convergent minimization and modified Newton-like iteration with starting points provided from an initial rough approximation of the intersection curve. Since the coefficients of the intersection curve were derived in the Bernstein basis, these coefficients also describe a Bernstein surface whose intersection with the control plane is the required algebraic curve of intersection. This fact is used to obtain the approximate intersection curve by intersecting facets of the control polyhedron of the Bernstein surface with the control plane. The starting points are then obtained as the turning points of this approximate intersection curve. This procedure was in a position to provide all the turning and singular points of a variety of algebraic curves chosen for their complexity and diversity. However, since there is no guarantee that in general at least one starting point exists for every turning point nor that the iterative technique will converge to the appropriate turning point, we added a theoretical verification of the correctness of the above procedure. This verification is based on the idea that if some turning / singular point is missed, the derivative surface of the Bernstein control surface will have an intersection with the control plane signaling the existence of a zero derivative within a particular subdomain. Such an occurrence on some sub-patch obtained after subdividing at the already found significant points will trigger additional subdivision on the sub-patch and the earlier scheme repeated in this sub-patch to find the missing turning or singular point. In this manner, all turning and singular points are found within the resolution of the final subdivision subdomain.

The tracing of the intersection curve is then accomplished by splitting the control Bezier patch at all parametric lines passing through the significant points leading to a matrix of smaller subpatches. Each subpatch intersection, if not empty, contains monotonic curve segments that extend from border to border of the subpatch and are simpler to trace using subdivision methods (Prakash 1988; Prakash and Patrikalakis; Patrikalakis and Prakash 1990). Alternatively, a tree-like subdivision may be employed to reduce the number of subpatches that are required to make each subpatch describe a simple intersection curve (Kriezis et al. 1990b). The tracing of each such curve is accomplished by iterative refinement of the control polyhedron of the control surface describing this portion of the intersection curve and intersecting triangular facets of the control polyhedron with the control plane. The linear segments approximating the curve are then connected together using the connectivity information implied in the control polyhedron to make up the complete curve. Each point on the curve is then corrected for accuracy using a Newton iteration. When there are near singular situations within each simple domain, these are detected by the presence of intersections in all edges of a quadrilateral of the polyhedron and further refinement in that area is requested. Each of these curves is then combined with their neighboring segments to form complete intersection curves.

A variety of complex algebraic curves and actual intersection problems with diverse features were solved successfully using the technique described above. Our method of tracing algebraic curves is illustrated in Figure 2.1. The application of the method in the solution of intersection problems between algebraics (such as torii) and piecewise rational polynomial surface patches (such as rational bicubic B-splines) is illustrated in Figure 2.2.

The methods used in our work depend to a large extent on the availability of an explicit polynomial representation of the intersection curve. Our method has been tested successfully in the intersection of algebraic surfaces up to degree four and rational polynomial parametric surfaces up to degree three in each parameter, for which a representation of the intersection can be obtained both accurately and efficiently. Extension of the method to the intersection of other low order algebraics, possessing an easily derivable implicit representation, such as surfaces of revolution with planar rational polynomial low degree profile curves as well as conical or cylindrical ruled surfaces with low degree rational polynomial surfaces is direct. The above representation of the intersection curve required by the method described above, although theoretically available for all intersections between rational polynomial surfaces, is impractical to obtain in some important cases. For example, for intersections between rational biquadratic and bicubic patches, such a representation is difficult to compute efficiently and accurately, and alternate methods of obtaining the intersection were developed for such important cases, as outlined in Section 2.4. An alternative method would be to study modeling sculptured shape with surface representations that would lead to algebraic intersection curves of lesser degree compared to the intersections of the widely used rational biquadratics and bicubics. Modeling with low order piecewise algebraic surface patches using the B-spline representation within rectangular boxes provide such an example (Patrikalakis and Kriezis 1989). The advantages and limitations of these surface representation methods are discussed in an earlier paper (Patrikalakis 1990).

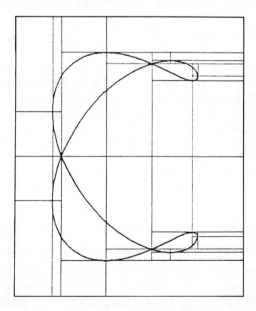

Figure 2.1. A degree 4 algebraic curve with three self-intersections (Kriezis et al. 1990b)

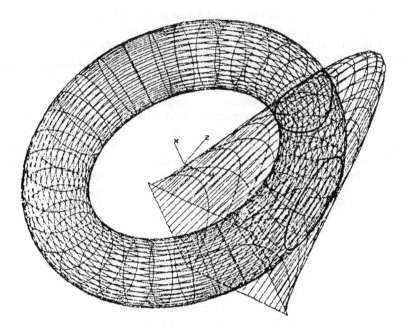

Figure 2.2. Torus and bicubic patch intersection with two loops (Kriezis et al. 1990)

2.4. Intersection of Rational Polynomial Surface Patches

2.4.1. Problem Statement

Our research on the problem of intersecting two rational polynomial surface patches defined over rectangular parameter spaces and expressed in the Bernstein basis is summarized in this section (Kriezis 1990; Kriezis et al. 1990a; Kriezis and Patrikalakis 1991; Wang et al. 1991). Our exposition is based on an update of an earlier summary paper (Patrikalakis 1991). Such surfaces (usually referred to as rational Bezier patches) arise, for example, by splitting rational B-spline surface patches into their rational polynomial subpatches. The present general problem is necessary in geometric modelers supporting free-form or sculptured surfaces. Rational B-splines are usually employed as a canonical geometric representation for creation, interrogation, storage and exchange of data in or between such modelers (Chryssostomidis and Patrikalakis 1988).

The above intersection problem can be viewed as the solution of a system of three non-linear relations, equating the three Cartesian coordinates of the two surfaces, $\vec{F}(u,v,s,t) = \vec{r}(u,v) - \vec{q}(s, t) = 0$, where $\vec{r}(u,v)$ and $\vec{q}(s,t)$ are the two parametric surface patch equations involved. Alternatively, the intersection set can be viewed as the set of points on the two surfaces with zero distance. For this purpose, the oriented distance function ϕ between an arbitrary point on $\vec{r}(u,v)$ and the surface $\vec{q}(s,t)$ may be introduced:

$$\phi(u,v) = \vec{n}_2 \left[\vec{Q}(\vec{r}(u,v)) \right] \cdot \{ \vec{r}(u,v) - \vec{Q}(\vec{r}(u,v)) \} \tag{2.1}$$

where $\vec{Q}(\vec{r}(u,v))$ is a point on surface $\vec{q}(s,t)$ which is the unique nearest point to the point $\vec{r}(u,v)$, and $\vec{n}_2$ is the unit normal vector on surface $\vec{q}(s,t)$ at point $\vec{Q}(\vec{r}(u,v))$. Note that $|\phi(u,v)|$ is the actual Euclidean distance of point $\vec{r}(u,v)$ from point $\vec{Q}(\vec{r}(u,v))$ on surface $\vec{q}(s,t)$, provided the vectors $\vec{n}_2[\vec{Q}(\vec{r}(u,v))]$ and $\{\vec{r}(u,v) - \vec{Q}(\vec{r}(u,v))\}$ are collinear (*collinearity condition*). In this case, point $\vec{Q}(\vec{r}(u,v))$ is the orthogonal projection of point $\vec{r}(u,v)$ on surface $\vec{q}(s,t)$ and the first- and second-order derivatives of ϕ (referred to as proper oriented distance function) may be computed *explicitly*. The intersection set between surfaces $\vec{r}(u,v)$ and $\vec{q}(s,t)$ is equivalent to the *zero set* of function ϕ, i.e. the set of points satisfying the implicit equation $\phi(u,v) = 0$, provided that $\phi(u,v)$ is proper.

There are special cases in which $\nabla\phi$ is not well defined. First, there may be more than one point $\vec{Q}(\vec{r}(u,v))$ on the surface $\vec{q}(s,t)$ nearest to point $\vec{r}(u,v)$. This occurs when $\vec{r}(u,v)$ belongs to the cut locus (Wolter 1985) of $\vec{q}(s,t)$. The cut locus is a generalization of the medial axis concept (Blum 1973; Patrikalakis and Gursoy 1990). It should be noted that for C' rational spline surfaces of at least degree 2 in each parameter which are regular (do Carmo 1976), the cut locus of $\vec{q}(s,t)$ stays away from $\vec{q}(s,t)$ and, therefore, all these points where $\nabla\phi$ is not well defined are away from the intersection set, see (Kriezis et al. 1990a) for a more detailed analysis. Second, when the surface $\vec{q}(s,t)$ has a finite boundary, the nearest point $\vec{Q}(\vec{r}(u,v))$ may lie on the border and the collinearity condition may not be satisfied. These types of points are always away from the intersection except from border intersection points, which are, however, explicitly computed by our methods. In practice, the presence of these points does not affect the reliability of our algorithms.

A crucial element of the intersection problem is the identification of all connected intersection components. The properties of ϕ can assist in the identification of intersection components. A closed loop in the intersection set of the two surfaces, corresponds to a closed level curve of ϕ in the parameter domain, i.e. $\phi(u,v) = c = 0$. If the domain D enclosed by such a curve is simply connected and ϕ is properly defined at all points in D, then that domain contains an *extremum* of $\phi(u,v)$, and consequently a *critical point* of ϕ. At a critical point $\nabla\phi = 0$. Therefore, the critical set of ϕ is directly related to the topology of the zero set of ϕ. If we could describe the structure of the critical set of ϕ, including ill defined regions, then we have sufficient information to identify all components of the intersection. Topological tools based on the rotation number of the vector field $\nabla\phi$ along a closed curve on the (u,v) parameter space are important to the solution of the intersection problem formulated above (see Section 2.4.2). The appropriate background theory may be found in (Krasnoselskiy et al. 1966; Arnold 1981). This theory is widely used in applications involving nonlinear dynamical systems. When the collinearity condition is valid, $\nabla\phi$ defined in the u, v parameter space assumes the following form (Kriezis 1990)

$$\nabla\phi(u,v) = \{ \vec{n}_2[\vec{Q}(\vec{r}(u,v))] \cdot \vec{r}_u(u,v), \vec{n}_2[\vec{Q}(\vec{r}(u,v))] \cdot \vec{r}_v(u,v) \}^T \tag{2.2}$$

where subscripts u, v denote partial derivatives and superscript T denotes transpose. The set $\phi = 0$ provides an alternative *implicit representation* of the intersection which is analogous to the algebraic curve of intersection defined in the parameter domain of one of the patches as described in Section 2.3. However, ϕ is not in general a polynomial function. The above field is also suggested by Cheng (1988) as useful in computing the intersection of two parametric surfaces and the vector field used by Markot and Magedson (1989) to compute singular points of the intersection using Newton iteration. The method developed by Cheng (1988), attempting to discover all connected components of the intersection, is based on the concept of connecting all critical points via gradient lines of ϕ. Unfortunately, this concept is not mathematically sound (see (Kriezis et al. 1990a) for details).

2.4.2. Significant Point Computation

In order to identify all connected components of the intersection curve, a set of important points on the intersection curve (*significant points*) can be defined. As seen in Section 2.3, such a set may include *border, turning and singular points* of the intersection and provides at least one point on any connected intersection segment and identifies all singularities. An alternative and more convenient set of such points, discussed in this section, sufficient to discover all connected components of the intersection, includes *border and collinear normal points* between two surfaces. Collinear normal points provide points inside all intersection loops and all singular points.

Border points: These are points of the intersection at which at least one of the parametric variables u, v, s, t takes a value equal to the border of the u–v or s–t parametric domain. The points with parametric values equal to the border of the s–t parametric domain are also called *termination points*. To compute border points, a piecewise rational polynomial curve to piecewise rational polynomial surface intersection capability is required. A combination of subdivision and numerical techniques has been used in our work to compute these points with high accuracy.

Collinear Normal Points: These are points on the two parametric surfaces at which the normal vectors are collinear. These points do not necessarily lie on the intersection, but if they do, they are also singular points. An alternative interpretation of collinear normal points can be obtained using ϕ. Most of the collinear normal points are critical points of ϕ, where $\nabla\phi = 0$, with ϕ not necessarily 0 there. If ϕ is proper at a point, then $\nabla\phi = 0$ at that point implies the presence of a collinear normal point pair there. There are some collinear normal points between two surfaces which are not *critical* points of ϕ, as they are not minimum distance point pairs. In this chapter we are interested in computing the collinear normal points between two surfaces, which are critical points of ϕ. In intersection problems, collinear normal points and critical points of ϕ may be used to signify the same concept, because after some subdivision, necessary in surface intersection, the extraneous collinear normal points, which are not critical points, become irrelevant.

The importance of collinear normal points in detecting the existence of closed intersection loops in surface intersections is well established during the last decade (Solomon 1985). A process for verifying absence of collinear normal vectors using an interval type of analysis was suggested by Sederberg et al. (1989) and Sederberg and Nishita (1989). The importance of computing collinear normal points and not just determining their absence, and a linearly convergent subdivision method to detect these points are also discussed by Sederberg et al. (1989) and Sederberg and Nishita (1989). Recently, Newton techniques to compute collinear normal points which lie on the intersection, (i.e. singular points) were developed by Markot and Magedson (1989). This method does not, however, provide a technique to automatically determine initial approximations for all these points. In our work, we have developed an effective method to compute initial approximations to collinear normal points. Direct numerical techniques (minimization and Newton methods) are subsequently used for the computation of these points. Such methods depend only on evaluations of the surface positions and their partial derivatives.

The theory of plane vector fields (Krasnoselskiy et al. 1966; Arnold 1981) may be used to determine these initial approximations. The vector field of interest is $\nabla\phi$ given in Equation 2.2. The *rotation number* of $V = \nabla\phi$ along a closed curve γ in the u-v parameter space is a useful concept. The rotation number $W(V,\gamma)$ counts the number of rotations performed by $\nabla\phi(\gamma(t))$ while the point $\gamma(t)$ moves along the curve γ on the parameter space of $\vec{r}(u,v)$. In the definition of rotation number, $\nabla\phi \neq 0$ on the curve γ is assumed. As can be seen in (Kriezis 1990), the following theorem is useful for the determination of approximations of critical points.

THEOREM 1: *If the rotation number of a continuous vector field $V = \nabla\phi$ along an arbitrary oriented continuous and closed curve γ bounding a simply connected domain D is non-zero, then there must exist at least one critical point of ϕ in domain D.*

$\nabla\phi$ is not continuous in a domain D if ϕ is not proper at a point in the interior of D. For intersection examples which are difficult to resolve (e.g. nearly coincident or tangent surfaces), we found that, after a small level of initial subdivision of both surfaces and elimination of non-intersecting subpatches using bounding boxes, $\nabla\phi$ is well defined and continuous at all points of the domain.

The first step in the determination of initial approximations to collinear normal points is the approximate computation of $\nabla\phi$ on a lattice of points in the parameter space of $\vec{r}(u,v)$. We use a coarse initial subdivision of the two parametric patches to provide a coarse approximation to the two surfaces. The use of bounding boxes assists in efficiently eliminating non-intersecting subpatches during this initial subdivision process. For each control point $\vec{r}_{ij}$ of the first surface, we calculate its Euclidean distance from all the control points of all the subpatches of the second surface $\vec{q}_{kl}$ and select the minimum distance pair. A pair of approximate minimum distance points is then identified in the parameter space of the two patches corresponding to the node values associated with the selected control points of the two subpatches. Our numerical experiments indicate that this procedure provides a good approximation of the nearest points after a coarse subdivision of the two surfaces (Kriezis 1990). As a result $\nabla\phi$ can be approximated at a lattice of points in the u–v parameter space by computing the right-hand side of Equation 2.2 at these points. Once the approximate $\nabla\phi$ is determined, Theorem 1 may be used to determine initial approximations for the collinear normal points. Every four neighboring points in the lattice of points form a quadrilateral, i.e. an oriented continuous closed curve in the u-v parameter space. We found that the rotation of $\nabla\phi$ around this quadrilateral can be approximated by computing the rotation of the vectors in the corner points of the quadrilateral. If the rotation number is non-zero, then the parameter values of the center of the quadrilateral are used as initial approximations for an accurate numerical computation of a critical point. Numerical methods based on minimization and Newton iterative techniques described in Kriezis (1990) have been developed and successfully applied in such computation. The objective of the above method is to provide an efficient automated way to compute collinear normal points, in order to provide at least one point inside all loops and all singularities. A more detailed analysis of the above method can be found in Kriezis et al. (1990a). However, there is no guarantee that, in general, at least one initial approximation exists for every collinear normal point, and that the iterative technique will converge to the appropriate collinear normal point.

To further enhance our confidence in identifying cases where the above numerical computations have missed a critical point,we may perform the following *verification* procedure based on the same concept as above but relying on accurate computation of rotation numbers as applied in appropriate subdomains of the full problem. Recall that in the simpler problem analyzed in Section 2.3, we subdivide (split) the domain at all available significant points obtained by some numerical computation and use a verification criterion based on derivatives of control surfaces in subdomains. This idea can be generalized to the problem addressed in this section. First, we split $\vec{r}(u,v)$ in a number of subpatches by using isoparameter lines passing through all available collinear normal points. This subdivision is performed sequentially in a manner similar to that alluded to in Section 2.3 (and described in some detail by Kriezis et al. (1990b) and the subpatches are kept in a tree structure exhibiting the same properties as those obtained in the simpler problem of the Section 2.3. Following this subdivision, each of the resulting subpatches are examined for the possibility of a missed collinear normal point in their interior. The bounding box of each of the subpatches of the first surface is compared with the bounding boxes of the subpatches of the second surface to determine the subpatches with no intersection. This is important in reducing the number of verification tests. Tight rectangular bounding boxes naturally oriented to the geometry of the subpatches are used to closely bound the subpatches (Kriezis 1990; Kriezis and Patrikalakis 1991) .

Each of the intersecting subpatches of the first surface is then examined for the existence of a missed critical point of ϕ in its interior using the rotation number of the $\nabla\phi$ on the boundary of the subpatch. If the rotation number is non-zero, then such a point may exist and needs to be identified. If the rotation number is zero, the present test is *inconclusive* since from the Poincare index theorem (Krasnoselskiy et al. 1966; Arnold 1981), the rotation of $\nabla\phi$ on the boundary of a region containing one saddle and one extremum point of ϕ is zero. Numerical experiments, however, suggest that missing of two neighboring critical points of ϕ with opposite index signs is infrequent (Kriezis 1990).

The rotation number of a vector field $V(u,v) = \{\chi,\psi\}^T$ along a closed curve γ can be determined using numerical quadrature from the Poincare formula (Krasnoselskiy et al. 1966; Arnold 1981):

$$W(V,\gamma) = \frac{1}{2\pi} \int\limits_{\gamma} \frac{\chi\,d\psi - \psi\,d\chi}{\chi^2 + \psi^2} \tag{2.3}$$

Since the rotation along a closed curve is an integer, we only need to evaluate this integral to within an error of less than 0.5 to determine the rotation. If any point on the boundary of the subpatch (except the corners) has a null vector, the above computation cannot be performed and the test is assumed to have failed. In order to avoid integrating over critical points which are already computed and are at corners of subpatches, the integration contour may be modified using a small tolerance to avoid the critical point (Kriezis 1990). This modification is acceptable for intersections with isolated critical points. The tolerance indicates the separation between critical points that we want to resolve. $\nabla\phi$ at the requisite number of points on the closed boundary curve in the u–v parameter space of the first surface necessary to compute (2.3) may be evaluated by first determining the point on the second surface $\vec{q}(s,t)$ which is at a minimal distance to a given point on the boundary curve. An alternative method to compute the integrand of (2.3) is to use differential equations describing the orthogonal projection of a closed curve of $\vec{r}(u, v)$ on $\vec{q}(s, t)$ and to compute $\nabla\phi$ at the resulting points. Differential equations governing the orthogonal projection of a curve on a surface can be found in Pegna (1989), Kriezis (1990) and Pegna and Wolter (1990). An exact method for computing the rotation number along a closed path of the special instance of vector fields involving polynomial functions with integer coefficients, may be based on (Sakkalis 1990), where a variation of Euclid's algorithm is employed.

If the rotation number on the boundary curve is non-zero, we search locally in the subpatch for a missed critical point using the same technique explained above but applied in the smaller domain. Once a new collinear normal point is determined, the subpatch is subdivided at this point and the verification test is performed recursively in the new subpatches until it is satisfied in all of them. This process is repeated until all subpatches of the first patch satisfy this test. The collinear normal point verification method described above, although only based on a *necessary condition*, has proven successful in a large number of complex intersections by discovering collinear normal points missed in a preliminary significant point computation without substantial computational expense (Kriezis 1990).

An alternate method for the computation of critical points of ϕ has recently been proposed by Wang et al. (1991). It relies on tracing out the curves $\phi_u = 0$ and $\phi_v = 0$ using differential equation techniques similar to those developed by Kriezis (1990) (as summarized in Section 2.4.3) and using the resulting traces of these curves plus a minimization technique to compute the intersections of these two curves, i.e. the critical points. Starting points found on the borders of the parameter domain by one-dimensional search techniques were used for tracing out these two curves using initial value differential equation techniques. The method was successful in a variety of complex cases involving a finite number of critical points to efficiently locate all such points. However, no theoretical proof exists that starting points on the border of the domain provide a sufficient set of starting points for a general case. Nevertheless, this process may be useful in efficiently identifying most critical points prior to the application of the more expensive sufficient conditions described below. In addition, just like the rotation number criterion outlined above, this method applies, under mild assumptions, to general parametric surface patches. In contrast, bounds necessitated by the sufficient conditions outlined below are only known for the simpler case of rational piecewise polynomial surface patches.

To provide a *sufficient condition* for absence of loops and singularities from an intersection, convex hull properties and bounds for the partial derivatives and normal vectors of rational B-spline surface patches can be employed. The following conditions are useful in this respect. If two at least C1 surfaces intersect in a closed loop, then there exists a normal vector on one surface which is *parallel* to a normal vector in the other surface (Sinha et al. 1985). Such a condition may be used to assist in selective subdivision of two surfaces to identify all intersection segments. If bounds to the normal vector directions of two subpatches do not intersect, these subpatches do not intersect in an interior loop and further subdivision is unnecessary. Furthermore, if two at least C^1 surfaces intersect in a closed loop (in both parametric spaces), then there exists a line which is perpendicular to both surfaces (*collinear normal vectors*), provided the inner product between any normal vector on one surface and any other normal vector on the other surface is never zero (Sederberg et al. 1989). The absence of a collinear normal line (i.e. absence of intersection loops)can often be deduced even though parallel normal vectors may exist. Interval type methods to bound a set of functions specifying collinearity to determine the existence or not of a collinear normal have been suggested (Sederberg and Nishita 1989). Similarly, if two at least C^1 surfaces intersect in a closed loop, then there exists a normal vector on one surface which is perpendicular to a tangent vector on the other surface (Sederberg and Myers 1988). Cones that bound the tangent directions of all curves of constant u or v in a rational B-spline patch (u, v bounding cones), and cones that bound all of the normal vectors on a rational B-spline patch (normal cone) have been proposed (Sederberg and Myers 1988). Using the normal cone, the tangent plane cone may be also defined by the following property. If its vertex is translated to any point on the surface, the tangent plane at that point will not cut the tangent plane cone. A criterion for evaluating existence of closed loops in the intersection curve may be formulated as follows. If the u or v cone from one of the surfaces lies completely within the tangent plane cone of a second surface then all v or u isoparameter curves of the first surface intersect the second surface at most once. This guarantees single valued intersection curves in v or u.

Experimentation with various possible bounds of partial derivatives and normal vectors of rational B-spline surface patches has shown that *rectangular pyramid bounds* may be constructed efficiently and are usually tighter than available alternatives by a significant factor. The details of the construction of pyramid bounds and comparisons with alternatives can be found in Kriezis (1990) and Kriezis and Patrikalakis (1990). The center vectors of the u and v rectangular pyramids of a rational B-spline patch may be also employed to define a coordinate system naturally oriented to the patch. Rectangular bounding boxes of the patch position defined in such a system are normally much smaller than bounding boxes in an arbitrary coordinate system. Such boxes provide an efficient way to eliminate non-intersecting subpatches generated in a subdivision process at small computational cost. Our experimentation with intersection problems has shown that numerical precomputation of most collinear normal points using the rotation number criterion developed above, splitting of the patches involved at such points, and application of sufficient conditions for loop and singularity detection relying on rectangular pyramids offer the potential of reliable intersection component detection at small computational expense. Comparison of the relative efficiencies of algorithms to detect collinear normal points based on various combinations of necessary and sufficient conditions for the detection of such points is recommended for further study.

2.4.3. Tracing Methods and Examples

Following the computation of significant points of the intersection, two methods for tracing the intersection curve of two surfaces have been developed (Kriezis 1990; Kriezis et al. 1990a; Kriezis and Patrikalakis 1991). The first method is a subdivision and faceting technique exploiting the convex hull properties of rational B-splines in combination with a local Newton refinement of the intersection to efficiently provide high accuracy. The second method is a marching technique and is based on the solution of a set of first order differential equations describing the zero level curves of the oriented distance function ϕ between two surfaces.

Our subdivision scheme starts after the two parametric surfaces are subdivided at the significant points and the verification criterion outlined in the previous section is possibly used. Approximate tracing of curve segments in a sub domain is based on approximation of subpatches by their control polyhedra and intersection of these approximations with each other. The approximation of the curve of intersection arising from the intersection of the two polyhedra is later refined using an efficient local Newton technique. The use of tight rectangular bounding boxes ensures fast elimination of non-intersecting subpatches.

Marching methods involve generation of sequences of points of an intersection curve branch by stepping from a given point on the intersection curve in a direction prescribed by the local differential geometry of the curve. Marching methods have been found to be a more efficient alternative to subdivision methods. In contrast to subdivision methods, they are simple to implement and do not generate large amounts of data during the solution process. The first difficulty with marching methods, in contrast to subdivision methods, is that they require starting points for every intersection branch. An important element of our work is the development of techniques to automatically determine these *starting points* on all connected intersection components and to identify the singular points of the curve. The second difficulty with marching methods is the selection of the step size. As noted in Section 2.2, incorrect *step size* may lead to erroneous connectivity of solution branches or even to endless looping in the presence of closely spaced features (Geisow 1983). Most recent marching methods make use of curvature analysis or power series expansions about each point of the intersection solution to control the step size.

A new marching technique was developed which transforms the intersection curve following (marching) problem to an equivalent initial value ordinary differential equation problem (Kriezis 1990; Kriezis et al. 1990a). The intersection curve between two surfaces can be considered as the zero level curve of the oriented distance function between the two surfaces. In addition, if a curve $\gamma(w)$ on a surface $\vec{r}(u,v)$ and its orthogonal projection on another surface $\vec{q}(s,t)$ are identical, then curve $\gamma(w)$ is an intersection curve of the two surfaces. Orthogonal projections of curves on surfaces are studied in (Pegna 1989; Pegna and Wolter 1990). These two views of an intersection curve provide the tools for the development of differential equations describing the intersection curve of two surfaces. There is a large amount of literature dealing with the numerical solution of initial value problems and there are some very good algorithms for the robust integration of the associated systems of first-order ordinary differential equations (Gear 1971; Numerical Algorithms Group 1989). These algorithms use adaptive techniques to select the proper integration order and marching step size and have proved successful in practice, particularly in areas where rapid variations and constrictions (near-singularities) of the curve exist.

Marching methods, just like subdivision methods, require special attention to reliably handle singularities. In our work,we have developed techniques for marching from ordinary order-two singular points (self-intersections) of general intersection curves $\phi = 0$ using the two asymptotic directions of the Hessian of ϕ at such points (Kriezis 1990; Kriezis et al. 1990a). The elements of the Hessian of ϕ can be computed *explicitly* in terms of partial derivatives of ϕ. The method can be extended to higher order singularities by using higher order partial derivatives of ϕ. Cusps, involving a single tangent direction, can be usually handled indirectly by arranging the sequence of marching towards rather than away from such points. Such an approach is expected to give correct results provided no two cusps occur within the same subdomain or if another significant point can be detected on a branch connecting them from which marching can be initiated. Analysis of tangent directions of an intersection curve at singular points is also useful in tracing intersection curves along which the two intersecting surfaces share a common tangent plane (e.g. models involving blending surfaces). Such cases involve infinite singular points at each of which there is a single tangent line. When this situation arises, the convex hull/subdivision based criteria for the detection of singular points naturally become unattractive. For such cases,we have, however, developed appropriate systems of ordinary differential equations describing the tangents to the curve, so that when a starting point is accurately known, these curves can be traced without difficulty. An experimental implementation of these systems has led to accurate results (Kriezis 1990).

The total computational cost of the intersection algorithms which use the two different tracing techniques mentioned above has been compared for a large number of complex and diverse intersections. In most instances, the marching algorithm outperforms the subdivision and Newton based algorithm by a significant margin in accurately computing intersection curves. The following observations may also be made. The marching algorithm increases in time complexity with an increase in the complexity of the intersection curve since it depends primarily on the number of intersection segments needed to be traced, while the subdivision algorithm depends less on the complexity of the intersection and is governed primarily by the number of intersecting subpatches of the two surfaces and the number of line to plane intersections performed.

Figure 2.3 presents the intersection of two biquartic Bezier patches (which are nearly coincident). The resulting intersection has four small loops in the parametric space of both patches.

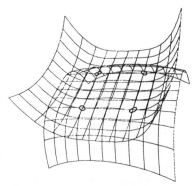

Figure 2.3. Intersection of two biquartic Bezier patches (Kriezis 1990)

2.5. Concluding Remarks on the Intersection Problem

Some important outstanding problems in the area of surface intersection computation are summarized in this section (Patrikalakis 1991). First, extension of our algorithms to handle intersections of complex general parametric surfaces such as offset, generalized cylinder, blending, and medial surfaces and surfaces arising from the solution of partial differential equations, or intersections of such surfaces with the basic algebraic and rational spline surfaces, commonly used in design, requires further study. Tracing of intersection curves by solving differential equations may be extended to handle general parametric surfaces known in a procedural fashion, intersections of surfaces exhibiting higher than tangent plane continuity, or higher order singularities. Such methods have, in many respects, been well addressed in the extant literature or the requisite methodologies are either of a classical nature or are currently being developed. However, a major difference between general parametric surfaces and rational B-spline surface patches, affecting the reliable interrogation of surface intersections, is the existence of a control polyhedron and associated convex hull properties and easily computable bounds for position, partial derivatives and normal vectors in the latter class. The development of efficient non-exhaustive detection conditions for significant points and verification of computation of all connected intersection branches to such complex parametric surface intersections is the key area requiring further study. The development of tight linear or non-linear bounds for positions, first and higher order partial derivatives, normal vectors and other relevant properties of general parametric surfaces,which can be computed rapidly is the dominant element in the efficient implementation of reliable feature detection conditions in such cases. Detection of surface overlap is a difficult special instance of surface intersection which also requires further study. Distance function and vector field ideas outlined here are expected to be useful in solving this complex intersection problem. The effects of floating point arithmetic on the implementation of intersection algorithms is an important area for basic research. Ways to enhance the precision of intersection computation and to monitor numerical error contamination ought to be explored. Alternative means of performing arithmetic, not relying on imprecise floating point computation alone, should also be explored as the demands for higher precision increase. Finally, the implementation of intersection algorithms in a parallel computation environment is an important research area, which will enhance our ability to perform design of complex systems at significantly reduced time scales in comparison to current capabilities. The general surface to surface intersection problem, although now becoming more well understood in some of its aspects and manifestations, remains a challenging computational problem, and much research is still required to achieve a good balance between the conflicting goals of reliability, accuracy, and efficiency in algorithms attempting to solve it.

2.6. Automated Shape Interrogation Using Medial Axis Transform

In this section we present the medial axis transform (MAT) as an automated shape interrogation method for geometric modeling applications including shape decomposition, adaptive surface faceting, finite element (FE) mesh generation and model creation. This section as well as Sections 2.7 to 2.9 briefly summarize our research in this area (Patrikalakis and Gursoy 1988; Patrikalakis 1990; Gursoy 1989; Patrikalakis and Gursoy 1990, Gursoy and Patrikalakis 1991a, 1991b). This interrogation method can automatically extract several important shape characteristics useful in engineering design and analysis,which can be effectively used in automating the FE modeling and discretization processes. These include:

- Detection of constrictions and their length scales in the problem domain allows the implementation of physically motivated and more efficient discretization of the problem domain. The choice of the initial FE mesh topology is an important factor from the efficiency point of view. To achieve rapidly convergent results,we usually have to refine a FE mesh in regions where the domain is narrow. Those regions, for example, are significant in structural mechanics, because stress concentrations usually occur in such areas. In fluid dynamics, those regions most likely give rise to flow separation.

- Extraction of holes in the problem domain and proximity information permits more effective discretization of the domain and this, in turn, would increase the accuracy of numerical results. Depending on the boundary and load conditions, a finer mesh should be used around holes in order to obtain accurate results.

- Decomposition of a complex shape into a set of topologically simple subdomains helps creation of FE models in an efficient and automated manner.

Detection of the above characteristics from the geometric representation provides important information especially to the FE analysis process. This type of information could also lead to the development of more automated FE mesh generators. If length scales of constrictions and other important shape characteristics of the problem domain are known, a mesh generator could be developed to adaptively select initial mesh topology and local mesh density. These capabilities are not available in existing FE preprocessors. Existing FE preprocessors frequently require interactive user input for the specification of significant shape characteristics some of which are introduced above. Our shape interrogation technique based on the MAT and introduced in Section 2.7 automatically extracts this information from geometric representations.

2.7. Medial Axis Transform

In this section,we introduce briefly main aspects of the MAT and also our methodology for MAT computation for two-dimensional shapes. Such shapes may either be physically planar shapes or represent the parameter space of a curved and, generally trimmed, parametric surface patch.More detailed discussions of these topics and related literature surveys on MAT algorithms can be found in Patrikalakis and Gursoy (1988), Gursoy (1989) and Patrikalakis and Gursoy (1990).

2.7.1. Overview of Medial Axis Transform

Blum (1973) has proposed the technique of MAT to describe biological shape. In this technique, a two-dimensional shape is described by using an *intrinsic* coordinate system. Every point p on the plane containing the shape may be associated with a nearest point on the boundary contour B. The Euclidean distance from a point p to the boundary set B is the distance from p to a nearest point P on B, $d(p,B) = \min \{ d(p,P) : P \in B \}$. Such a nearest point exists because our shape is a closed subset of the Euclidean space. For a particular set of points the minimum distance is not achieved uniquely. Such points are equidistant from two or more points on the boundary contour. This set of points together with the limit points of this set constitute the *medial axis* (MA) or *skeleton* or *symmetric axis* of the shape (see Figure 2.4). We consider here only points in the interior domain bounded by B. For example in Figure 2.4, we have the relationship for an interior point a, $d(a,B) = d(a,b) = d(a,c)$. This definition of the MAT is equivalent to Blum's definition of the MAT (Blum 1973). Blum defines the MA of a closed curve B in the Euclidean plane to be the set consisting of the centers of all *maximal* disks which fit into the domain bounded by B. The metric interpretation of the MA provides a natural basis for building a complete description of the shape. On the MA, S, of a boundary B, we define a function taking values in the set of non-negative real numbers equal to the distance of point $p \in S$ from B. This function r(p) is called *radius function* (RF) or *disk function* of MA. According to Blum,shape may be described procedurally by means of its MA and the associated RF. Namely, given the MA and associated RF of a shape we can exactly reconstruct it. It can be shown that, given a MA, we can uniquely recover the original shape by taking the union of all disks with radius equal to the RF and centered on the MA (see Figure 2.4).

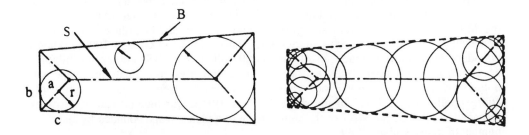

Figure 2.4. The medial axis transform of a planar shape

The concept of MA is related to the closest neighborhood problems in computational geometry (Preparata and Shamos 1985). Given a set of n elements e_i (e.g. points), we can associate every element e_i with a particular subregion r_i in which every point is closer to that element e_i than to all other elements of the set. These individual subregions r_i are referred to as *Voronoi regions*.

The boundaries of the Voronoi regions comprise the *Voronoi diagram* (VD) of the given set. In essence, the VD of a set in a certain region decomposes the region into a finite number of subregions ("influence" regions of elements in the set). Construction of the MA can be referred to as the solution of the closest boundary point problem. The MA of a planar convex polygon decomposes it into a set of subregions each of which is the nearest neighborhood of a boundary edge. Thus, MA and VD are closely related. In the case of a convex polygon, they are identical to each other. If a polygon is non-convex, including *re-entrant corners* on its boundary contour, then the VD of the polygon is a superset of the associated MA. In this case, the difference between the MA and VD is that the MA does not include edges of the VD incident at the re-entrant corners. A re-entrant corner of a polygon is a vertex at which the internal polygon angle is greater than π. If the angle is less than π the corner is called *convex vertex*.

Using the MAT as a shape interrogation technique, we can effectively decompose complex shapes into subregions as we present in the sequel. Those subregions can be reduced to either four-sided or three-sided simple subdomains. This process constitutes the starting phase of our FE meshing scheme (Gursoy 1989; Gursoy and Patrikalakis 1991a, 1991b), in which a complex shape is decomposed into coarse subdomains.

2.7.2. A Computational Methodology for the Medial Axis Transform

In this section, we briefly present our methodology to compute the MAT of connected two-dimensional shapes bounded by closed curved boundaries. The two-dimensional shape can either be planar objects or the parameter space of a curved trimmed surface patch. For the latter case, the parameter space is used in the MAT computation and results are mapped to three-dimensional space via the surface equation of the parametric patch. The boundary of a region (or shape) is defined by an exterior loop and one or more interior loops (i.e. contours), if the region of interest is multiply connected. Each loop of the boundary is composed of an ordered set of boundary elements (curve segments and vertices). The algorithm developed for the MAT computation covers straight line and circular arc boundary curves exactly (Patrikalakis and Gursoy 1988; Gursoy 1989; Patrikalakis and Gursoy 1990). When the boundary of a shape is made up of rational B-spline (NURBS) curves, the algorithm developed in (Patrikalakis 1989) may be used to adaptively approximate the shape with a polygon within a given precision, which can in turn be used for the derivation of an approximation of the MAT of the shape (Gursoy 1989). Our method can be also easily extended to compute the MAT of the complement of a planar shape bounded by an arbitrary number of loops (Gursoy 1989).

If the boundary contour of a planar shape is composed of re-entrant vertices, straight line segments and circular arcs, with arbitrary radii, then the MA of this shape, in general, consists of straight line segments and arcs of conics (i.e. parabola, ellipse, and hyperbola (Blum 1973)). The MA branch $S(e_i, e_j)$ of two boundary elements e_i and e_j is the locus of the points equidistant from e_i and e_j. Descriptions of conic MA branches and their parametric representations, useful for tracing purposes, are presented in (Patrikalakis and Gursoy 1988; Gursoy 1989). The conic branches of MA can degenerate to straight line segments or circles.

In our computational methodology, we can analytically define the MA between two boundary elements in terms of conic sections. By intersection of adjacent MA branches, we determine end points on each MA branch, also called *branch points*. In this way, we obtain the MA branch associated with the two boundary elements. The distance from a point on a MA branch to one of its associated boundary elements gives the value of the RF at that point.

It can be shown that there are three distinct types of branch points in MAT computation (Montanari 1969). An initial branch point of a contour is a vertex at which the equal distance offsets of precisely two non-adjacent boundary elements are tangent to each other. RF attains a minimum value at the initial branch point. Such points identify **constrictions** of shape. An *intermediate* branch point of a contour is a vertex which is equidistant from three or more boundary elements. A final branch point is a special case of an intermediate branch point at which the RF has a local maximum. Such points identify local maxima of the "thickness" of shape. Detailed discussion of our computation methodology briefly summarized in this section, an algorithm for MAT computation and data structures used in the implementation can be found in Patrikalakis and Gursoy (1988), Gursoy (1989) and Patrikalakis and Gursoy (1990).

2.7.3. Medial Axis Transform as a Shape Decomposition Technique

MA branches and the initial boundary contour decompose a shape into a set of subregions.If the given shape is convex those resulting subregions are also convex. For a non-convex shape, some subregions are not convex. Introducing *Voronoi edges* and *cuts* at initial branch points as shown in Figure 2.5, we can further subdivide such non-convex subregions to obtain convex or *pseudo-convex* subregions. Voronoi edges of a given VD are the edges that are incident at re-entrant corners and flat vertices of the boundary contour of a planar shape. A *flat vertex* of a boundary contour of a planar shape is a junction point of two adjacent boundary elements at which the interior angle is equal to π. A *cut* at an initial branch point is a straight line segment connecting the two non-adjacent boundary elements generating the initial branch point and orthogonal to these boundary elements. A pseudo-convex region is an area whose closed boundary can be offset (in a direction normal to the boundary using the grass-fire wavefront concept (Blum 1973)) until the area becomes nil without splitting the area into separate components. A pseudo-convex region involves no bottleneck type narrow part, and the RFs associated with MA branches have no local minima other than at the end points of the MA branches that generated the region. As shown in Figure 2.5, subregions can be further divided into topologically simple subdomains using a set of straight line segments which are indicated by the dotted lines in this figure. These lines are generated by projecting the branch points on the boundary elements associated with them. The resulting subdomains are either three or four sided.

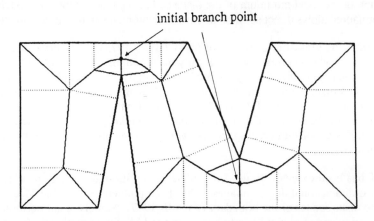

Figure 2.5. Decomposition of a non-convex shape into simple subdomains

2.8. Applications of the Medial Axis Transform

The MAT is an effective method to extract geometric characteristics of a shape. In this section, we identify several applications of the technique to various problems encountered in engineering design and manufacturing based on an earlier paper (Patrikalakis and Gursoy 1990). Inclusion of these capabilities into geometric modeling systems could significantly increase their functionality.

In a Boundary Representation, the data necessary to describe holes (internal loops in faces) are explicitly present in the data base of the model. But the extent of the holes in the region and the length scale of their proximity with respect to each other and the external boundary of the region is not readily available information in existing geometric models. The MAT can be effectively used to *isolate holes* and to extract such *proximity information*.

Since the MA of a shape is the local symmetry axis, it is at equal distance from the boundary on both sides. This basic property of the MA provides solutions to design and manufacturing problems involving *constrictions, clearances and general arrangements*.

Symmetry is a fundamental shape characteristic. Symmetry information and knowledge of presence of similar subcomponents in a shape can be employed effectively to reduce complexity and increase efficiency in many diverse engineering problems, such as in storage involving representations of patterns with symmetry (Tanimoto 1981) and substructuring and use of *super finite elements* in a FEA context (Kardestuncer and Norrie 1987). For detection of symmetry various methods have been proposed (Eades 1988). The MAT may be used to extract not only symmetry information but also to discover similar subcomponents of complex shapes. Encoding MA information may be applicable in a multiresolution approach for shape and symmetry analysis (Pizer et al. 1987).

The RF associated with a MA branch can be used to determine *constrictions* at which the RF attains a local minimum. The RF determines the length scale (thickness) of such constrictions. Using this information we can determine proximity of various parts of the boundary of a shape with respect to each other. For example, this process allows computation of the local minimum of the distance between an internal and external contour. Such information allows direct solution of *clearance* problems in design and manufacturing.

If we consider the grass-fire analogue of MAT (Blum 1973),we observe that the grass-fire ends at locations which correspond to a locally maximum distance from the boundary. Using the grass-fire analogue, the MA is generated procedurally as the set of points at which grass-fire wavefronts originating from two boundary elements intersect. Such points are called *maximum thickness points* (MTP). The RF associated with such points gives the maximum local thickness of the region. This information is potentially useful in general arrangement problems in design of cluttered spaces as well as in manufacturing applications such as molding analysis.

The MAT has been extensively used in pattern recognition and image processing areas to analyze two-dimensional digital images. It has been pointed out that the MAT is extremely sensitive to disturbances of the boundary (Pavlidis 1977). Namely small perturbations on the boundary can give rise to significant changes in the MA. Some publications consider this to be a disadvantage of the MAT. However, this sensitivity of the MAT to perturbation of the boundary shape could be exploited to compare objects in order to identify similarities and differences. It could also be used to classify different variations derived from a basic shape (Bookstein 1979).

The VD decomposes a shape into a set of subregions (closest-point Voronoi regions or influence regions of the components of the boundary of a shape). In two dimensions, each MA branch is associated with two adjacent subregions. The RF associated with the MA branch defines the geometry of the two subregions. In a manner analogous to a CSG model, we can hierarchically represent such a decomposition and call it as the "*MAT tree*" (see Figure 2.6). In this approach, the MA branches and the RF represent area primitives and the shape is defined as the union of the primitives. We can arrange the area primitives,so that when the tree is traversed in ascending order, the value of the area associated with each leaf of the tree (i.e. subregion of the shape) increases. In other words, the shape is represented by including shape characteristics into the MAT tree in an order starting from smaller characteristics and moving towards larger ones. Thus, this shape representation can be regarded as a multi-resolution approach.

VD's and regions, the MA and information regarding constrictions may be used to provide an elegant automated solution to general arrangement problems such as the design of geometry of distributive systems in cluttered spaces. For example, the above information can be used to find various paths within the region for the solution of arrangement problems of distributive systems such as piping.

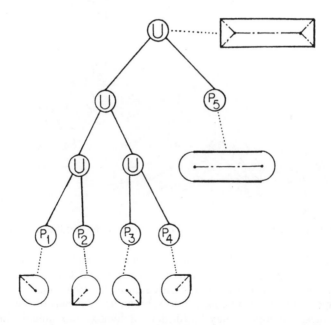

Figure 2.6. The medial axis transform tree of a simple planar shape

The grass-fire analogue of the MAT and subregions defined by the VD of a planar shape may be used to plan and determine numerical control (NC) tool paths. For this purpose, a technique addressing simply connected shapes bounded by straight line segments and circular arcs is addressed by Persson (1978). This approach is based on the determination of influence regions of the boundary edges of planar shapes and does not directly employ the MAT concept. However the MAT can be seen to be the fundamental underlying concept which allows extension of his approach to multiply connected regions. More recent work along these lines is reported in Held (1990).

The MA and associated RF may also be considered to be a shape representation method rather than a method of shape interrogation. Such a representation method would be similar to (but not exactly the same) shape description techniques based on generalized cylinders (sweeps). In a similar direction, the MA and the associated RF can be used to idealize shapes for structural analysis purposes (Gursoy 1989). For example, an elongated slender object may be idealized as a rod using its MA, and the MA may be subsequently discretized to obtain an approximate FE model of the object. Identification of an object as slender may be made by verifying that the ratio of the maximum of the RF over a branch of the MA divided by the length of the branch is below an appropriate threshold. Therefore, the MAT can be used as a technique to automatically create indirect models. The RF directly provides us with the information to compute a good approximation of the bending, tensile and torsional stiffness properties of elongated structures. This approach leads to a first order solution of complex analysis problems in an automated and efficient manner (Gursoy 1989).

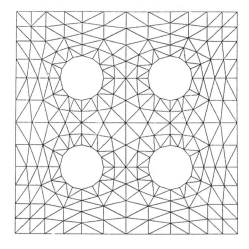

Figure 2.7. Finite element discretizations using medial axis transform

Finally, Voronoi regions, the MA and the associated RF can be used to aid in automation of domain discretization for finite element analysis (Patrikalakis and Gursoy 1988; Gursoy 1989; Patrikalakis and Gursoy 1990; Srinivasan et al. 1990) (see Figure 2.7). Given a complex shape, we may decompose it into subregions by means of the VD. As we saw in Section 2.7, these subregions may be further subdivided into simpler three or four-sided subregions. Such subregions are easier to discretize in comparison to the full domain. Occasionally, the above process gives rise to subregions with high aspect ratios inappropriate for further discretization and FE analysis. Ways to eliminate this problem are described in (Gursoy 1989; Srinivasan et al. 1990; Gursoy and Patrikalakis 1991a). Also the RF can be used to automatically identify the relevant local length scales of the region (e.g. maximum thickness points and constrictions) and to distribute key nodes in a physically motivated non-uniform manner (mesh gradation information). These nodes can then be used for fine triangulation using Delaunay methods or, more directly, the simple three or four - sided subregions may be discretized using standard mapping techniques. The details of the FE meshing technique we developed along these lines can be found in Gursoy (1989), Gursoy and Patrikalakis (1991a, 1991b). An example is shown in Figure 2.8. This example involves coarse subdivision and fine triangulation (meshing) of the parameter space of a trimmed surface patch and mapping of the resulting mesh to three dimensions via the patch equations. The above process can be viewed as the first iteration of an automatic mesh generation scheme. On the second iteration, the mesh is locally refined to account for the boundary and loading conditions of the problem. Several important advantages of this scheme include the capability to extract shape characteristics and length scales in a fully automated manner, a direct way of defining super finite elements and a substructuring capability, and spatial addressability of resulting discretizations using simple subdomains.

2.9. Summary and Concluding Remarks

We have presented the MAT as a shape interrogation method to automatically extract several geometric characteristics of two-dimensional shapes with a curved boundary. The two-dimensional shape can either be planar objects or the parameter space of a curved trimmed surface patch. For the latter case, mapping of the MA to three-dimensional space via the surface equation allows surface discretization. Such discretization may be used for the processing and visualization of trimmed surface patches or for finite element analysis of shell-type objects.

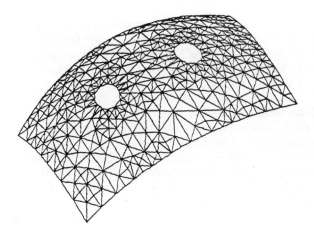

Figure 2.8. Finite element meshing of a trimmed surface patch

This scheme can effectively extract several important shape characteristics useful for design and analysis tasks. We have also identified several applications of the technique in geometric modeling.

Extension of these techniques to higher dimensions (MAT on curved surfaces and within three-dimensional volumes) is feasible and a subject of current research (Gursoy 1989; Hoffmann 1990). However, such extension is expected to be computationally intensive due to substantial increases in combinatorial and algebraic complexity of the process in higher dimensions. In addition, the MA of an object in three dimensions, in general, involves mixed dimensional entities (such a MA generally comprises connected distinct vertices, curved edge segments and surface patches as MA branches). Thus, representation of such a complex structure within a volume would require sophisticated Boundary Representation techniques capable of handling non-two-manifold and mixed dimension situations (Weiler 1986; Rossignac and O'Connor 1990). Even though there are major difficulties in MAT computation in higher dimensions, the MAT is a very rich topic involving interesting research problems. This technique promises elegant solutions to many potential problems in engineering design, analysis, animation and scientific visualization of physical phenomena.

Acknowledgements

Support for the research activities of the MIT Ocean Engineering Design Laboratory in the area of shape interrogation has been provided in part by the following funding institutions in the USA: MIT Sea Grant College Program (project nos.NA86AA-D-SG089 and NA90AA-D-SG-424); the Office of Naval Research (project nos. N00014-87-K-0462 and N000-91-J-1014); the National Science Foundation (project nos. DMC-8706592 and DMC-8720720); the General Electric Company; and the Doherty Professorship. Mr B. A. Moran assisted in the preparation of this chapter.

References

Abhyankar SS, Bajaj CL (1988) Automatic parametrization of rational curves and surfaces iii: Algebraic plane curves, *Computer Aided Geometric Design*, 5, pp.309-321.

Arnold VI (1981) *Ordinary Differential Equations*, MIT Press, Cambridge, MA

Arnon DS (1983) Topologically reliable display of algebraic curves, *ACM Computer Graphics*, Vol.17, No3, pp.219-227.

Bajaj CL, Hoffmann CM, Hopcroft JE, Lynch RE (1988) Tracing surface intersections, *Computer Aided Geometric Design*, 5, pp.285-307.

Barnhill RE, Farin G, Jordan M, Piper BR (1987). Surface/surface intersection, *Computer Aided Geometric Design*, 4, pp.3-16.

Barnhill RE, Kersey SN (1989) A marching method for parametric surface / surface intersection, *Computer Aided Geometric Design*, 7, pp.257-280.

Blum H (1973) Biological shape and visual science (part I), *Journal of Theoretical Biology*, 38, pp.205- 287.

Bookstein FL (1979). The line skeleton, *Computer Graphics and Image Processing*, 11, pp.123-137.

Canny J (1990) Generalized characteristic polynomials, *Journal of Symbolic Computation*, 9, pp.241- 250.

Chen YJ, Ravani B (1987) Offset surface generation and contouring in computer-aided design, *Journal of Mechanisms, Transmissions, and Automation in Design*, ASME Transactions, Vol.109, No3, pp.133-142.

Cheng KP (1988) Using plane vector fields to obtain all the intersection curves of two general surfaces, in: Strasser W, Seidel H (editors) *Proc. Theory and Practice of Geometric Modeling*, pages 187-204, Springer, New York.

Chryssostomidis C, Patrikalakis NM (1988) Geometric modeling issues in computer aided design of marine structures, *Marine Technology Society Journal*, Vol.22, No2, pp.15-33.

de Montaudouin Y, Tiller W, Vold H (1986) Applications of power series in computational geometry, *Computer Aided Design*, Vol.18, No10, pp.514-524.

do Carmo MP (1976) *Differential Geometry of Curves and Surfaces* Prentice-Hall, Inc., Englewood Cliffs, NJ.

Eades P (1988) Symmetry finding algorithms, in: Toussaint GT (editor) *Computational Morphology*, pages 41-51, Holland, 1988. Elsevier Science Publishers, Amsterdam.

Farouki RT (1986) The characterization of parametric surface sections, *Computer Vision, Graphics and Image Processing*, 33, pp.209-236.

Gear W (1971) *Numerical Initial Value Problems in Ordinary Differential Equations*, Prentice Hall, Inc, Englewood Cliffs, NJ.

Geisow A (1983) *Surface Interrogations*, PhD thesis, School of Computing Studies and Accountancy, University of East Anglia, Norwich NR47TJ, UK, July.

Gursoy HN (1989) *Shape Interrogation by Medial Axis Transform for Automated Analysis*, PhD thesis, Massachusetts Institute of Technology, November.

Gursoy HN, Patrikalakis NM (1991a). *An automatic coarse and fine surface mesh generation scheme based on the medial axis transform: Part I algorithms* Technical Report 91-2, MIT Ocean Engineering Design Laboratory, Cambridge, MA, January.

Gursoy HN, Patrikalakis NM (1991b). *An automatic coarse and fine surface mesh generation scheme based on the medial axis transform: Part II implementation*, Technical Report 91-3, MIT Ocean Engineering Design Laboratory, Cambridge, MA, January.

Held M (1990) *On the Computational Geometry of Pocket Machining*, PhD thesis, University of Salzburg, Department of Mathematics and Computer Science, Austria, May.

Hoffmann CM (1989) *Geometric and Solid Modeling: An Introduction*, Morgan Kaufmann Publishers, Inc., San Mateo, CA.

Hoffmann CM (1990) *How to construct the skeleton of CSG objects*, Technical Report CSD-TR-1014, Purdue University Computer Sciences Department, W. Lafayette, Indiana.

Kardestuncer H, Norrie DH (1987) *Finite Element Handbook*, Mc Graw Hill, New York.

Krasnoselskiy MA, Perov AI, Povolotskiy AI, Zabreiko PP (1966) *Plane Vector Fields*, Academic Press, New York.

Kriezis GA (1990) *Algorithms for Rational Spline Surface Intersections*, PhD thesis, Massachusetts Institute of Technology, Cambridge, MA, March.

Kriezis GA, Patrikalakis NM (1991) Rational polynomial surface intersections, *Proc. 17th ASME Design Automation Conference*, Miami, FL, September (to appear)

Kriezis GA, Patrikalakis NM, Wolter FE (1990a) *Topological and differential equation methods for rational spline surface intersections*, Technical Report 90-3, MIT Ocean Engineering Design Laboratory, Cambridge, MA, March. Revised October.

Kriezis GA, Prakash PV, Patrikalakis NM (1990b) A method for intersecting algebraic surfaces with rational polynomial patches, *Computer Aided Design*, Vol.22, No10, pp.645-654.

Lane JM, Riesenfeld RF (1980) A theoretical development for the computer display and generation of piecewise polynomial surfaces, *IEEE Transactions PAMI*, Vol.2, No1, pp.35-46.

Levin JZ (1979) Mathematical models for determining the intersections of quadric surfaces, *Computer Vision, Graphics and Image Processing*, 11, pp.73-87.

Markot RP, Magedson RL (1989) Solutions of tangential surface and curve intersections, *Computer Aided Design*, Vol.21, No7, pp.421-429.

Montanari U (1969) Continuous skeletons from digitized images, *Journal of the Association for Computing Machinery*, Vol.16, No4, pp.534-549.

Numerical Algorithms Group (1989) Oxford, UK, *NAG Fortran Library Manual*, mark 13 edition.

Patrikalakis NM (1989) Approximate conversion of rational splines, *Computer Aided Geometric Design*, 6(2), pp.155-165.

Patrikalakis NM (1990) Shape interrogation, in: Chryssostomidis C (editor) *Proceedings of the 16th Annual MIT Sea Grant College Program Lecture and Seminar, Automation in the Design and Manufacture of Large Marine Systems*, October, Cambridge, MA, Hemisphere Publishing Co, New York, pp.83-104.

Patrikalakis NM (1991). Interrogation of surface intersections, in: Barnhill RE (editor) *Geometry Processing*, Philadelphia, PA. Society for Industrial and Applied Mathematics. To appear.

Patrikalakis NM, Gursoy HN (1988) *Skeletons in shape feature recognition for automated analysis*, Technical Report 88-4, MIT Department of Ocean Engineering Design Laboratory, Cambridge, MA, June.

Patrikalakis NM, Gursoy HN (1990) Shape interrogation by medial axis transform, in: Ravani B (editor) *Proceedings of the 16th ASME Design Automation Conference: Advances in Design Automation, Computer Aided and Computational Design*, Chicago, IL, Vol. I, New York, ASME, pp.77-88.

Patrikalakis NM, Kriezis GA (1989) Representation of piecewise continuous algebraic surfaces in terms of B-splines, *The Visual Computer*, Vol.5, No6, pp.360-374.

Patrikalakis NM, Prakash PV (1987) *Computation of algebraic and polynomial parametric surface intersections*, Technical Report MITSG 87-19, MIT Sea Grant College Program, Cambridge, MA.

Patrikalakis NM, Prakash PV (1990) Surface intersections for geometric modeling, *Journal of Mechanical Design, ASME Transactions*, Vol.112, pp.100-107.

Pavlidis T (1977) *Structural Pattern Recognition*, Springer, Berlin.

Pegna J (1989) Interactive design of curvature continuous fairing surfaces, in: Patrikalakis NM (editor) *Proceedings of the 8th International Conference on Offshore Mechanics and Arctic Engineering*, The Hague, The Netherlands, volume VI, ASME, New York, pp. 191-198.

Pegna J, Wolter FE (1990) Designing and mapping trimming curves on surfaces using orthogonal projection, in: Ravani B (editor) *Proceedings of the 16th ASME Design Automation Conference: Advances in Design Automation, Computer Aided and Computational Design*, Chicago, IL, Vol. I, New York, ASME, pp. 235-245.

Persson H (1978) NC machining of arbitrarily shaped pockets, *Computer-Aided Design*, Vol.10, No3, pp.169- 174.

Petersen CS (1984) Adaptive contouring of three-dimensional surfaces, *Computer Aided Geometric Design*, 1, pp.61-74,.

Pizer SM, Oliver WR, Bloomberg SH (1987). Hierarchical shape description via the multiresolution symmetric axis transform, *IEEE Transactions on PAMI*, Vol.9, No4, pp.505-511.

Prakash PV (1988) *Computation of Surface-Surface Intersections for Geometric Modeling*, PhD thesis, Massachusetts Institute of Technology, Cambridge, Massachusetts, May.

Prakash PV, Patrikalakis NM (1988) *Surface-to-surface intersections for geometric modeling*, Technical Report MITSG 88-8, MIT Sea Grant College Program, Cambridge, MA.

Preparata FP, Shamos MI (1985) *Computational Geometry:An Introduction*, Springer, New York.

Rossignac JR, O'Connor MA (1990) SGC: A dimension-independent model for point sets with internal structures and incomplete boundaries, in: Wozny MJ, Turner JU, Preiss K (editors) *Geometric Modelling for Product Engineering*, Elsevier Science Publishers, Amsterdam, pp.145-180.

Rossignac JP, Requicha AAG (1987) Piecewise-circular curves for geometric modeling, *IBM Journal of Research and Development*, Vol.31, No3, pp.296-313.

Sakkalis T (1990) The Euclidean algorithm and the degree of the Gauss map, *SIAM Journal of Computing*, Vol.19, No3, pp.538-543.

Sakkalis T (1991) The topological configuration of a real algebraic curve, *Bulletin of the Australian Mathematical Society*, 43, pp.37-50.

Sakkalis T, Farouki R (1990) Singular points of algebraic curves, *Journal of Symbolic Computation*, 9, pp.405-421.

Sarraga RF (1983) Algebraic methods for intersections of quadric surfaces in GMSOLID, *Computer Vision, Graphics and Image Processing*, 22, pp.222-238.

Sederberg TW (1984) Planar piecewise algebraic curves. Computer Aided Geometric Design, 1, pp.241-255.

Sederberg TW, Anderson DC, Goldman RN (1984). Implicit representation of parametric curves and surfaces, *Computer Vision, Graphics and Image Processing*, Vol.28, No1, pp.72-84.

Sederberg TW, Christiansen HN, Katz S (1989) An improved test for closed loops in surface intersections, *Computer Aided Design*, Vol. 21, No.8, pp.505-508.

Sederberg TW, Meyers RJ (1988) Loop detection in surface patch intersections, *Computer Aided Geometric Design*, 5, pp.161-171.

Sederberg TW, Nishita T (1989) *Direct approximation of surface patch intersection curves*, Technical report, Brigham Young University, Provo, UT, January.

Sinha P, Klassen E, Wang KK (1985) Exploiting topological and geometric properties for selective subdivision, *Proceedings of ACM Symposium on Computational Geometry*, ACM, pp.39-45.

Solomon BJ (1985) *Surface Intersection for Solid Modelling*, PhD thesis, Clare College, University of Cambridge, Cambridge, UK.

Srinivasan V, Nackman LR, Meshkat SN (1990) *Automatic mesh generation by symmetric partitioning of polygonal domains: I. algorithm*, Technical Report RC 16132, IBM, Yorktown Heights, NY, September.

Tanimoto SL (1981). A method for detecting structure in polygons, *Pattern Recognition*, Vol.13, No6, pp.389- 394.

Thomas SW (1984) *Modeling Volumes Bounded by B-Spline Surfaces*, PhD thesis, Department of Computer Science, University of Utah, Salt Lake City, Utah.

Varady T (1983) Surface-surface intersections for double-quadratic parametric patches in a solid modeller, *Proceedings of the U.K. - Hungarian Seminar on Computational Geometry for CAD/CAM*, Cambridge University.

Wang Y, Gursoz EL, Chen JM, Prinz FB, Patrikalakis NM. (1991) Intersections of parametric surfaces for next generation geometric modeling systems, in: Turner JU, Pegna J, Wozny MJ (editors) *Product Modeling for Computer Aided Design, Proceedings of the IFIP TC5/WG5.2 Working Conference on Geometric Modeling*, To appear.

Weiler KJ (1986) *Topological Structures for Geometric Modeling*, PhD thesis, Rensselaer Polytechnic Institute, Troy, NY.

Wolter FE (1985) *Cut Loci in Bordered and Unbordered Riemannian Manifolds*, PhD thesis, Technical University of Berlin, Department of Mathematics.

3

Object-oriented Design of Dynamic Graphics Applications

Enrico Gobbetti and Russell Turner
Computer Graphics Laboratory, Swiss Federal Institute of Technology, Lausanne

3.1. Introduction

The continued improvement and proliferation of graphics hardware for workstations and personal computers has brought increasing prominence to a newer style of software application program. This style relies on fast, high quality graphics displays coupled with expressive input devices to achieve real-time animation and direct-manipulation interaction metaphors. Such applications impose a rather different conceptual approach, on both the user and the programmer, than more traditional software. The application program can be thought of increasingly as a virtual machine, with a tangible two- or three- dimensional appearance, behavior and tactile response. In the following chapter, we use the term *dynamic graphics* to refer to this new style of program, which encompasses not only the now familiar mouse-based windowing applications but also real-time animation, interactive 3D, and virtual reality software.

Dynamic graphics techniques are now considered essential for making computers easier to use, and interactive and graphical interfaces that allow the presentation and the direct manipulation of information in a pictorial form is now an important part of most of modern graphics software tools. The range of applications that benefit from this techniques is wide: from two-dimensional user interfaces popularized by desktop computers like Apple's Macintosh or the NeXT computer, to CAD and animation systems that allow the creation, manipulation and animation of complex three-dimensional models for purposes of scientific visualization or commercial animation. Future possibilities include the latest virtual environment research that permits an even more intuitive way of working with computers by including the user in a synthetic environment and letting him interact with autonomous entities, thanks to the use of the latest high-speed workstations and devices.

Unfortunately, the creation and the implementation of such dynamic applications are a complex tasks: these systems have to manage an operational model of the real or virtual world, and simulate the evolution of this model in response to events that can occur in an order which is not predefined. They must handle multi-threaded dialogues with the user that are essential for direct manipulation interfaces, and make extensive use of many asynchronous input devices, ranging from the common keyboard and mouse to sophisticated 3D devices such as the Spaceball, Polhemus or DataGlove.

It was soon recognized that the classical approach of functional decomposition was not well suited for building these kinds of applications and that object-oriented techniques were more appropriate for this domain (Kay 1977). In the following sections we will explain the reasons that lead to this point of view, and present an overview of some of the important object-oriented design principles, issues and techniques that are involved in the construction of dynamic graphics systems.

3.2. Object-oriented Graphics

3.2.1. Background

The relevance of object-oriented concepts for the purpose of building dynamic graphics applications has been recognized since computer graphics began, and many of these concepts were introduced by researchers working in the field of computer graphics. The beginning of modern interactive graphics are found in Sutherland's Ph.D. work about the 2D interactive drawing system Sketchpad (Sutherland 1963) which introduced concepts such as creation of objects by replication of standard templates, hierarchical graphic structures with inheritance of attributes, and programming with constraints that can be considered as precursors of object-oriented technologies (Foley et al. 1990).

In the late 1960s, Alan Kay was working at the University of Utah on FLEX, a project for building "the first personal computer to directly support a graphics and simulation language" (Kay 1977) based on the central ideas of the programming language Simula (Dahl and Nygaard 1966) which can be considered the immediate ancestor of modern object-oriented languages. This work was continued later at the Xerox Palo Alto Research Center (PARC) where he helped to create a hardware and software system called Dynabook. The hardware part of Dynabook later became the Xerox STAR. The software part of Dynabook became the language Smalltalk (Goldberg and Robson 1983). These have become the basis of modern graphical user interfaces.

The Smalltalk example showed that object-oriented techniques are ideally suited for dynamic graphics, but the performance problems raised by the fact that Smalltalk is an interpreted (rather than compiled) and typeless language, limited for a while the main impact of this new methodology to the field of user interfaces. In fact, almost all workstations to appear since the early 80s come with some sort of object-oriented user interface toolkit.

3.2.2. Dynamic Graphics

As dynamic graphics applications become larger, more sophisticated, and move increasingly into the 3D realm, their software engineering problems have become acute. It is increasingly evident that software design must make more use of assemblies containing standard components that can be reused and extended from project to project.

The recent availability of new compiled object-oriented languages such as C++ (Stroustrup 1986), Objective C (Cox 1986) and Eiffel (Meyer 1987) make it possible for a new generation of dynamic graphics applications to emerge with fully object-oriented architectures. Such a development would be welcome because object-oriented design techniques seem to be the most promising solution to these problems.

3.2.3. Design Approach

In order to build any dynamic graphics application, from a simple two-dimensional user-interface manager to a complex three-dimensional animation system, three major problems have to be solved.

- How to describe and manage the model that the application is supposed to manipulate?
- How to render this model?
- How to obtain animation and interactive control?

A good solution to these questions should result in a system that is highly efficient, reusable and extensible. The object-oriented paradigm suggests that all relevant information should be encapsulated within objects. This leads to a major conceptual shift in design from a functional decomposition approach, in which the basic unit of modularization is the algorithm, to a data decomposition approach, in which the basic unit of modularization is the data structure.

This new approach is actually a very intuitive one for most dynamic graphics applications, and it is quite natural to break an application up into objects representing subsystems and assemblies, each with its own appearance and behavior. There is, however, no unique solution to this problem, and the design of a good system structure is a problem that requires careful examination. In fact, as object-oriented graphics matures, and the basic problems such as languages and implementation are solved, larger design issues will increasingly dominate. The remaining sections will discuss some of these important issues and suggest some solutions for the problem of object-oriented design for dynamic graphics applications.

3.3. The Graphical Model

3.3.1. The Need for a Graphical Model

Since interactive and dynamic graphics must respond to real-time input events as they happen, it is usually impossible to know when and in what order the events will come. Therefore, at any moment during the execution of a dynamic application the entire state has to be explicitly maintained in a global data structure.

A common example of this principle is the simple one of drawing a graphical figure on the screen. In traditional graphics libraries, the programmer draws a circle by calling one of the circle drawing routines, which has the immediate effect of making the circle appear on the screen. However, there is no record that the circle exists, so in an event-driven system, subsequent events can not know about the circle, and it is the application programmer that has to explicitly take care of maintaining this information.

In an object-oriented system, however, a circle is drawn by first creating a circle object and placing it in the graphical hierarchy, then issuing a redraw command. In this way, the graphical state of the system is always known from one event cycle to the next: every visible figure on the screen (windows, widgets, geometric figures, etc.) is an object fitted into a single graphical database. All details of the object's appearance (dimensions, color, position, etc.) are maintained as state variables within the object data structures themselves. If the screen needs to be refreshed, this can be done by traversing these data structures.

3.3.2. Two-dimensional Models

The first object-oriented design for modeling two-dimensional graphics was Smalltalk's class libraries (Goldberg and Robson 1983). Many later object-oriented graphics and user-interface toolkits were inspired by this example. For example, Macintosh's MacApp classes, using an object-oriented version of Pascal (Schmucker 1986), NeXT Inc.'s NextStep written in Objective-C (Webster 1986) and the University of Zürich's ET++ (Weinand et al. 1989), written in C++, were all strongly influenced by the original Smalltalk design.

Two dimensional geometric models are utilized by a wide range of applications such as editable drawing programs, desktop publishing and data display. Often, 2D models are closely integrated with windowing system models and interaction objects or widgets, so that 2D models form the basis for most user-interface toolkits. The basic libraries of the Eiffel language (Interactive Software Engineering 1989) offer a simple example of object-oriented encapsulation of the concepts needed for representing two-dimensional models and will be presented here.

 Graphics programming in Eiffel is based on four basic notions: *worlds, figures, devices* and *windows.*

A *world* is the description of a two-dimensional reality, part of which will be displayed, under some representation, on a graphical medium. It has an origin and a coordinate system and represents the entire two-dimensional plane.

Figures are components of the world. They are geometrical entities, such as circles, rectangles or strings of text, whose size and position are expressed in world coordinates.

Devices are portions of the computer screen that have their own coordinate system and are used to display partial representations of worlds.

Finally, *windows* serve to establish the correspondence between the components of a world and their graphical representation of the device. Windows are defined by two rectangles: one in world coordinates, that defines the portion of the world that is captured by the window, and one in device coordinates, that defines the part of the device that is used for display.

The class and instance relationships of Eiffel figures are shown in the following diagram. This type of diagram represents classes as boxes and relationships between them as lines. The cardinality of the relationship is indicated by circles at the end of the lines. A filled circle represents a cardinality of zero to n, an unfilled circle represents a cardinality of zero or one, and no dot represents a cardinality of one. Subclass relationships are represented with arrows directed from the subclass to the superclass.

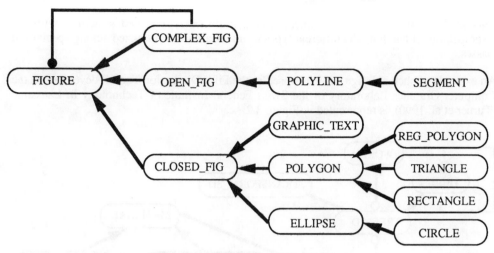

Figure 3.1. Two dimensional figures

Complex figures may contain any number of figures or other complex figures, forming an unlimited hierarchy. This hierarchy, which it should be stressed is an instance hierarchy and not a class hierarchy, allows complex figure objects to be arranged in a tree. Since each figure has its own coordinate system, the programmer can place graphical objects within the figure's local coordinate system and allow the default drawing methods to calculate the global coordinates.

Figures can therefore be said to inherit the coordinate systems of their parents, demonstrating a form of instance (as opposed to class) inheritance. Other characteristics can be inherited by figures through the instance hierarchy such as foreground and background colors and other drawing characteristics.

3.3.3. Three-dimensional Models

Several class hierarchies have been proposed for representing three-dimensional scenes. These designs strive to provide good encapsulations of the concepts useful for modeling, rendering and animating the types of complex objects that are necessary for dynamic graphics applications. Examples are proposed by Fleischer and Witkin (1988), which describes an object-oriented modeling testbed, Grant et al. (1986), which presents a hierarchy of classes for rendering three-dimensional scenes, and Hedelman (1984) which proposes an object-oriented design for procedural modeling.

Three-dimensional dynamic graphics systems are typically concerned with the animation of models arranged in a hierarchical fashion (see Chapter 4). Such systems usually need to maintain the following kinds of information in their graphical data structures:

- the shapes of the models, described in a local reference frame;
- their position, orientation and scale in Cartesian space;
- the hierarchical relation between the different reference frames;
- the rendering attributes of the different models.

This kind of knowledge can be encapsulated in an object-oriented structure, with the responsibility of handling the different types of information decentralized among specialized classes.

An example of such a design, which is used in the Fifth Dimension Toolkit developed at the Computer Graphics Laboratory of the Swiss Federal Institute of Technology in Lausanne (Turner et al. 1990), is represented in Figure 3.2.

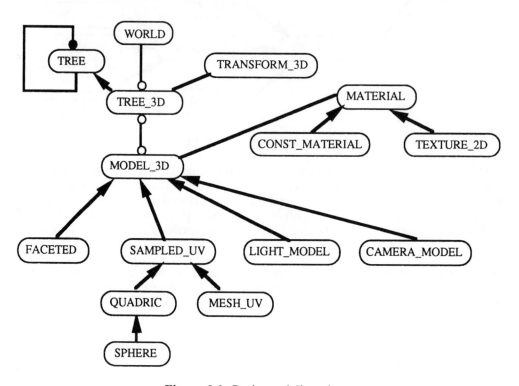

Figure 3.2. Basic modeling classes

Four basic concepts can be identified in this diagram.

- The *world* represents the three-dimensional scene that applications manipulate and contains all the information that is global to a scene such as the global illumination parameters and the geometric hierarchies that are being manipulated.
- The *three-dimensional models* are encapsulations of the concept of a physical object having a shape in the Cartesian space. The different subclasses of MODEL_3D define different ways to describe and manipulate this shape, such as FACETED, whose instances represent geometric objects composed of triangular facets and SAMPLED_UV, whose instances are parametric objects sampled on two local coordinates.
- *Materials* represent the way to give an optical behavior to the models. Examples are CONST_MATERIAL, which allows an object to be rendered with constant illumination parameters over the whole surface, and TEXTURE_2D, which allows the

specification of surface properties that vary according to two texture coordinates. Default mappings exist for every kind of shape.

• The *transformation hierarchy* is used to specify the position of the objects in the world

All the state information about the model being manipulated can be maintained within this graphical hierarchy. Inheritance and polymorphism are used to handle in a simple and efficient way the different types of graphical objects and materials. The addition of new types of graphical objects, for example, is done by defining new subclasses of MODEL_3D and specifying the relevant operations. Programs that were able to manipulate graphical objects before this extension will be able, without any need for recompilation, to also manipulate scenes containing the new type of object.

3.4. Rendering

3.4.1. Should Graphical Objects Draw Themselves?

The modeling hierarchies presented in the previous section are examples of how to organize and maintain data structures in two and three-dimensional dynamic graphics applications. The next step in the object-oriented design process is to package this information together with operations defining how the data structures should be manipulated. These packages define classes that represent the operational model of the simulated world (Meyer 1988).

For dynamic graphics applications, two of the most important types of operations are implementing the visual appearance and dynamic behavior of the different graphical objects. An important design question that arises is: where should the graphical appearance and dynamic behavior be encoded? In simple 2D architectures they are usually encoded directly in the model. For example, a slider object class will contain methods to redraw the slider in its current position and to update the position of the slider according to the position of the mouse. For more sophisticated applications, particularly in 3D, it usually becomes necessary to move this functionality out into separate classes. This is because one of the main goals in designing good component graphical objects is that they be reusable and extensible. To do this most effectively, they need to be general purpose, small and uncomplicated, encapsulating enough functionality to be useful without being difficult to reuse. Complex behavior requires complex design, and often more classes have to be added to the system in order to package some additional functionalities. The decentralization principle that underlies object-orientation can be applied at any level.

3.4.2. Rendering 2D Graphics

An example of how the rendering operation should be separated from the graphical object itself can be taken from the domain of device independent 2D graphics. Suppose there are a number of different geometrical object classes (e.g circles, rectangles, lines) which need to be rendered on different types of devices. However, some devices have hardware support for certain types of geometries, while others require implementation in software. If the rendering operation is implemented within the object, then each object has to be modified when a new device is added.

Where should this information be maintained and how can it be made accessible for the drawing function? The simple polymorphism obtained by defining a rendering function for every graphical object is not sufficient for handling this case, where the action to be performed depends on so many other factors. A better solution is to create new classes to handle the information related to rendering, such as type of algorithm and type of representations, and to use inheritance to create specific versions, such as ray-tracing, wire-frame, and Gouraud shading. Dynamic binding can be used to choose the right implementation among all the possibilities. This method was introduced in the two-dimensional graphic classes of Smalltalk-80 (Ingalls 1986).

3.4.3. Rendering a Three-Dimensional Scene

If we analyze the problem of rendering a three-dimensional scene, it is clear that, as in the 2D device-independent graphics example, implementing the rendering operation within graphical objects is not entirely satisfactory for several reasons.

- Many different algorithms for drawing graphical scenes may coexist in the same system: examples are ray-tracing, radiosity, or z-buffering techniques. The details about these techniques should not be known by every object.
- Rendering may be done using several output units, such as a portion of the frame buffer or a file, and all this knowledge should not be spread out among all the graphical objects.
- Several rendering representations, such as wire-frame or solid, may be selectable on a per graphical object basis. The same object may be viewed by several different windows at the same time, each view using a different representation.

An example of a design that uses separate modeling and rendering classes can be found in the Fifth Dimension Toolkit. Figure 3.3 shows the basic structure of its rendering classes.

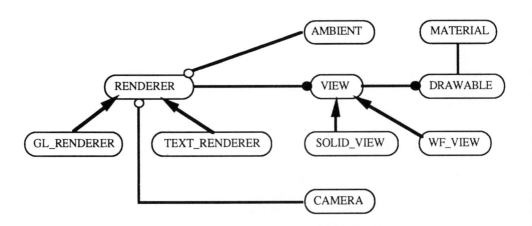

Figure 3.3. Basic rendering classes

Five basic sorts of classes can be identified.

- *Renderers* (instances of subclasses of the RENDERER abstract class), that represent a way to render entire scenes. The code for actually rendering three-dimensional scenes is implemented here.
- *Cameras* (instances of subclasses of CAMERA) that are objects able to return viewing information, such as the CAMERA_MODEL class.
- *Ambients* (instances of subclasses of AMBIENT, such as the WORLD) that are objects able to return global illumination informations.
- *Drawable models* (instances of subclasses of DRAWABLE, such as MODEL_3D in the modeling cluster) that are visible objects having position and shape.
- *Representations* (instances of subclasses of VIEW), that define how a drawable object should be represented.

In this architecture, the representation objects act as intermediaries between the drawable models and the renderer, telling the renderer what technique (e.g. wireframe, solid) should be used to render each graphical object. The drawable models maintain only geometric information about the shape and position of the graphical object. The material objects attached to the drawable models maintain information about the optical properties of their surfaces. The camera object maintains geometrical viewing information used to project the drawable models into screen coordinates.

In order for a renderer object to be able to display a single graphical object, it must consult all of these other types of objects to determine the necessary drawing algorithm. This is done not through conditional statements but rather by using a dispatch method inherent to the object-oriented programming mechanism of dynamic binding called multiple polymorphism (Ingalls 1986). The following diagram shows an example of application of this method.

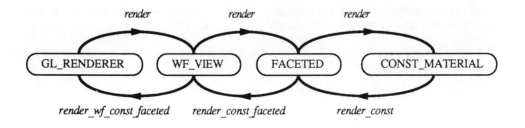

Figure 3.4. Multiple dispatching

As the diagram shows, rendering a single object involves setting off a chain of message invocations, passing through the representation, drawable model and constant material objects, ultimately resolving to the appropriate rendering method. In this way, the composition of the instance data structure automatically determines the rendering algorithm.

3.5. Dynamics and input

Animated and interactive behavior are among the most confusing and poorly understood aspects of computer graphics design. These can actually be thought of together as the fundamental problem of dynamic graphics: how to modify graphical output in response to real-time input? Viewed in this way, input from the user results in interactive behavior, while input from other data sources or timers results in real-time animated behavior.

There are at least two reasons why dynamic behavior can be so difficult to design. Unlike graphical entities, which can be easily modeled with data structures, dynamic behavior is more difficult to visualize and tends to be buried within algorithms. Secondly, there are at least three different software techniques for obtaining real-time input: asynchronous interrupts, polling and event queues. The challenge of dynamics in object-oriented design is: how to design and encode the behavior of graphics programs as easily as we can design and encode their visual appearance. To do this, we have to first try to construct a clear and understandable basic model of dynamic program behavior and then build a set of higher-level concepts on top of it.

3.5.1. Event-Driven Model

Most modern object-oriented graphics systems obtain their real-time input in the form of events in an event queue. Event queues are generally the preferred method, although some systems, such as the original Smalltalk, use polling and others, such as X windows (Nye 1988), allow a mixture of the two.

Applications built using a purely event-driven input model usually consist of two sections: initialization and event loop. In the first section, the initial graphical data structures are built up. In the second section, events are responded to by changing the state of particular graphical objects, creating new objects, destroying existing ones, or by redisplaying the screen. This results in an application which is dynamically coherent, that is, after each cycle of the event loop, the entire data structure is up-to-date and consistent with itself.

Assuming a purely event-driven model, the basic application algorithm then takes the form of an event loop as follows:

```
loop forever
    Go into wait state;
    Wake up when event happens;
    Respond to event;
endloop
```

In such a structure, the dynamic behavior is implemented in the section *Respond to event*. This is usually referred to as *event handling*.

3.5.2. Representing Events

How should this event driven model be represented in an object-oriented design? A common way is to represent each event as an instance of an event object which contains all the appropriate data associated with the event. Although this representation is useful for creating event queues, it is not always the most appropriate. Different types of events can contain completely different sorts of data, requiring a separate subclass for each type of event. More importantly, the event instances themselves are short-lived and if more than one instance exists at a time, there is a possibility that the data structures will become incoherent.

Once an event has been removed from the queue and needs to be handled, it can be represented as a message. This is quite natural because the act of sending a message is, like an event, a temporal, one-time occurrence. The parameters of the message contain the event data and the receiver of the message is some object which is able to handle the event. The entire event loop then consists of gathering the next event, converting it to a message and sending the message to an event handling object.

3.5.3. Event Handlers and Messages

Given the representation of events as messages, the problem of dynamic behavior becomes one of event handling. Good object-oriented design, however, suggests that event handling should be decentralized so that the task is split up among the various objects affected by the event. Each object implements its event handler in the form of event methods, one for each type of event recognized by the object. These methods effectively encapsulate the object's dynamic behavior, allowing it to be inherited and reused like its other characteristics. A more sophisticated approach involves moving the dynamic behavior into a separate object, called a controller, which implements behavior. This is analogous to the separation of the rendering operation described in the previous section.

3.5.4. Distribution of Events

Just as the encapsulation of an object's graphical appearance allows higher-level graphical assemblies to be constructed from components, an assembly's dynamic behavior can be built up from the behavior of its component parts. To do this effectively, a mechanism must be used to distribute the events properly to the component objects. The standard solution to this, used for example in the Xt toolkit (McCormack and Asente 1988), is to distribute the events to the objects according to a predefined algorithm. In the Xt toolkit, which calls its user-interface objects *widgets*, the distribution is based on the widget's location on the screen and the position of the mouse. The widget has a certain amount of control over the distribution of events, by choosing whether to absorb the event or pass it on to an object underneath. It can also generate secondary "software" events by placing new events on the queue.

Although screen-based event distribution works quite well for 2D user-interface objects, there are several problems in generalizing the technique and applying it to 3D interactive graphics. The method of distributing the events is quite centralized and highly specialized for graphical user interface events. For user-interface objects, which usually occupy a rectangular region of the screen, the event can be distributed to whichever object the mouse is on top of. For 3D objects, less well defined graphical objects, or non-graphical objects, there is no particular way of distributing the events. There are only a limited number of types of events and these carry information specific to traditional input devices such as the mouse and keyboard. Finally, it is difficult for objects to control the distribution of secondary events since they must be placed back on the central queue.

3.5.5. Decentralized Event Distribution

A general solution to these shortcomings can be found in NextStep's target/action metaphor (Webster 1989). In NextStep's InterfaceBuilder, user-interface objects communicate via *action* messages which have a single parameter, the source. This source is the object which sent the action message and can be queried by the receiver of the message, or *target* object, for any associated data. User interface objects can be *bound* together so that when, for instance, a slider object is moved, it sends an action message to a second slider so that the two move in tandem.

This representation introduces the concept of an event being a signal between two connected objects, a source and a target, much as two IC chips communicate via a signal on a connecting wire. The only information transmitted by the event itself is its type, represented by the selector name. Any other data must be explicitly queried from the source by the handler of the event. This eliminates the need for various different data structures for each type of event. The data is contained in the source object and it is up to the handler to decide which type of information to look for.

By extending action messages to include all types of events, a decentralized event distribution mechanism can be created in which every event has a source and a target. The fact that events have to come from somewhere suggests a software architecture in which every input device or source of real-time data is represented by an object. Rather than having a *Mouse Moved* event and a *Spaceball Moved* event, we instead can have a single *New Value* event which can come from either the Mouse or the Spaceball object. This helps to support reusability, because device objects can be interchanged easily, and decentralization, because the event generating code is distributed among the various device objects. It also supports "virtual" device objects such as graphical widgets because there is no syntactic difference to the handler between "software" events coming from a virtual device and *real* events coming from a real device.

3.6. Building Applications

3.6.1. Object-Oriented Toolkits

In the previous sections we outlined some of the object-oriented principles that form a basis for the design of dynamic graphical software and presented how these techniques help produce software components that are more extensible and reusable. Providing large libraries of such components is a common solution for helping application programmers in their work. Object-oriented component libraries, often called *toolkits* or *toolboxes,* have been proposed in several fields, user interface software being perhaps the most influenced by this kind of approach.

User interface toolkits, whose design, look and feel are greatly influenced by the seminal example of Smalltalk's system, remain one of the major commercial successes of the application of the techniques presented in this chapter. Some examples are Apple Macintosh's Toolbox (Apple Computer 1985) and Xt for the X windowing system (McCormack and Asente 1988) and Sun's SunView (Sun Microsystems 1986). These kinds of libraries offer to application programmers a collection of reusable user interface components, such as windows, buttons and sliders, and can be easily used from non-object-oriented application programs. Much of the code of typical applications built on top of such toolkits is merely concerned with the creation and the assembly of instances of predefined components, and with the handling of the relevant events.

One consequence of this approach is that the object-oriented design process tends to shift from the traditional top-down to a bottom up strategy. In fact, the major effort in object-oriented graphics programming often is put into designing a good set of general-purpose graphical objects, such as a user interface toolkit, which are only later combined to form applications. This is conceptually similar to modern digital electronic design where more effort is put into designing the modular IC chip components than into the finished circuits containing them. Cox (1986) has emphasized this analogy.

However, simply calling a lower-level toolkit is not an entirely satisfactory solution to the problem of software reuse. Because of the similarity of the overall structure of dynamic graphics applications and the similarities between subsystems within the same domain, it should be possible to simplify the task of building up applications from scratch.

3.6.2. Application Frameworks

It is possible to exploit this similarity of structure by creating *frameworks* that define and implement the object-oriented design of an entire system such that its major components are modeled by abstract classes. High level classes of these frameworks define the general protocol and handle the default dynamic behavior, which is usually appropriate for most of the cases. Only application-specific differences have to be implemented by the designer through the use of subclassing and redefinition to customize the application. The reuse of abstract design which is offered by this solution is even more important than the obvious reuse of code.

The idea of frameworks was developed at Xerox PARC by the Smalltalk group, and the first widely used framework was based on the model–view–controller (MVC) concept of design found in Smalltalk-80 (Krasner et al. 1988).

3.6.2.1. The Model–View–Controller Framework

The MVC framework is based on a uniform model of representing interactive graphical objects. To construct such an interactive object, three specific components, named *view*, *controller*, and *model* are required.

- The *view* object is concerned with rendering: and must know how to convert the important aspects of the model to a visible form.
- The *controller* object implements dynamics and provides the mechanisms that interpret input events as commands and updates the model accordingly.
- The *model* object maintains the information of the application domain and provides the interface that allow controllers and views to access it.

A model can be associated with many view–controller pairs and generic utilities are provided by the different classes of the framework to establish the connections between components and to propagate changes to maintain coherence. Figure 3.5 illustrates the behavior of MVC classes.

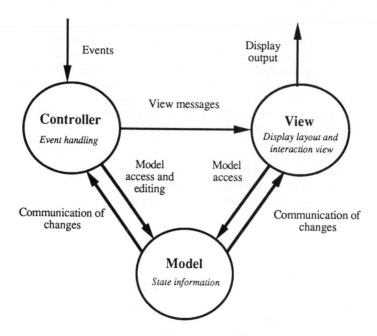

Figure 3.5. Model–view–controller behavior.

An application program using the MVC paradigm is made by providing concrete subclasses of the Model, View, and Controller abstract classes to implement the behaviors specific to the application. These concrete classes usually must provide the implementation of a limited number of deferred methods, the rest being already supplied by the framework.

The separation between modeling, rendering and dynamics that has been described in the previous sections of this chapter is enforced by the MVC paradigm. This fundamental division of powers may become a particularly useful concept in the design of future dynamic graphics application frameworks.

3.6.2.2. Other Frameworks

A number of user interface frameworks have been implemented on the basis of the MVC design, such as MacApp (Schmucker 1986) that handles all aspects of Macintosh applications, and ET++ (Weinand et al. 1989) that offers similar features for Unix workstations.

One major advantage of this approach is that the guidelines for the user interface can be implemented in software, guaranteeing a uniform interface for all the applications and increasing in this way their user-friendliness. Such guidelines can be developed by teams composed of specialists from different domains (designers, psychologists, programmers) and an improvement in these guidelines can be incorporated into the framework with a great benefit to all of the applications.

Although most of the frameworks focus on user interfaces, this design technique, which is perhaps the most impressive realization of object-oriented ideas, can potentially be used in other application domains. A relatively unexplored research area is the development of application frameworks for 3D dynamic graphics applications. As 3D and interaction metaphors become better understood, the form that such application frameworks would take may become more obvious.

3.6.3. Interactive Construction of Applications

The use of frameworks provides a tangible basis for realizing a long sought dream of software engineering: interactive creation of application programs. Although completely interactive software construction is at very best a long way off in the future, some promising attempts have been made to build systems for specifying aspects of 2D user interfaces. These software construction tools are usually referred to as user interface design systems.

Perhaps the most promising of these to be marketed commercially is the Interface Builder application, which is part of the NextStep environment on the NeXT computer. The Interface Builder is particularly interesting because not only does it allow standard user-interface objects to be created and edited interactively (in a manner similar to an interactive drawing program) but it allows certain aspects of their assembled behavior to be specified as well. Using the target/action metaphor described in the previous section, the InterfaceBuilder allows connections to be specified graphically (by interactively drawing a line) between objects so that the data output of one object is automatically sent to the input of another. This allows a major part of the larger assembled behavior, if not the detailed individual behavior, of a group of objects to be designed and constructed without programming a single line of code.

3.7. Conclusions

The challenge of building dynamic graphics applications that realize the full potential of modern computer graphics hardware remains immense. Object-oriented design techniques, however, provide a significant advance toward the creation of reusable and extensible software components and assemblies for dynamic graphics construction. As object-oriented techniques become more accepted and as language and implementation issues are resolved, more attention can be focussed on the larger design issues. Application frameworks provide a structure into which software components can be assembled. General design principles, in particular the MVC metaphor, provide a basis for a more rigorous and well understood dynamic graphics design methodology. These principles can themselves form the basis for increasingly automated interactive software construction tools for building the next generation of dynamic graphics applications.

Acknowledgements

We wish to thank David Breen and Kurt Fleischer for their suggestions in the research and our colleagues Angelo Mangili and Francis Balaguer for reviewing the text.

References

Apple Computer (1985), Inc., *Inside Macintosh*, Addison-Wesley, Reading MA.

Cox BJ (1986) *Object Oriented Programming: An Evolutionary Approach*, Addison-Wesley, Reading, MA.

Dahl OJ, Nygaard K (1966) SIMULA -- an ALGOL-Based Simulation Language, *Communications of the ACM*, Vol.9, No9, pp.671-678.

Fleischer K, Witkin A (1988) A modeling Testbed, *Proc. Graphics Interface '88* pp.127-137.

Foley J, van Dam A, Feiner S Hughes J (1990) *Computer Graphics: Principles and Practice* (2nd ed), Addison Wesley, Reading MA.

Goldberg A, Robson D (1983) *Smalltalk-80: The Language and Its Implementation*, Addison-Wesley, Reading, MA.

Grant E, Amburn P, Whitted T (1986) Exploiting classes in Modeling and Display Software, *IEEE Computer Graphics and Applications*, Vol.6, No11.

Hedelman H (1984) A Data Flow Approach to Procedural Modeling, *IEEE Computer Graphics and Applications*, Vol.4, No1.

Ingalls DHH (1986) A Simple Technique for Handling Multiple Polymorphism, *Proc. ACM Object Oriented Programming Systems and Applications '86*.

Interactive Software Engineering (1989) *Eiffel: The Libraries*, TR-EI-7/LI.

Kay AC (1977) Microelectronics and the Personal Computer, *Scientific American*, Vol.237, No3, pp.230-244.

Krasner GE, Pope ST (1988) A Cookbook for Using the Model-View-Controller User Interface Paradigm in Smalltalk-80, *Journal of Object-Oriented Programming*, Vol.1, No3, pp.26-49.

McCormack J, Asente P (1988) An Overview of the X Toolkit, *Proc. ACM SIGGRAPH Symposium on User Interface Software*, pp.46-55.

Meyer B (1987) Reusability: The Case for Object-Oriented Design, *IEEE Software*, Vol. 4, No. 2, pp.50-64.

Meyer B (1988) *Object-Oriented Software Construction*, Prentice-Hall, Englewood Cliffs, NJ.

Nye A (1988) *Xlib Reference Manual*, O'Reilly & Associates Inc., Newton, MA.

Schmucker KJ (1986) *Object Orientation*, MacWorld, Vol.3, No11, November, pp.119-123.

Stroustrup B (1986) An Overview of C++, *SIGPLAN Notices*, Vol.21, No10, pp.7-18.

Sun Microsystems (1986) *SunView Programmer's Guide*, Sun Microsystems, Mountain View, CA.

Sutherland I (1963) *Sketchpad, A Man-Machine Graphical Communication System*, Ph.D. Thesis, Massachusetts Institute of Technology, January.

Turner R, Gobbetti E, Balaguer F, Mangili A, Thalmann D, Magnenat-Thalmann N (1990) An Object Oriented Methodology Using Dynamic Variables for Animation and Scientific Visualization, *Proceedings Computer Graphics International 90*, Springer Verlag, Tokyo, pp.317-328.

Webster BF (1989) *The NeXT Book*, Addison Wesley, Reading, MA.

Weinand A, Gamma E, Marty R (1989) Design and Implementation of ET++, a Seamless Object-Oriented Application Framework, *Structured Programming*, Vol.10, No2, pp.63-87.

4

3D Hierarchies for Animation

Ronan Boulic and Olivier Renault
Computer Graphics Laboratory, Swiss Federal Institute of Technology, Lausanne

Geometric representation associated with computer-assisted modeling has proven to be very usefull to visualize and understand the structure and behavior of a wide spectrum of entities (Foley et al. 1990). But if we examine the scope of the current 3D geometric models, we notice that they tend to embrace a static view of the information structure. In this chapter, we are particularly interested in stating the requirements for the modeling of complex 3D environments with mobile components. Such a modeling approach has to integrate a dynamic view of these components such that specific goals can be acheived in space and time. A key requirement is to provide a representation of relative motions and this can be addressed through the use of hierarchical modeling.

In the first section we review some geometric models and the PHIGS graphic standard which could be considered suitable for the modeling of 3D hierarchies. Then, we focus on the representation of mobility as it was first studied in robotics. The following sections are dedicated to an overview of the related technical requirements and to their application to a data hierarchy. The last section covers the general techniques of interaction and animation of 3D hierarchies .

4.1. Existing Hierarchical Geometric Models

Some geometric models are, by definition, 3D hierarchies. This is the case of the octree and CSG representations. We now present briefly these hierarchical approaches and then study their scope and their adequacy to the requirement of relative motion representation.

4.1.1. Octree

The octree representation is a subset of the cell decomposition technique, in which a solid is decomposed into arbitrary cells and is represented by each cell in the decomposition. Octree representation gives a 3D systemization to this cell decomposition.

Octrees are a 3D extension of the 2D quadtrees. Figure 4.1 shows the octree representation of a solid. The hierarchical tree results in a recursive decomposition of a cubic region into eight equally sized octants, which are cubic regions. If a cube is partially full, it is decomposed; if a cube is empty or completely full, it is not decomposed. A complex scene, made of several objects, can be decomposed in two ways:

(a) the complete scene is considered as a whole and is decomposed using one global frame,

(b) the objects are decomposed into their local frame and the complete scene is decomposed into the global frame using the bounding box of the objects; in this case there are two levels of decomposition.

One problem with the octree representation is that even small changes require recalculating the data system. If one object of the scene is in motion we see that, for the first case, all the decomposition must be built again and for the second case only the global decomposition using the bounding box must be redone. In both cases this updating of the representation of the scene is heavily time-consuming. Furthermore, octree representation doesn't integrate the relative positioning of objects. Octree representation may be suited for static scenes and for optimization of high CPU-consuming algorithms as ray-tracing or path planning.

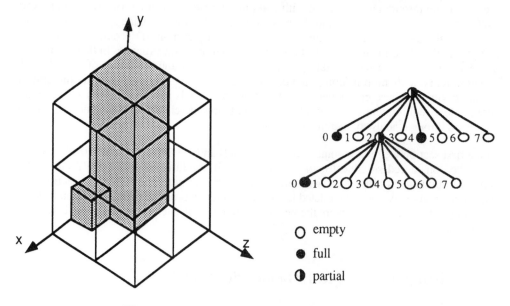

Figure 4.1. Octree representation of a 3D object

4.1.2. Constructive Solid Geometry (CSG)

CSG is a generalization of cell decomposition. Solids are created by assembling primitive volume objects along with three boolean operators: union, intersection and difference. Figure 4.2 gives an example of CSG representation.

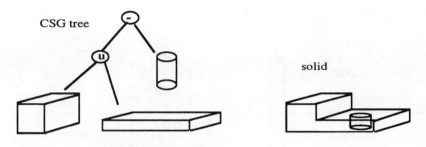

Figure 4.2. CSG decomposition of a 3D object

Objects are represented as binary trees, called CSG trees. Each terminal node is composed of a primitive object and a transformation (translation, rotation, scaling); each non-terminal node is either a boolean operator or a transformation which operates on the subnodes. This model, with its intuitive editing and its relatively compact storage of objects, is one of the most used representation for solid modeling in commercial packages.

CSG offers the feature of positioning objects of a complex scene relative to each other. The ability to edit the nodes allows independent motions of the components of a scene.

However, CSG presents two drawbacks for use in animation. First, its binary tree structure: scenes used in animation are easily describe with n-ary trees, as shown by Figure 4.3. The conversion of a n-ary tree into a binary tree leads to a less tractable representation. Finally, the main drawback is that CSG lacks of representation of mobility.

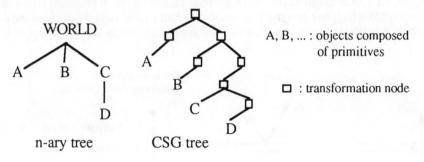

Figure 4.3. Conversion from n-ary tree to CSG tree

4.2. Representation of Mobility

This topic has been studied in the robotics field where control of articulated chains is the major goal. From a general point of view the relative mobility of two objects can be described with joints possessing from one to six *degrees of freedom (DOF)*. Figure 4.4 shows the usual joints with their number of degrees of freedom. Any of the multiple DOF joints can be decomposed into a series of one DOF joints.

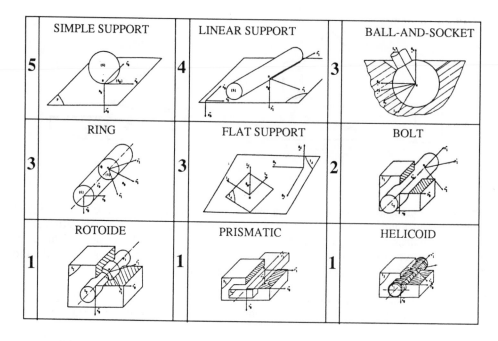

Figure 4.4. Usual joints representing relative mobility of two objects

Therefore, it is only necessary to have some representations for one DOF joints so as to be able to represent a more complex one. Such a representation has been proposed (Denavit and Hartenberg 1955) which has become a common standard in this field. It employs only four parameters to describe the relative position of two axes of motion as shown on Figure 4.5.

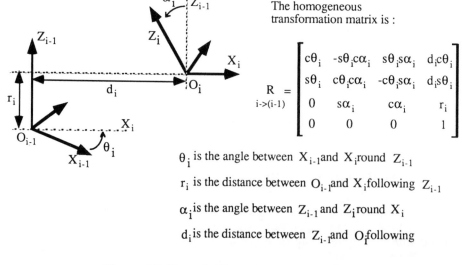

The homogeneous transformation matrix is :

$$R_{i \rightarrow (i-1)} = \begin{bmatrix} c\theta_i & -s\theta_i c\alpha_i & s\theta_i s\alpha_i & d_i c\theta_i \\ s\theta_i & c\theta_i c\alpha_i & -c\theta_i s\alpha_i & d_i s\theta_i \\ 0 & s\alpha_i & c\alpha_i & r_i \\ 0 & 0 & 0 & 1 \end{bmatrix}$$

θ_i is the angle between X_{i-1} and X_i round Z_{i-1}

r_i is the distance between O_{i-1} and X_i following Z_{i-1}

α_i is the angle between Z_{i-1} and Z_i round X_i

d_i is the distance between Z_{i-1} and O_i following X_i

Figure 4.5. Denavit–Hartenberg (DH) notation

The parameters can easily be derived from the typical chain structures of robotics which are a succession of parallel or perpendicular axes of motion. Although widely used in robotics, these parameters have some drawbacks as pointed out by Sims and Zeltzer (1988):

- By convention: the axis of motion of a link is the z axis of the preceding link in the chain, which can be confusing.
- This representation is directional in the sense it has to be covered from the base to the end of the chain to derive the global transformation matrices.
- It is not possible to utilize it for a tree structure or a closed loop.

An alternative principle of representation can be proposed to deal with this last point. It needs a set of seven parameters based on a decomposition in two parts:

- a constant part specifies the *shape* of the segment , with six parameters,
- a variable part specifies a one DOF motion (one parameter) along the new z axis.

This decomposition principle is used by Sims and Zeltzer (1988) which retains the position and orientation of the axes of motion as the shape and one more parameter for the degree of freedom.The fact that it is less directional than DH notation makes it very interesting for animation as further developed in Section 4.4.3 .

4.3. The PHIGS Standard

In this section we will present PHIGS (Programmer's Hierarchical Interactive Graphical System), an ISO standard for computer graphics programming. PHIGS allows to build, manipulate and visualize interactively 3D graphics data, providing the user with hierarchical data organization and editing capabilities.

4.3.1. Background

The design of PHIGS started in the early 80s. From the beginning PHIGS has been conceived as a standard. In an abstract way, a standard can be defined as a set of rules permitting exchange of information through an interface, and so, independent development of the entities on both side of the interface. Thus, PHIGS has been designed as an interface between interactive applications that need complex graphics and graphics systems. It provides the application developers with a set of functionalities to manipulate and display their application models. Developing with PHIGS assures the programmers of the portability of their applications among different systems.

There are two worldwide official 3D graphic standards at the programmer-system level: GKS and PHIGS. GKS started as a 2D graphic standard and has been extended to 3D (GKS-3D) to meet the evolution of the graphic hardware. Basically PHIGS and GKS are constructed on a common set of graphic concepts and terminology, and PHIGS can be considered as a superset of GKS. The major differences between these two standards, concerning our topic, are (Shuey et al. 1986):

- GKS only offers a one-level, flat data organization,
- PHIGS allows more flexible, easier dynamic modifications of the graphic database.

4.3.2. Structure Hierarchy

In PHIGS, the basic organizational building blocks of graphic models are called structures. A structure consists of structure elements. A structure element can represent output primitives, attributes, viewing selections, modeling transformations or structure invocations. The graphic primitive elements are defined in their own coordinate system, called the modeling coordinate system. Modeling transformations convert the modeling coordinate space of the output primitives to world coordinate space. PHIGS allows multiple, cumulative modeling transformations. Attributes are used to define the appearance of the output primitives. A structure invocation element, called an EXECUTE–STRUCTURE element, is used to produce a directed acyclic graph (DAG).

To be displayed, a structure must be posted to the workstation. The display traverser goes over and executes elements of a posted structure one after the other; it applies the transformations, assigns attributes to the primitives and displays the output primitives. Attributes are modal: an attribute value specified by an attribute element is applied to all the primitives uncounted by the traverser until the next attribute element changes its value.

When an EXECUTE–STRUCTURE element is uncountered by the traverser the following actions occur:

(1) the traversal of the current structure is suspended,
(2) the state of the attributes values is saved,
(3) the executed structure (and all the structures it executes) is completely traversed,
(4) the attributes values are restored to the state saved before the executed structure was traversed,
(5) traversal of the parent structure is resumed.

Traversal binding permits inheritance. An invoked structure inherits the defined attribute values and transformations of its parent structure. As a consequence of (4), a structure affects only those structures subordinated to it.

4.3.3. Limitation of PHIGS

Structure hierarchy in PHIGS allows the sharing of data. This sharing functionality can be useful to spare storage space but at the expense of independent management of the instances. As an example, we can construct a robot with an upper body invoking the same arm structure twice. Specification of modeling transformations before each invocation allows the left and right arm to be moved separately. If, in the arm structure, we add a call to an object structure so that the arm "holds" the object, both left and right arm will hold it. To avoid this we have to define two arm structures, one for the left and one for the right, each invoked only once. This is a classical tradeoff between instantiation of structure (multi-invocation of a same structure) and characterization (duplication of the structure) in structure hierarchies.

Although structure hierarchy allows inheritance of transformations and attributes, and so could be compared to procedure hierarchy, it lacks a general parameter-passing mechanism and a general flow-of-control construct. Furthermore, inheritance rules are very simple and do not support complex operations on solids as deformations. In fact, the PHIGS hierarchy is a data hierarchy extended with an elementary parameter passing mechanism but restricted from the dynamic editing point of view (Foley et al. 1990).

PHIGS carries some graphic limitations due to its early 80s conception. PHIGS+, an on-going extension of PHIGS, tries to overcome these limitations by proposing new primitives (e.g. surface B-splines), better rendering (e.g. shading and different types of light), and limited control over the flow of execution of the structures.

4.4. Data Hierarchy: a Case Study

Unlike PHIGS structure hierarchies, data hierarchies can be managed dynamically. Although their flexibility has to be inscribed in the data themselves, for example using flags, this approach is still very convenient and, as such, widely used for scene representation.

4.4.1 Homogeneity vs Integration of Information

In the introduction, we stressed the fact that we were interested in modeling scenes which are basically complex, evolving environments. Such an entity has to integrate many different type of information, usually application dependant. How can we keep some homogeneity within the description of a 3D hierarchy with such an open stipulation ?

The first idea for matching the homogeneity requirement is to define a basic structure which is common to all the entities of the hierarchy. It retains the geometric, topological and display informations sufficient to set a frame in a 3D space within a hierarchy. We call it a node_3D (Figure 4.6).

In this way, one typed structure can be associated to a node_3D to represent additional functionalities. If a node_3D has no associated information it is said to be of NEUTRAL type ; it can be used as an intermediate frame to identify some specific location. The next paragraph describes how the typed data are partitioned into two families to further ensure the geometric integrity of the structure.

4.4.1.1. The Skeleton

As we cannot make any *a priori* statement on what the information to integrate is, none of the application-dependent information can be part of the internal structure of the hierarchy. Therefore we partition the typed data into two families.

(1) A small set of types are used to construct the internal and mobile part of the hierarchy which is called from now on the *skeleton* (Figure 4.6). The idea is to provide some autonomous structures with respect to external information depending on the application.

(2) All other information is considered as external to the structure and attached as *terminal* nodes to the skeleton. Figure 4.6 shows two such basic types.

Members of the skeleton family are the following.

NEUTRAL: retains all the informations to set an intermediate 3D frame.

JOINT: describes a one DOF joint either translational or rotational. As stated in section 4.2., the other usual joints can be constructed with a series of such node_3D.

FREE: it is possible to use six JOINT node_3D to completely define the position and orientation of a corps in space. The corresponding chain is well fitted to coordinated treatments as those provided in robotics. Yet, the orientation is under some kind of Euler sequence which always has some singularity. Another drawback is the fixed suite of orientation angles which may not be suited to user needs. That's why the FREE type has been introduced to specify locally some arbitrary geometric transformation. It is useful in the editing stage but also in animating some independent objects. For example, a human body can be built of JOINT for the bony skeleton while its motion with respect to some external support will be defined with a FREE node_3D.

4.4.1.2. General and Application-Dependent Terminal Types

Although terminal data are typically application-dependent, we can at least bring out two basic types to relate this approach to classic geometric modeling and to provide some graphic display.

FIGURE: This type is used to integrate informations about geometrical modeling of static structured "objects". A choice of such a model, or family of models, has to match with the necessities of the application.

        For example in a robotics application: a CSG model allows the derivation of physical properties and a Boundary representation a fast display. A Design application can managed numerous representations as spline curves, surface patches etc.

        We actually use a Boundary representation which retains a polygonal surface representation in a local frame. This representation is associated with various display and management procedures.

CAMERA: This is one major critical link between data and user because the user accesses to 3D information via a 2D projection . There must be some compensation to the loss of dimension by high interactivity and suitable working modes. Flexibility of the viewing and viewed points is essential to access to hidden information .

We only present here some of the basic operating lookat modes. The camera model retains the classic data of projection type and parameters, near and far planes, zooming coefficient, and a local transformation. This latter is used in conjunction with a lookat mode, three additional parameters and an entry point on a view node_3D. Four lookat modes are of primary interest.

Default mode: the local transformation is the identity matrix so the camera motion is the one of its father node_3D (any node_3D of the hierarchy).

Lookat_to_the view_node: the viewing direction of the camera is set to look at the view node, usually a reference up-vector is used to gear the twist angle along the viewing direction.

Lookat_from_view_node: the local transformation is set to look around from the location of the view node.Two coefficients are interpreted as two polar angles to orientate the direction of viewing.

Bubble_lookat_to view_node: this mode is derived from the virtual sphere principle: the camera is always pointing to the origin of the view node and moving around on a sphere (two parameters) of constant radius (one parameter)

Some extended modes of camera motion can be found in Turner et al. (1991).

Figure 4.7 (see color section) shows a layout of an application based on this decomposition principle. All the squares in the 2D viewport represent a node_3D and are used for selecting. Examples of color codes are: white for NEUTRAL, orange for JOINT, red for CAMERA.

Other types of terminal data can be developed to meet the qualifications of the application, for example: LIGHT for rendering, SOLID for dynamic computation, CONSTRAINT for motion control.

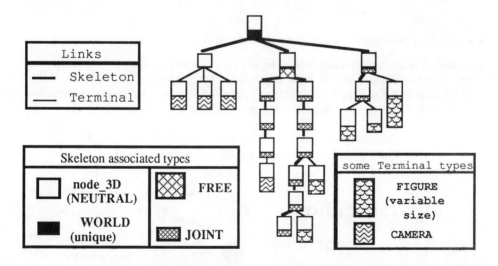

Figure 4.6. node_3D, skeleton and some typed data

4.4.2. Calculus Efficiency vs Memory Space

In the classical space-time tradeoff, we definitely favour the calculus efficiency against memory space. This will be justified in the following design choices for geometric information.

4.4.2.1 Homogeneous Coordinate System

First of all, we use a homogeneous coordinate system (Figure 4.8). Although this approach presents an elegant way of unifying coordinate transformations by simple concatenation of homogeneous matrices, it is also guided by the fact that more and more workstations provide some hardware management of such matrices. More advanced ones even provide a matrix stack to minimize the traversal cost of the application hierarchy.

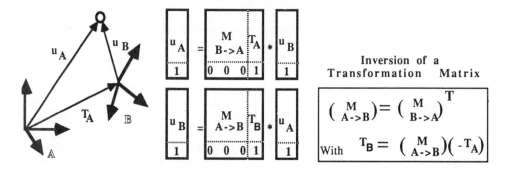

Figure 4.8. Coordinate system transformation with homogeneous representation

4.4.2.2 Direct-Inverse Transformations (DIT)

The second major assumption related to geometric manipulation is the extensive use of coordinate transformations **in both direction**. That's why we introduce the DIT entity which retains both the **D**irect and **I**nverse **T**ransformations between two coordinate systems. The convention is relative to the node_3d possessing the DIT (Figure 4.9):

  • The Direct (dir) Transformation goes away from the proprietary node_3D.
  • The Inverse (inv) Transformation comes to the proprietary node_3D.

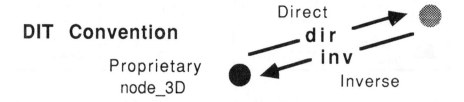

Figure 4.9. DIT orientation convention with respect to the node_3D it belongs to

4.4.2.3. Local Transformations

We have agreed to the decomposition principle (cf Section 4.2) to represent the relative mobility of two objects. A constant initial DIT localizes each node_3D with respect to his father node. In addition, some types of node_3D (JOINT, FREE, CAMERA...) may hold a variable DIT. These are applied after the initial transformation (Figure 4.10).

4.4.2.4. Global Transformations

In addition to the local DIT, each node_3D hold a global DIT, also called reference DIT, with respect to a Reference node_3D. This latter is usually the root of the hierarchy (Figure 4.10).

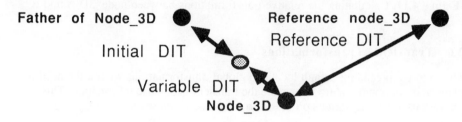

Figure 4.10. Basic local and global DIT maintained by a node_3D

The increased cost due to the updating of this information pays off as soon as we need to visualize the scene because it holds the equivalent concatenation of the traversal of the hierarchy. Then, if we wish to display the scene as viewed from a CAMERA node_3D, we just have to update the geometric pipeline matrix stack as follows:

(1) Only once: multiply the top of the matrix stack with the inverse matrix of the camera reference DIT.

(2) For each node_3D of the hierarchy:

    (a) push the matrix stack and multiply it by the Direct matrix of the node_3D reference DIT,
    (b) send the display commands expressed in its local frame,
    (c) pop the matrix stack.

Many other algorithms can benefit from this information, in fact, as soon as any relative transformation has to be evaluated (Figure 4.11). For example, editing the lookat transformation for a camera, geometric reasoning, obstacle avoidance.

4.4.2.5. Memorization of Variable Information

As soon as the user wants to control realistically the evolution of a variable over time he needs to evaluate its current first and second derivatives. For this purpose, the JOINT and FREE types memorize the two previous values of their degrees of freedom. Some utilities can take profit of this memory buffer to retrieve and reconstruct up to the second previous state of the hierarchy.

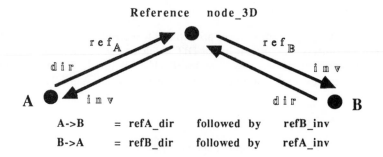

$$A \to B \quad = \text{refA\_dir} \quad \text{followed by} \quad \text{refB\_inv}$$
$$B \to A \quad = \text{refB\_dir} \quad \text{followed by} \quad \text{refA\_inv}$$

Figure 4.11. Calculating the relative transformations between node_3D A and B

4.4.2.6. Transient Transformations

In addition to the preceding default local and global transformations we felt the need of one complementary optional feature to manage the transient geometric information. This feature may be very useful along various processes from edition to simulation.

In the editing process of working on some complex structure to obtain a specified attitude, the user is likely to appreciate an incremental approach, viewing both the current configuration while interactively editing a transient one. Once he is satisfied with the transient attitude he can validate it and it becomes the new current attitude.

In a simulation context, many algorithms work within a prediction–correction scheme. The current state of the system is maintained while the prediction and the correction are evaluated on the transient state. If it succeeds the correction is shifted to the current state. If it fails, a new transient prediction is evaluated, usually from the current state and a shorter timestep.

We have chosen to optionally retain a transient variable DIT for JOINT and FREE node_3D. In such a case it forces a transient global DIT to be retained for any influenced node_3D in the hierarchy. This transient global DIT is also evaluated with respect to the reference node_3D. Figure 4.12 (see color section) shows the edition of a leg posture: in magenta the current leg configuration and in red the transient left leg configuration. The user is interactively setting the transient and current left knee flexion.

Combined with the memorization of variable informations the transient information greatly improve the real-time efficiency of animation algorithms.

4.4.3. Topology and Animation

A hierarchical topology orientates the propagation of motion from the root to the terminal nodes. This property suits structures in which the base is fixed in the world frame, but is this always the case ? Let us first recall that a base, or root of motion, can be any node of the hierarchy except the WORLD node which is needed as an invariable reference. What happens if we want to represent some structure whose "behavior" induces a variable root of motion. For example where should be the root of motion for a human body ? And how can we change it if required by the animation ?

Most authors have stressed the ability to change the motion root of a hierarchy. For Kroyer (1986), the primary action devoted to the structure should be localized at the root, the secondary actions being tuned after the primary one. For example, in the context of a human body structure, he chooses a BODY root localized at the base of the spine to define a walking motion. He justifies this by the fact this action clearly determines a forward motion of the body center of gravity which is close to the BODY node. Moreover he advises setting the root of the hierarchy at one hand if the human model has to hang at some bar. His approach of walking is not shared in Ridsdale et al. (1986) where the root of motion turns alternatively from the foot in contact with the floor to the next one. It has the clear advantage to prevent the supporting foot from going into the floor but conversely it is really difficult to control the speed of the body. That is why most of the walking studies refer to the first approach with some additional functionalities (cf Section 4.3.2).

Besides, authors are divided between those who prefer to redefine the topology of the hierarchy as Kroyer (1986), Cary et al. (1990) and Ridsdale et al. (1986) and those who rather redefine the traversal of the hierarchy, Van Baerle (1986) and Sims and Zeltzer (1988). This latter approach is more suitable in a context of dynamic location of the motion root and we actually subscribe to it.

4.4.3.1. Docking

Let us examine now how we can define a root of motion different from the topoligical root. This operation is called **docking** and the root of motion the **dock** node.

As the WORLD frame is invariant in space, we can see from Figure 4.12 that each child-hierarchy of the WORLD node_3D can be manipulated independently. This can be useful to organize complex scenes where each of these child-hierarchies can be assigned to a specialized functionality. For example for an animation set-up there can be some independent human structures, separate lights, cameras and decor configurations.

In this simple docking context, the traversal procedure which updates the global DIT checks if each WORLD child node_3D is in docking mode. Then it eventually deviates from the default downward chaining of transformations to an alternative upward and downward chaining beginning at the dock node_3D (Figure 4.13). The necessary information is kept with the WORLD data within a dynamic list of DOCK data. It comprises the root and dock entry points and the dock initial and local DIT with respect to the father node_3D of the root.(Figure 4.13).

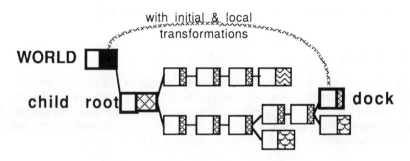

Figure 4.13. Information to retain for simple docking

A more general approach is to decentralize these DOCK data to permit local docking of a branch inside the hierarchy. In such a case, all node_3D should maintain their docking status either *root / dock / else* and an entry point to a shared DOCK structure.

4.4.3.2. Sharing

Considering the design choices we have made for the geometrical and topological informations, sharing can easily be performed on terminal data types.

The terminal node_3D holds an horizontal node_3d list of all the terminal node_3d sharing the same typed data (Figure 4.14). With this sharing scheme, the instances can still be characterized geometrically and visualized independently.

Proposing a sharing scheme for sub-hierarchies requires some additional features and management, particularly for the global transformations. How can we describe global situation of multiple instances? Duplication of these transformations would be hard to maintain at the level of each shared node_3D with respect to the corresponding father nodes of the sub-hierarchy root . A better solution is to reference all the global transformations of a shared sub-hierarchy to its root node_3D ; thus they become sub-global transformations. The final WORLD transformation is then obtained by concatenation of the sub-global transformations.

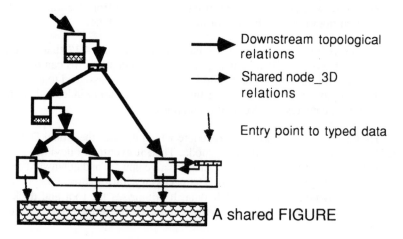

Figure 4.14. node_3D sharing scheme of terminal typed data

4.4.3.3. Editing

It is sometimes necessary to modify the topology to transfer the motion control of a branch from its current father to a new one ; this is the typical case of "pick and place" tasks in robotics. Transfer is a rather straightforward operation unless the desired new father node_3D is a terminal one. In such a case a NEUTRAL node_3D can be created with the same location and the same father and the transferred branch is attached to it.

4.5. Animation Techniques

4.5.1. Control Spaces

Let us give some definitions before going further:

- The whole set of local transformations corresponds to the **configuration space** of the structure. Its dimension, noted **n**, is the sum of all the degrees of freedom.

- The global transformation corresponds to the **situation space** of a node_3D. It is six dimensional for full specification of the position and orientation of a node 3D.

In addition to these spaces and their derivative spaces, other control spaces can be used as force-torque subject to having the necessary inertial data (they could be in a SOLID type).

4.5.2. Geometric Control

By construction of the hierarchy, specification of configuration is the default control mode. Local transformations are defined and global transformations are updated depending on the traversal direction (Boulic and Renault 1991).

Specification of situation is the inverse problem but it may have zero, one, a finite number or an infinite number of solution(s). In robotics, most of the commercial robots match a few well known chain structures for which there exist specialized algorithms to deal with this issue. When the robot has as many degrees of freedom as cartesian dimensions to control, there is always a finite number of solutions. The final choice is made with some additional stipulation as elbow *high* or *low* etc. A higher level stipulation is to evaluate the feasibility of some trajectory beginning at the desired situation (Borrel 1986).

We need an alternative method to cover the general context with any kind of chain structures. This method has also to deal with **redundant** systems with more degrees of freedom than cartesian dimensions to control, leading to an infinite number of solutions. A local approach based on a linearization of the system at the current state can be used to obtain a configuration solution close to the current one. This tool is widely used in robotics and animation (Cary et al. 1990) and is called inverse kinematics.

4.5.3. Kinematic Control

4.5.3.1. Keyframe

Keyframe methods control the evolution of some parameters over time with only a reduced list of key_values of the parameters set at key_time. This defines some *control points*. Traditionally, key_times are expressed by a frame number of an animation film but this is no more a requirement. There exist a few interpolation or approximation functions based on groups of four control points with some additional qualitative parameters such as tension, and bias (Magnenat-Thalmann and Thalmann 1990).

4.5.3.2. Functional Models

The previous parametric animation method becomes limited for the representation of complex coordinated motions. For this reason many authors (Zeltzer 1982; Girard and Maciejewski 1985; Sims and Zeltzer 1988; Boulic et al. 1990b; Maiocchi 1991) stress the need for functional model providing some higher level input parameters from which low level parameters values are automatically derived. The idea is to build an animation system with a library of such models and composition operators. To date most of the researches focused on human or animal locomotion. The recent models usually combine configuration and situation control with inverse kinematics (cf next section).

Another related approach, although less fundamental to the understanding of the motion, is data acquisition with rotoscopy (Maiocchi and Pernici 1990) with further editing or composition. It usually lacks a real functional level input (as speed for walking motion, for example).

4.5.4. Inverse Kinematics

Considering the problem of modifying the situation of a node_3D with an opened chain, the general discrete form of the solution provided by inverse kinematics is

$$\Delta q = J^+\Delta x + (I-J^+J)\,\Delta z \qquad (4.1)$$

Δq is the solution of the equation in the configuration variation space.

Δx describes the *main task* to realize in term of a variation of the situation of the controlled node_3D. (Figure 4.15 a,b,d: a translation in the cartesian plane).

I is the identity matrix of the configuration variation space (n x n)

J is the Jacobian matrix associated to the controlled system

J^+ is the unique pseudo-inverse of J providing the minimum norm solution which realizes the *main task* (Figure 4.15 a,b).

$(I-J^+J)$ is a projection operator on the *kernel* of the application describing the main task

Δz describes a *secondary task* in the space of variation of configuration; this task is partially realized via the projection on the *kernel*. In other words, the second part the of equation does not modify the achievement of the main task for any value of Δz (Figure 4.15 c has a null vector as main task to materialize the kernel space). Usually Δz is calculated so as to minimize a cost function.

If the dimension of the main task is m, then the kernel is (n–m) dimensional in the configuration variation space. This information is fundamental to evaluate the potential of the secondary task.

Some secondary tasks that have been used in robotics are avoiding joints limits (Borrel 1986), and optimizing maneuverability. In animation it is applied in the same way and as an interactive tool to tune a configuration while respecting a fixed situation for the controlled node_3D. For example, Girard and Maciejewski (1985) fix the pelvis and foot location and fine tunes the intermediate configuration of the leg via the secondary task. More recently, Boulic et al. (1990a) propose a methodology of correction of predefined motions. The idea is to retain the most of an initial motion by direct kinematics while applying some simple constraints to be fulfilled by inverse kinematics. This methodology, currently under investigation, is interested in providing a mixed kinematic control allowing both direct and inverse transitions.

4.4. Dynamic Control

There has been considerable interest in the introduction of dynamic control for complex structures (Isaacs and Cohen 1987; Wilhems 1990). This kind of control of hierarchy is well treated as long as there are no closed loops or complex interactions (as in walking between feet and floor). In such context, authors have used a mixed kinematic and dynamic control scheme (Girard 1987; Sims and Zeltzer 1988; Maiocchi 1991).

Furthermore, such a force-torque control space shall be suitable to interactive specification only when there exist appropriate devices to provide input and output of this nature.

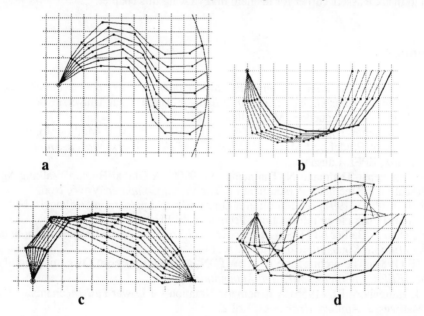

Figure 4.15. (a) and (b) main task only, (c) secondary task with null vector main task, (d) same main task as (b) with arbitrary secondary task

4.5. Limitations of Hierarchical Structure

As pointed out in the previous section, the representation and management of closed loops is close to going beyond the scope of hierarchical representation. That is why most mechanical simulation systems represent solid systems by a connected graph with solid objects as nodes and joints as arcs (Hégron 1988; Cremer 1989).

In fact, numerous fields of geometric modeling require graph structures to represent networks or complex layouts such as electrical circuits, chemical plants and molecules.

4.6. Conclusion

We have reviewed the basic requirements and the scope of modeling complex 3D environments with hierarchies. Although designed for such purpose the PHIGS standard doesn't address all the key issues as flexibility, calculus efficiency, integration of new functionalities, such as cameras and rendering, and motion root modification. In a second part, we have presented a framework for data hierarchy that tries to embody these qualifications. The last section terminates with a classification of the available motion techniques.

Acknowledgement

We wish to thank Russell Turner for his help in reviewing this chapter.

References

Borrel P (1986) *Contribution a la modélisation géométrique des robots manipulateurs. Application a la conception assistée par ordinateur*, Thèse d'Etat, Université des Sciences et Techniques du Languedoc , Montpellier.

Boulic R, Magnenat-Thalmann N, Thalmann D (1990) A New Methodology for the Correction of Predefined Motions", *EUROGRAPHICS Workshop on Animation and Simulation*, EPFL Lausanne.

Boulic R, Magnenat-Thalmann N, Thalmann D (1990b) A Global Human Walking Model with real time Kinematic Personification, *The Visual Computer*, Vol 6, No6.

Boulic R, Renault O (1991) Modélisation d'objets hiérarchiques tridimensionnels, Notes du XII Cours Postgrade en Informatique Technique, EPFL, Lausanne.

Cary BP , Zhao J , Badler NI (1990) *Interactive Real-Time Articulated Figure Manipulation using Multiple Kinematic Constraints*, ACM.

Cremer JF (1989) The architecture of NEWTON, a general purpose Dynamics simulator, *Proc. IEEE Conf. on Robotics and Automation*.

Denavit J, Hartenberg RS (1955) A Kinematic Notation for Lower Pair Mechanisms Based on Matrices, *J. Applied Mechanics*, Vol 22.

Foley J, Van Dam A, Feiner S, Hughes J (1990) *Computer Graphics Principles and Practice*, Second edition, Addison-Wesley, Reading, MA.

Girard M, Maciejewski AA (1985) Computational Modeling for the Computer Animation of Legged Figures, *Proc. SIGGRAPH '85, Computer Graphics*, Vol.19, No3, San Francisco, CA.

Girard M (1987) Interactive Design of 3D Computer-Animated Legged Animal Motion, *IEEE Computer Graphics and Applications* , Vol.7, No6.

Hégron G (1988) *Animation de systèmes de corps rigides*, Notes de cours de Computer Animation International 88, Genève.

Isaacs PM, Cohen F (1987) Controlling dynamic simulation with kinematic constraints, behavior functions and Inverse Dynamics, *Proc. SIGGRAPH '87, Computer Graphics*, Vol.21, No4.

Kroyer B (1986) Animating with a Hierarchy, *SIGGRAPH '86Course notes of the Seminar on Advanced Computer Animation*.

Magnenat-Thalmann N, Thalmann D (1990) *Computer Animation: Theory and Practice*, second edition, Springer Verlag, Tokyo.

Maiocchi R, Pernici B (1990) Directing an Animated Scene with Autonomous Actors, *The Visual Computer*, Vol. 6, No6, Springer Verlag, Heidelberg.

Maiocchi R (1991) A knowledge-based approach to the synthesis of human motion, in: Kunii (ed.) *Modeling in Computer Graphics*, Springer Verlag, Tokyo.

Ridsdale G, Hewitt S, Calvert TW (1986) The Interactive Specification of Human Animation, *Proc. Graphics Interface and Vision Interface '86*.

Sims K, Zeltzer D (1988) A Figure Editor and Gait Controller for Task Level Animation, *SIGGRAPH '88 Course notes on Synthetic Actors*.

Shuey D, Bailey D, Morrissey TP (1986) PHIGS: A Standard, Dynamic, Interactive Graphics Interface", *IEEE Computer Graphics and Application*, Vol.6, No8.

Turner R, Balaguer F, Gobetti E, Thalmann D (1991) Physically-based interactive camera motion using 3D input devices, *Proc of CGI '91*.

Van Baerle S (1986) Character Animation: Combining Computer Graphics and Traditional Animation, *SIGGRAPH '86 Course notes*.

Wilhelms J (1990) Dynamic Experiences, in: Badler N, Barsky B, Zeltzer D (editors) *Making Them Move*, Morgan Kaufmann Publishers, pp.265-279.

Zeltzer D (1982) Motor Control Techniques for Figures Animation, *IEEE Computer Graphics and Applications*, Vol.2, No9, pp.53-59

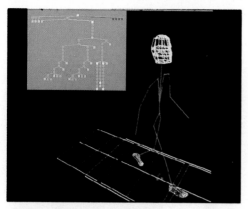

Figure 4.7. Data hierarchy: decomposition principle in skeleton and terminal node_3D

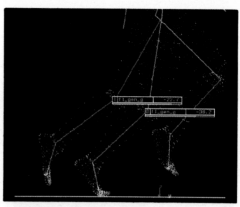

Figure 4.12. Transient transformation: edition of the left leg at knee flexion

Figure 5.4. Navigation through composition mechanism. The picture shows the process of revealing the contents of an image node 'Amah' (means a domestic servant) by navigating through the high-level composite node 'Chinese Immigrants' and its member composite node 'Occupation'. A composite node is shown as a window containing a set of named icons representing its members

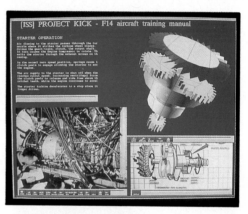

Figure 5.5. An interface of KICK. The display shows the details of an aircraft engine in four different media (text, 3D graphics, image and video)

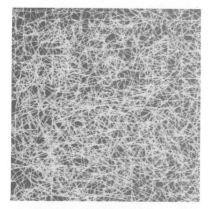

Figure 8.1. A mesh generated by a computer

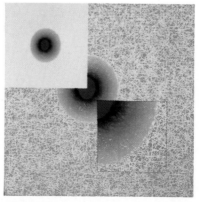

Figure 8.3. Generation of the ''nijimi'' image

Figure 8.16. Three auditory ossicles reconstructed using the triangulation method with Gouraud shading (Nomura et al. 1989)

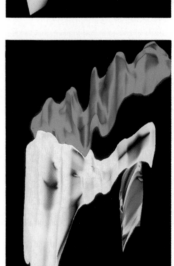

Figure 8.15. Three auditory ossicles reconstructed by a homotopy corresponding to a cardinal spline surface

Figure 8.14. Three auditory ossicles reconstructed by a straight-line homotopy

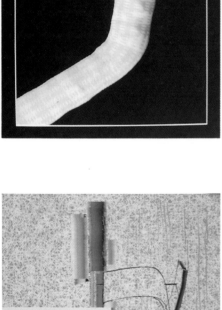

Figure 8.9. (a & b) Animation of wrinkle formation processes

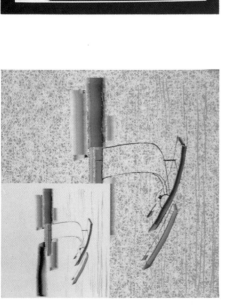

Figure 8.4. A computer-generated "sumie" with the 'nijimi' effect

Figure 9.1. Visualizing the flow over a wing with animated particles

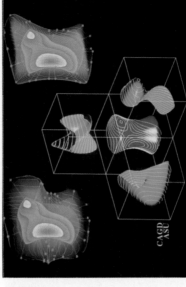

Figure 9.2. Radiation treatment (image courtesy of Fuchs, Levoy and Pizer)

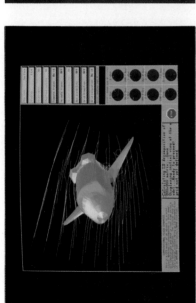

Figure 9.3. Choropleth and radially projected surface graph of a function defined over a sphere

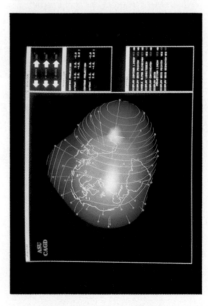

Figure 9.15. Various methods for visualizing surfaces-on-surfaces: choropleth graph, radially projected and orthogonally projected surface graphs and hypersurface projection graph

Figure 10.1. Wolkenhaus. Design created with volumes and parameterized elements, Hugo Doenz using ArchiCAD; rendering Sharon Refvem

Figure 10.2. Interactive design with volumes and parametric elements, Thomas Kämpfer using ArchiCAD; visualization Shen Guan Shih with Stalker

Figure 10.3. Wolkenhaus, roof terrace, design Hugo Doenz using ArchiCAD; rendering Sharon Refvem with personal visualizer

Figure 10.4. Model of a proposed design for Carnegie Mellon University, using substitution and instantiation; design Pierre Zoelly with Stephen Ciulla; modeling, substitution using AutoCAD and visualization using Stalker by Gerhard Schmitt

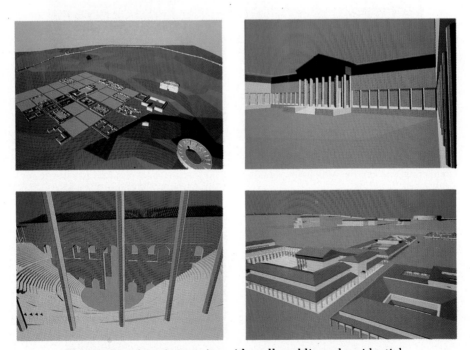

Figure 10.5. Aventicum, city with wall, public and residential buildings (top left), view of the temple (top right), view of the theater (bottom left), view of the forum (bottom right)

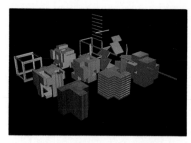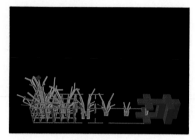

Figure 10.6. Types and levels of detail; object level Jürg Buman (left), CH 91 Urs Hirschberg (right); rendering Eric van der Marc with Wavefront Advanced Visualizer

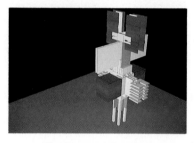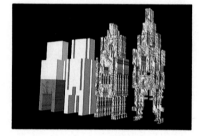

Figure 10.7. Combination of types and level of detail; design Gernot Schulz; rendering Eric van der Marc with Wavefront Advanced Visualizer

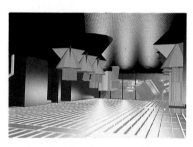

Figure 10.8. Models of types and levels of detail inserted into the exhibition space of the ETH Zürich; design Patrick Schaad; rendering Eric van der Marc with Wavefront Advanced Visualizer

Figure 10.9. Building types inserted into the context model of Winterthur, entire model inserted into the exhibition space of the ETH Zürich; rendering Eric van der Marc with Wavefront Advanced Visualizer

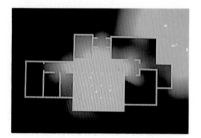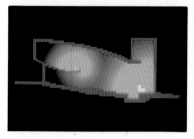

Figure 10.10. Experiments with cellular automata programs. Sound propagation in a building plan (left) and in a building section (right); program Shen Guan Shih on Silicon Graphics

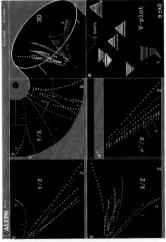

Figure 11.1. Standard projections. Two views (Y/X and ρ′/Z) of a typical high multiplicity event measured in the TPC of the ALEPH detector at LEP/CERN

Figure 11.2. Methods of representing 3D data. A cluster of tracks from the event of Figure 11.1 is shown in different projections: as perspective 3D picture, as front- (Y/X), side- (Y/Z) and top-view (X/Z), as ρ′/Z and as V-plot. The lines in the 3D picture represent the visible speed of the hits, if the event is rotated

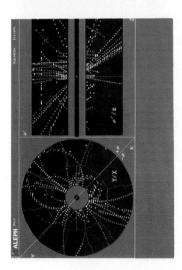

Figure 11.3. Check of tracks with the V-plot. The event of Figure 11.1 is shown as V-plot, where a box shows the selected hits, which are then drawn in enlarged sections of Y/X and ρ′/Z and as a magnified section of the V-plot. Y/X is shown cleaned and not cleaned

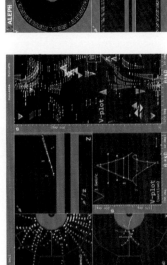

Figure 11.4. Simulation of an event with very high multiplicity. Y/X, ρ′/Z and V-plot of 1000 hits. The box on the V-plot shows the selected hits, which are shown in the cleaned Y/X view and as a magnified section of the V-plot

Figure 12.1. "Deilcraft Curio Design" by Semmania Luk Cheung, © Design Vision, Toronto, Canada

Figure 12.3. "Frank the Snake" by Gavin Miller and Michael Kass, © Apple Computer Inc., Cupertino, California

Figure 12.2. "Eric the Dynamic Worm" by Gavin Miller, Freddi Gitelman and Andrew Pearce, © Alias Research Inc., Toronto, Canada

5

Hypermedia: A New Approach to Multimedia Information Retrieval

Tat-Seng Chua
National University of Singapore

Hypermedia refers to a set of technologies that deals with a new way of organizing and providing associations between related pieces of information. Although many systems that claimed to be hypermedia have been developed, the concept of hypermedia is still constantly being defined and revised. This chapter reviews the features and limitations of the current generation of hypermedia systems, and explores five fundamental issues on hypermedia system research. It also discusses the components and architecture of a dynamic hypermedia system, and describes efforts towards developing such a system.

5.1. Introduction

Hypermedia is a technology recently evolved to tackle the problem of organization and access of multimedia information. Instead of organizing information as a continuous sequential flow of data, hypermedia encodes information into small self-contained units called nodes. Related nodes are linked together using machine supported links, giving rise to an associated information network as shown in Figure 5.1. Instead of accessing information by searching through indexes or turning pages, the users of such system access information by selecting links through trails of associated information. It is these machine processible links that gives the power to the hypermedia system. The type of information that can be handled in a hypermedia system is diverse: including static media such as text, image and graphics; dynamic media such as sound, video and animation; and variable media such as the spreadsheet.

Hypermedia in its basic form is most consistent with one particular way of accessing information–exploration. It has the potential to deliver new freedom to the users in exploring large amounts of multimedia information at their own pace and according to their interests. Through the interface, the users may examine a 3D graphics model; study its associated textual descriptions; view a simulation of its operations; watch a video on how it is being used in an actual environment; and, examine other relevant information. All these can be done easily through a consistent direct manipulation interface. A diagram illustrating how this scenario may be carried out is shown in Figure 5.5 (see color section). Hypermedia thus fits in well with the trends of giving more power to the users in using the system. Because of this, it is an ideal tool for learning and simulation.

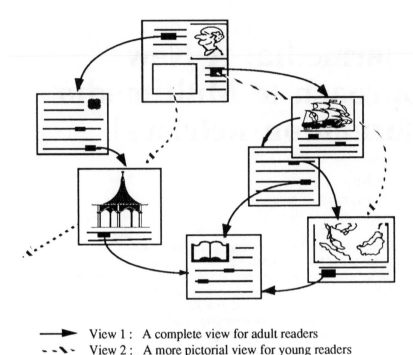

—▶ View 1 :   A complete view for adult readers
- -◣- View 2 :   A more pictorial view for young readers

Figure 5.1. A hypermedia information base

The full potential of hypermedia can only be realized by looking beyond the traditional uses of computers and the confined of printed media (Yankelovich et al. 1985). Among the potentials of the hypermedia technology are: (a) it permits the user to interact with the system to view and compose information in a non-linear and associative manner; (b) it permits the information presentation to be dynamic–both in terms of what is to be presented and how it is presented; (c) it enables the information to be "active" in which the user may interact directly with the information to perform operations such as traversing a link, activating an associated program, or initiating a simulation and, (d) it provides a consistent basis of linking and viewing large quantities of heterogeneous information. It is the realization of these potentials that led the early researchers (eg. Nelson 1967) to envision the creation of a huge information system that electronically links all the world's information together.

Current generation of hypermedia systems is still a long way away from realizing these potentials. The purpose of this chapter is to discuss the features and limitations of the current systems, and outlines the issues and efforts towards developing a new generation hypermedia system.

5.2. The Current Generation of Hypermedia Systems

5.2.1. Current Systems and Applications

The idea of hypermedia is not new. It was first proposed by Bush (1945) in the form of a "trail blazer" that permits the users to move quickly between related pieces of information. The first serious attempt to build a hypermedia system took place in 1968, when Engelbart (Engelbart and English 1968) demonstrated his Augment system in which he worked collaboratively on a hypertext document with a colleague 500 miles away. In the 20 years since Engelbart's demonstration, both interest and activity in hypermedia have grown steadily. Many research prototypes and commercial hypermedia systems have been developed. A good survey of the current state of development in hypermedia systems can be found in Conklin (1987).

Among the commercial products that have emerged over the last few years are: Apple's HyperCard (Goodman 1987); OWL International's Guide (Brown 1987); Cognetics's Hyperties (Shneiderman 1987); Scribe's KMS (Akscyn et al 1988); and, IBM's Linkway (IBM 1989). These are mainly general purpose systems aimed at aiding users in processing multimedia information, although most systems support only text and image properly. These systems provide only minimal support for browsing. None of the system provides graphical display of the hyperbase structure. Instead, they rely on bookmarking and history trail facilities to aid users in orientating within the hyperbase. In addition to the general systems, many of the above-mentioned hypermedia features have also been integrated into the interfaces of products like the Symbolics Document Examiner (Walker 1985), and Lotus's Agenda—a personal information manager.

Many research prototypes have also been developed over the same period. They include the Intermedia from the Brown University (Yankelovich et al. 1988); NoteCards from Xerox PARC (Halasz et al. 1987); Neptune from Tektronix (Delisle and Schwartz 1987); gIBIS from MCC (Conklin and Begeman 1988); and Medical Handbook from Washington University (Frisse 1988). These research prototypes are more focussed in terms of applications. They are developed respectively to support large scale interactive teaching (Intermedia); information gathering and analysis (NoteCards); large scale software engineering projects (Neptune); decision support and early decision deliberation (gIBIS); and, on line retrieval of medical information (Medical Handbook project). These research prototypes are mainly used as vehicles to investigate specific issues in hypermedia research. They are usually multi-window-based and support a more complete set of functions than the products. For example, most prototypes support the graphical display of the whole or part of the hypermedia structure, permit user customization of the hyperbase, and provide extension capability.

In addition to the systems, many application prototypes have also been developed to demonstrate the use of dynamic and 3D media in futuristic applications. The use of video as an active medium were explored in the Elastic Charles (Brondmo and Davenport 1989) and Aspen Movie Map (Lippman 1980) projects, where users may interact directly with the video to control the display of the video sequences. The Interactive SIGGRAPH Proceedings (Phillips 1990) attempts to use a wide variety of media including sound, video, animation to capture the richness and complexity of the SIGGRAPH conference experience. Finally, in KICK (Serra et al 1991), users may interact directly with 3D graphics and video to retrieve multimedia information through a consistent direct manipulation interface.

5.2.2. Common Features of Existing Systems

Despite the differences in applications and emphasis of the existing hypermedia systems, a number of features common to most systems can be identified. These common features are discussed in terms of: information creation, organization, presentation, interaction and retrieval.

Information Creation and Organization. Most systems organize information based on the node-and-link model, where the basic entities are a set of nodes interconnected by a set of links. Through the hypermedia editor, the user can create new nodes and add new links to any node. The user can also alter the contents of the nodes or the attributes of the links. Links are mostly generated and maintained manually by the users.

Information Presentation and Interaction. Most systems use the book metaphor as the main user interface. As with the book, the main access points in these systems are the table-of-contents and indices. System facilities are provided to enable users to place bookmarks on important nodes to re-visit; highlight certain passages; take notes; and keep track of sequence of nodes visited by users (history trail) for back tracking purposes. Most systems support or provide hooks to support the display of text, image, graphics, sound and video. However, other than text and image, most systems treat other media merely as passive media. Most research systems are multi-window based, and use graphs of information network to guide users in navigating the hyperbase.

Information Retrieval. In terms of information retrieval, most systems emphasize how browsing can be more effectively supported on the node-and-link model. Browsing can be accomplished in three ways by: (a) following the links within the nodes; (b) selecting appropriate nodes on the graph; and (c) examining the nodes stored in the history list and bookmarks. Information can also be accessed by searching the network for a logical combination of strings, keywords or attribute values.

5.2.3. Limitations of the Current Systems

The present generation of hypermedia system is based on the node-and-link model. Although the node-and-link model is very simple, flexible and efficient, it is too low level to support large scale information seeking needs that hypermedia technology promise to deliver. In particular, the current generation of hypermedia systems lacks supports for the following:

(a) User-orientation within the information network. One of the most fundamental problems in hypermedia system is the problem of getting "lost" when the size of the information exceeds 1000 nodes (Conklin 1987). The user gets lost when he does not know where he is; where he is heading to; or how he may reach a known location.

(b) Support for high-level abstraction of information. The high-level abstraction provides a way of representing a group of nodes and links as an unique entity with well defined syntactic and semantic properties. Successively higher levels of abstraction should be possible to reduce the vast quantity of nodes into a small number of well defined concepts. With better management, these high-level nodes can be used to provide context to users during browsing, thus further alleviating the disorientation problem.

(c) Facilities to help users to better organize and classify information. The existing system relies entirely on the users to create and maintain the links between nodes. The manual process of creating links is a major effort (Glushko 1989). In addition, if links are to be created and maintained by different authors for different parts of the information base, some inconsistency in the way in which the information units are links would arise. Such inconsistency will aggravate the problem of disorientation in the hyperbase.

(d) Intelligent presentation and filtering of information. This requires the ability of the system to decide not only what or how much information to present to the user, but also how it should be presented. Current hypermedia systems do not provide the necessary deductive capabilities to support these features.

(e) Consistent access and interaction of multimedia information. One essential attribute of hypermedia is that its information is "active", that is, the user may interact with the information directly by clicking (using a mouse on a conventional workstation) on the region of interest to perform operations like retrieving more information. For almost all existing systems, this paradigm works only for static 2D media such as text, image and graphics. Sound, video and 3D graphics are only passive media introduced to supplement the information provided by static media. No information seeking operations may be performed on these media.

5.3. Issues in Hypermedia Research

In an attempt to overcome these limitations, many agenda for hypermedia research have been proposed in the areas of system building (Halasz 1988) and usability (Waterworth and Chignell 1989). This chapter discusses five areas of research considered to be important by the author towards building a new generation hypermedia system.

The first is towards the use of semantics and high-level structure to provide better browsing support for the users. The use of frame formalism (Minsky 1967) as the basic mechanism to supplement the node-and-link model of the hypermedia system has been considered by Loo (1988), and extended by Koh and Chua (1989). In that prototype, frames are used as the underlying mechanism to structure information, and to control the user interface and information presentation. To provide better focus to the users, Nanard et al. (1988) proposed the use of frames mechanism to extract, organize and present a subset of information based on the user's interests. The use of composition as a mechanism to group multiple nodes with the same semantics has also been attempted (Garg and Scacchi 1988, Chua and Lai 1991). Compositions can be used as the basis of structuring information, and to guide user's browsing activities. In Serra et al (1991), a model has been described for integrating multimedia information based on 3D graphics hierarchies. The use of 3D model as the basis for organizing information provides natural supports for abstraction and facilitates the consistent organization and interaction of multimedia information.

The second is towards the integration of powerful search and query facilites to the hypermedia systems. Current generation of hypermedia systems rely mainly on exact-match boolean keyword search, which has been found to be unsatisfactory for hypermedia applications (Crouch et al. 1989). New search facilites based on content and structure are required (Halasz 1988). In content search, all nodes and links in the network are considered as independent entities and are examined individually for a match to a given query. The content search generally uses the partial-match query-based techniques (referred to as IR techniques) to perform the automatic analysis of the text contents against the user's query (Salton and McGill 1983). One approach suggested by Salton (1988) is to use IR techniques to automatically maintain the keyword indices and the linkage between relevant pieces of information. The structure search, on the other hand, examines the hypermedia structure for sub-networks that matches a given pattern. The structure search has been explored by Consens and Mandelzon (1989), in which a visual language, Graphlog, is used to express the structural query. Although the basic approaches of the content and structure search are quite different, future hypermedia search engine is likely to combine both approaches. One early attempt to combine both search approaches is the electronic medical book described by Frisse (1988), in which IR techniques are used in conjunction with the built-in hypermedia structure to find a most suitable starting point for a user to start browsing.

The third is towards the development of a dynamic hypermedia system. Current hypermedia model is static in nature, in which the sequencing of information and the associations between information chunks are fixed. The static nature of hypermedia model tends to have difficulty with changing information and variations in user's information needs. A solution to this problem is to incorporate the concept of dynamic links. A dynamic link is defined as one where the linkage between related nodes is determined at run-time based on the context and contents of the nodes. One way to implement the dynamic links is to develop a powerful search engine which could achieve a retrieval accuracy of over 80%. To achieve such accuracy, knowledge-based IR techniques must be used (Belkin and Croft 1987). An early attempt to use a knowledge-based IR model to generate the dynamic links has been described in Wang and Chua (1990).

The fourth is towards the development of a more effective user interface (UI). The development of navigation tools to aid user-orientation within the information network based a node-and-link model has been attempted by many authors. The navigation tools aim to present an overview of the hypermedia network structure to the users. Variations of such tools that have been developed ranging from 2D graph browsers (Halasz et al. 1987) and overview maps (Feiner 1988), to 3D network navigator (Fairchild et al. 1988). Although these tools are useful for exploratory navigation, they have been found to be unwieldy for large hyperbase (Monk 1989). To handle the problems of viewing large and complex network structures, various graph abstraction techniques are proposed, including the fisheye view (Furnas 1986), node clustering (Fairchild et al. 1988), and the dynamic presentation of abstract network views using nested box approach (Travers 1989). As we move towards providing higher level abstractions for the hyperbase, the use of high level abstract map, with landmarks denoting the major concepts available in the system, can be used to aid user-orientation. The use of physical metaphors to provide a consistent interface in the way that the users are familiar with in their daily life is also gaining popularity. Many existing hypermedia systems feature their interfaces based around some sort of metaphor, such as an encyclopaedia, box of cards, an electronic library, or a guided tour. However, a single metaphor is likely to be insufficient to present the different views of the future hyperbase. The use of multiple and possible hierarchical metaphors to handle different aspects of information presentation for different categories of users may be desirable (Waterworth and Chignell 1989). A hypermedia system with an extendable interface and supports a variety of metaphors is likely to be essential for future hypermedia applications.

The fifth is towards a more seamless integration of multimedia information into the hypermedia environment. Hypermedia advocates the direct manipulation of information on the screen. This paradigm works well for text and graphics because their contents are encoded in discrete, manipulatable units such as phrases or graphics entities. This is not the case for media such as image and video. For these media, additional encodings of their contents such as the overlaying simple polygons or graphics models on regions of interests must be carried out (Serra et al. 1991). The use of dynamic media gives rise to additional issues of handling temporal links, and interaction in a dynamic situation. Brondmo and Davenport (1989) describe the use of moving icons along with video presentation to permit users to traverse within video information during playback. Serra et al. (1991) discuss the synchronization of 3D animation with video sequences to facilitate direct manipulation of video contents. The inclusion of 3D graphics and animation gives rise to interesting issues of manipulating and simulating in a 3D virtual world. The inclusion of these media enriches the range and scope of applications of hypermedia systems.

5.4. Towards A New Generation Hypermedia System

5.4.1. A Dynamic Hypermedia Model

From the above discussion, a model for a new generation hypermedia system can be evolved. The new hypermedia system will be characterized by its support for dynamic information structure and high-level information abstraction. An outline of a model is shown in Figure 5.2.

Node :== Simple_Node I Composite_Node

Simple_Node :== [Content_Object]$^{1-n}$, Node_Type, Attribute_Set

Attribute_Set :== KEYWORDS, [SUMMARY], [FORMAT] [ ]...

Node_type :== TEXT I IMAGE I GRAPHICS I ANIMATION I SOUND I VIDEO I ..

Composite_Node :== Node_set, Attribute_set

Node_Set :== [Node I Query_Spec]$^{1-n}$

Node_Context :== Node, Link_Set

Link_Set :== [Link]$^{0-n}$

Link :== Link_Source, Link_Destination, Link_Type, Attribute_Set

Link_type :== ASSOCIATION I STRUCTURAL I SEQUENTIAL I
                REFERENTIAL I ...

Link_Source :== Node_id, [Content_Object_id]

Link_Destination :== Node_id, [Content_Object_id] I Query_Spec

Query_Spec :== Free_Text I Type_Description I ...

Figure 5.2. The definition of a dynamic hypermedia model

The basic entities in this model are a set of nodes interconnected by a set of links. The nodes are self-contained and independent of each other. Two classes of nodes are provided—the simple and the composite node. A simple node is defined as consisting of a set of attributes and content objects. The contents of a simple node can be of any medium type. A composite node consists of one or more simple or composite nodes. Composition is provided as a mean to composing high-level nodes by inclusion. The contents of a composite node may be pre-defined or specified through some query descriptions. In the latter case, the composite node is dynamic as its content is composed at run-time using a hypermedia search engine. All nodes are treated as first class objects in the system. They may be used as link destinations and subject to the same set of operations.

Links are used to provide associations between nodes. Various types of links can be supported including the association, structural, sequential and referential links (Chua and Lai 1991). The source and destination of a link may be fixed to a node or part of a node (see Figure 5.1). As with the contents of a composite node, the destination of a link may also be made dynamic by using a query specification. Such link is known as a dynamic link. The destination of a dynamic link is again determined at run-time using the hypermedia search engine.

In this model, nodes and links are treated as separate entities and they joined together only in a node context. A node context consists of a simple or composite node and a set of links. The set of links exist only within the context of the node in which it is defined. Outside the context of the node, the set of links does not exist. This link semantic permits a node to be included in more than one composition and exhibits different association behavior in different compositions. For example, a node about a person A may be included in two different composite nodes called Family_of_A and Company_of_A. While within the context of the composite node Family_of_A, node A contains association links to his parents, brothers, and sisters. However, within the context of the composite node Company_of_A, node A only maintains associations to his superior, his colleagues, and his work interests. Thus such a mechanism facilitates better sharing of nodes and clearer semantics of the nodes and links within the context of a composition.

5.4.2. The Architecture

The architecture of a new generation hypermedia system that incorporates the above model is shown in Figure 5.3. The architecture consists of six layers: the node and link layer; the search and information retrieval layer; the dynamic composition and linking layer; the presentation layer; the application-based structuring layer; and, the user profiling layer.

The lowest layer provides the basic support for the management of the set of nodes and links in the system. The set of nodes includes both simple as well as composite nodes. The next layer implements the knowledge-based search engine for retrieving the subset of nodes and links based on the user's request. The search engine is used to support the next higher layer for providing dynamic composition and linking supports. This layer aims to support the customization of information (through dynamic composition) and the automatic association between related nodes. At the presentation layer, various tools are provided for defining the presentation styles and metaphoric interface of the hyperbase. A range of metaphors can be made available to cater for different variety of applications. The application-based layer deals with application specific presentation and structuring of information. It provides utilities for defining new types of nodes and links, and their presentations. Lastly, the user profiling layer maintains the user profiles, and determines the presentation as well as a suitable subset of information to be presented to the users.

It should be noted that the model and architecture described above refer only to a general framework of how high-level abstraction and dynamism may be introduced into the hypermedia system. The actual formalism for high-level abstraction and search engine is implementation dependent.

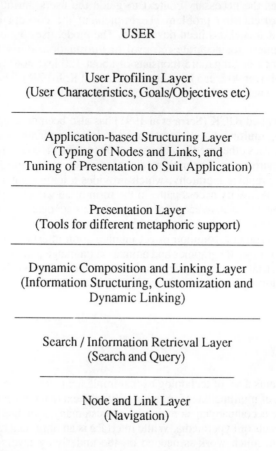

USER

User Profiling Layer
(User Characteristics, Goals/Objectives etc)

Application-based Structuring Layer
(Typing of Nodes and Links, and
Tuning of Presentation to Suit Application)

Presentation Layer
(Tools for different metaphoric support)

Dynamic Composition and Linking Layer
(Information Structuring, Customization and
Dynamic Linking)

Search / Information Retrieval Layer
(Search and Query)

Node and Link Layer
(Navigation)

Figure 5.3. The architecture of a dynamic hypermedia system

5.4.3. Hypermedia Prototypes

Two hypermedia systems based on the above architecture has been developed at the National University of Singapore. The first system aims to investigate the issues of high level abstraction and dynamism in the hypermedia system. The design of the system using the frame formalism has been discussed in detail in Koh and Chua (1989). To provide the necessary high-level abstraction in the system, a composition editor has been developed (Chua and Lai 1991). Through the interface of the editor, the user can freely create composite nodes and define their contents. Various types of compositions may be defined in a recursive manner. Once the compositions are defined, operations may be performed on them to view, expand, abstract or traverse their contents, or find other nodes with similar contents. Users may navigate within the hyperbase by expanding the compositions defined by the authors. A typical screen snapshot during a navigation process through the composition mechanism is shown in Figure 5.4 (see color section). As shown in Figure 5.4, the composition mechanism provides the necessary context to guide the users during browsing, and thus alleviating the disorientation problem. To implement the concept of dynamic links, a knowledge-based IR model has been developed. The model uses the domain knowledge to expand the user's query for accurate retrieval of information. Early results based on the domain of the History of Singapore (consists of about 120 text nodes) indicate that a high retrieval accuracy of over 90% can be achieved (Koh and Koh 1991). This result demonstrates that the concept of dynamic linking is feasible in a specific domain.

A separate system called KICK (Serra et al 1991) has also been developed to investigate the issues of integrating multimedia information for training applications. The system is based on 3D graphics, but uses other media such as text, image and video to provide a complete and realistic learning environment. The multimedia information is organized using a model based primarily on a 3D graphics hierarchy, which provides a natural interface for the users to access information. Auxiliary access paths in the form of network are provided by means of other media to enable associative access of information as advocated by hypermedia. A major concern of this system is to permit consistent interactions of different media, including images and video, through a common direct manipulation interface. Techniques have been developed to superimpose 3D graphics and animation on image and video media to make this possible. Two industrial training applications have been developed using this prototype. The interface of the prototype for an aircraft training application is shown in Figure 5.5 (see color section).

5.5. Summary

Hypermedia represents a set of technologies that implements the concept of free associations between a large set of multimedia information. With the excitement generated by multimedia presentation and the accompanying commercial interest, many current efforts are concentrated on the interface aspects of hypermedia. While interface is an important and integral part of the hypermedia system, much work is needed on the underlying layers of the system. This chapter presents the need for more research in these areas. In particular, this chapter discusses current efforts towards providing high-level abstraction, better integration of multimedia information, and dynamism in the hypermedia system. A model and the architecture of a dynamic hypermedia system have also been described. It is believed that progress in this direction will lead to a more usable hypermedia system.

Acknowledgements

The author would like to acknowledge the support and contributions of the Hypermedia group at the Institute of Systems Science, National University of Singapore, for the various concepts presented in this chapter.

References

Akscyn R, McCracken D, Yoder E (1988), KMS: A Distributed Hypermedia System for Managing Knowledge in Organizations, *Comm of ACM*, Vol.31, No7, pp.820-835.

Belkin NJ, Croft WB (1987), Retrieval Techniques, in Williams ME (Ed), *Annual Review of Information Science and Technology (ARIST)*, 22, pp.109-145.

Brondmo HP, Davenport G (1989), Creating and Viewing the Elastic Charles - A Hypermedia Journal, *Hypertext II*, Jun, York, UK.

Brown PJ (1987), Turning Ideas into Products: The Guide System, *Proc Hypertext'87 Workshop*, Chapel Hill, NC, pp.33-40.

Bush V (1945), As we may Think, *Atlantic Monthly*, Vol.176, No1, pp.101-108.

Chua TS, Lai EPM (1991), Supporting Composition in a Hypermedia Environment, submitted to Hypermedia Journal for publication.

Conklin J (1987), Hypertext: An Introduction and Survey, *IEEE Computer*, pp.17-41.

Conklin J, Begeman ML (1988), gIBIS: A Hypertext Tool for Exploratory Policy Discussion, *ACM Trans Office Infor System*, pp.140-152.

Consens MP, Mandelzon AO (1989), Expressing Structural Hypertext Queries in GraphLog, *Proc Hypertext'89*, pp.269-292.

Crouch DB, Crouch CJ, Andreas G (1989), The Use of Cluster Hierarchies in Hypertext Information Retrieval, *Proc Hypertext'89*, pp.225-237.

Delisle NM, Schwartz MD (1987), Contexts - A Partitioning Concept for Hypertext, *ACM Trans on Office Infor. Systems*, Vol.5, No2, pp.168-186.

Engelbart DC, English WK (1968), A Research Centre for Augmenting Human Intellect, *AFIPS Conf Proc*, 33(1), The Thompson Book Co, Washington, D.C.

Fairchild KM, Poltrock SE, Furnas GW (1988), SemNet: 3D Graphics Represntations of Large Knowledge Bases, in Guindon R (ed) *Cognitive Science and Its Applications for Human-Computer Interaction*, Lawrence Erlbaum Associates, Hillsdale, NJ.

Feiner S (1988), Seeing Forest for the Trees: Hierarchical Display of Hypertext Structure, *Proc of Conf. on Office Infor Systems*, ACM, pp.205-212.

Frisse ME (1988), Searching for Information in a Hypertext Medical Handbook, *Comm of ACM*, 31(7), pp.880-886.

Furnas G (1986), Generalized Fisheye Views, *Proc CHI'86 Human Factors in Computing Systems*, Boston, MA, pp.13-17.

Garg PK, Scacchi W (1988), Composition of Hypertext Nodes, *Proc of 12th Intl Online Information Meeting*, London, UK, pp.63-73.

Glushko RJ (1989), Design Issues for Multi-Document Hypertexts, *Proc Hypertext'89*, Nov, pp.51-60.

Goodman D (1987), The Complete HyperCard Handbook, Bantam, Toronto.

Halasz FG (1988), Reflections on Notecards: Seven Issues for the Next Generation of Hypermedia Systems, *Comm of ACM*, Vol.31, No7, pp.836-852.

Halasz FG, Morgan TP, Trigg RH (1987), NoteCards in a Nutshell, *Proc ACM CHI+GI'87*, Toronto, Canada, pp.45-52.

IBM (1989) - The IBM Linkway User's Manual, *IBM*.

Koh CK, Koh CC (1991), Dynamic Hypertext System: A Concept-based Information Retrieval Model, *Third Year Project Dissertation*, Department of IS/CS, National University of Singapore.

Koh TT, Chua TS (1989), On the Design of a Frame-based Hypermedia System, *Hypertext II*, Jun, York, UK.

Lippman A (1980), Movie Maps: An Application of the Optical Videodisc to Computer Graphics, *SIGGRAPH'80 Proc*, ACM.

Loo JPL (1988), Hypertext is Here to Stay, *ISS Systems Catalyst*, Sep, pp. 3-4.

Minsky M (1967), A Framework for Representing Knowledge, in P. Winston (Ed.), *The Psychology of Computer Vision*, McGraw-Hill, New York, pp. 211-277.

Monk A (1989), Getting to a Known Locations in a Hypertext, *Hypertext II*, Jun, York, UK.

Nanard J, Nanard M, Richy H (1988), Conceptual Documents: a Mechanism for Specifying Active Views in Hypertext, *ACM Conference on Document Processing Systems*, (New Mexico), Dec, pp.37-42.

Nelson TH (1967), Getting it Out of Our System, in Schecter G (ed), *Information Retrieval: A Critical Review*, Thompson Books, Washington DC.

Phillips D (1990), Interactive SIGGRAPH Proceedings: A New For of Publication, *Computer Graphics*, Vol.24, No1, pp.59-61.

Salton G (1988), Automatic Text Indexing Using Complex Identifiers, *ACM Conference on Document Processing Systems*, (New Mexico), Dec, pp.135-144.

Salton G, McGill MJ (1983), Introduction to Modern Information Retrieval, *McGraw-Hill*.

Serra L, Chua TS, Teh WS (1991), A Model for Integrating Multimedia Information Around 3D Graphics Hierarchies, to appear in *The Visual Computer*.

Shneiderman B (1987) - User Interface Design and Evaluation for an Electronic Encyclopedia, in Salvendy G (ed), *Cognitive Engineering in the Design of Human-Computer Interaction and Expert Systems*, Elsevier Science Publishers, pp. 207-223.

Travers M (1989), A Visual Representation for Knowledge Structures, *Proceed of Hypertext'89*, ACM Press, Nov.

Walker JH (1985), The Document Examiner, *SIGGRAPH Video Review*, Edited compilation from CHI'85: Human Factors in Computing Systems, Toronto, Canada, Apr.

Wang X and Chua TS (1990), Support for Search and Dynamic Linking in a Hypertext Environment, *ISS Internal Report*.

Waterworth JA, Chignell MH (1989), A Manifesto for Hypermedia Usability Research, *Hypermedia*, Vol.1, No3, pp.205-234.

Yankelovich N, Haan BJ, Meyrowitz NK, Drucker SM (1988), Intermedia: The Concept and the Construction of a Seamless Information Environment, *IEEE Computer*, Vol.21, No1, pp.81-96.

Yankelovich N, Meyrowitz NK, van Dam A (1985), Reading and Writing the Electronic Book, *IEEE Computer*, Vol.18, No10, pp.15-32.

6

Virtual Environments

Francis Balaguer and Angelo Mangili
Computer Graphics Laboratory, Swiss Federal Institute of Technology, Lausanne

The last decade has been marked by the development of the computer as a tool in almost every domain of human activity. One of the reasons for such a development was the introduction of human-friendly interfaces which have made computers easy to use and learn. The most successful interface paradigm so far has been the Xerox Parc Desktop metaphor popularized among computer users by the Macintosh. However, if the desktop metaphor is well suited to interacting with two-dimensional worlds, it starts to show limitations when interacting with three dimensional worlds. Recently, various specialized research programs on advanced concepts for human–machine interaction have focused on this problem and have gradually made possible the development of new input devices and displays for interacting with remote or computer generated worlds. Rather than keyboard input, interaction is based on voice, gesture and hand manipulation; displays are rethought to closely match human vision capabilities yielding in the development of head mounted or head coupled display concepts. The goal is to simulate operator presence in remote or computer synthesized worlds. In this chapter, we present this new interface metaphor, the perceptual and technological requirements to simulate it, 3D input devices and displays, and 3D interaction techniques.

6.1. Virtual Reality

6.1.1. Historical Background

Virtual reality (VR) is not a new concept even if the oxymoron "artificial reality" was recently introduced by Krueger (1983). Sutherland (1965) introduced the key concepts of immersion in a simulated world, and of complete sensory input and output, which are the basis of current VR research. At MIT, at the beginning of the 1980s, a limited three-dimensional virtual workspace in which the user interactively manipulates 3D graphical objects spatially corresponding to hand position, was developed (Schmandt 1983). In 1984, NASA started the VIVED project (Virtual Visual Environment Display) and later the VIEW project (Virtual Interactive Environment Workstation). As described in Fisher et al. (1986), the objective of the research at NASA Ames is to develop a multipurpose, multimodal operator interface to facilitate natural interaction with complex operational tasks and to augment operator awareness of large-scale autonomous integrated systems. The application areas on which NASA Ames focuses, are telepresence control, supervision and management of large-scaled information systems and human factors research. Even though NASA's research interested researchers, VR was not introduced to the general public until June 6, 1989 at two trade shows by VPL and Autodesk. Both companies presented devices and head-mounted displays for interacting with virtual worlds. Since then, VR has captured the public imagination and lots of work has been done to explore the possibilities of VR in new areas of application such as medicine, chemistry, scientific visualization.

6.1.2   Application

VR is more than just interacting with 3D worlds. By offering presence simulation to users as an interface metaphor, it allows operators to perform tasks on remote real worlds, computer generated worlds or any combination of both. The simulated world does not necessarily have to obey natural laws of behavior. Such a statement makes nearly every area of human activity, a candidate for a VR application. However, we can identify some application areas as more straightforward than others.

6.1.2.1. Telepresence, Telerobotics

Hostile environments such as damaged nuclear power plants make it difficult or impossible for human beings to perform maintenance tasks. However, for the foreseeable future, robots will not be intelligent enough to operate with complete independence, but will require operator intervention to perform tasks in changing or unanticipated circumstances (Zeltzer 1990). Telepresence aims to simulate the presence of an operator in a remote environment to supervise the functioning of the remote platform and perform tasks controlling remote robots. In supervisory control modes, a VR interface provides the operator with multiple viewpoints of the remote task environment in a multi-modal display format that can be easily reconfigured according to changing task priorities. The operator can investigate the remote site either free-flying or through telerobot mounted cameras. To perform remote operations that cannot be performed autonomously by robots, the operator can switch to interactive control. In this telepresence mode, he is given sufficient quantity and quality of sensory feedback to approximate actual presence at the remote site. The operator's stereoscopic display is linked to the robot 3D camera system and his arm is made spatially correspondent with the robot arm. NASA Ames developed a telepresence prototype application where the operator interacts with a simulated telerobotic task environment (Fisher et al. 1986).

6.1.2.2. Large Data Set Exploration

Many three-dimensional applications in scientific visualization consist of the study of multi-dimensional physical phenomena. In such systems, the computer model generates data representing the behavior of the model under special initial conditions. Study of complex phenomenon such as a thunderstorm requires a tremendous volume of data which raises the problem of data interpretation. In scientific visualization, the VR interface can help scientists explore the multi-dimensional graphical representation of their data at various levels of detail using interactive camera control and stereoscopic displays. The scientist is free to fly within his simulation data and therefore to focus interest on any part of its simulation, to study it in detail or to allocate supercomputer time for a more precise simulation (Brooks 1988).

6.1.2.3. Architecture Walkthrough

One application area of VR can be architecture. Brooks (1986) and Airey et al. (1990) presented a system to explore virtual buildings, designed but not yet constructed. The object of the system was visualization of the building to permit the architect to prototype a building and to iterate with his client on the detailed desiderata for it. Using a video projector for a wider field of view, stereo techniques and a special 3D device, he enabled the user to interactively walk-through the virtual building as if it was built. Even if in that case, the purpose of the application was presentation of an already designed building, an extension of such an application can be thought of as a tool to help the designer visualize and explore the spaces he is creating as part of the design process.

6.1.2.4. Other Areas

Examples in previous sections are not exhaustive. At the University of North Carolina, they explore the use of head-mounted displays in areas such as molecule analysis and medical imaging (Chung et al. 1989). Nasa Ames build a system to interactively explore the surface of Mars based on Viking images (Jackoby 1990) and apply VR to information management (Fisher et al. 1986). At the Human Interface Technology Laboratory (HITL) of the University of Washington, they are working on VR for air traffic controllers where the controller would be able to see with a head-mounted display every plane in the sky around the airport and would be able to start a radio connection with the plane by touching its 3D graphical representation (Stewart 1991).

6.1.3. Perceptual Requirements for a Virtual Reality System

We humans are experienced in interacting with three-dimensional worlds. Our sense of vision enables us to orient ourselves in space, and provides others cues for locomotion and communication. Our mind is highly trained to interpret images and communication is often more effective through images, graphs, diagrams than through words. Traditional computer configuration allows us to interact visually with virtual worlds through a window (the screen) on that world. We can change what we see on the window, but the window itself remains static in our own world. The virtual world resides inside the computer, we are exterior to it.

The major characteristic of VR is inclusion: being surrounded by an environment. VR places the participant within information. This simulation of presence inside a computer generated world introduces a general paradigm shift in the way we perceive the interaction task with the machine. Bricken (1990) gives the HITL's opinion on changes of perspective introduced by simulation of presence:

"The extension of field of view coupled with stereoscopic display produces the feeling that we cease from viewing a picture on the screen to start experiencing the sensation of being in a place. We shift from external users exercising rights to internal participant exercising responsibilities, from observing to experiencing, from interfacing with a display to inhabiting an environment. This sensation of being surrounded make us forget about the virtuality of the world we are exploring."

Every human–machine interaction task is a bi-directional communication between a user and the machine. The user specifies input and the computer responds to it by updating its output.

What are the input and output channels required to realize simulation of presence? In a traditional computer configuration, inputs and outputs are well defined. Input is specified through the keyboard and the mouse while output consists of updating a display. VR, which assumes the fact that human beings are well equipped to interact with 3D worlds, wants to make users interact with virtual worlds in the same way they interact with real worlds, thus making the interaction task much more natural and reducing training. Observing the way we interact with the real world, it is possible to identify the new input and output channels required to simulate immersion.

- **output** channels are those by which humans receive information from the world. They correspond to our senses: vision, touch and force perception, hearing, smell, taste. Analyzing crudely how we use our senses, we can say that vision is our privileged mean of perception, while hearing is mainly used for verbal communication, to get information from invisible parts of the world or when vision does not provide enough information. Touch and force perception is essential for interacting with another object during manipulation tasks while smell and taste are mostly secondary. Therefore, critical output channels are graphical display, audio output, touch and force information output. Visual feedback must match as closely as possible human vision capabilities, i.e. binocular vision, and wide field of view. Audio feedback must be able to synthesize sound, to position sound sources in 3D space and can be linked to a speech generator for verbal communication with the computer. Touch feedback must transmit force data necessary for precise manipulation.

- **input** channels are those with which humans emit information and interact with the environment. We interact with the world mainly through locomotion and manipulation. We communicate information by means of voice, gestures and facial expressions. Gestural communication as well as locomotion make full body motion analysis desirable. However, hand motion tracking is sufficient for almost every applications as the hand offers many more degrees-of-freedom (DOF) concentrated in a small area than any other part of the body. Moreover, the fact that the hand is our privileged manipulation tool make hand motion tracking a critical input for interacting with virtual worlds. Viewpoint specification requires real time motion tracking of the user's head, and eventually eye, in order to update displayed stereo images in coordination with user movements. Verbal communication with the computer or other users makes voice input necessary.

Figure 6.1 presents output and input channels of a typical VR computer configuration.

6.2. Interaction Devices for Virtual Reality

Currently, a set of devices, hand measurement hardware, head-mounted displays, as well as 3D audio systems, speech synthesis or recognition systems are available on the market. At the same time, many research labs are working on defining and developing new devices such as force-feedback devices, tactile gloves, eye-tracking devices, or on improving existing devices such as head-mounted displays and tracking systems. In the next sections, we are going to present various existing devices and a perspective of development for the future.

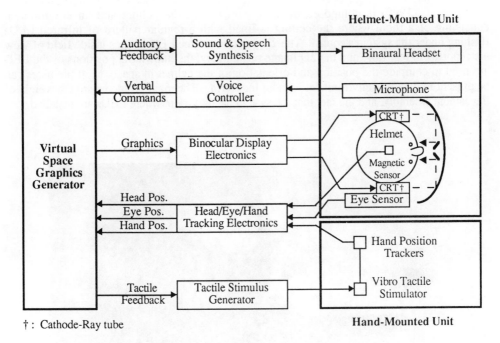

Figure 6.1. Virtual reality computer configuration (Furness 1987).

6.2.1. Tracking Devices

Commercial and experimental 3D position tracking devices have used acoustic, magnetic, mechanical, and optical methods for reporting 3D position and orientation.

Acoustic systems use the time-of-flight principle to estimate the position of an object in space. Because the speed of sound varies if ambient air density changes, these systems have poor accuracy over a large range. Furthermore, it is difficult to use them to measure orientation.

Mechanical linkage systems have been built in the past (Sutherland 1968). Not only have they a limited working range, but the friction inertia of the system and the mechanical linkage attached to the user greatly restrict its motion.

Magnetic tracking devices have been the most successful and the Polhemus 3Space Isotrack, although not perfect, is the most common one. A source generates a low frequency magnetic field detected by a sensor (see Figure 6.2). The main problems with the Polhemus, is that its performance is affected by any conducting materials present in the environment. Moreover, the Polhemus has a limited working range (~ 1 m^3) and a update rate (~ 16 Hz) which is barely enough for interactive applications.

Although most optical tracking systems seem to have failed as commercial products for VR, the method is appealing mainly because it is relatively insensitive to environmental distortions and has a large working environment. The optical tracking system presented by Wang et al. (1990) is composed of three cameras on the helmet and an environment consisting of a room where the ceiling is lined with a regular pattern of infrared LEDs flashing under the system's control. The 2D positions of the LED images inside field of view are reported in real-time and the 2D image position and the known 3D positions of the LED are used to compute the position and orientation of the helmet in space. Multiple users can be present in the same environment without interfering. The main problems are the weight of the camera assembly, and the fact that the system needs a room where LEDs are installed.

Figure 6.2. Polhemus source and sensor

6.2.2. Head-Mounted Displays

Most head-mounted display systems developed in the last decade (Chung et al. 1989), present the rich 3D cues of head-motion parallax and stereopsis. Head-mounted displays, designed to take advantage of human binocular vision capabilities, present the general following characteristics:

- headgear with two small display devices (generally LCD color screens), each optically channeled to one eye, for binocular vision.
- special optics in front of the screens, for wide field of view
- a tracking system for precise location of the user's head in real time.

Figure 6.3 presents the internal components of an head-mounted display developed at NASA Ames. Displays are small LCD TV screens and the computer output has to be predistorted to compensate for the radial distortion introduced by the wide angle optics.

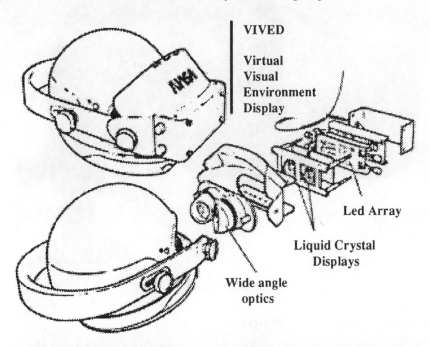

Figure 6.3. Virtual environment display system (Reproduced from Fisher et al. (1986)).

Figure 6.4. A see-through head-mounted display

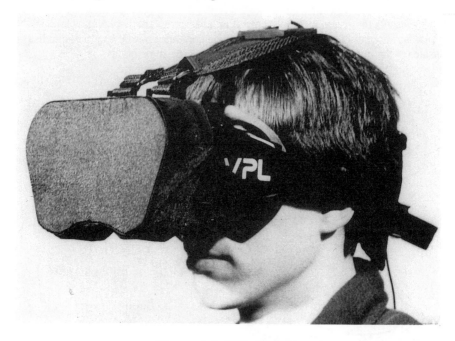

Figure 6.5. VPL EyePhone

6.2.3. Hand Measurement Devices

Hand measurement devices must sense both the flexion angles of the fingers and the position and orientation of the wrist in real-time. Image based techniques have been used to measure both channels directly from observation of user movement. However, since interpretation of the moving images is required, this technique tends to be slow and imprecise, even when LEDs are used to identify key points on the user to simplify image processing task (Ginsberg and Maxwell 1986). The Z-glove (Zimmerman et al. 1987) from VPL Research, performed position tracking with electronics transducers mounted on side of the palm. This method of tracking fails if there is not a direct line-of-sight between the transducers and the set of three receivers.

Currently, the most common hand measurement device is the DataGlove (see Figure 6.6) from VPL Research. The DataGlove consists of a lightweight nylon glove with optical sensors mounted along the fingers. In its basic configuration, the sensors measure the bending angles of the joints of the thumb and the lower and middle knuckles of the others fingers, and the DataGlove can be extended to measure abduction angles between the fingers. Each sensor is a short length of fiberoptic cable, with a light-emitting diode (LED) at one end and a phototransistor at the other end. When the cable is flexed, some of the LED's light is lost, so less light is received by the phototransistor. Attached to the back is a 3Space Isotrack system (see previous section for description) to measure orientation and position of the gloved hand. This information, along with the ten (fifteen to measure abduction angles, in the extended configuration) flex angles for the knuckles is transmitted through a serial communication line to the host computer. Knuckle data can be sampled at up to 60 Hz.

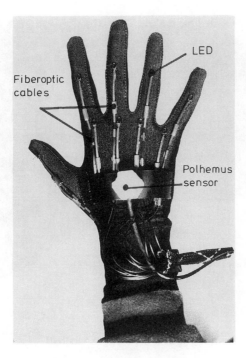

Figure 6.6. VPL DataGlove

6.2.4. Other Devices

The DataGlove and head-mounted displays are not the only devices to have been developed in the last few years.

Some people have tried to extend the concept of the mouse to 3D. Called a wand or bat in the literature, 3D mice (Ware and Jessome 1988) are generally built around a Polhemus tracker. Some buttons are sometimes added to the device. The problem of such devices is that they are absolute position devices. You must move the hand grabbing the device, according to the movement desired for the object. This is often tiring and requires a bit of concentration, especially when the display upgrade rate falls under 10 Hz.

In order to address this problem, Spatial Systems designed an incremental device called the Spaceball (see Figure 6.7). It is composed of a rigid sphere containing strain gauges mounted on a plastic base in order to offer a comfortable rest position for the operator hand and arm. The position and orientation are specified by rotating or pushing the sphere in a certain direction. Although the sphere moves only slightly, the force and torque applied are measured and an incremental position and orientation is transmitted, at a configurable rate, to the host computer. The Spaceball is well suited to moving objects or virtual cameras in three-dimensional space. The metaphor based on the fact that the ball you grab is the object you want to move is easy to integrate, thus requiring reduced training.

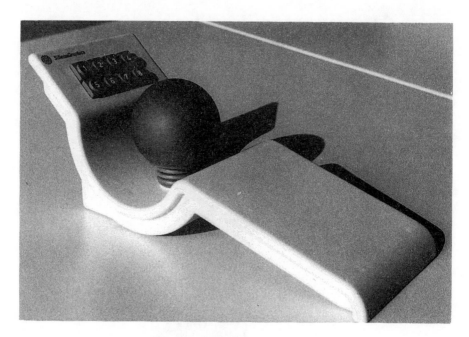

Figure 6.7. The Spaceball

6.2.5. Perspectives

Even if the hardware presented above is a tremendous step towards the VR computer configuration presented in part one (see Figure 6.1), many major problems remain unresolved to achieve full effectiveness:

- *developing high-resolution color displays*. The technology used in current head-mounted displays is mainly based on LCD screens for reasons of weight and energy consumption. The resolution is too low (less than video resolution) for high quality images. Even if we can expect higher resolution LCD screens and video standard in the future, some people have taken a totally different approach. HITL has engaged a research project on using laser beams to display the pictures directly on the retina, hence solving the problem of resolution and wide field of view.

- *developing headgear* of a reasonable size and weight, that allows a wide-screen view of the graphics display screen superimposed on the real world. This is a difficult optical problem. The wide angle optics used nowadays make superposition of computer images onto the real-world difficult because the real-world pictures have to be predistorted to compensate for the radial distortion introduced by the optics.

- *developing tracking systems* that have the range of a room with 1 mm resolution and response time of a few milliseconds or less. An ultimate tracking system would require real-time high precision tracking of multiple persons in a large environment. It should also be insensitive to interference from the environment. Even if some progress has been made with the optical tracker, the ultimate tracker is still far in the future.

Other research focuses on creating force-feedback devices (Minsky et al. 1990; Iwata 1990; Luciani 1990), eye trackers (Jacob 1990), tactile feedback gloves, and on improving graphics performance of workstations (Fuchs et al. 1989). Even if a real VR system is still far off, existing devices allow us to build real and useful applications and to study the software tools needed for interaction.

6.3. Interaction Techniques

Interacting with three-dimensional worlds is not fundamentally different from interacting with two dimensional worlds, in terms of interaction tasks. Basic interaction tasks are still the same. We still need to specify a viewpoint, to select objects and to position them in space, to specify values, states, or text (Foley et al. 1990). However, in order to simulate presence, the mouse has been replaced by hand measurement hardware which has become the main input channel for interacting with the virtual world. How shall we use this device combined with tracking information to specify viewpoint, values and states? How shall we use direct manipulation to position an object? How can we control objects with many degrees of freedom? Solving these complex problems is the aim of current research. Hence, the next sections will present a starting point for a solution based on the work of Zeltzer at MIT. We present the different levels of abstraction that can be used to model objects in a virtual environment, and how the DataGlove can be used for direct manipulation of each type of object.

6.3.1. Abstraction of a Privileged Device, the Glove

When using an input device, one can poll directly the input channels and hard code a meaning for each of them according to the program current state. If such an approach is possible with a simple device such as the mouse, it is much more difficult to poll a device such as the DataGlove because of its 10 or 15 DOF for the hand plus 6 DOF for position and orientation. The DataGlove must be abstracted into a virtual device at the software level, which sends out higher level events.

The DataGlove comes with a library that polls the hardware and composes event records containing flexion angles, location of the hand, a timestamp and a posture number. Postures are identified by correlating finger angles and posture numbers using a lookup table. At MIT, Studmann et al. (1989) evaluated the abstraction proposed by VPL as not sufficient for whole hand interaction because VPL offers only direct manipulation and state input through postures. Studmann identified three ways of approaching whole hand interaction:

- as a method for direct manipulation where the user guides object of the virtual world as if he would manipulate elements of the real world.

- as an abstracted graphical input device such as a button, valuator, or locator.
- as a gestural language.

Studmann analyzed hand motion in terms of its basic components: hand position and orientation, finger flexion angles, and organized the components into a taxonomy of hand motion summarized by the following table (Figure 6.8).

Hand position & orientation	Finger flex angles		
	don't care	motionless fingers	moving finger
don't care		**finger posture** (button) *e.g. fist*	**finger gesture** (valuator)
motionless hand	**hand posture** (3D gesture)	**oriented posture** *e.g. thumbs/down*	**oriented gesture** *e.g. bye-bye vs. come here*
moving hand	**hand gesture** (contunuous 3D locator)	**moving posture** *e.g. banging fist or a salute*	**moving gesture** *e.g. strong come here*

Figure 6.8. Hand motion taxonomy (Studmann et al. 1989)

The first row and first column of the table, correspond to conventional logical input devices. Whole hand input can be used in terms of the existing interaction metaphor. Finger postures offer a natural way to initiate events and set modes of interaction. Flex angles can be used as valuators and the hand itself is used as a 3D cursor. The lower 2x2 part of the table corresponds to more complex composite movements that are familiar from everyday social interactions. These do not really correspond to classical input metaphors. Recognition of gestures requires the use of artificial intelligence pattern matching because a gesture will never be reproduced exactly the same way twice. Gestures could be associated with some actions (like bye-bye with quit).

As use of classical interaction metaphors is well defined in the literature (Foley et al. 1990), the next section will present the use of direct manipulation with the various types of objects populating the virtual world.

6.3.2. Direct Manipulation (Guiding)

Guiding requires the user to provide the parameters required by some program. Guiding is interactive and direct and requires real-time system response. Typically in interacting with virtual environments, guiding is useful when positioning objects in space, or to specify a viewpoint. As guiding techniques require detailed specification of movement by the user, real-time feedback is necessary.

6.3.2.1. Viewpoint Specification

In previous sections, we pointed out the importance of the visual output channel to create the illusion of presence. On the other hand, viewpoint specification is a key technique which must be as natural and intuitive as possible so that the user is no longer conscious of it and can concentrate on the application task.

The head motion input channel provides all the information required for viewpoint specification. The kinesthetic correspondence between the user's head and the virtual camera viewpoint provide a highly naturalistic for of interaction. However, such a straightforward spatial correspondence is not always desirable or possible. Unconstrained motion with respect to real space is necessary for large displacement purposes. Several recent papers have proposed and studied the use of various kinematic or dynamic metaphors (Ware and Osborne 1990), Turner et al. 1991), such as "flying-vehicle", to control the virtual camera motion using a six DOF devices. Hence, we can think of the virtual camera as a two part mechanism, one part is a mechanical system which embodies the behavior of the metaphor, the other part is the camera itself with a 3 DOF mount for local rotations. Then the camera is controlled through two input channels, hand motion can be used to control the metaphor while head motion is used to control local rotation while moving. Hence, using a flying vehicle metaphor, the hand can be used to specify direction and speed of motion, while head motion is used to allow the user to look around while flying.

It is generally accepted that no one particular type of camera control metaphor is appropriate for all tasks. Scene exploration, object inspection and editing do not have the same requirements in terms of camera motion. In telepresence applications, on the other hand, user movements are constrained by the ability of the robot to move in the real world.

6.3.2.2. Object Manipulation

In graphical simulations, guiding is useful as a means to specify the details of object motion. However, since humans are not very good at attending to more than a few tasks at once, the power of guiding tools diminishes rapidly as the number of simultaneous DOF to be controlled increases. A solution to this problem is abstraction to hide irrelevant details so that the user can focus on general concepts appropriate to the task at end.

Zeltzer (1990) has identified four levels of abstraction (structural, procedural, functional, agents) from passive objects (structural), to autonomous objects (agents), and analyzed how direct manipulation should be used with each level of abstraction. At the structural level, the object is described as its kinematic structure and physical attributes. Procedural abstraction is a mechanism for defining processes that control rigid or non rigid object motion, such as collision detection, inverse kinematics, forward dynamics or elastic deformation, independently of the structure of the object. Functional abstraction consists of associating procedures with objects or object subassemblies. Functional units allow decomposition of many DOF system such as a human body, into a set of small, constrained, manageable subsystems with fewer DOF. For example, we can define a walk functional unit where we associate the lower part of the body with a walk engine (Boulic et al. 1990). Since the action to be performed is known, functional constraints can be applied so that the walking subsystem can be controlled with fewer parameters. The higher level of abstraction consists in defining agents. An agent is composed of a structural definition, a set of functional units that defines its behavior repertoire, and some means for selecting and sequencing behaviors according to variation in environment.

At a structural level, direct control of the object motion can be useful when few DOF are involved, especially if we consider that we are highly accustomed to position and orient objects using our hands. Thus, the DataGlove can be really useful to manipulate objects, at least through manipulation of the root node of the kinematic hierarchy. Guiding procedural abstraction consists of supplying a stream of value as input to procedures which are subsequently applied to models. Direct manipulation of the camera can be performed this way by "plugging" the output of a device such as the DataGlove or the Spaceball to the input of a controller which will apply the transformation on the camera object. Guiding functional units is similar to guiding procedural abstractions. Controlling agents through direct manipulation consists of changing the environment to vary its behavior by, for example, specifying a position to reach through the use of a 3D locator, or using the 3D locator as an obstacle for the agent to avoid.

6.4. Conclusion

In this chapter, we have presented the application fields of VR for the short term future. We have identified the perceptual requirements for a VR computer configuration in order to simulate presence, examined the currently available devices and their limitations in offering complete sensory input–output. We have studied the problem of interacting with three dimensional worlds, focusing on direct manipulation of objects and viewpoint through the use of the DataGlove.

Major problems remain. Improvement of current head-mounted displays and real-time trackers is necessary to reach full simulation of presence. On the software side, simulation of presence and new device capabilities require the definition of new interaction metaphors for direct manipulation of objects, and the development of techniques to associate them with behaviors. On-going research is addressing these problems and some progress can be expected in the foreseeable future. However, the current technology allows developers and application designers to increase the effectiveness of 3D application interfaces, hence increasing users creativity and comfort while reducing training requirements.

Acknowledgements

We would like to thank Russell Turner, Enrico Gobbetti and Ronan Boulic for their help reviewing this chapter.

Notes

DataGlove™, EyePhone™ are registered trademarks of VPL Research Inc, Redwood City, CA, USA.

3Space™, Isotrack™ are registered trademarks of Polhemus Navigation Sciences, Colchester, VT, USA.

Spaceball™ is a registered trademark of Spatial Systems Inc.

References

Airey J, Rohlf JH, Brooks Jr FP (1990) Towards Image Realism with Interactive Update Rates in Complex Virtual Building Environments, *Proceedings ACM Siggraph Symposium on Interactive 3D Graphics*, 1990, Vol.24, No2, pp.41-50.

Boulic R, Magnenat-Thalmann N, Thalmann D (1990) A Global Human Walking Model with Real-time Kinematic Personification, *The Visual Computer*, Vol 6(6), Dec. 1990, Springer, pp.344-358.

Bricken W (1990) Virtual Reality: Directions of Growth, Notes from the Siggraph 1990 Panel, *usenet paper, group sci.virtual-worlds*, Nov.

Brooks Jr FP (1986) Walkthrough - A Dynamic Graphics System for Simulating Virtual Buildings, *Proceedings 1986 ACM Workshop on Interactive Graphics*, Oct 23-24, pp.9-21.

Brooks Jr FP (1988) Grasping Reality Through Illusion - Interacting Graphics Serving Science, *Proceedings CHI 88*, May 15-19, pp.1-11.

Chung JC, Harris MR, Brooks Jr FP, Fuchs H, Kelley MT, Hughes J, Ouh-young M, Chung C, Halloway RL, Pique M (1989) Exploring Virtual Worlds with Head-mounted Displays, *Non-Holographics True 3-Dimensional Display Technology, SPIE Proceedings*, Vol 1083, Los Angeles CA, January 15-10.

Fisher SS, McGreevy M, Humphries J, Robinett W (1986) Virtual Environment Display System, *Proceeding 1986 Workshop on Interactive 3D Graphics, ACM*, pp.77-87

Foley J, van Dam A, Feiner S, Hughes JF (1990) *Computer Graphics, Principles and Practice*, Second Edition, Addison-Wesley, Reading, MA.

Fuchs H, Poulton J, Eyles J, Greer T, Goldfeather J, Ellsworth D, Molnar S, Turk G, Tebbs B, Israel L, (1989) Pixel-Planes 5: A Heterogeneous Multi-processor Graphics System Using Processor-Enhanced Memory, *Proceedings SIGGRAPH 1989*. Vol 23, No3, ACM Press, pp.79-88.

Furness III TA (1987) Designing in Virtual Space, *Chapter in System Design*, Editors: Rouse W.B., Boff K.R., North-Holland, Amsterdam, pp.127-143.

Ginsberg CM, Maxwell D (1986) Graphical Marionette, *Motion: Representation and Control*, Editors: Badler N.I, Tsotsos J.K, Elsevier Science Publishing, Amsterdam, pp.303-310.

Iwata H (1990) Virtual Reality with Force-feedback: Development of Desktop Virtual Space with Compact Master Manipulator, *Proceeding SIGGRAPH 1990*, Vol 24, No4, pp. 165-170.

Jackoby R (1990) More Virtual Reality Work at NASA Ames, *usenet paper, group sci.virtual-worlds*, Nov.

Jacob RJK (1990) What You Look Is What You Get: Eye Movement-Based Interaction Techniques., *Proceedings CHI conference, 1990, Empowering People*, Seattle Washington, ACM Press, pp 11-18.

Krueger (1983) *Artificial Reality*, Addison-Wesley, Reading, MA.

Luciani A (1990) Physical Models in Animation. Towards a Modular and Instrumental Approach, *Proceedings of Eurographics Workshop on Animation*, Lausanne, Switzerland.

Minsky M, Ouh-young M, Steele O, Brooks Jr FP, Behensky M, (1990) Feeling and Seeing: Issues in Force Display, *Proceedings ACM Siggraph Symposium on Interactive 3D Graphics*, 1990, 24(2), pp 235-243.

Stewart D (1991) Through the Looking Glass into an Artificial World -- Via Computer., *Smithonian Magazine*, Vol.21, No10, pp.36-45.

Studmann DJ, Zeltzer D, Feiner S (1989) Hands-on Interaction with Virtual Environments, *Proceedings of the ACM SIGGRAPH Symposium on User Interface Software and Technology*, Williamsburg, Virginia, Nov. 13-15, ACM Press, pp.19-24.

Sutherland IE (1965) The Ultimate Display, *Proceedings IFIP Congress 1965*

Sutherland IE (1968) A Head-mounted Three Dimensional Display, *1968 Fall Joint Computer Conference, AFIPS Conference Proceedings*, Vol 33, pp.757-764.

Turner R, Balaguer F, Gobbetti E, Thalmann D (1991) Physically-based Interactive Camera Motion Control Using 3D Input Devices, *Proceedings Computer Graphics International 91*, Boston, MA.

Wang J, Chi V, Fuchs H, (1990) A Real-time Optical 3D Tracker For Head-mounted Display Systems, *Proceedings ACM Siggraph Symposium on Interactive 3D Graphics*, 1990, Vol.24, No2, pp.205-215.

Ware C, Jessome DR, (1988) Using the Bat: a six-dimensional mouse for object placement, *IEEE CG&A* Vol 8, No6, pp.65-70.

Ware C, Osborne S, (1990) Exploration and Virtual Camera Control in Virtual Three Dimensional Environment., *Proceedings ACM Siggraph Symposium on Interactive 3D Graphics*, Vol.24, No2, pp.175-183.

Zeltzer D (1990) Task-level Graphical Simulation: Abstraction, Representation, Control, Chapter in: Badler NI, Barsky BA, Zeltzer D (editors) *Making them Move. Mechanics, Control, And Animation of Articulated Figures*, Morgan Kaufmann Publishers, San Mateo, CA.

Zimmerman TG, Lanier J, Blanchard C, Bryson S, Harvill Y, (1987) A Hand Gesture Interface Design, *Proceeding CHI'87*, pp.189-192.

7

Tools and Techniques for Scientific Visualization

R.A. Earnshaw
University of Leeds

A summary of mathematical tools and methods to provide the basis for scientific visualization is presented. Computational resources currently available now allow mathematical models and simulations to become increasingly complex and detailed. This results in a closer approximation to reality, thus enhancing the possibility of acquiring new knowledge and understanding. Processes that formerly separated out simulation and design can now bring them together. Control over fine simulations, interactivity, and computer performance mean that vast amounts of multidimensional data can be generated. The representations of such data need to be carefully chosen.

The combination of Mandelbrot sets, computers, and computer graphics has provided a powerful toolset for exploring the complex plane and the behavior of dynamical systems and to gain comprehension of what has formerly been unimaginable. This has contributed greatly to our understanding of both mathematics and complex systems, and has been well documented (e.g. Peitgen and Richter 1986; Crilly et al 1991). This phenomenon is illustrative of an important point: computer graphics has provided a powerful tool to uncover mathematical and physical behavior, and in turn the techniques have provided the basis for developments in computer modeling and the representation and visualization of natural objects.

7.1. Introduction to Scientific Visualization

"The purpose of computing is insight, not numbers", wrote the much cited Hamming (1962). Scientific Visualization is an amalgam of tools and techniques that seeks to promote new dimensions of insight into problem solving using current technology.

Visualization utilizes aspects in the areas of computer graphics, user- interface, image processing, design, and signal processing. Formerly these were independent fields, but convergence is being brought about by the use of analogous techniques in the different areas.

Visualization highlights applications and application areas because it is concerned to provide leverage in these areas to enable the user to achieve greater exploitation of the computing tools now available. In a number of instances visualization has been used to analyze and display large volumes of multi-dimensional data in such a way as to allow the user to extract significant features and results quickly and easily. Tools and techniques in this area are therefore concerned with data analysis and data display, with perhaps provision for the display of data changes with respect to time. One of the fundamental goals of scientific visualization is to enable the user to explore the the information inherent in the data, by providing alternative methods of analysis and presentation.

Such tools benefit by the availability of modern workstations with good performance, large amounts of memory and disk, and with powerful graphics facilities—both in terms of range of colors available and also speed of display by the workstation. This close coupling of graphics and raw computation power is a powerful combination for those areas where visual insight is an important part of the problem-solving capability.

Such workstations now offer substantial computation power coupled with high speed 3D graphics. These facilities can be exploited to significant advantage in application areas such as modeling, simulation, and animation. Real-time dynamical simulation can involve the processing and display of large amounts of data, and often the only effective analysis of the performance or validity of the model is through visual observation.

Such workstations provide the computation power to process the data, and the high speed graphics pipeline can transform this into graphical images, often in real time. In those cases where additional computational resource is required, the calculation can be off-loaded on to a supercomputer, or other advanced workstations with spare capacity, and the resulting image down-loaded for viewing (and perhaps even interaction) when it is ready.

Useful references are McCormick et al (1987, 1989), Frenkel (1988), Nielson et al. (1990), and Thalmann (1990).

7.2. Background to Display Algorithms

Early work on display algorithms concentrated on points, lines, and curves in two dimensions. Earnshaw (1983,1985,1987) provides a summary of a wide range of algorithms for converting one, two, three-dimensional data into appropriate pictorial representations. This included points, lines, curves, characters, contours and surfaces. Different representations may be chosen for different mathematical or modeling reasons. For example, if it is desired to represent a set of points in a 2D plane by a curve, then some of the possibilities are as follows.

(i)   Single-valued or multi-valued in either coordinate

(ii)   Shape and axis independence on transformation (e.g. rotational invariance)

(iii)   Smoothness and fairness—mathematical, aesthetic, or model-based

(iv)   Global and local control of shape

(v)   Use of approximation functions

The importance of a particular characteristic is often related to the requirements of the application area under consideration, so it is possible to select an approach which satisfies the prime requirement. For example, if is required to rotate the defining points of the curve and for the curve to maintain the same shape (e.g. for design applications) then this is a constraint on the methods that can be used. If the points have error bounds on them, then it is often more appropriate to use an approximating curve.

Further information on these methods may be found in Brodlie (1980, 1985).

Sabin (1985) provides a comprehensive survey of contouring, looking at the kinds of data patterns that occur, surface interpolation aspects, and techniques for drawing the contours.

Texts by Rogers and Adams (1990) and Rogers (1985) provide a detailed coverage of mathematical and procedural elements for computer graphics. Principles are also covered in detail in Foley et al. (1990a). A tutorial paper (Earnshaw 1987) provides an overview of mathematical procedures used in computer graphics, modeling, and fractals.

7.3. Display Techniques

Rogers and Earnshaw (1987, 1990) summarizes a range of current hardware and software techniques available in computer graphics and modeling.

This section summarizes possible approaches for the representation and display of points, lines, curves, and surfaces. Volumes are treated in a further separate section.

7.3.1. Points, Lines and Curves

We usually require some kind of interpolated function to be fitted to the data points, such as described in Section 7.2. Cubic splines (in 2D) or bi-cubic splines (3D) have been used with great success because of their shape properties and smoothness. However, for design purposes where local control of the shape of an area is required, then Bezeir and B-spline curves have proved to be very useful. Lancaster and Salkauskas (1987) provides a summary of curve and surface fitting.

7.3.2. Surfaces

If the value of a function is defined by two parameters (e.g x, y), then the resulting surface can be sampled by a grid or the data can be scattered. Various algorithms have been devised to convert the latter case into the former by interpolation methods. The gridded data can then be interpolated to produce a function defining a surface (e.g. bicubic spline). This can be displayed as a contour map (where lines of constant height mark the "shape" of the surface), as a colored contour map (where colors fill in the areas of constant height between contour lines), or a surface view (where a 3D representation of the surface is displayed by means of a mesh or a color shaded surface). In the latter case, the use of color needs to be considered carefully (e.g. Sabella 1988), as this can have an impact on the way the data is interpreted when the final image is displayed. Contouring approaches are summarised in Sabin (1985).

Many current graphics and visualization packages have comprehensive facilities for contouring and surface plotting from a wide range of data sets. There are also facilities for allowing for constraints in the data, e.g. fault lines or discontinuities.

7.3.3. Algorithms

The Floating Perimeter Algorithm (Wang and Staudhammer 1990) solves the hidden-line and hidden-surface problem on grid surfaces, such as graphs of bivariate functions. Foley et al. (1990b) discuss techniques for the visualization of a scalar-valued function defined over a spherical domain.

7.3.4. Higher-level Functions

Techniques for modeling such as NURBS (Non-uniform rational B-splines) are regarded as being at a somewhat higher level and beyond the scope of this chapter. This is more properly regarded as part of the general are of geometric modeling, where the primary concern is with the representation and definition of a set of objects and their subsequent manipulation and analysis (see Mortenson 1985; Woodwark 1986; Earnshaw et al. 1987; Earnshaw 1988)

7.3.5. Higher Dimensions and Further Parameters

Helman and Hesselink (1990) discuss the visualization of vector fields, an area of great importance for computational fluid dynamics. A data set can have three velocity components, with pressure and density, and perhaps also temperature. Choosing a representation to convey this information is non-trivial. Where time is also a variable, then animation can be used in the presentation of the results.

7.3.6. Animation

For the presentation of the results of simulations or for comprehension of complex 3D information, then animation can help in the visualization process. Animation includes time-varying position (motion dynamics), shape, texture, color, and transparency. Current work is exploring effective methods for the display of large 2D and 3D data sets of multi-dimensional information.

Useful references are Magnenat Thalmann and Thalmann (1990) and Chapter 21 of Foley et al. (1990a).

7.3.7. Software for Visualization

Upson et al. (1989) and Dyer (1990) describe two software systems for visualization of data sets. The first, called the Application Visualization System (AVS), is designed to enable applications combining interactive graphics and high computational requirements to be easy to develop for both programmers and non-programmers. Software components are combined into executable flow networks or directed acyclic graphs, to construct applications. These modules implement specific functions such as filtering, mapping, or rendering. Execution can be controlled by a direct-manipulation user interface. This style of use is becoming increasingly the norm for those who require to drive large systems, but who do not wish to program.

The second, called Animation Production Environment (apE) provides a dataflow toolkit for scientific visualization (i.e. converting generic scientific data into graphical forms).

Many other systems are available on a variety of platforms, both workstation and desk top, and more systems are currently being designed

7.4. Tools for Volume Visualization

Volume rendering is used to view 3D data without the usual intermediate step of deriving a geometric representation which is then rendered. The volume representation uses voxels (volume elements) to determine visual properties, such as opacity, color, and shading at each point in the computational domain. Several images are created by slicing the volume perpendicular to the viewing axis at a regular interval and compositing together the contributing images from back to front, thus summing voxel opacities and colors at each pixel. By rapidly changing the color and opacity transfer functions, various structures are interactively revealed in the spatial domain.

Volume visualization is elaborated in Upson and Keeler (1988), Levoy (1988), Drebin et al. (1988), Gallagher and Nagtegaal (1989) and Levoy (1990).

A number of projects in the USA have demonstrated the benefits to medical and surgical planning from these new techniques. Further information may be found in Frenkel (1989), Kaufman (1990), and Upson (1991).

7.5. Fractals and Chaos

Fractal techniques have been successfully used in modeling and computer graphics (e.g. Fournier et al. 1982; Barnsley 1988; Peitgen and Richter 1985; Peitgen and Saupe 1988; Crilly et al. 1991) and have produced realistic images of waves, clouds, natural terrain, trees, fire etc (Batty 1985). Batty (1991) also shows how these techniques can be used to model geographic and demographic entities such as cities and populations. They are also currently being used to provide the basis for image compression algorithms that allow subsequent regeneration with little loss of visible information (Barnsley and Sloan 1988). In the modeling of complex dynamical systems fractal methods are being used with some success. Chaotic systems have the appearance of unpredictability, but can be simulated by precise mathematical laws (Crilly et al. 1991).

7.6. Tools for Non-Scientific Use

Tools such as those described in this chapter can be also used by those whose primary interest is not in the scientific content of the information presented, but rather the creative or aesthetic value.

Barlow et al. (1990) outlines how artists create effects and explores issues at the interface between art and science.

Artists and sculptors have been using computer-assisted tools for a number of years (Lansdown and Earnshaw 1989) and these tools often promote new and unexpected ways of creating and developing images and objects. Thus visualization tools are not confined to scientific visualization but can be used in all areas where the user is seeking to create and manipulate information via visual means.

7.7. Conclusions

In this chapter we have reviewed tools and techniques for scientific visualization, concentrating on methods for representing data as points, lines, curves, surfaces, or volumes. These methods are generally concerned with the visual representation of discrete date rather than image data or user-defined structures. Tools and techniques for image analysis and image processing are beyond the scope of this present chapter. However they are very important, and many of the techniques that have been developed within the context of signal and image processing have important uses and and applications within the area of scientific visualization.

Although we have been concerned with visual representation, it is worth noting that other parallel and complementary methods are currently being investigated, including the use of non-visual representations (e.g. sound). Multimodal representations are also being considered.

From the software point of view, we are observing the increasing availability of a wide variety of tools for scientific visualization on both low-end platforms (e.g. PC and Macintosh) and also on high-end workstations.

Advanced input–output devices such as 3D mice, data gloves, and other "virtual reality" tools are also beyond the scope of this chapter and are part of the growing field concerned with user interfaces and human factors in visualization. These are likely to have a major impact on the way scientific visualization facilities are mediated to the user.

A further area of importance is the correct handling of data containing known errors or uncertainties, and the incorporation of these into the scientific visualization process. In addition, it is essential to minimize the introduction of other errors (e.g. aliasing artefacts) in the visualization process, as has been pointed out by Drebin et al (1988) in the context of volume rendering, as the results then give a misleading picture of the actual data being analyzed. One can end up with doubly unfortunate situation, namely the omission of known errors in the data, and the introduction of other (different) errors in the data! Both of these are undesirable.

The references given below provide more detail on the various mathematical techniques outlined in this chapter.

References

Barlow H, Blakemore C, Weston-Smith M (Eds) (1990) *Images and Understanding: Thoughts about Images, Ideas and Understanding*, Cambridge University Press, Cambridge, UK.

Barnsley M (1988) *Fractals Everywhere*, Academic Press, New York.

Barnsley MF, Sloan AD (1988) A Better Way to Compress Images, *Byte Magazine*, January, pp.215-223.

Batty M (1985) Fractals-Geometry between Dimensions, *New Scientist*, Vol 105, No 1450.

Batty M (1991) Cities as Fractals: Simulating Growth and Form, in: Crilly AJ, Earnshaw RA, Jones H (eds) *Fractals and Chaos*, Springer-Verlag, Berlin.

Brodlie, KW (Ed) (1980) *Mathematical Methods in Computer Graphics and Design*, Academic Press, New York.

Brodlie, KW (1985) Methods for Drawing Curves, in: Earnshaw RA (ed.) *Fundamental Algorithms for Computer Graphics*, Springer-Verlag, Berlin.

Crilly AJ, Earnshaw RA, Jones H (Eds) (1991) *Fractals and Chaos*, Springer-Verlag, Berlin.

Drebin RA, Carpenter L, Hanrahan P (1988) Volume Rendering, *ACM SIGGRAPH 88*, pp.65-74.

Dyer Scott D, (1990) A Dataflow Toolkit for Visualization, *IEEE Computer Graphics & Applications*, Vol 10, No 4, pp.60-69.

Earnshaw RA (Ed), Bresenham JE, Pitteway MLV, Kilgour AC, Forrest AR (1983) *Display Algorithms*, Report No 189, Dept of Computer Studies, University of Leeds, pp.89.

Earnshaw RA (Ed) (1985) *Fundamental Algorithms for Computer Graphics*, NATO ASI Series, Vol F17, Springer-Verlag, Berlin.

Earnshaw RA (1987) The Mathematics of Computer Graphics, *The Visual Computer*, Vol 3, No 3, pp.115-124.

Earnshaw RA, Parslow RD, Woodwark JR (Eds) (1987) *Geometric Modeling and Computer Graphics - Techniques and Applications*, Technical Press, Gower Publishing, UK.

Earnshaw RA (Ed) (1988) *Theoretical Foundations of Computer Graphics and CAD*, Springer-Verlag, Berlin, Vol F40.

Foley JD, van Dam A, Feiner SK, Hughes JF (1990) *Computer Graphics - Principles and Practice*, Addison-Wesley, Reading, MA, 2nd Edition.

Foley TA, Lane DA, Nielson GM, Ramaraj R (1990) Visualizing Functions over a Sphere, *IEEE Computer Graphics & Applications*, Vol 10, No 1, pp.32-40.

Fournier A, Fussel D, Carpenter L (1982) Computer Rendering of Stochastic Models, *Communications of the ACM,*, Vol 25, pp.371-384

Frenkel KA (1988) The Art and Science of Visualizing Data, *Communications of the ACM*, Vol 31, No 2, pp.110-121.

Frenkel KA (1989) Volume Rendering, *Communications of the ACM*, Vol 32, No 4, pp.426-435.

Gallagher RS, Nagtegaal JC (1989) An Efficient 3D Visualization Technique for Finite Element and other Coarse Volumes, *ACM SIGGRAPH 89*, pp.185-194.

Hamming R (1962) *Numerical Methods for Scientists and Engineers*, McGraw-Hill, New York.

Helman J, Hesselink L (1990) Representation and Display of Vector Field Topology in Fluid Flow Data Sets, in Nielson G. M., B. Shriver, L. Rosenblum, (Eds) *Visualization in Scientific Computing*, IEEE Computer Society Press, Los Alamitos, CA.

Kaufman A (Ed) (1990) *Volume Visualization*, IEEE Computer Society Press, Los Alamitos, CA.

Lancaster P, Salkauskas K (1987) *Curve and Surface Fitting, An Introduction*, Academic Press, New York.

Lansdown RJ, Earnshaw RA (Eds) (1989) *Computers in Art, Design and Animation*, Springer-Verlag, Berlin.

Levoy M (1988) Display of Surfaces from Volume Data, *IEEE Computer Graphics & Applications*, Vol 8, No 3, pp.29-37.

Levoy M (1990) Efficient Ray Tracing of Volume Data, *ACM Transactions on Graphics*, Vol 9, No 3, pp.245-261.

McCormick BH, DeFanti TA, Brown MD (Eds) (1987) Visualization in Scientific Computing, *ACM SIGGRAPH Computer Graphics*, Vol 21, No 6, Nov.

McCormick BH., DeFanti TA, Brown MD (Eds) (1989) Visualization in Scientific Computing, *IEEE Computer*, Vol 23, No 8.

Magnenat-Thalmann N, Thalmann D (1990) *Computer Animation: Theory and Practice*, Springer-Verlag, Berlin, 2nd edition,.

Mortenson M (1985) *Geometric Modeling*, Wiley, Chichester, UK.

Nielson GM, Shriver B, Rosenblum L, (Eds) (1990) *Visualization in Scientific Computing*, IEEE Computer Society Press, Los Alamitos, CA.

Peitgen HO, Richter P.H (1986) *The Beauty of Fractals: Images of Complex Dynamical Systems*, Springer-Verlag, Berlin.

Peitgen H-O and D. Saupe, *The Science of Fractal Images*, Springer-Verlag, 1988

Rogers DF (1985) *Procedural Elements for Computer Graphics*, McGraw-Hill, New York.

Rogers DF, Adams JA (1990) *Mathematical Elements for Computer Graphics*, McGraw-Hill, New York, 2nd Edition.

Rogers DF, Earnshaw RA (Eds) (1987) *Techniques for Computer Graphics*, Springer-Verlag, Berlin.

Rogers DF, Earnshaw RA (Eds) (1990) *Computer Graphics Techniques - Theory and Practice*, Springer-Verlag, Berlin.

Sabella P (1988) A Rendering Algorithm for Visualizing 3D Scalar Fields, *ACM SIGGRAPH*, pp.51-58.

Sabin MA (1985) Contouring - State of the Art, in: Earnshaw Ra (ed) *Fundamental Algorithms for Computer Graphics*, Springer-Verlag, Berlin.

Thalmann D (Ed) (1990) *Scientific Visualization and Graphics Simulation*, JohnWiley, Chichester, UK.

Upson C (1991) Volumetric Visualization Techniques in: Rogers DF, Earnshaw RA (eds) *State of the Art in Computer Graphics - Visualization and Modeling*, Springer-Verlag, Berlin.

Upson C, Faulhaber T, Kamins D, Laidlaw D, Schlegel D, Vroom J, Gurwitz R, van Dam A (1989) The Application Visualization System: A Computational Environment for Scientific Visualization, *IEEE Computer Graphics & Applications*, Vol 9, No4, pp.30-42.

Upson C, Keeler M (1988) V-Buffer: Visible Volume Rendering, *ACM SIGGRAPH*, pp.59-64.

Wang SL, Staudhammer J (1990) Visibility Determination on Projected Grid Surfaces, *IEEE Computer Graphics & Applications*, Vol 10, No 4, pp.36-43.

Woodwark J (1986) *Computing Shape*, Butterworths, Guildford, UK.

Part 2

Visualization Problems and Applications

8
Visualization Modeling: Making Visualization a Creative Discipline

Tosiyasu L. Kunii and Yoshihisa Shinagawa
University of Tokyo

8.1. Introduction

8.1.1. Why Make Visualization a Creative Discipline ?

Computer science is a relatively young discipline, with much potential for new findings. Computer graphics, particularly raster graphics, as a discipline is one of the most progressive area in computer science and is further young. Visualization is a recent prominent offspring of computer graphics, thus, visualization is a young[3] discipline, and is growing extremely rapidly. Partly because of the speed of growth and partly because of the lack of knowledge on how to make it better disciplined, it is blurred and getting more and more blurred as the application areas expand to cover almost anything. They include science, technology, medicine, art, entertainment, sporting, economics, law, history, sociology and politics. Words such as scientific visualization, engineering visualization and medical visualization can be seen everywhere. It is certainly an advancement of knowledge to be able to visualize what we could previously only imagine.

The problem here is clear and so is the remedy. The problem is in the lack of an academic discipline to discover or invent a small number of *essential visualization models* systematically out of rich but diverse visualization practice. The remedy is the *creative discipline* for *discovery or invention of essential visualization models*. The models are also called the *theories*. For people who wish to visualize something, the situation has reached the critical point. They have to work with individual visualization cases without dependable guidelines or theories, and even worse, often without the support of methods and tools. As a guarantee that the theories to work correctly, the discipline includes the proofs to show that the theories or models truly cover the diversity and multiplicity of visualization.

Were we to learn from the traditionally established academic research areas which have been successful to build creative disciplines to continue to grow the areas based on a limited number of clear and fundamental models, it is meaningful to look into the *nature of creativity* in these areas. Let us examine the creation process itself first, and see how creation is accomplished.

8.1.2. The Three-Step Model of Creation

There are two types of creation: discovery and invention. The former is creation as in the fields of natural science and mathematics, while the latter is creation as in the field of engineering. Generally, the creative process can be divided into three steps:

STEP 1   World

                  ↓   Derivation process

               A set of assumptions

STEP 2   ↓   Construction process

               Model

STEP 3   ↓   Model testing process

               Proof

In the first step, the real world is observed, from which observations *a set of assumptions* sometimes called a *hypothesis* are derived. The hypothesis is the basis of invention or discovery. The second process, the construction process, is to construct a *model* from the hypothesis. Since it must be proven that the model satisfies the hypothesis, the *testing* process of the model against the hypothesis constitutes the last step. The result of the process provides a proof of the correctness of the model. The process of creation described above is referred to as the *"three-step model of creation"* in what follows.

Next, we will apply the three-step model of creation to invention and discovery in existing fields: mathematics, natural science and engineering.

8.1.3. Creation in Mathematics

In the field of mathematics, it can be described as follows:

STEP 1   Thought

                  ↓   Derivation process

               A set of axioms

STEP 2   ↓   Construction process

               Theory

STEP 3   ↓   Proof process

               Proof

The world in the field of mathematics is that of thought. A set of assumptions correspond to the *a set of axioms*. Non-Euclidean geometry was born from the doubt of whether the axiom concerning the non-intersection of parallel lines is really necessary. Theories in mathematics such as set theory include *theorems* built from the axioms, and *proofs* are given to validate them against the axioms or previously proved theorems.

8.1.4. Creation in Natural Science

What about natural science? The world in the field of natural science is nature and a set of assumptions derived are called the *hypothesis*. In physics, for example, it was assumed that particles were in fact waves. Quantum *theory* formalized this assumption, providing a model as a wave equation called the Schrödinger equation. The proof was completed when the electron beams were observed to interfere as waves. This last step was achieved through *experimental discovery*. To summarize, discovery in the field of natural science is accomplished according to the three-step model as follows:

STEP1   Nature

          ↓   Derivation process

          Hypothesis

STEP 2   ↓   Construction process

          Theory

STEP 3   ↓   Experiments and observation

          Experimental discovery, new observation

8.1.5. Creation in Engineering

Next, we discuss the three-step model in the field of engineering. In this case, the steps are as follows:

STEP 1   Artificial

          ↓   Derivation process

          A set of requirements

STEP 2   ↓   Construction process

          Engineering model

STEP 3   ↓   Test process

          Invention

The world we consider here is the world of the artificial. The set of *requirements* defines what structure and which functions are necessary. Next, an *engineering model* is constructed which satisfies the requirements. Finally, the proof that the model satisfies the requirements is in the form of an *invention*. For example, in the case of semiconductor phenomena, the proof came in the form of the invention of transistor.

8.1.6. The Three-Stage Model of Hypothesis Derivation

Let us elaborate the first and most difficult step at which we derive assumptions from the world we deal with. From what was the axiom of parallel lines derived? From where was the wave hypothesis of matter brought? If we wish visualization to be a creative discipline, we must understand the first step. What is then the process of forming a hypothesis? It is described as follows in three stages.

(1) Construction of a prototype object model: brief observation of a particular object (or phenomena) and construction of a prototype *object model* which abstracts the basic structure of the object.

(2) Construction of a prototype typical object model: brief observation of a group of objects (or phenomena) which share a certain abstract structure of the prototype object models. Then the group is an object type, and the common abstract structure shared is the prototype *typical object model*. Note here that at this stage a set of prototype object models obtained at the previous stage has been assumed to hold and has served as the *hypothesis*.

(3) Construction of a prototype essential object model: brief observation of the prototype typical object models obtained at the previous stage to find a distinct structure common to all of them. If found, it serves as the prototype *essential object model*, and the model thus derived is assumed to be applicable to all the objects (or phenomena), and serve as the hypothesis for the next step of creation, modeling. Please remind here again that a set of prototype typical object models obtained at the previous stage has been assumed to hold and has served as the hypothesis of this stage.

We have briefly considered the creative process in the light of the step of hypothesis derivation. The result of the consideration above concludes that *modeling is the key even in the first step of creation, hypothesis formation*. More specifically, hypothesis formation and modeling evolve alternately. This shows the recursive nature of modeling. The implication is that modeling is the true fundamental and common process of creation. There are cases where hypothesis formation is done rather in an *ad hoc* manner or intuitively without any modeling. However, a well done hypothesis derivation essentially completes the model construction at the prototype level, and is superior to the *ad hoc* and intuitive approaches. To understand modeling, particularly in visualization, the following section discusses an examples of prototype modeling in art painting. Prototype modeling, although it is rather primitive and crude, is the very initial process of creation, and from which the rests should evolve as formulated above.

8.2. Modeling Irregularity—A Case Study of Diffuse Painting in Black Ink, "SUMIE"

First, let us see how to discover a model for visualization of physical phenomena. The basic method to do this is to abstract the key visual properties of the behavior of physical objects. This section presents a case study of discovering a typical model to cover wide varieties of interesting phenomena in art, science and engineering by abstracting *regularity* from *irregularity*. One typical irregularity model is selected which abstracts regularity from *irregularity* in a rather general type of physical phenomena: *diffusion of particles through an evaporating irregular channel*. In art, this type of phenomena includes diffuse painting in black ink, called "sumie". In science, geology of land formation through soil deposition. In engineering, VLSI functioning through electronic propagation on a silicon wafer. We choose a case of diffuse painting "sumie" which we can observe in detail by using our current facility, and model the phenomenon of ink diffusion through a sheet of paper. The importance of the typical model makes the case study worth serious research.

In diffuse painting (called "sumie" in Japanese), an effect called "nijimi" is the most remarkable feature which is produced by letting ink diffuse through absorbent paper. The diffusion of the ink usually results in a delicately blurred image. How can we model the "nijimi" effect to visualize it? So far, we have completed a prototype model (Guo and Kunii 1991). First, we carried out the physical analysis of the construction of the paper as an *irregular* mesh of fibers, and modeled it as a homogeneously random system. We also analyzed and modeled the characteristics of ink flow, and the interaction of the *irregular* fiber mesh with the liquid and the ink pigment particles. The interaction includes the particle adsorption. Although the aggregated phenomena causing the effect are fairly complex, a simple filter model leading to a three area schema works fine as explained below. The model testing through visualization is completed, and statistical testing against the real images is under way.

8.2.1. Modeling the Irregular Mesh of Painting Paper

For modeling the nature of *irregularity* characteristic to the fiber meshes of particular types of paper used in black ink painting, the applicability of the principles of a *homogeneously disordered system* proposed by Ziman (1979) is assumed. The basic idea of the homogeneously disordered system is simple. First, the *order* and *disorder* in the paper fiber meshes have to be identified and modeled. In the physical situation F of the fiber mesh system at some point r, the *order* is the *regularity* incorporated by making F exactly or approximately reproduced at every point homogeneously (namely, *regularly*) positioned at the interval of R like a lattice. In a form,

$$F(r+R) \sim F(r) \qquad (8.1)$$

The situation function F and the range R are related to the properties of the system. Now a mesh is created by dividing a field into several regions at the interval of R and distributing the fibers according to the homogeneity rule such that for each region the average fiber distribution is the same. Now, the *disorder* or *irregularity* is brought in such that the fiber distribution varies randomly within each region. In Figure 8.1 (see color section), a mesh created by the model of homogeneous disorder is shown. The *disorder* or *irregularity* considered so far is the first order approximation of disorder, and the second and higher order approximation can be easily added by bringing the irregularity or randomness gradually into the interval R and F.

8.2.2. Modeling Ink Diffusion through an Irregular Mesh

During the formation of "nijimi", the change in ink density occurs through various interactions of the ink with the mesh. Black ink is a typical *colloid*. A colloidal liquid is made by mixing very fine particles of solid with water. For instance, black ink is made by mixing powdered carbon and glue with water. We assume that a colloidal liquid is modeled by the distribution of the size and number of the particles in it.

For understanding of the phenomena behind the "nijimi" effect, let us look at the aspects of the spectacular complexity of the phenomena. When the carbon particles diffuse through the irregular paper fiber mesh, the particles smaller than the mesh size and free from the stereoscopic hindrance still cannot move through the mesh unless the adhesive power of the mesh fibers is less than the carrying power of water. The *irregularity of the mesh* brings in the local variation of the particle movement and the water flow. Further, the particles adhered by the fibers regulate the adhesive power of the fibers. Whether the regulation is positive or negative depends on the types and states of the fibers and particles. The gravity deposits the particles on the mesh. Water evaporation while seeping through the paper prevents particle movement by decreasing the carrying power of water gradually and finally fixes the particles on the fibers when dried up. The carrying power is coming from the water flow which again is coming from the gravity, the adhesive power of the fibers and also from the physical nature of water being in the liquid state. The posture of the paper such as whether it is laid flat, vertical or oblique, changes the effect of the gravity on the water flow and on the particle deposit.

A brief consideration so far allows us to characterize the complicated phenomena behind the "nijimi" effect in diffuse painting "sumie" as a typical class of phenomena, "*transportation of particles through evaporating irregular channels*". In "sumie", the particles are the carbon particles of black ink, and the irregular channels are the irregular mesh of paper as shown in Figure 8.1 (see color section). Other phenomena which appear to belong to the type and under study are *soil erosion and deposition during land formation* in geology, and *electronic charge propagation on a VLSI wafer* in electronic engineering.

We now model "sumie" painting to abstract only the major features of "nijimi". The painting paper is assumed to be laid flat. When the ink colloid starts to diffuse through the mesh, the observable change of the particle density of the colloid occurs at the starting points. Only such particles that are smaller than the space between the paper fibers can seep through the mesh carried by water. It is as if a filter is embedded in the mesh. The influence of the filter effect results in a change in the particle density, and hence in a change in image intensity. This *filter model* characterizes the major feature of the particle–mesh interaction in "sumie" to produce the "nijimi" effect, and is a case of the *stereoscopic hindrance model* which serves as a kind of *typical model* and is itself a case of *geometric model* which is the *essential model*.

Suppose we assume the applicability of the filter model. Then, as explained in Section 8.1.6, we can use it as the *hypothesis* to construct a "nijimi" effect model. During the diffusion process, three areas of different particle density should be formed: the initial area where the ink is applied, the filter area through which the ink seeps through the paper and the diffusion area where only the particles smaller than the average size of the spaces between fibers exist. Thus, the filter model as the hypothesis leads us to the construction of the *three area schema model* of the "nijimi" effect.

In the filter area, assuming the existence of fairly plenty of water in the area, the gradation of the image intensity can be roughly calculated form the distribution of the particle sizes and the number of particles of each size. Next in the diffusion area, the scarcity of the amount of water makes the situation rather delicate and complex. The image intensity depends not only on the particle distribution but also heavily on the characteristics of the liquid flow and particle adsorption in the mesh. According to the physical principle of adsorption, the quantity of adsorbed particles is in proportion to the surface area of the solid. The particle adsorption also varies with the irregular structure of the mesh as seen in Figure 8.1 (see color section). Due to the characteristics of liquid flow and uneven particle adsorption in the *irregular* mesh, the delicate and often subtle local variation of intensity is produced in diffusion images.

To simplify the modeling of the image intensity variation, we analyzed the structure of meshes and classified the irregularity of mesh structures into a number of individually distinct cases. For each case, the state of liquid flow and particle adsorption is decided dynamically, and then the intensity is calculated to generate the pixel types (Figure 8.2). For visualizing the result of "transportation of particles through evaporating irregular channels", this *pixel* type model is assumed to serve well to model the types of visual *irregularity* in the diffuse paintings of "sumie".

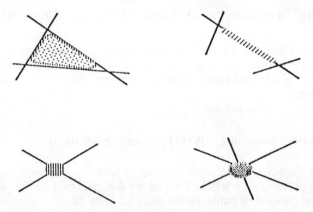

Figure 8.2. The classification of the *irregularity* of the mesh structures as the *pixel types*

8.2.3. Image Generation for Model Testing

Using the pixel type model, we now generate "sumie" to test that the generated "sumie" actually simulates the visual reality. For generating the delicate images of "nijimi", it is required to capture, represent and display the details which go beyond the resolution of the physical screen. Our simulation schema, as illustrated in Figure 8.3 (see color section), is therefore designed to complete an image in two steps. The first step is to generate a fine and detailed image on the logical screen in the computer memory space based on the pixel type model. The second step is to transform the logical image to the physical display image which has the resolution of the physical display screen. The transformation can be completed for each pixel of the logical image simply by averaging the intensities of neighboring pixels. This transformation is the first order approximation, and the type of transformation model based on the *logical-to-physical object mapping* is required for improved image quality at the edges of the objects painted. The object mapping is itself based on object modeling and is under study.

We have used the pixel type model to generate "nijimi" on painting strokes. The original stroke corresponds to the initial area, while the extended parts denote the filter and diffusion areas. Figure 8.4 (see color section) shows an example of black ink painting generated by a computer. In the upper part of the painting, there are some strokes, which describe the fog over the lake. These blurred strokes are created with the effect of "nijimi".

The examples of generated images shown serve as the preliminary tests of the modeling through visualization. They appear to come close to the visual reality to indicate the validity of the modeling of painting paper as a homogeneously disordered system and the modeling of the "nijimi" effect by filters and then pixel types. Further testing of the scientific validity of the proposed modeling is in progress by statistically comparing the spatial distribution of the fibers and pixel types in the real and generated images. The test covers both the dynamic images being painted to validate the model of the diffusion process and the final paints to validate the terminal state of the process.

8.3. Modeling Singularity—A Case Study of Garment Wrinkling

This section shows another example of discovering a typical visualization model by abstracting *singularity* from *non singularity*. When we model some phenomena with very many elements to consider and highly complex, this type of abstraction makes modeling far simpler and clearer.

8.3.1. Complexity Modeling, Wrinkles and Singularity

One example is cosmology, the main concern of which is to model the beginning and evolution of the universe as a whole. Singularity theory is playing the central role there. Look at the initial creation of matter in the universe from the state of homogeneous energy distribution in space. Since the energy is equal to the mass of matter multiplied by the light speed twice, the creation of mass is modeled as the creation of a *wrinkle* in the energy space where homogeneous energy distribution was broken and high energy concentration is taking place at the locations where matter exists. The birth of matter is modeled by the birth of *singularity*. Garment wrinkle creation is modeled the same simply by replacing the word "energy" by "cloth" and changing the scale factors.

The advantage of taking garment wrinkles as an example to study is in their handiness. To model the shapes of garment wrinkles, it is not practical to simulate their behavior by directly solving differential equations because a garment also belongs to an object composed of extremely many components. We prefer to use some *global information* to reduce the amount of computation.

The existence of wrinkles can serve as the global information (Kunii and Gotoda 1990a, 1990b). When a garment is deformed, wrinkles are formed or extinguished. Shape changes are mainly observed around wrinkles while the other parts of the garment remain unchanged. In fact, the geometry of the wrinkles and of the other parts are different: at the wrinkles both metric and curvature change, whereas at the other parts metric is preserved and only curvature changes. This observation implies a potential key hypothesis of the wrinkles as the *indexes* of global shape change.

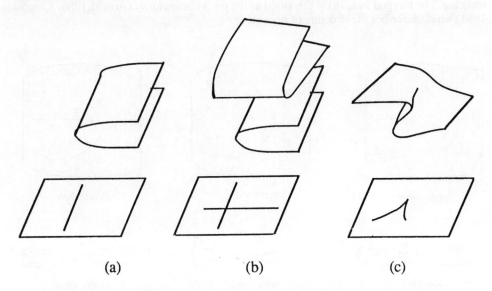

Figure 8.5. Typical signs: (a)a fold, (b)crossing lines and (c)a cusp

The *hypothesis* that "the wrinkles are the *indexes*" is used to construct a model of garment wrinkling by employing a mathematical method known as *singularity theory* (Arnold 1986). This theory provides a mathematical foundation to handle the qualitative geometric changes of a given system. The basic idea of singularity theory is in considering a singular set of surface-to-surface mapping. More specifically, a series of projections of a given surface are taken and analyzed. Figure 8.5 shows three typical types of projections. In the framework of singularity theory, our particular interest is related to contours. The theory shows that the *signs* depicted in Figure 8.5 are the only *stable* patterns in general, and the other types of signs are *unstable*, namely, if we take a projection from a slightly different direction, the pattern is decomposed into some combinations of the stable signs shown in Figure 8.5.

An important point here is that one can distinguish general types of signs which are *stable* from special types of signs which are *unstable*. If no *a priori* knowledge is assumed on the surface to be analyzed and if a projection is taken in an arbitrary direction, then the sign to be observed is almost always one of those in Figure 8.5. The other types of signs are too rare to be observed. However, if the surface does have a special structure, we can expect that the rare types of signs are also observed. We conclude here that "*the stable signs can serve as the indexes of surface projections*".

8.3.2. Singularity Signs in Garment Wrinkling

When a garment wrinkles, in most cases the following signs appear in the projections: *cusps, folds* and *crossing lines*. As shown in Figure 8.6, however, there are special instances where the other types of signs emerge by changing the directions of viewing a given shape.

This figure shows a situation where (a)a cusp and a fold approach to each other, (b)then merge, and (c)finally depart from each other. Note that (a) and (c) show different configurations: the lines that form the cusp and the fold are exchanged in the process of merging. The merged state (b) is classified as the *p+ +c singularity* (Arnold 1986; Kergosien 1981) which describes the structure of *branching*.

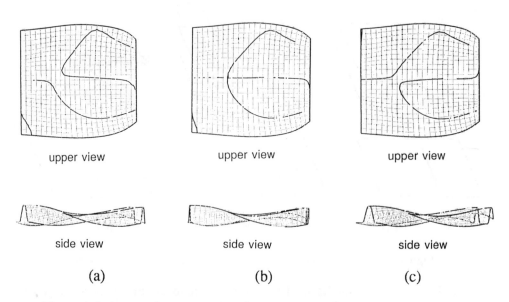

upper view

side view

(a)   (b)   (c)

Figure 8.6. A case where p+ +c singularity emerges: (a) fold and cusp, (b) p+ +c singularity, and (c) fold and cusp

The same p+ +c singularity also describes the structure of vanishing. Branching and vanishing are complementary to each other. A point on a surface can be a branching point when it is looked from one side, and can be a vanishing point when it is looked from the other side. Since this singularity is very rare, the behavior of the points corresponding to this type of singularity is far more greater constraints than the behavior of the other points. Such points are the *characteristic points* of garment wrinkles. They serve as the *primary indexes* of the global shape change. By specifying the local structures around the characteristic points, more realistic garment wrinkle images can be synthesized. This characteristic point model serves as the hypothesis of the next step to construct the typical model through further abstraction.

8.3.3. Modeling Primitives of Wrinkles

As explained above, the *local structures around the characteristic points remarkably influence the global structures of garment wrinkles*. Since the number of characteristic points is small, great *data compression* can be achieved by representing a wrinkle surface as a collection of characteristic points and the *local* structures around them.

The basic sets of modeling primitives are the positions and the types (branching or vanishing) of characteristic points. These sets of primitives alone, however, are not sufficient to reconstruct the original shape from the compressed data in a satisfactory way. Our choice is to add the *contours* that are associated with the special singular configurations (see Figure 8.7) as another set of modeling primitives. This enables us to restrict the number of possible wrinkle shapes to be reconstructed. As a matter of fact, the next section of this chapter is entirely dedicated to the theme of *modeling surface reconstruction from contours*. Note here that contours are not necessarily on planes. For specifying the contours, we choose several sample points and interpolate the coordinate values between those points by a curve such as a spline function.

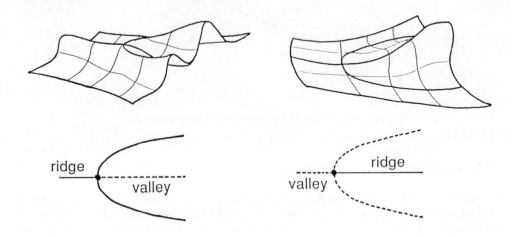

Figure 8.7. Wrinkle modeling primitives

It is usually observed that several wrinkles appear on the garment cloth, and become connected with each other or diminish at their ends. Our modeling primitives can describe such a complex situation: connections can be represented by branching points and diminishings by vanishing points. Such a description yields a graph named a *wrinkle graph*, as shown in Figure 8.8, where vertices correspond to the characteristic points and edges to the associated contours. This graph adequately abstracts the *essential* structure of a wrinkling phenomena. As a way of abstract representation, it is free from any geometrical or physical differences of the modeled objects, and thus serve as a *typical model* of wrinkling phenomena in general.

8.3.4. Preliminary Model Testing through Wrinkling Animation

To carry out a preliminary testing of the wrinkling model, two examples of wrinkle formation processes are animated as shown in Figure 8.9 (see color section). A case of wrinkles formed around the arm of a jacket is used. The first basic parameter is the angle between the human forearm and the upper arm at the elbow. To test the model in the simplest situation first, we assume the situation where the characteristic points are not newly created or destroyed during the process of wrinkle formation. Based on this assumption, we also include the initial configuration of the characteristic points as the second parameter of this animation. The animated result approximates the visual reality. Further testing is planned for garment drapery and human facial wrinkles.

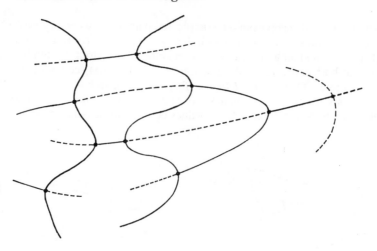

Figure 8.8. A wrinkle graph of modeling primitives

8.3.5. Challenges and Temptations

Historically, the success of computer architecture has been always based on localizing information to be processed. Computation speed gain has been mainly depended on the *information locality model* devising a program counter in the Von Neumann architecture and a page counter in the virtual memory architecture. The locality in our wrinkling modeling, thus provides the basis of possible "singularity computer architecture" as a challenge.

Although it is an open problem, one of the largest challenge and temptation is testing the wrinkling modeling of the creation of the universe against the computer graphics-based four-dimensional visualization of the astronomical observation. Challenges to open problems is the privilege of voluntary scientists.

8.4. Essential Object Modeling—A Case Study Based on the Homotopy Model

This section discusses how to construct an essential model from typical models. A method often used for this purpose is to provide a general concept for abstracting a common structure from the existing typical models to cover them as the special cases. In the following, we show a case to unify various *surface models* which are *typical models* into a single and new *essential model* called the *homotopy model.*

8.4.1. Surface Reconstruction from Contours as a Typical Problem

What we look into is a very popular and typical problem of *surface reconstruction from contours* , which also appeared in Sections 8.3.3 and 8.3.4. In the medical field, it is of great significance to reconstruct the entire surface shape of a human organ from a set of contours in the cross-sections derived from the slices or CT (including MRI) devices because it is difficult to envisage the three dimensional structure of the organ by viewing individual cross-sections. In geography, the reconstruction of three dimensional topography from maps is a daily work. The similar situation exists in mechanical and architectural CAD to reconstruct three-dimensional objects from two-dimensional drawings.

The following discussions do not limit contours to be on planes. This generality is advantageous when modeling objects, particularly to characterize surfaces by ridges, valleys and saddles as shown in the previous section.

For the surface generation, the triangular tile technique has been popular; triangular patches are generated between the adjacent contours that are approximated by linear line segments as shown in Figure 8.10 (Fuchs et al. 1977; Christiansen and Sederberg 1978; Boissonat 1988; Kaneda et al. 1987). A spline approximation has also been used (Wu et al. 1977). These two models are typical surface models.

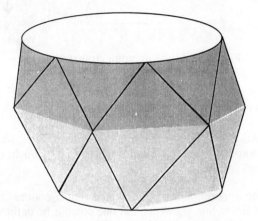

Figure 8.10. Triangulation method

The homotopy model (Shinagawa et al. 1989; Shinagawa and Kunii 1991) is based on a family of functions called a homotopy, and both the triangular tile technique and the spline approximation become the special cases. Furthermore, it overcomes their drawbacks which are serious as explained later. The homotopy model can be thought of as an *essential model*. The existing methods consider each contour line as a set of line segments or as a set of control points of spline functions. In the homotopy model, contour lines are considered as shape functions and the surface generated is the locus of the homotopy that transforms the function of one contour to that of the other (see Figure 8.11). This enables us to handle the problem continuously, not necessarily discretely.

The *homotopy model* consists of the *continuous toroidal graph representation* of the relationship between the neighboring contours and the *homotopic generation* of surfaces from the representation. To be more precise, the continuous toroidal graph defines how each contour line is parametrized as a function and also defines the correspondence between the adjacent contours.

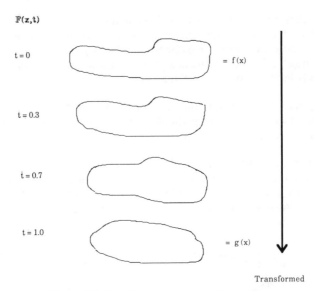

Figure 8.11. Homotopic transformation

8.4.2. Discrete Toroidal Graph Representation

Let us study the toroidal graph representation in more detail. First, we examine the original discrete version of the toroidal graph representation proposed by Fuchs et al. (1977) before we extend it to a continuous version.

In the original discrete version, first it is assumed that a contour line is approximately modeled by a string of linear line segments. Let one contour be defined by a sequence of m distinct contour points $P0$,...,$Pm-1$, and the other contour by a sequence of n distinct contour points $Q0$,...,$Qn-1$. The orientations of both loops are assumed the same.

Triangulation must satisfy the two rules (Christiansen and Sederberg, 1978): if two points of the same contour are to be defined as the vertices of the same triangle, they must neighbor on each other on the contour line; also, no more than two vertices of any triangle may be recruited from the same contour line.

Fuchs et al. reduced the two rules into one in graph theory. They represented the mutual topological relations of triangles in a *toroidal graph*, which is adopted as the basic representation in our model. In this graph, vertices correspond to the set of all possible spans between the points $P0$,...,$Pm-1$ and the points $Q0$,...,$Qn-1$, and the arcs correspond to the set of all the possible triangles (see Figure 8.12). The graph of an acceptable surface has exactly one vertical arc in every row and exactly one horizontal arc in every column. There are two kinds of acceptable surfaces: one is homeomorphic to a cylinder and the other homeomorphic to two cones. In our model, for simplicity, we limit us to the former case unless otherwise noted. Fuchs et al. proved that the toroidal graph of an acceptable surface homeomorphic to a cylinder is connected, and for every vertex of the graph, one arc is incident to it and one arc is incident from it.

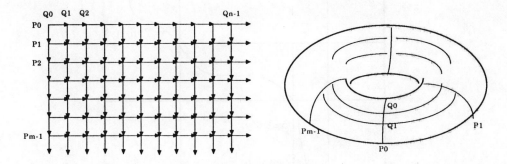

Figure 8.12. The discrete toroidal graph representation (Fuchs et al. 1977)

8.4.3. Continuous Toroidal Graph Representation and the Homotopy Model

Now we are ready to generalize the discrete toroidal graph by abstracting the features *essential* for reconstructing surfaces from contours. First of all, the lower and upper contours are represented by parameters x and y. The points on the contours are designated by shape functions f(x) and g(y) whose domains are the interval [0, 1]. In the continuous toroidal graph, the horizontal and vertical distances between the two vertices of the continuous toroidal graph represent the differences of the parameter values (the values of x and y) between the two vertices. When a path passes through (x,y) where f(x) is the coordinate value of a point P and g(y) is that of a point Q, it means that P and Q is connected by a homotopy.

Generally, a surface is represented by a concatenation of monotonously increasing functions as shown in Figure 8.13. The decision of this path is itself an interesting theme (Shinagawa and Kunii 1991). The toroidal graph that represents triangular patches is expressed as a concatenation of step functions. This can be considered as an approximation of the monotonously increasing functions in the discrete case. The spline approximation method is represented by the function y = x on the continuous toroidal graph. This can be considered as an approximation of the monotonously increasing functions in the piecewise continuous interpolation case. Thus, the continuous toroidal graph abstractly models the basic key feature of these typical approximation models.

Using the continuous toroidal graph representation, the *homotopy model* generates the surface patch between the adjacent contours by connecting the corresponding points on each contour by a *homotopy*. In other words, in this model, all the points on a contour have their corresponding points on the adjacent contours, and a homotopy is used for connecting the corresponding points like fibers. Here, the correspondence is represented by the continuous toroidal graph. Then, the homotopy model is more than the generalization of the typical surface approximation models. Essential surface operations such as taking the first-, second- and higher order-derivatives to identify the surface properties (including the peaks, pits, ridges, valleys and saddles) can be defined on the surfaces generated by the homotopy model as needed, qualifying the homotopy model to be an essential model.

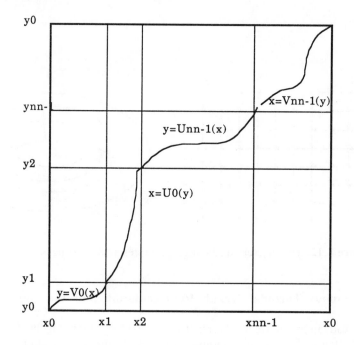

Figure 8.13. Continuous toroidal graph representation

8.4.4. Visualization

This section presents the results of testing the homotopy model against the very complex surface structure of the three auditory ossicles (malleus, incus and stapes) of a human ear. Figure 8.14 (see color section) shows the case where the outline curves are approximated by the cardinal spline and the surface is generated by a straight-line homotopy. Figure 8.15 (see color section) shows the same objects reconstructed by using a homotopy that corresponds to the cardinal spline surface. The outline curves are approximated by the cardinal spline. Figure 8.16 (see color section) shows the same objects reconstructed by Christiansen's triangulation method with Gouraud shading. The shape is ambiguous in the details.

8.5. Conclusions

Although young[3], visualization certainly has provided enough evidence to convince us that it can be disciplined. In modeling the visualization of the physical phenomena in diffuse painting, the physical and singular phenomena in garment wrinkling, and the mathematical structures in reconstructing surfaces from contours, we have seen the three-step model of creation works quite reliably to make visualization disciplined. We humbly present the result of our observation as volunteers to advance knowledge in visualization, and extend our invitation to everybody interested.

References

Arnold VI (1986) *Catastrophe Theory*. 2nd edition, Springer-Verlag, Berlin.

Armstrong MA (1983) *Basic Topology*, Springer-Verlag, New York, p.88, pp.103-105, p.169.

Boissonnat JD (1988) Shape Reconstruction from Planar Cross Sections, *Computer Vision, Graphics, and Image Processing*, Vol. 41, No. 1, pp.1-29.

Christiansen HN, Sederberg TW (1978) Conversion of Complex Contour Line Definitions into Polygonal Element Mosaics, *(Proc. SIGGRAPH, Computer Graphics,* Vol. 12, pp.187-192.

Fuchs H, Kedem ZM, Uselton SP (1977) Optimal Surface Reconstruction from Planar Contours, *Comm. ACM* Vol. 20, No. 10, pp.693-702.

Guo Q, Kunii TL (1991) *Modeling the Diffuse Paintings of `Sumie.'* in: *Kunii TL (ed) Modeling in Computer Graphics (Proc. IFIP TC5/WG5.10 Working Conference on Modeling in Computer Graphics)*, Springer-Verlag, Tokyo, pp.329-338.

Kaneda K, Harada K, Nakamae E, Yasuda M, Sato AG (1987) Reconstruction and Semi-Transparent Display Method for Observing Inner Structure of an Object Consisting of Multiple Surfaces, in: Kunii TL (ed) *Computer Graphics 1987* Springer-Verlag, Tokyo, pp.367-380.

Kergosien YL (1981) *Topologie Differentielle*, Comptes Rendus, 291, I, pp.929-932.

Kunii TL, Gotoda H (1990a) Modeling and Animation of Garment Wrinkle Formation Processes, in: Magnenat-Thalmann N and Thalmann D (eds.) *Computer Animation' 90,* 131-147, Springer-Verlag, Tokyo.

Kunii TL and Gotoda H (1990b) Singularity Theoretical Modeling and Animation of Garment Wrinkle Formation Processes *The Visual Computer*, Vol. 6, No.6, pp.326-336.

Nomura Y, Okuno T, Hara M, Shinagawa Y, Kunii TL (1989) Walking through a Human Ear. *Acta Otolaryngol* (Stockholm) 107, pp. 366-370.

Shinagawa Y, Kunii TL, Nomura Y, Okuno T, Hara M (1989) Reconstructing Smooth Surfaces from a Series of Contour Lines Using a Homotopy, in: Earnshaw RA, Wyvill B (ed) *New Advances in Computer Graphics*. Springer-Verlag, Tokyo, pp.147-161.

Shinagawa Y, Kunii TL (1991) The Homotopy Model: A Generalized Model for Smooth Surface Generation from Cross Sectional Data, *The Visual Computer*, Vol.7, No2, to appear

Strassmann S (1986) Hairy Brushes, *Proc. ACM SIGGRAPH, Computer Graphics*, Vol. 20, No.4, pp.225-232.

Wu S, Abel JF, Greenberg DP (1977) An Interactive Computer Graphics Approach to Surface Representation, *Comm. ACM*, Vol.20, No.10, pp.187-192.

Ziman JM (1979) *Models of Disorder - The Theoretical Physics of Homogeneously Disordered Systems*, Cambridge University Press, Cambridge, UK.

9

On the Topic of Interactive Scientific Visualization

Gregory M. Nielson
Arizona State University

9.1. Introduction

This chapter is on the topic of interactive scientific visualization. It is intended to be an introduction and tutorial to certain aspects of this area; namely those related to applications where the user interacts with the model and drives the simulation in hopes of "gaining new insight" or "creating a new design." The primary interface for this interaction is the visual images viewed by the user and the subsequent input based upon the user's perception and interpretation of these images. The emphasis here is on applications which involve physical models in three dimensional space, thus including the very important class of problems concerned with modeling and understanding phenomenon occurring in the real world.

The chapter is organized as follows. The next section describes three prototypical application examples. Abstraction and generalization of these examples leads to a simple, information flow model which is used for three purposes. It serves as an initial step in the direction of unifying this subarea of scientific visualization. Secondly, it serves as an organizational framework for the third section of this article where the various phases of each of the three examples are described; thus giving the reader a sampling of the various aspects and techniques of this topic. Thirdly, this information flow model provides a rather natural means of segmenting the workload of an application of this type. In the forth section, one of the three prototypical examples is analyzed in this regard and estimates of computing and network requirements are discussed.

9.2. Examples of Interactive Steering

9.2.1. Example A: Wing Design

An engineer is designing a new wing for an airplane (see Figure 9.1 in the color section). An initial description of the wing is formulated and the physical situation is modelled with partial differential equations. These equations are solved and the results are observed by watching the animation of particles flowing through the domain and past the wing. The initial design is determined to be unsatisfactory and so changes to the wing surface geometry are made and the new flow is observed. This continues until the engineer is satisfied with the design.

9.2.2. Example B: Radiation Treatment Design

A medical practitioner is designing a radiation treatment for a tumor (see Figure 9.2 in the color section). MR data has been collected. Using volume visualization techniques, the practitioner can take a non-invasive view into the patient and determine the location of the area needing treatment. By interactively simulating the application of the treatment the practitioner can determine the parameters of the treatment (direction, focus, intensity, etc.) so that extraneous exposure is minimized.

9.2.3. Example C: Environmental Data Perusal

Temperature, humidity, concentration of certain chemicals and a variety of other variables have been measured at various location on the surface of the Earth (see Figure 9.3 in the color section). These measurements are known at regular intervals over a period of time. An environmentalist is interested in perusing this data in hopes of detecting some global trends; both temporal and physical. The data is modeled by a mathematical function with parameters and displayed over the background of the Earth. The user animates it through time and interactively changes the viewing position and the parameters of the mathematical model.

All three of these examples contain the very basic loop of modern scientific discovery consisting of a model or abstract description of the phenomena followed by observation and subsequent modification and refinement of the model.

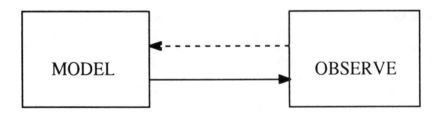

Figure 9.4. Basic iterative loop of scientific discovery

For these three examples, there is a strong emphasis on the visual interface and so it is possible to refine the model and identify an additional phase which is positioned between the modeling and observation phases and provides the two-way interface between these phases. In this phase, information is "derived" or "extracted" from the model and used to create the image for the user. In the case of the wing design example, this phase involves taking the solution of the Navier–Stokes equations (which is a 3D vector field) and "graphing" it by animating weightless particles flowing through it. In the radiation treatment example, it requires taking the raw MR data and smoothing/fitting this data and then "graphing" the resulting trivariate function using volume visualization techniques along with some means of representing the region of treatment. In the environmental data example, the modeling function is "graphed." The computations required depend upon the type of graph that is chosen. Two possibilities are a choropleth (commonly used for weather reports) and a radially projected surface graph. Both types are shown in the image of Figure 9.3. Since this phase is analogous to the computation of a simple, univariate function, $y = F(x)$, in preparation for the display of a conventional graph of F, we call this the "graph evaluation" phase.

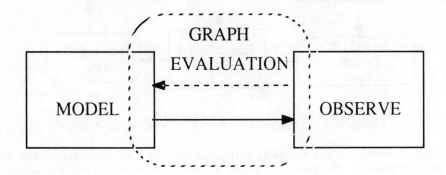

Figure 9.5. Visual interface for interactive modeling

If the data which is passed from one phase to the other is also added, we have the basic information flow model shown in Figure 9.6.

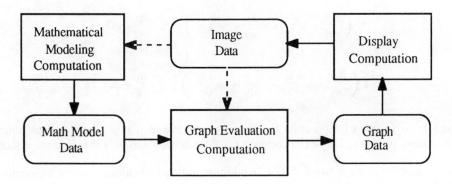

Figure 9.6. Information flow model for interactive scientific visualization

9.3. Further Description of the Three Examples

In the following three subsections, each of the three examples are more fully described; particularly with respect to the phases of the the information flow model: mathematical modeling, graph evaluation and display.

9.3.1. Wing Design, Example A

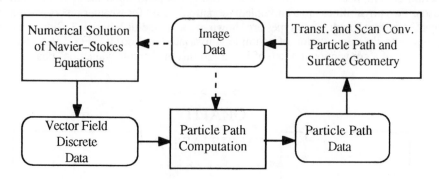

Figure 9.7. Information flow model for wing design example

One type of **mathematical modeling** is physical modeling which, in very simple terms, involves expressing the laws of physics in terms of mathematical equations. The mathematical model for the wing design example uses the basic equations of fluid dynamics. These are the Navier–Stokes equations,

$$r\left(\frac{\partial u}{\partial t} + u\frac{\partial u}{\partial x} + v\frac{\partial u}{\partial y} + w\frac{\partial u}{\partial z} \right) = X - \frac{\partial p}{\partial x} + m\nabla^2 u$$

$$r\left(\frac{\partial v}{\partial t} + u\frac{\partial v}{\partial x} + v\frac{\partial v}{\partial y} + w\frac{\partial v}{\partial z} \right) = Y - \frac{\partial p}{\partial y} + m\nabla^2 v \qquad (9.1)$$

$$r\left(\frac{\partial w}{\partial t} + u\frac{\partial w}{\partial x} + v\frac{\partial w}{\partial y} + w\frac{\partial w}{\partial z} \right) = Z - \frac{\partial p}{\partial z} + m\nabla^2 w$$

where $\vec{V}$ = (u, v, w) represents the velocity vector and p is a scalar valued function representing pressure. The scalar constant r is fluid density and m is the dynamic viscosity.

The external forces are $\vec{F}$ = (X, Y, Z). In addition to these equations, there is the continuity equation,

$$\text{div } \vec{V} = \nabla \cdot \vec{V} = \frac{\partial u}{\partial x} + \frac{\partial v}{\partial y} + \frac{\partial w}{\partial z} = 0 . \qquad (9.2)$$

The overall problem is to solve for $\vec{V}$ and p as functions of time t and the three spatial variable (x, y, z). Using vector notation, the equations of (9.1) take on a more compact form,

$$r\left(\frac{\partial \vec{V}}{\partial t} + (\vec{V}\cdot\nabla)\vec{V} \right) = -\nabla p + m\nabla^2\vec{V} + \vec{F} . \qquad (9.3)$$

Boundary conditions for the wing design problem must be specified on the surface of the airplane. They are used to reflect the condition that the velocity of the flow is equal to the velocity of the airplane at this interface and far from the airplane, the velocity must approximate the free stream conditions. If $\dfrac{d\vec{A}}{dt}(t)$ represents the velocity of the airplane, then the boundary conditions are

$$\vec{V}(x, y, z, t) = \frac{d\vec{A}}{dt}(t) = 0, (x, y, z) \in S ,\qquad (9.4)$$

where S represents the surface of the airplane. In general boundary conditions are extremely important. In order to include them completely, it is often necessary to have a mathematical representation of the boundary, which, in many physical models, is some geometric object. In the wing design example, a mathematical representation for the surface of the airplane is required. The mathematical representation of free-form surfaces is fairly well developed. Trimmed, non-uniform, rational B-splines (NURB) are rapidly becoming the standard for surface modeling systems. A NURB can be represented in parametric form as

$$S(u,v) = \frac{\sum\limits_{ij} b_{ij}N_i(u)N_j(v)}{\sum\limits_{ij} w_{ij}N_i(u)N_j(v)}\qquad (9.5)$$

where $N_i(u)$ and $N_j(v)$ are the standard, univariate B-splines, b_{ij} are points in 3D which serve to control the shape of the surface and w_{ij} are weights associated with each control point which can further affect the shape of the surface. Trimming a NURB simply means to restrict the domain as shown in Figure 9.8.

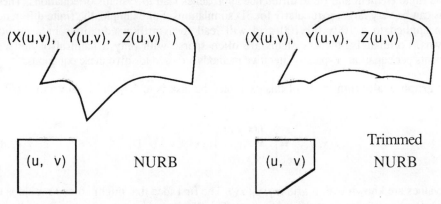

Figure 9.8. Trimmed non uniform, rational B-spline

We now turn to the problem of solving the mathematical modeling equations. In general the PDEs that arise in physical models do not lend themselves to exact, explicit solutions. Numerical methods must be used. There are two well known general approaches; finite difference schemes and finite element methods. Finite difference schemes utilize a grid on the domain. The PDE is replaced with an approximation where derivatives are replaced by approximations based upon differences. This yields a system of equations where the unknowns are the values of the solution function at the grid values. For example, the following approximations might be used:

$$u_x \cong .5(u_{i+1,j,k}-u_{i-1,j,k}), \; u_y \cong .5(u_{i,j+1,k}-u_{i,j-1,k}), \; u_z \cong .5(u_{i,j,k+1}-u_{i,j,k-1})$$

$$\nabla^2 u = u_{xx}+u_{yy}+u_{zz} \cong \{u_{i+1,j,k} - 2u_{i,j,k} + u_{i-1,j,k}\} +$$

$$\{u_{i,j+1,k} - 2u_{i,j,k} + u_{i,j-1,k}\} + \{u_{i,j,k+1} - 2u_{i,j,k} + u_{i,j,k-1}\} \tag{9.6}$$

where $u_{i,j,k}= u(x_i, y_j, z_k)$ and (x_i, y_j, z_k) is a grid point. Finite element methods assume a general form for the solution

$$u(x,y,z) = \sum_{i=1}^{n} a_i b_i(x,y,z) \tag{9.7}$$

consisting of a linear combination of "trial" functions $b_i(x,y,z)$. The trial functions are defined in a piecewise manner over a decomposition of the domain and are required to have only a small region of support. The next step is compute the a_i , $i = 1, \ldots$, n. This is done, for example, by requiring that the representation of (9.7) satisfy the PDE at n discrete locations.

Both the finite element and finite difference approaches lead to systems of equations. These systems can be very large; particularly for 3D simulations. For example, the finite difference scheme applied to a 100x100x100 grid will lead to a million equations in a million unknowns. Fortunately, these systems are often sparse with only a handful of nonzero coefficients per equation. Typically, iterative methods are used to solve these equations.

For the **graph evaluation** phase of this example, the task is to "graph" a 3D vector field

$$V(x, y, z) = \begin{pmatrix} u(x,y,z) \\ v(x,y,z) \\ w(x,y,z) \end{pmatrix}, (x, y, z) \in D, \tag{9.8}$$

where values are known over a grid (x_i, y_j, z_k). The first idea that might come to mind is to draw a collection of arrows at the grid points. This "hedgehog" type of display turns out to have very limited value in learning about a vector field. The picture gets too crowded and one can not see the "forest for the trees." A deformation map also attempts to convey the information in a vector field. Animating particles that follow along the paths of streamlines is another choice. Streamlines are curves in space $P(t) = (x(t), y(t), z(t))$ which are tangent to the vector field, that is,

$$P'(t) = (x'(t), y'(t), z'(t)) = V(x(t), y(t), z(t)) = V(P(t)). \qquad (9.9)$$

This is, of course, an ODE (ordinary differential equation) which can be numerically solved by conventional methods. For example, using Euler's method, the path of a particle released at $P_0 = (x_i, y_j, z_k)$ is computed by

$$P_{n+1} = P_n + hV(P_n), n = 0, 1, \ldots \qquad (9.10)$$

where h is the step size and P_k denotes the approximation to $P(kt)$. In order to compute $V(P_k)$, it will be necessary to use some interpolation technique. A particularly simple choice is to use trilinear interpolation over each voxel.

Once the choices and computations of the graph evaluation phase have been completed, it is usually a rather standard problem of computer graphics to **display** the actual images. The typical graph evaluation phase produces "graphic primitives" which can be displayed by well developed and widely available techniques. Points, lines and polygons are typical primitives. For this example, it is required that an animation of the path of a particle be displayed over the background of the airplane. This requires the transformation and rendering of the particle paths and the polygon boundaries (usually triangles or quadrilaterals) of these geometric primitives. The typical processing of polygons passes them through a viewing pipeline consisting of a transformation from the three dimensional coordinates of the modeling domain to the two dimensional coordinates of the display screen. The pixels interior to this polygon are then colored according to some illumination function. The hidden surface computations and the clipping of primitives must also occur during this phase.

9.3.2. Radiation Treatment, Example B

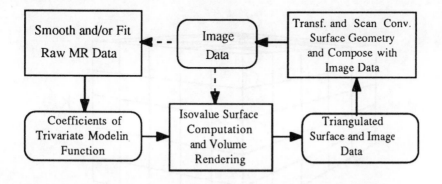

Figure 9.9. Information flow model for radiation treatment example

There are several techniques which produce data for noninvasive medical imaging. This includes positron emission tomography (PET), magnetic resonance imaging (MRI) and ultrasound. All of these produce a three dimensional array of values, F_{ijk}; $i = 1, \ldots, N_x$;

$j = 1, \ldots, N_y$; $k = 1, \ldots, N_z$. These are intensity values associated with data site positions in 3D space, V_{ijk}. The **mathematical modeling** phase of this type of example involves the determination of a trivariate function, $F(x, y, z)$, that is intended to represent the relationship implied by this data. This means that $F(V_{ijk})$ approximates or is equal to F_{ijk}. If the data sites form a cuberille grid (Figure 9.10), $V_{ijk} = (x_i, y_j, z_k)$ then the mathematical model might be as simple as inferring that F is piecewise trilinear over each of the voxels of the cuberille grid. In order to get a smoother modeling function, a triple tensor product cubic spline can be used to fit the cuberille grid data. If the data is not on a cuberille grid, then methods of interpolation or approximation of scattered, trivariate data need to be used. Some recent work on least squares techniques for trivariate data is covered by Nielson and Dierks (1991) and the topic of trivariate scattered data interpolation is discussed by Nielson et al. (1991).

The first part of the **graph evaluation** phase requires the computation of isovalued surfaces of the modeling function, $F(x, y, z)$. Isovalue surfaces are the trivariate analogues of the widely used topographical contour maps and choropleth temperature maps associated with weather reports. They consist of the collection of points in the domain where the function takes on a certain specified value; that is $S_k = \{ (x, y, z) : F(x, y, z) = k\}$. Isovalue surface plots, enhanced with transparency and other features are very useful for analyzing a trivariate relationship. Usually S_k will be a collection (often one) of surfaces. For an arbitrary trivariate function, F, it could be rather difficult to compute the isovalue surfaces exactly. Most algorithms compute an approximation to Sk, consisting of a collection of triangles. First, the function is evaluated over a cuberille grid (x_i, y_j, z_k) to yield the values $F(x_i, y_j, z_k) = F_{ijk}$. The vertices of S_k can then be compute from these values by assuming the the function varies linearly over the edges of the cuberille grid. These vertices are then joined into polygons on the surface of the voxel and then split into triangles. Some cases are shown in Figure 9.11. The algorithms based upon this approach described by Lorenson and Cline (1987) has some problems in the manner in which it handles certain ambiguous cases. One way to avoid this problem is to decompose each voxel into 5 (or 6) tetrahedra (see Figure 9.12) and to assume linear variation on each of these tetrahedra.

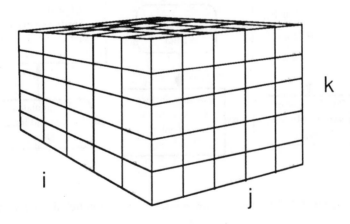

k

i

j

Figure 9.10. Cuberille grid data.

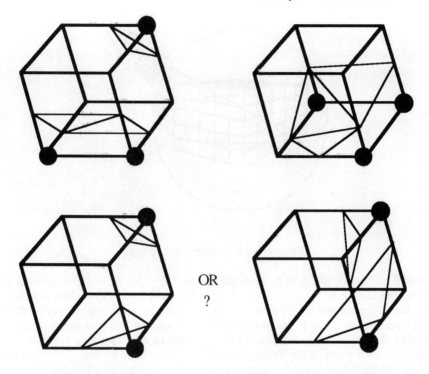

Figure 9.11. Some cases for trilinear interpolation along edges

OR
?

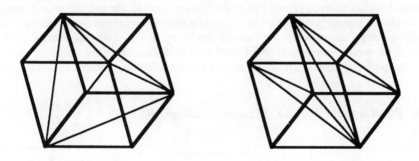

Figure 9.12. Decomposition of voxel into five or six tetrahedra

In the above discussion, we assumed that the modeling function, F, is evaluated on a cuberille grid in order to get the data F_{ijk} to use for the computation of the triangulated approximation to contour surfaces. In some some cases, the values F_{ijk} are provided directly by the raw data, so there is really no fitting process taking place except from the viewpoint that there is an inferred trivariate function based upon piecewise trilinear interpolation from the cuberille grid of points. Even in this case, it is often desirable to "evaluate" a cuberille grid to obtain a new cuberille grid which is much coarser. For example, it may be desirable to "reduce" a grid of size 256x256x113 to one of size 100x100x100. This will lead to fewer triangles for the approximation of the isovalue surface which means quicker computations and a surface that can be animated with less computing power.

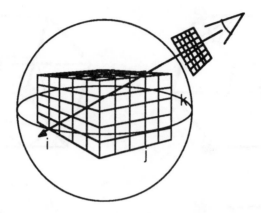

Figure 9.13. Volume rendering.

The second portion of the **graph evaluation** phase for this example requires a volume rendering (see Drebin et al. 1988, Fuchs et al. 1989 and Levoy 1988). This is a method of viewing the entire volume of 3D data in a single image. In some ways it can be thought of as being similar to an X-ray in that it allows the viewer to see inside of the data and observe objects that are not normally visible. An image is produce by casting a ray from the view point through each pixel of the display screen into the volume of data. The ray penetrates certain voxels and based upon the data values there, values are computed at various points along the ray. These values are composed with a user provided "transport function" and certain other values to obtain a single color for the pixel associated with this ray. The potential benefits of volume rendering are tremendous. Being able to take a non-invasive view inside the human body allows medical practitioners to perform diagnostics and treatment schedules heretofore impossible. Volume rendering is very compute intensive and many applications require interaction. Real time volume rendering is not presently possible, but due to the potential benefits, it is sure to be a reality in the near future.

9.3.3. Environmental Data Perusal, Example C

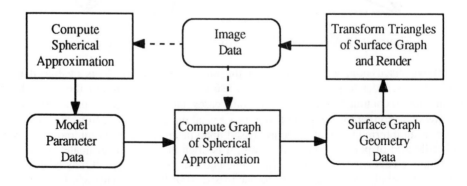

Figure 9.14. Information flow model for environmental data example

The **mathematical modeling** portion of this example requires the mathematical fitting of data that has been measured at various locations on the Earth. For mathematical purposes, the Earth is assumed to be a unit sphere $S = \{ (x, y, z) : x^2 + y^2 + z^2 = 1 \}$ and that the data sites are denoted by $P_i \in S$ with associated dependent data values F_i, $i = 1, \ldots, N$. In terms of this notation, the problem is to determine a function, F, defined on S such that $F(P_i)$ approximates or equals F_i, $i = 1, \ldots, N$. Approximation methods could be based upon least squares techniques but these methods are not very well developed in this area at this point in time. Interpolation methods, where $F(P_i) = F_i$, $i = 1, \ldots, N$ are more developed. In the past few years, several methods for interpolating data over a spherical domain have been described. The minimum norm network method has proven to be a very effective method (Franke and Nielson 1991) and Nielson and Ramaraj (1987) have discussed this method as it applies to the spherical domain. The application of this method requires the solution of a 2Nx2N linear system of equations; but it is sparse (approximately 12 nonzero coefficients per equation) and can be easily solved by iterative methods.

We now discuss the **graph evaluation** phase for this example where it is required to "graph" a scalar valued function whose domain is a sphere. One possibility is a choropleth as shown in Figure 9.3 (see color section). A conceptually simple, but computational expensive way to compute such a graph is to take each pixel in image space and determine where it is on the sphere and then evaluate the modeling function there in order to get the proper color. Another approach (and the one used to produce the image of Figure 9.3) is based upon computing polygon approximations to the contour curves lying on the spherical domain, S_k $= \{ (x, y, z) : x^2 + y^2 + z^2 = 1 \text{ and } F(x, y, z) = k \}$. This is done by approximating the domain with a number of smaller regions and then assuming that the function has a very simple representation over these regions. The image of Figure 9.3 (see color section) uses an approximation consisting of a collection of triangles and assumes that the function varies linearly over each triangle. Contour curves then become line segments and so a polygon approximation to the contour curves is achieved. While contours are useful, there can be certain properties of a function which are difficult to detect from contours. For example, a collection of concentric circles might be representing a conic shaped surface or a nice smooth exponential bump; it is hard to tell which. Additional graphs can reveal additional information. The radially projected, transparent surface graph of Figure 9.3 uses the same triangulation of the sphere as the choropleth and the dependent function values are scaled so that the minimum value lies on a unit sphere and the maximum lies on a sphere of radius two units. More discussion on the techniques leading to graphs of the type shown in Figure 9.3 (see color section) can be found in Foley et al (1990).

An interesting and very useful extension of the above problem is the case where the data is measured (or by some other means given) over an arbitrary surface. For example pressure measurements over the wing of an airplane or voltage gradients over the surface of a human brain. Because the domain is a two-dimensional surface and because it is common to refer to a bivariate function as a surface, this is referred to as the **surface-on-surface** problem. One recently developed technique for solving this problem is the domain mapping method described in Foley et al. (1990). In a nutshell, this method maps the problem to a spherical domain, solves it there using some spherical method, and then maps it back. An example of a surface-on-surface is shown in Figure 9.15 (see color section) where the domain is the apple core shaped surface. The upper left shows a radially projected surface graph and the upper right shows a surface graph that is projected perpendicularly to the domain. In the center is an example of a new method of viewing surfaces defined over surfaces. It is called a

hypersurface projection graph. More discussion on this technique can be found in Nielson et al. (1991).

9.4. Computational and Network Requirements

In this section, we are interested in the problem of distributing the workload of an interactive scientific visualization project among the various resources of a network. The phases of the information flow model provide a convenient means to partition the overall workload. Estimates of the requirements of each phase can be made and then used to predict overall performance and to adjust parameters and configurations in an attempt to best satisfy the demands. Only one of the the above three examples is examined here. The other two examples can be analyzed in a similar manner. The estimates are done in two steps. First, several key quantities are identified and given variable names. The requirements are then formulated in terms of these variables. The second step gives specific requirements by assigning actual values to the variables. This second step may be done several times.

Consider the wing design example. The mathematical modeling portion involves the numerical solution of the Navier–Stokes equations based upon a finite difference scheme. The first assumption is that the problem is steady. This means that $\frac{d\overrightarrow{V}}{dt} = \frac{dp}{dt} = 0$, and so these unknown functions do not depend upon the time variable t. A cuberille grid is specified by three resolution parameters N_x, N_y and N_z. This specifies the grid (x_i, y_j, z_k) with $i = 1, \ldots, N_x; j = 1, \ldots, N_y; k = 1, \ldots, N_z$ and

$$x_i = x_{min} + \frac{i-1}{N_x-1}(x_{max} - x_{min})$$

$$y_j = y_{min} + \frac{j-1}{N_y-1}(y_{max} - y_{min}) \tag{9.11}$$

$$z_k = z_{min} + \frac{k-1}{N_z-1}(z_{max} - z_{min}).$$

The unknowns, that are eventually computed, are the values of the discrete vector field $(u_{ijk}, v_{ijk}, w_{ijk}) \cong V(x_i, y_j, z_k)$ and the discrete pressure values $p_{ijk} \cong p(x_i, y_j, z_k)$. This gives a total of $4 \cdot N$ unknowns where $N = N_x \cdot N_y \cdot N_z$ is the number of positions in the cuberille grid. Actually the number of unknowns could be less than this because some of the positions lie in the interior of the airplane and will not be involved as unknowns after the boundary conditions are imposed on the surface of the airplane, but, as far as estimates for this type of analysis are concerned, it is close enough. Using approximations like those of equation (9.6), a large nonlinear system of equations results. This system will be solved by an iterative method. It is assumed that it takes K iterations to converge to the required accuracy and that each iteration requires μ operations per equation to compute the updated iterate. After the discrete version of the Navier–Stokes equations are solved, only the discrete vector field data is passed on to the particle integration portion of the software. It is assumed that a total of P, weightless particles are released and that each one is stepped through the ODE solver a total of R times. The computation cost of each step is assumed to be v floating point operations. If Euler's method is used, for example, the bulk of the work is the evaluation of $V(P_n)$ which we assume is done by trilinear interpolation on the voxel containing P_n. It is assumed that the number of vertices required to represent the triangulated geometry of the surface of the airplane is V. Since it is a closed surface, the number of triangles is approximately $2 \cdot V$. Three additional variables are used for representing the requirements of handling the conventional display of these graphical primitives: π represents the number of operations to scan convert a triangle, λ represents the number of operation to scan convert a line and τ represents the number of operations to transform and clip a 3D point to 2D screen coordinates.

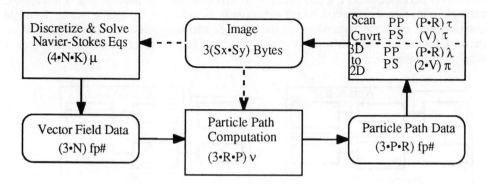

Figure 9.16. Estimates of workload for wing design example. PP = Particle Pathes, PS = Polygon Surface.

Some choices for the variables of Figure 9.16 lead to the requirement in Figure 9.17.

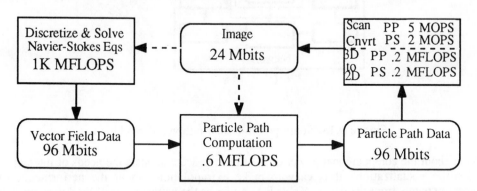

Figure 9.17. Workload of typical CFD problem, per frame, with the values Nx=Ny=Nx = 100, K = 10 , R = 100 , P = 100 , V = 10,000 μ = 25 FLOPS, v = 20 FLOPS, τ = 20 FLOPS, λ = 500 OPS, π = 1000 OPS

How to distribute the workload? A few possibilities are indicated in Figure 9.18. The nomogram of Figure 9.19 is useful for doing some quick estimates and for some "what if" situations. If animation speeds of approximately 10 frames per second are desired then the configuration of Figure 9.18a indicates that the connection between the workstation and the supercomputer must be able to sustain speeds of approximately 10 Mbits/sec. This choice also implies that the "host" be able to sustain approximately 10,000 MFLOPS/sec and that the workstation be capable of transforming and rendering 100,000 polygons and 100,000 vectors per second. A division that is likely to be rather common in the future is indicated by Figure 9.18b. Here all the numerical simulation, graph computation and 3D to 2D transformation are done on the resources of the network and only 2D primitives are passed to the X-window server. This would require network speeds of approximately 3 to 4 Mbits/sec and server performances of approximately 70 MIPS in order to provide animation for this example. Another distribution worth mentioning is indicated by Figure 9.18c. Here the computations are done somewhere in the network and image files are passed around the network for various users to view. Animation within this context requires network speeds of nearly a gigabit per second.

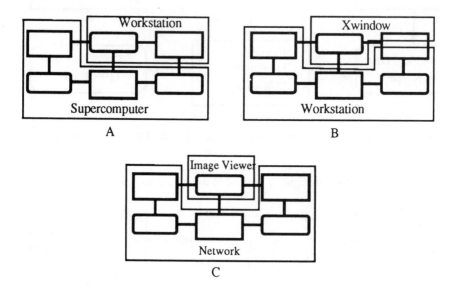

Figure 9.18. Some possible distributions of workload

What about the computational power of the future to accommodate the needs of interactive scientific visualization? It is easy to make extrapolations about the performance of supercomputers from the data of Table 9.1. As far as the workstations of the future go, Jim Clark of Silicon Graphics may have the best crystal ball around. Today, SGI's high-end system VGX can display a million polygons/vectors per second and has the computing power of 30 MIPS/5 MFLOPS for the single processor version and extends up to 200+ MIPS/30+ MFLOPS for the eight processor version. At a recent CEO panel at VISUALIZATION '90, "Visualization- The Next Decade", Clark predicted that through the use of multi/micro RISC processors, high-end workstations ($150,000.00) will approach a GFLOP (1,000,000,000 floating point operations per second) performance in the next two to three years. He also made some other interesting predictions (announcements) for the low end. He described the multimedia machine of the future as a device which integrates the capabilities of (1) full 3D, interactive, real time computer graphics, (2) full motion video, (3) image processing capabilities, (4) fully integrated geometric text and (5) full CD, digital sound. He predicts that this will be available in a portable notebook sized device with motion sensors in the next five to ten years for a price less than $5000.

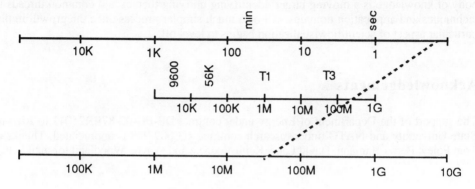

Figure 9.19. Nomogram

	Cray 1	X-MP/2	X-MP/4	Cray 2	YMP	Cray 3	Cray 4
Year	1976	1982	1984	1985	1988	1989	1992
MFLOPS	160	420	840	1.7 K	2.5 K	16 K	128 K

Table 9.1. Performance statistics of Cray supercomputers

9.5. Summary

The information flow model consisting of the three phases of mathematical modeling, graph evaluation and display has been useful for this article. In general, this whole idea of information/data flow coupled with the visual programming provides an extremely effective means for the user to interact with mathematical modeling problems. Both AVS (see Upson et al. 1989) and apE (see Dyer 1990) use this idea extensively and there is sure to be more of this type of software coming. The mathematical modeling portion could also benefit from this influence (see Ford and Chatelin 1987).

This whole process of deciding how to "graph" the data and how to perform the required computations in order to render this "graph" is a challenging problem in scientific visualization. Many believe that this the central problem of scientific visualization. Haber and McNabb (1990) view this as a process of mapping the data to an abstract visualization object (AVO). There is also the viewpoint that information is being "extracted" or "derived" from the data. The general idea of having an algorithm find interesting things in the data and then concentrate the viewers attention accordingly is very important in scientific visualization. An example is the work of Helman and Hesselink (1989) in the area of flow visualization where they determine critical points, classify them by the eigenvalues of the Jacobian and then present this information, along with some interconnection topology, to the user. The current situation for this aspect of scientific visualization is that there is a rapidly growing collection of tools, techniques, ideas and methods without much structure. Several authors have tried to unify the concepts, identify the principles and, in general, put some structure to the whole process, but this is an extremely difficult task; particularly when the body of knowledge is a moving target. Identifying unifying themes and common threads in techniques and application domains will be a much simpler process once the growth in this particular aspect of scientific visualization begins to level off.

Acknowledgements

The support of the Department of Energy under contract DE-FG-02-87ER25041 to Arizona State University and NATO under research contract RG 0097/88 is appreciated. Thanks to Tom Foley, Bernd Hamann, David Lane, Keith Voegele and Wayne Woodland for their help.

References

Drebin R, Carpenter L, and Hanrahan P (1988) Volume rendering, SIGGRAPH 88 Conference Proceedings, *Computer Graphics*, Vol. 22, No. 4, pp. 65-74.

Dyer S (1990) A dataflow toolkit for visualization, *Computer Graphics & Applications*, Vol 10, No. 4, pp. 60-69.

Foley T, Lane D, Nielson G and Ramaraj R (1990) Visualizing functions over a sphere, *Computer Graphics & Applications*, Vol. 10, No. 1, pp. 32-40.

Foley T, Lane D, Nielson G , Franke R and Hagen H (1990) Interpolation of scattered data on closed surfaces, *Computer Aided Geometric Design* 7, pp. 303-312.

Ford B and Chatelin F (Eds) (1987) *Problem solving environments for scientific computing*, North Holland, Netherlands.

Franke R and Nielson G (1991) Scattered data interpolation and applications: a tutorial and survey", in: H. Hagen and D. Roller (Eds) *Geometric Modeling: Methods and Their Application*, Springer, Berlin.

Fuchs H, Levoy M, and Pizer S (1989) Interactive Visualization of 3D Medical Data, *Computer*, Vol. 22, No. 8, pp. 46-51.

Haber, R and McNabb D (1990) Visualization idioms: A conceptual model for scientific visualization systems, in: G. Nielson and B. Shriver (Eds) *Visualization in Scientific Computing*, IEEE Computer Society Press, Los Alamitos.

Helman J and Hesselink L (1989) Representation and Display of Vector Field Topology in Fluid Flow Data Sets, *Computer*, Vol. 22, No. 8, pp. 27-36.

Kaufman A (Ed) (1990) *Volume Visualization*, IEEE Computer Society Press, Los Alamitos.

Kaufman A. (Ed) (1990) *Visualization '90 Conference Proceedings*, IEEE Computer Society Press, Los Alamitos

Levoy M (1988) Display of surfaces from volume data, *IEEE Computer Graphics and Applications*, Vol. 8, # 3, pp. 29-37.

Lorensen W and Cline H (1987) Marching cubes: A high-resolution 3D surface construction algorithm, *SIGGRAPH 87 Conference Proceedings, Computer Graphics*, Vol. 21, No. 4, pp. 163-169.

Nielson G and Dierks T (1991) Analysis and visualization of scattered volumetric data, *Proceedings of SPIE*, #1259, pp. 20-32.

Nielson G, Foley T, Hamann B and Lane D (1991) Visualization and Modeling of Scattered Multivariate Data, *Computer Graphic & Applications*, Vol. 11, No. 3, pp. 47-55.

Nielson G and Ramaraj R (1987) Interpolation over a sphere, *Computer Aided Geometric Design*, Vol. 4, pp. 41-57.

Nielson G and Shriver B (1990) *Visualization in Scientific Computing*, IEEE Computer Society Press, Los Alamitos.

Upson C.(Ed) (1989) *Proceedings of the Chapel Hill Workshop on Volume Visualization*, Chapel Hill, NC.

Upson C, Faulhaber T, Kamins D, Laidlaw D, Schlegel D, Vroom J, Gurwitz R, van Dam A (1989) The application visualization system: A computational environment for scientific visualization, *Computer Graphics & Applications*, Vol. 9, No. 4, pp. 30-42.

10

Computer Graphics in Architecture

Gerhard N. Schmitt
Department of Architecture, Swiss Federal Institute of Technology, Zürich

10.1. Introduction

Computer graphics applications in architecture extend from computer aided drafting to the automatic generation of a virtual architectural reality. The chapter begins with some critical reflections on the history of the new medium in architecture and then concentrates on the traditional use of computer graphics, models of transition and computer graphics in presentation. Computer graphics in design is the second focus illustrated by two examples: the reconstruction of a Roman city and a contemporary urban project. Selected research directions including visualization, cellular automata and case-based reasoning are outlined at the end.

We give preference to the use of computer graphics in architecture as an active tool for design rather than reducing it to presentation purposes. To this end, we develop rapid visualization programs that support decision making during the design process. We also consider computer graphics the most important tool to demonstrate similarities and relations between building performance factors.

10.2. Traditional Computer Graphics in Architecture

Two individuals set ambitious goals for computer aided design and graphics more than 20 years ago and implemented them in prototypical form. Sutherland's (1963) Sketchpad represented one of the first uses of interactive computer graphics for design applications. The architecture machine group that developed around Negroponte (1970) discussed design automation possibilities. The MIT Media Lab, Carnegie Mellon University and UCLA now have a tradition in partial design automation.

The gap between the early prototypes and architectural praxis of the early 1970s was extreme. Pioneers who used CAD in architecture were under pressure to justify the financial and human investment while attempting to define and improve basic modeling tools as Kemper (1985) describes. Justification became easier with the proliferation of reasonably fast personal computers in the late 1980s. Computer graphics became an increasingly important part of modeling systems. While an office could justify powerful but expensive systems with an hourly cost of over $50 for highly paid partners—who most likely could not use the system to its fullest extent—investment justification for PC based CAD packages with hourly costs of about $5 was less difficult.

10.2.1. From Paper to Screen

Until recently, paper was the predominant external medium on which architectural design ideas were generated, communicated, and stored. It still is the medium for legal documents that define the scope, execution and communication of a project from planning through building. It is therefore natural that the first CAD applications concentrated on moving paper representations to similar computer representations. Two-dimensional drawing systems are the most widely used CAD applications. The opportunities that Charles Eastman demonstrated with the GLIDE project (Eastman and Henrion 1977) are not implemented in most CAD programs. Until today, isolated problem solutions that answer specific questions characterize the computer aided design and construction process. This approach also duplicates the immense communication problems of traditional design processes.

10.2.2. Editing and the Time Factor

Two motivations lead to the introduction of CAD in architectural offices after 1980. Proponents of the "idealistic" approach expect to gain time for the improvement of architectural quality and to create the possibility of alternative evaluation by automating routine tasks. The "pragmatic" approach aims at rationalization of the design process in order to improve the financial situation of architectural offices.

To date, most of the expectations of the idealistic approach have not been realized due to the absence of truly interactive design support systems (Schmitt et al. 1990). However, the pragmatic and partial automation of documentation processes has led to a high level of acceptance in architectural offices. In the United States, more than three quarters of the architectural firms have installed CAD systems of some form. The single most successful application is the creation and editing of two-dimensional drawings. In this respect similarities to the introduction of word processing programs into the office environment are obvious.

The university situation is different and might point to the future direction in offices as well. Programs that support interactive three-dimensional modeling and rendering tools dominate the teaching labs. Integration issues including the linking of graphical and non-graphical databases are a standard part of CAD teaching. Teaching and research can concentrate on principles without facing the complexity barrier posed by concrete architectural projects. Architectural practice cannot afford to accept solutions in principle. It must deliver completely documented and specified answers to complex problems.

10.2.3. Unfulfilled Expectations

Even the simplest building is composed of several thousand individual parts of varying complexity. Present limitations of machine performance necessitate the abstraction of the design process and its documentation as much as the medium paper resulted in the established abstractions of orthogonal projection and notation. As architects and researchers define the specifications of the ideal modeling support system, display and processing technologies are still far behind expectations. Even today's fastest systems do not allow interactive design with knowledge-based and fully shaded complex building objects. The necessary abstractions represent a significant administrative and program management overhead in dealing with CAD systems.

The introduction of computers in architectural offices has created a new class of employees, the CAD operators. One reason for the establishment of this position is the complexity of early CAD environments. A designing architect could not possibly handle CAD in addition to design, administration and acquisition tasks. Although this reason has lost some of its significance through software and hardware advances, the proliferation of networks and shared data bases has added new time consuming tasks. The second, more serious reason for the necessity of CAD operators is the weakness of all existing commercial systems in terms of semantic communication. Human adaptation to program capabilities is a fact, machine adaptation to design problem solution only a future possibility.

The disappointment of architects is understandable. Medium size offices now require a CAD operator to translate sketches and drawings into the machine, an operator to extract it from the drawing database for presentation, a systems operator to maintain security and document backups as well as an up-to-date level of capital intensive equipment to compete with other offices. They require service bureaus to generate renderings and promotional presentation videos. Basically, most of the goals that Sutherland and Negroponte defined as machine activities can only be achieved by hiring very specialized operators to form a human interface between architect and program.

10.3. Models of Transition

As research and practice discover more applications for computer graphics, the view of the design process and the process itself change. The tool begins to influence the task. Visualization has improved the understanding of complex relations in architecture and can lead away from the one-dimensional view of performance factors in design.

10.3.1. The Discovery of the AEC Market

The graphic quality which the architecture, engineering and construction (AEC) professions require for documentation and communication was prohibitively high for the early CAD packages. Fragmentation and individualistic needs characterize the AEC market and the associated sectors, although they account for more than one third of the gross national product of industrialized countries. Readily available standard packages, which were useful in mechanical engineering, chemistry and medicine, did not meet with the necessary acceptance of large numbers or of financially strong AEC firms in order to be economically feasible.

Again powerful microprocessors which made CAD workstations affordable for small offices changed market conditions in favor of architectural CAD packages. Since the mid 1980s a rapidly growing number of architecture specific modeling programs have entered the market. In Switzerland alone more than 60 architecture related CAD packages are available.

This development brings with it the advantages of increased competition and a general improvement in quality. The disadvantage is the proliferation of a range of file formats which are only partially compatible. In addition, each CAD program aimed at architectural practice incorporates a particular design strategy which might not be obvious at the time of purchase, but consequently impacts work in the office later on.

10.3.2. From Single Applications to Integration

Computer graphics in architecture has begun to influence document illustration, graphical data bases, presentation drawings, and performance simulation. Each application was developed separately with different goals in mind. The viewer must be able to interpret the graphic result. Extraction of knowledge from graphic representations remains a human task. Teaching a design studio or attempting to complete a building project from design through construction with the help of the computer demonstrates integration problems. Integration on the lowest common denominator such as DXF files or ASCII files does not solve the problem of information reduction between applications. Strategic integration approaches exemplified by the STEP consortium do address the problem, but may be years away from implementation (Gielingh 1989).

10.4. Computer Graphics in Presentation

Computer graphics in presentation requires a completed architectural design as input. Because presentation and rendering packages are often separated from modeling software, the same person rarely creates design and presentation images. It is more likely for small and medium size offices that external firms produce realistic renderings and videos.

10.4.1. From Model to Projection

The introduction of computer graphics has almost reversed the traditional handling of three-dimensional objects in architecture. Although designers think in three dimensions, drawings were the two dimensional projection of this process and three-dimensional physical models were then built based on those drawings. It is now common to model and visualize design ideas three-dimensionally. The extraction of two-dimensional orthogonal projections from these three-dimensional models seems a trivial task. But traditional documentation requirements have developed a high degree of specialization in architecture which standard CAD packages are often unable to duplicate. Therefore, either the documentation standards must be adjusted to the capabilities of the new medium or, from a multi-dimensional model, document specific extractions must be made. The latter implies the storage of additional information in the model which has no meaning for the three-dimensional representation but is necessary to uniquely specify the required orthogonal projections.

Most architectural CAD packages implement the second approach. The advantage of extracting plans from three-dimensional representations is the reduced risk of errors compared to traditional methods of revision. A disadvantage is the inherent redundancy of information. Well developed CAD programs solve this problem by separating the graphic and non-graphic data base.

10.4.2. Rendering

Rendering is the last step in architectural presentations and has the purpose of communicating a realistic image of the proposed design to laymen. Rendering is a specialized activity. Architectural presentation is also the art of abstraction. It took three hundred years to evolve the level of presentation quality which defines the present professional practice. In general, abstractions allow faster and more precise manipulations. Renderings depict the final state of the design with a low level of abstraction which is more difficult and time consuming to manipulate. The designer's requirement is the seamless integration of sketching, modeling, and rendering. The structure of available commercial programs does not cover these requirements which in turn causes problems with their acceptance for design purposes.

Realistic renderings are becoming a competition for physical models which represent a significant cost factor in the final presentation of the architectural idea. The advantage of computer renderings is a generally shorter generation time and a higher degree of material realism, their disadvantage is the loss of the three-dimensional and haptic quality of built models.

10.4.3. Video

The use of videos for existing architecture in the form of physical model walk-throughs has a long history. Computer generated wire frame videos preceded animations featuring surface models. Several minute long videos of fully rendered architectural models stress the limits of even the fastest available computers. They are therefore not yet a presentation medium for the average office, rather for service bureaus specializing in animation production. The combination of real scenery and simulated architecture has become a widely accepted application used to demonstrate contextual responses of proposed buildings and to display issues related to scale and human interaction.

10.5. Computer Graphics in Design

Architectural design is one of the most challenging applications for computer graphics. Researchers and architects describe design as a dynamic process that incorporates not only imagination and intuition but also formal top-down and bottom-up approaches which the new medium is able to support. Computers in design must support interactivity, semantic and multi-dimensional modeling.

10.5.1. Interactive Computer Graphics

Design relies on the availability of different representations of the same design object. Interactive computer graphics must therefore not only fulfil rapid manipulation of models but also allow the view of these models through semantic filters. Otherwise, it would just translate a traditional representation method at a very high cost to another medium. Researchers concluded that interactivity demands a response time of less than 0.5 seconds. Redraw speeds on full color screens are still an obstacle for this goal. Even the introduction of "large" screens does not offer the same amount of information space that a drawing board presents.

These limitations have consequences on the structure of the design process in that designers must follow certain rules. It is not clear at this point whether or not this presents a disadvantage because it forces the designer to organize her or his ideas. The relative freedom of object manipulation in two-dimensional drawing and painting programs still contrasts with the rigid modeling requirements of three-dimensional packages. Architecture can learn significantly from applications in medicine about the viewing of design objects through semantic filters: a scan of a part of the human body displays various aspects that are of interest for specific purposes. Similar results appear when the infrared image of a building, depicting heat loss is overlaid with the geometric model.

10.5.2. From Idea to Model

Architects learn to create and manipulate the model of an entire building in their memory. This includes syntactic and semantic aspects, the ambience of the design and specific design intentions. The computer should support the designer by communicating his ideas precisely and in understandable form. It should also offer appropriate feedback for further development of design alternatives. It is therefore most cumbersome to step from this high level of unity in the human mind to the regeneration of design line by line. In fact, this process can discourage designers from employing computers in the design process.

For this reason we focus on the development of intelligent modelers that provide loosely structured objects which are similar to the information clusters that experienced designer work with as Akin (1986) points out. For teaching design we have integrated a set of intelligent modeling tools into a commercial CAD program: a database of three-dimensional design elements, a collection of parameterized objects, tools to define and execute shape grammars and fractal algorithms, relational prototypes, and fully interactive building prototypes.

10.5.3. Multidimensional Modeling

Although a building should be more then the sum of its parts, it is constructed of individual members. In combination, composite building parts such as exterior walls influence the performance of a building. We therefore need the capability to analyze architecture seen through individual filters such as building cost, energy consumption, maintenance aspects, building management, and occupants satisfaction. Visualizing these factors is a goal that still is in the very early stages of implementation. Computer graphics serves as the common visualization medium.

10.6. Selected Computer Aided Design Strategies

We decided to apply the theory to practical design problems in an architectural studio where students work in an environment of UNIX workstations and visualization machines. In using two examples we present the application of computer aided design in architecture. The first example describes the reconstruction and redesign of the Roman town of Aventicum in Switzerland, the second example is the exploration of object creation with computer aided substitution and instantiation tools.

10.6.1. Aventicum: From Data Bases to Prototypes

Aventicum, founded in 8 B.C. was an important Roman city in western Switzerland and had, at the beginning of the third century more than 20000 inhabitants. A large wall surrounded the regular roman layout of the city. The "cardo maximus" and the "decumanus maximus" were the main axes. Archaeologists have partially excavated the forum and and adjacent areas. We did not intend to produce a complete reconstruction but rather a plausible redesign based on urban Roman architecture north of the Alps. The following is a synopsis of the course that we offered and the description of the computer methods and tools we employed.

Data bases of existing elements. Unique artifacts found during excavation are placed into a data bank of three-dimensional elements. They are available for use in design from pop-up slides activated on the screen or on the digitizing tablet. Students use existing elements to reconstruct a Roman room as closely as possible.

Data bases of parameterized elements. Instances of architectural building elements often differ in only few characteristics or parameters. We specify the range of acceptable difference and provide a collection of elements with parameters attached. Students graphically select an element from the data base, define the parameters, and insert the element in the model. With this approach they construct more complex objects such as entire buildings.

Shape grammars and fractals. Shape grammars are the graphical equivalent to production systems. Fractals are a sub-category of shape grammars as they rely on the recursive execution of one shape rule. Stiny (1981), Flemming (1986), Mitchell (1990) and Schmitt (1988) describe their applications to design. Students use them mainly for experimentation and for the creation of landscapes and trees. More interesting applications are possible whenever the syntax rules are known and suffice for the generation of form.

Relational Prototypes. These are two- and three-dimensional functional prototypes for which the topology is known and fixed but the geometry is variable. We selected the example of a Roman bath where the functions are defined and well known but where the size, proportion and location of spaces may vary within limits. The relational prototype program "knows" which spaces are allowed next to each other and which are not. It does not allow that spaces overlap and enforces rooms to stay within proportional and size ranges. It finally checks the completeness of the design.

Prototypes. Intelligent prototypes may include properties from all previous methods. They contain parameters that can vary within ranges and are connected by relational constraints. Modifying one parameter can cause the entire object to change in many respects. In the theater prototype, for example, changing the number of seats will influence the height of the building, possibly its radius as well as the number and location of exits. The Roman temple is another example for a prototype. In this case, students select temple types from a menu and define all geometric parameters graphically.

For the final project, each student selected a city block or insula or one of the public buildings. Using existing excavation results or literature sources, they proposed a reconstruction, using the methods described. At the end of the semester we inserted the insulae, the forum, the theater, the temple, the baths and city wall into the terrain model to perform a walk-through of the entire city.

10.6.2. Winterthur: Classes, Objects, and Substitution

The purpose of this studio is the exploration of methods that traditional paper based design does not offer. Computer graphics is the tool that controls success and provides three-dimensional and dynamic feedback. The studio problem is to propose new designs for a large inner city industrial area in Winterthur, Switzerland. Students have one semester to learn the method and its application in the following steps:

Creation of objects. Students create objects based on traditional and new methods: modeling with individual surfaces, extrusion of closed polygons, defining complex objects by selecting continuous patterns from square grids.

Types. Students specify types of objects to define design intentions. Types should be recognizable as individual and distinct objects. In a next step students construct a table of types which appears on a pop-up slide menu.

Levels of detail. For each type, students develop various levels of detail. These instances become children of the type. They can depict the same type in higher degrees of detail, or they may form alternatives to the original type.

Context. Students insert types at the lowest level of detail into the context of the existing city of Winterthur. They can be merely symbolic placeholders for more complex objects to develop later.

Massing model. First massing models develop within the context. Geometric transformations scale, rotate, and re-position the inserted types.

Substitution. Students develop the individual types into higher degrees of realism and detail by substituting the types by their higher degrees of detail. At any time, the designer can turn an existing building from the context into a new type.

Alternatives. Types can also be substituted by alternatives which are stored in the same manner as levels of detail. A second alternative is the substitution of one type with another.

Final result. The final result is the site with the completed new design on which the students can perform a logical zoom: to demonstrate the development of the project they substitute the inserted objects with lower level of detail or with the alternatives that emerged during the design process.

10.6.3. New Graphics Tools

For the design studios we developed computer tools in AutoLISP to support particular design processes. The tools are available in the form of pull-down menus and pop-up slides in the AutoCAD environment. Three-dimensional modeling occurs within the commercial CAD package. For the interactive visualization of design results we developed Stalker (Shih 1990), a C program using the Silicon Graphics GL graphics library. The interface is implemented in Display Postscript and offers interactive menus for definition and manipulation of files, layers, colors and materials. Stalker also supports an additional function key pad and a dial box with dials for view manipulations and navigation. Stalker accepts any DXF file.

10.7. Selected Research Areas

Given enough interest from the design and construction market, it takes 10 to 15 years for proven research results to reach the bug-free implementation level in commercial programs. Some of the research directions in visualization and architectural generation will therefore not be on the desktop of architects until the next century.

10.7.1. Visualization

Architecture is a science of purposeful change, not of keeping the status quo under all circumstances. During the design process architectural visualization must support the rapid development and transition of ideas and their consequences in terms of building performance. Holography and virtual reality, once they reach an acceptable level of performance, are appropriate tools for this.

10.7.2. Cellular Automata

This is a class of programs with possible implications for architecture and planning that have not yet been explored. Cellular automata can be modeled after natural growth processes. Individual cells behave like simple computers which in certain time intervals change their state as a reaction to external conditions. The information for the state transformation is inherent in the cells. Thus certain cells will develop well while others decay because of adverse conditions. As a further step, information of the more successful cells—if several classes of cells exist—can form the origin of a new generation of cells which could be "smarter".

Applications could be the development of a new city in a region with high population growth. In this case, every building, apartment or work place could react as a living cell that must actively cooperate and compete with the neighboring cells. Every building or complex needs light, air, access and protection from adverse conditions. A simulation could accept local environmental conditions and expects the "planting" of a design cell containing growth information. After this, the growth process can commence, based on built-in genetic information. Contrary to the present planning practice they would not simply cover a given area; rather interactions between cells would occur. Many might "die" because of lack of light, sun or quietness, others would concentrate in areas of better conditions. At points of overly intensive concentration, a counterreaction might occur. In a few cases, a stable condition may develop after several thousand cycles in which balance between cells and the context evolves. Simulations of this kind are not possible with traditional means and require the availability of computer graphics.

10.7.3. Case-based Reasoning

The traditional knowledge representation paradigm of Artificial Intelligence is that of general production rules. For applications in domains like design, however, it is close to impossible to construct a coherent set of rules for representing a large amount of knowledge, and it is not clear how to formulate knowledge needed to produce a complete design in the form of general rules. Furthermore, Schank (1982) describes that there is strong psychological evidence that people do not reason from general rules alone, but refer to the memory of previously solved similar problems. This observation has led to the paradigm of case-based reasoning (CBR), which helps eliminate some of the deficiencies of rule-based systems.

In a larger context, CBR can be thought of as an alternative to automatic machine learning systems which learn production rules by generalizing from examples. In CBR, generalization takes place only at the time that the knowledge is to be used. This bypasses two major problems of machine learning, namely that it is often not clear what rules should be learned from a particular example, and to what degree these rules should be generalized. The latter problem also poses itself in the CBR approach, in that it must be decided if a particular case can be applied to the current problem. However, it is much easier to solve because of the limitation of the comparison to two examples.

In order to apply a previous case to a new problem, it is necessary to match the problem structures of old and new cases. Existing systems for CBR do this by first computing a causal analysis of the given case with respect to the problem at hand, and then matching aspects of this causal structure to the problem. This still requires general knowledge of the domain, usually provided in the form of a traditional rule-based system. The problem of constructing the knowledge base for this task is much simpler than the original one: since we require only an analysis instead of a synthesis, it can be constructed in a principled way based on known scientific theories. Furthermore, it is not necessary for this knowledge to be complete: a missing analysis can cause the system to miss a possible match, but this is not a problem provided the catalogue of cases is large enough.

A first prototype of an architectural CBR system exists at the Swiss Federal Institute of Technology in Zürich and Lausanne. Computer graphics is used to validate the architectural quality of the new, adapted case that automatically develops from an existing case. Computer graphics is indispensable to visualize the results which in architecture cannot be expressed with any other means.

Figures 10.1–10.10 (see color section) show architectural designs.

Acknowledgements

The author wants to thank Shen Guan Shih who developed Stalker, Leandro Madrazo who was instrumental in the design of the course, Annelies Zeidler, Maia Engeli, Laura Lee, Sharon Refvem, Claude Vezin, Chen Cheng Chen, Bharat Dave, Hansuli Matter and Eric van der Marc. Special thanks to Boi Faltings and Kefeng Hua from the Laboratoire d'Intelligence Artificielle at EPF Lausanne.

References

Akin Ö (1986) *Psychology of Architectural Design*, Pion, London
Eastman C and Henrion M (1977) GLIDE: language for design information systems, *Proc. ACM SIGGRAPH '77*, ACM, New York
Flemming U (1986) The role of shape grammars in the analysis and creation of designs, in: Y. Kalay (ed), *Computability of Design*, John Wiley, New York, pp. 245-272
Gielingh I W (1989) Computer Integrated Construction, a major STEP forward, *Proc. 2nd International Symposium on Computer Aided Design in Architecture and Civil Engineering*, Barcelona, Spain
Kemper A M (1985) *Pioneers of CAD in Architecture*, Hurland/Swenson, Pacifica, CA
Mitchell W (1990) *The Logic of Architecture*, MIT Press, Boston, MA
Negroponte N (1970) *The Architecture Machine*, The MIT Press, Cambridge, MA
Schank R (1982) *Dynamic Memory - A Theory of Reminding and Learning in Computers and People*, Cambridge University Press, Cambridge, UK.
Schmitt G (1988) *Microcomputer Aided Design*, John Wiley, New York
Schmitt G, Flemming U and Madrazo L (1990) *Design Support Systems*, Archithese 3-90, pp. 28-37
Shih S G (1990) Stalker, *CAAD Wintersemester 1990/91*, Lehrstuhl für Architektur und CAAD, ETH Zürich, pp. 89-92
Stiny G (1981) An introduction to shape and shape grammars, *Environment and Planning B*, Vol. 8, 1981, pp. 343-351
Sutherland IE (1963) *Sketchpad: a man-machine graphical communication system*, Thesis 296, Department of Electrical Engineering, Massachusetts Institute of Technology, Cambridge, MA.

11

A New Concept for Visual Analysis of Three Dimensional Tracks

H. Drevermann and C. Grab[1]
CERN, Geneva

D. Kuhn[2]
*Institut für Experimentalphysik
der Universität Innsbruck*

B.S. Nilsson
Niels Bohr Institute, Copenhagen

R.K. Vogl[2]
*Institut für Experimentalphysik
der Universität Innsbruck*

The importance of visual event analysis in the process of evaluating collision phenomena in elementary particle physics is described. Shortcomings of most of the conventional methods for visual analysis when representing three dimensional space points are discussed.

An alternative method, the V-plot, based on the representation of individual space points by lines is presented here. It is shown, that this plot leads to an easily recognizable track pattern and allows for a local estimation of the significant track characteristics, namely of origin, momentum and charge. The versatility of this plot is exemplified using events from the ALEPH detector installed at the LEP-Collider at CERN.

11.1. Introduction

The research in elementary particle physics is predominantly based on the investigation of collisions between two particles at high energies. The collision process takes place at subnuclear scale; it is studied usually through detailed analysis of the particles emerging from

---

[1] Present address: IMP, ETH Zürich
[2] Supported by grant of FWF

the interaction. Along their trajectories, points, called hits, are recorded in highly sophisticated detectors.

The easiest way to illustrate such collisions, called events, is by showing a picture of the hits. An example from the ALEPH experiment (Decamp et al. 1990) at the LEP collider at CERN is displayed in Figure 11.1 (see color section). The data come from a subdetector of ALEPH, the time projection chamber, TPC. This chamber is able to measure hits in all three dimensions X, Y, Z. The figure was produced by the graphics program DALI (Drevermann and Grab 1990).

The trajectories — tracks — are reconstructed by pattern recognition methods from the measured hits. Origin, momentum, charge and type of the outgoing particles are then determined and characteristic features of the whole event are derived.

The algorithms for these procedures are complex and, although they are quite reliable, one needs independent methods to check the results. One of the best methods to fulfill this task is the *visual analysis* of events, i.e. the use of the human pattern recognition capability and imagination. Visual analysis may even go beyond the capabilities of existing algorithms in recognizing specific event features. However, the human brain can be misled by:

- relying on false assumptions,
- being unaware of the loss of relevant information,
- being biased by a suggestive result, etc..

Therefore one needs clear pictures, which effectively and unambiguously present the data to the human operator.

Visual checking is important in the development phase of experiments. In the running phase, where millions of events can be registered, visual inspection is reduced to events of special interest and to routine checking of small subsamples.

There exist many programs for visual analysis based predominantly on conventional 2D and 3D methods. However, since these methods were mostly optimized for general applications, their results are often insufficient especially for complicated events. Therefore, experimentalists are sometimes discouraged to apply visual techniques. This situation is expected to be even worse in the future, because events will get more and more complicated mainly due to the increasing number of particles per event.

It is the aim of this chapter to present a new visual representation, which facilitates considerably the task of visual analysis and expands its application to complex events.

The methods have been developed especially for displays of particle collisions. This is justified by the size of experiments and the large number of users in this field. The program DALI was written to be used on inexpensive simple workstations.

It is beyond the scope of this chapter to present generalizations of these methods to other fields of research. Nevertheless it is hoped that new developments may be inspired.

11.2. Event Analysis

The reaction shown in Figure 11.1 (see color section) in two views is a typical high multiplicity event. For ease of interpretation, hits associated to the same track are given the same colour in all views; unassociated hits are white, hits rejected for the calculation of the track parameters are grey.

The tracks are curved as the TPC is embedded in a homogeneous magnetic field, the radius of the curvature being a function of the particle momentum: high momentum tracks are less curved than low momentum ones. Using this event as an example, objectives and techniques of visual event analysis will be discussed.

The aim of visual event analysis is to answer the following general questions:

- Are single tracks found and well reconstructed?
  Errors occurring during reconstructing may e.g. be:
  - A track is not found; a track is faked from noise etc..
  - One track is split into two; two tracks are joined together into one.
  - Good hits are not associated to the track; hits are wrongly associated.
  - Associated points are erroneously rejected or kept for the fit.

- How are tracks related in space?
  Items deserving special attention are:
  - Two tracks cross in space.
  - Two tracks may originate from the same space point.
  - The endpoint of one track is the starting point of another one.

- What is the event structure?
  - Are there tracks clustering in space?
  - How are clusters of tracks and/or single tracks related in space?

- Are tracks and clusters associated to tracks and clusters registered in
  other subdetectors? This question is discussed elsewhere (Drevermann and Grab 1990).

In all cases it is essential to estimate charge, track momentum and track origin.

For visual analysis it is mandatory to know beforehand what tracks look like in the different representations to be used.

11.2.1. Helix Equations

Due to the specific layout of the ALEPH experiment (B-field parallel to the direction of the incoming colliding beam-particles, denoted as z-axis), an outgoing charged particle with

momentum $\vec{P}$ produced in the collision moves along a helix — axis in z-direction — starting from the collision point at the origin of the coordinate system. Such a helix is described by the following equations:

$$X = c \, P_t \, (\cos (\alpha_0 + \Delta\alpha) - \cos \alpha_0),$$

$$Y = c \, P_t \, (\sin (\alpha_0 + \Delta\alpha) - \sin \alpha_0), \qquad (11.1)$$

$$Z = c \, P_z \, \Delta\alpha,$$

with
$$\vec{P} = (P_x, P_y, P_z), \qquad P = \sqrt{P_x^2 + P_y^2 + P_z^2}, \qquad P_t = \sqrt{P_x^2 + P_y^2} \qquad (11.2)$$

$$\Phi_0 = \text{arctg}\left(\frac{P_y}{P_x}\right), \qquad \Theta_0 = \text{arctg}\left(\frac{P_t}{P_z}\right), \qquad \alpha_0 = \Phi_0 + 90^\circ \qquad (11.3)$$

where $\Delta\alpha$ is a track parameter, the sign of which depends on the charge q of the particle: $\Delta\alpha > 0$ for negative and $\Delta\alpha < 0$ for positive particles in the case of ALEPH. The constant c depends on the strength of the magnetic field and has the sign of the charge q, so that always $c\Delta\alpha > 0$. By use of cylindrical and spherical coordinates:

$$\rho = \sqrt{X^2 + Y^2}, \qquad R = \sqrt{X^2 + Y^2 + Z^2} \qquad \Phi = \text{arctg} \left(\frac{Y}{X}\right) \qquad \Theta = \text{arctg} \left(\frac{\rho}{Z}\right) \qquad (11.4)$$

the equations take a more simple form:

$$\Phi = \Phi_0 + \Delta\Phi, \qquad Z = 2 \, cP_z \, \Delta\Phi, \qquad \rho = 2 \, c \, P_t \, \sin(\Delta\Phi) \qquad (11.5)$$

where $\Delta\Phi = \frac{1}{2}\Delta\alpha$ serves as track parameter with the same sign conventions as $\Delta\alpha$. Approximating $\sin (\Delta\Phi)$ by $\Delta\Phi$ one arrives at:

$$\rho \approx 2 \, c \, P_t \, \Delta\Phi, \qquad R \approx 2 \, c \, P \, \Delta\Phi, \qquad \Theta \approx \Theta_0 \qquad (11.6)$$

Most particles have a sufficiently large momentum to justify the above approximation, i.e. the curvature of their track in the detector is sufficiently small.

11.2.2. Track Pictures in Different Projections

A projection is defined here by the variables connected to the abscissa and to the ordinate; for example, in the Θ / Φ (Mercator -)projection Θ is the variable of the ordinate and Φ of the abscissa.

From the above equations one recognizes that the picture of a helix is:

- a section of a circle in Y/X, the radius of which is proportional to P_t;
- a section of a sin-function in Y/Z, X/Z or more general in any projection onto a plane containing the Z-axis (the momentum cannot be estimated);

- a cycloid in a so-called 3D projection (the momentum cannot be estimated);
- a straight line in Φ/Z with a slope proportional to $\frac{1}{P_z}$.

For tracks, where the approximation $\sin(\Delta\Phi) \approx \Delta\Phi$ holds, it is:

- a straight line in ρ/Z (the momentum cannot be estimated);
- a vertical straight line in (anything)$/\Theta$ (the momentum cannot be estimated);
- a straight line in Φ/ρ, Φ/R with a slope proportional to $\frac{1}{P_t}$, $\frac{1}{P}$ respectively.

If $\sin(\Delta\Phi)$ cannot be approximated by $\Delta\Phi$, i.e. a track has low momentum or does not pass through the origin, the track images get curved.

In any projection a three dimensional space point — a hit — is represented by a point on a two dimensional screen. Hence, all projections suffer from the fact that information is lost; this is also true, if perspective pictures are used. The power of perspective pictures lies in the fact that for known objects the missing information is substituted by the human brain from previous experience. No such assumptions can be made for hits or tracks. It is a major concern of visual analysis to overcome the problem of loss of information. In the following, various solutions will be studied.

11.2.3. Conventional Projections

In Figure 11.2 (see color section) a perspective picture of a group of tracks in the cylindrical TPC is shown. On an appropriate graphic station allowing fast rotations of 3D data, the lost information can be retrieved through the speed of the points during a smooth rotation of the event. Neighbouring points in the projection are close to each other in space, if they have similar speed. In static pictures the speed of the points can be represented by a line, the length of which is proportional to the speed. This is seen in the 3D picture of Figure 11.2, where the speed due to a rotation around a horizontal axis through the center in the picture plane is displayed. (Note that it can e.g. be deduced that the yellow track (2) is a continuation of the red one (1).)

Such a picture is truly three dimensional in a more general sense, because hits are represented by lines with three degrees of freedom; i.e. their position and length, from which X,Y,Z can be recalculated. With the complexity of high multiplicity events, however, pictures like this are unusable as the lines may be hidden by each other.

Another commonly used method keeps the full 3D information by showing several projections side by side. The best perception of a track — a helix arc — is obtained, if it is seen from two sides: from the side, where the track looks straight and from the orthogonal side, where it shows its full curvature.

If several projections are applied, one uses normally the front view (Y/X), side view (Y/Z) and top view (X/Z). For the effective visualization of a whole event all three views are needed. It can in fact be seen from Figure 11.2 that the pair of green tracks is curved in Y/X and X/Z and is straight in Y/Z, whereas the red (1) and the yellow track (2) are curved in Y/X and Y/Z and are straight in X/Z. In general one finds that different pairs of projections are needed for different tracks.

Since the magnetic field bends the particle trajectories perpendicular to $\vec{\rho}$ and $\vec{Z}$, the projection ρ / Z displays all tracks simultaneously from the "straight side". This can be seen in Figure 11.2. For the whole event, Y/X and ρ / Z can therefore be regarded as *"orthogonal views"*.

However, tracks opposite in Y/X may have the same ρ, Z and therefore be superimposed in ρ / Z, which complicates the picture. This is overcome by dividing all hits into two groups depending on their Φ-value. In Y/X of Figure 11.1 (see color section) the two regions are separated by a white line: for all hits above and below this line, ρ / Z and $-\rho / Z$ are displayed respectively. This projection is called ρ' / Z here, i.e. $\rho' = \pm\rho$ according to Φ. In DALI the direction of the separating line can be modified interactively. In addition, it has been shown (Drevermann and Grab 1990), that Y/X and ρ' / Z are the most adequate projections to display a detector of cylindrical form as ALEPH. Therefore they are used as standard projections in this experiment.

However, it is often difficult to associate hits and tracks to each other in the different views. One of the intentions in developing the V-plot was to overcome this disadvantage.

11.2.4. The Three-Dimensional V-plot

The 3D projection in Figure 11.2 (see color section) was recognized as three dimensional because space points are represented by lines with three degrees of freedom. A similar procedure leads to the V-plot, an example of which is shown in Figure 11.2.

In the V-plot each space point is represented via two points connected by a line. The picture originates from a Φ/Θ projection of the hits. However, instead of drawing a point at the Φ, Θ position of the hit, a horizontal line is drawn there symmetrically to the left and the right with a total length of $2kD$. Here, $D = R_{max}(\Theta)-R$ is the distance between the hit and the — cylindrical — outer TPC surface. The factor k is determined interactively to produce a clear picture. This leads to a V shaped pattern for single tracks as seen in Figure 11.2. It should be emphasized here that the V-plot is drawn hit by hit without making use of any information from other hits or from the association of hits to tracks except for the colouring.

The V-plot may also be regarded as the superposition of two projections in one picture, namely

$$\Phi / (\Theta \pm k(R_{max}(\Theta)-R)) \tag{11.7}$$

for the right arm and the left arm of the V respectively. Therefore, the picture of one arm of a V is identical to the track picture in Φ/R apart from a linear transformation (Note that $\Theta \approx \Theta_0$ = constant). Since in the projection Φ/R tracks are approximately straight lines with a gradient proportional to $\frac{1}{P}$, the same is true for the V: the arms of the V are straight and the opening angle is a measure for the track momentum P.

The track leaves the TPC at the Φ, Θ -position of the tip of the V (D=0). The charge of a particle is reflected by an increase or decrease of Φ with R: in ALEPH downwards V's belong to positive particles, upward V's to negative ones.

The X, Y, Z position of each hit can be recalculated from the line position and its length. Therefore the V-plot can be regarded as a three dimensional picture combining a Φ/R and a Φ/Θ projection.

11.2.4.1. Analysis with the V-plot

Figure 11.3 (see color section) shows a V-plot of all hits of the same event as in Figures 11.1 and 11.2. The tracks of the outgoing particles are clearly visible in the form of V's.

In the following, some examples for the application of the V-plot taken from Figures 11.2 and 11.3 are given:

Even without exploiting the V-plot in detail, one can simply use it for visual analysis as an efficient *tool to isolate* tracks or groups of tracks from all others for better visualization in other views.

- By use of a rubber band cursor, as provided by most graphics programs, a rectangular area around a group of tracks can be defined as e.g. seen in Figure 11.3 (see color section). This contains enough information for the program to create the standard projections (Y/X and ρ'/Z) as shown in Figure 11.3. The pictures are cleaned by selecting only those hits, which lie inside the rectangular box in the V-plot. For comparison Y/X is shown cleaned and not cleaned.

A more advanced application of the V-plot is the *check of the correct association* of hits to tracks.

- In Figure 11.3, the white lines drawn through the points show the tracks as reconstructed by program, which failed for the red track, although in Y/X it is suggested as a correct solution. Only by a careful study of this projection one recognizes that one hit (point 2) of the red track does not belong to it and that some unassociated (white) points should be added to it. In contrast, this is immediately obvious from the section of the V-plot, which is shown magnified in Figure 11.3 (see color section). It is seen there that point 2 does not belong to the red track and that the white (unassociated) points do belong to it. Point 1 belongs to both tracks, that means both tracks cross in space. This observation is a good example for visualization of the *space relation of tracks*.

Other cases of *space relations* are due to decays of particles, which manifest themselves by two tracks with a common origin other than the collision point, or by a kink between two connected tracks. The observation of such patterns is a main concern of visual analysis.

- Examples are found again in Figure 11.2 (see color section). From the 3D picture and the Y/X projection one gets the impression that the pair of green tracks originates from the same point in the TPC; the same seems to be true for the pair of blue tracks. Especially from the V-plot it is obvious that this interpretation is only correct for the green pair and not for the blue pair, where no line is common for the two blue V's.

- It is also obvious from the V-plot that the red (1) and the yellow track (2) are represented by different V's, i.e. they are different tracks. The end of one is the start of the other in space. A kink is visible between the two tracks. In the V-plot, the kink angle is strongly *enhanced* compared to the other projections, which facilitates the detection of such phenomena.

Due to the simple interpretation of the V's given above the V-plot is a powerful tool for the *estimation of the relevant physical quantities* of tracks: charge, momentum and origin.

- Onto its enlarged sections in Figures 11.2 and 11.3 (see color section) V-patterns of 2 and 1 GeV/c respectively are drawn. By comparing it to the opening angles of the V's one can estimate the momenta of the tracks. The red track at $\Phi \approx 90^\circ$, $\Theta \approx 40^\circ$ in Figure 11.3 does not form a V with straight arms, which means that it does not originate from the collision point.

Finally the V-plot gives a good *overview of the event structure*.

- The V-plot in Figure 11.3 (see color section) is used as an example. The cluster at $\Phi \approx 60^\circ$, $\Theta \approx 150^\circ$ has six tracks, three of them with relatively high momentum. Opposite to it ($\Phi \to 180^\circ+\Phi$, $\Theta \to 180^\circ-\Theta$) are two clusters of tracks at $\Phi \approx 250^\circ$, $\Theta \approx 50^\circ$ and $\Phi \approx 140^\circ$, $\Theta \approx 25^\circ$: one with eight tracks and one with five tracks of rather low momentum. Three isolated tracks are perpendicular to the beam axis ($\Theta \approx 100^\circ$). Some particles of very low momentum spiral inside the TPC.

These examples demonstrate clearly, that the V-plot is a powerful tool to deal with the problems of event analysis as described in Section 11.2.

11.2.5. Track Detection Efficiency

Visually, a track is easy to detect and to distinguish from other tracks and from noise if:

- the track pattern to be looked for is simple;
- the distance between track points is small;
- the noise in the neighborhood of the track is low.

These requirements are met to a high extent by the V-plot due to the simple V pattern and the high *track concentration* when applied to data from the TPC and similar detectors.

Comparing the V-plot of Figure 11.3 to Y/X in Figure 11.1 (see color section), which both show the same event, the superiority of the V-plot in this respect is easily realized.

11.3. Application of the V-plot in Future Experiments

Compared to ALEPH, future experiments will be even more complex, and in particular the number of tracks will increase considerably. For a number of reasons, a TPC will not be usable at the colliders being built or planned. In order to get an idea of the feasibility of visual analysis for such experiments, a possible layout of a future subdetector, capable of measuring hits in three dimensions, was simulated by using the outer part of the TPC only. For this configuration, an event containing about 300 tracks was simulated by adding up the hits of many real events. This event is shown in Figure 11.4 (see color section). The hits are coloured by one out of eight colours. The colour number N is calculated as a function of the hit angle Θ ($N=1+MOD(1.5\cdot\Theta,8)$ with Θ in degrees), that means, no information of the association between hits and tracks is used. In Y/X and ρ'/Z the hits evenly fill the space, where hits can be recorded. Practically no track can be recognized. In contrast the V-plot shows clearly distinguishable V patterns.

If a set of tracks is isolated via the V-plot (see the rectangle in the V-plot), the corresponding cleaned Y/X projection becomes significantly clearer. The magnified section of the V-plot is even better. It shows the same hits as in the cleaned Y/X view, but grouped together in a suitable way for *track identification* and analysis.

In the cleaned Y/X projection the curvature of tracks can no longer be estimated visually, as tracks look straight. Nevertheless, charge and momentum could still be estimated from the distance by which linearly extrapolated tracks miss the interaction point. However, this procedure is obviously difficult to perform visually. In addition, this method necessitates the display of the collision point — a *global picture* of the event —, which reduces the screen area available for the display of the hits.

In contrast, the two V-plots in Figure 11.4 allow the sign of charge and the momentum to be estimated from the information contained in the track pattern itself, i.e. *locally*.

If this simulation is not too unrealistic, it can be deduced, that only three layers may be enough to supply sufficient track information for visual analysis and hence for track reconstruction by program.

11.4. Conclusions

Visual analysis is an important tool to check and complete the computer treatment of the large amount of events produced in elementary particle physics.

The standard *orthogonal* projections Y/X and ρ'/Z are to be preferred, if the track number is sufficiently low and *intuitive comprehension* of the event is important. The benefit of these projections becomes more and more restricted with increasing track multiplicities.

A powerful alternative is the V-plot, which is a synthesis of two projections in one picture. It has the following characteristics:

- three dimensional points (hits) are mapped onto lines with three degrees of freedom.
- tracks are represented by the linear arms of the V pattern
- track patterns are highly concentrated.

Although being an abstract representation of an event, hence being not intuitively understandable, it has the following substantial advantages:

- for single tracks:
  . easy track identification;
  . easy check of association of hits to tracks;
  . simple local evaluation of the relevant track characteristics;

- for pairs of tracks: easy recognition and identification of
  . crossing of tracks in space,
  . common track origin outside collision point,
  . continuation of one track by another;

- for events: easy identification of
  . clusters of tracks,
  . correlation between clusters;

- easy isolation of tracks for further display by conventional views.

The three-dimensional V-plot proves to be a powerful tool for visual analysis, where unambiguous and efficient transfer of data to the human brain is required.

Acknowledgements

The successful construction and running of the ALEPH-detector by the collaboration provided the events for which the methods described in this chapter were developed.

Our special thanks are due to G. Kellner, S. Orteu, G. Waltermann and R. Xu for their valuable contributions and to J. Knobloch, D. Schlatter and J. Steinberger for helpful comments and constant encouragement.

References

Decamp D et al. (1990) ALEPH Collaboration, ALEPH: A Detector for Electron-Positron Annihilations at LEP', *Nucl. Instr. Meth.*, A294, 121.
Drevermann H, Grab C (1990) Graphical Concepts for the Representation of Events in High Energy Physics, *Int.Jour.Mod.Phys.*, C1, pp.147-163.

Part 3
Rendering of Natural Phenomena

12

The Simulation of Natural Phenomena

Gavin Miller
Apple Computer Inc., California

12.1. Introduction

This paper reviews a number of areas of computer graphics concerned with the animation and rendering of natural phenomena. The inspiration for studying natural forms and processes springs from three properties which they possess: complexity, subtlety and beauty. The complexity arises from the vast amounts of detail created spontaneously by natural processes. These can involve large amounts of matter broken up into a myriad of pieces, such as snowflakes on a mountain. Alternatively, the amount of matter may be modest, but the complexity of design arises as a result of complex geological processes, such as with a piece of marble, or as a result of biological processes arising from the information content of a piece of DNA. Complexity alone is a severe challenge for the would-be simulation system requiring massive amounts of storage and computer time.

If complexity were the only problem, existing techniques would be adequate to simulate all events and forms seen in nature. However, the problem of subtlety stands in our way. All computer simulations require an approximation of the processes seen in nature. Some approximations may not be recognized as such until an example is found in nature which is outside the domain of the model. For instance, what is a completely general surface reflectance model? At one extreme are the simple procedural approximations such as diffuse or Phong shading. At the other extreme is a table driven approach in which n-dimensional arrays are used to store data digitized from nature. Digitized data has it limitations. What are the effects of blending two such materials together? If the surface material belongs to a parametric family of similar materials, one table has to be stored for each member of that family. An appropriate analytic model makes explicit the degrees of freedom which may be manipulated by the user to define similar materials. In the case of surface textures, just digitizing a material may be fine if the surface to be rendered is the same shape as the original. But if the texture is to be applied to a different shape, is it assumed to permeate space, like a wood grain, or is it a surface attribute, like scales on a reptile? Again the problem arises of how to generate a similar material with subtly different properties.

Finally, the beauty of natural phenomena is sufficient reason to study them. By understanding the way that natural processes work, an animator is given the tools to create realistic-looking films with interesting variations. A sunset may be accelerated to take only a few seconds, without the water being made to move ridiculously fast. Alternatively, a product may be enhanced with naturalistic designs or visualised as if manufactured from natural materials.

12.2. The Appearance of Surfaces

The appearance of surfaces depends on a number of factors including the lighting conditions, the surface reflectance function and the surface texture. The surface reflectance function defines how a particular piece of material will scatter light when illuminated from particular directions (Hall 1988). The surface texture characterises the changes to the reflectance function over the surface as the mixture of materials change. In the case of bump and displacement mapping, the texture can modify the surface normal and position as well. Different materials in nature have their own particular models for surface reflectance functions and textures.

12.2.1. Wood

"Solid textures" use the surface (x,y,z) position to compute some shading parameter of a surface. A large number of useful effects can be produced in this way. Image extrusions are particularly effective since they allow the combination of painting techniques and 3D rendering. A simple extrusion is achieved by using the surface x-coordinate to index into the image x-coordinate and the surface y-coordinate to index into the image y-coordinate. The extrusions can be made more interesting by the addition of a noise offset to the coordinates before indexing into the image. One useful form of noise to use is a cubic lattice of random numbers interpolated using biquadratic b-splines. This is similar to the noise function in Perlin (1985a). As in Perlin's paper, a fractal noise may be generated by adding successively scaled versions of the noise function together. However, unlike Perlin, it is not recommended to take the absolute value of the noise function at each scale

$$f = \sum_{i=0}^{n} \frac{N\ (2^i\ x,\ 2^i\ y,\ 2^i\ z)}{2^H} \qquad (12.1)$$

$$n = \frac{-\log\ (\Delta x)}{\log\ (2)} \qquad (12.2)$$

Where Δx is the extent of the surface in world space for that pixel and H is a ratio which determines the fractal dimension of the signal. Values of H greater than or equal to 0.5 give interesting looking marble for a wide variety of colorful input images. On the other hand, to create convincing wood effects it is necessary to start with an image which looks reasonably like a cross-section through a tree. A simple radial function may be built up by adding randomly spaced rings for each season of growth. Each ring period corresponds to a ramp function in the intensity. Also, on such an image, a number of small dark dots should be applied which correspond with the xylem passing up through the stem. Extruding such images with no noise functions leads to completely straight wood grain which can look rather artificial. Adding a 3-D noise function to the image x and y indices can lead to a more natural looking texture. A value of *H* less than 0.25 is more realistic for most kinds of wood. A second key component is an image which shows the cross-section through a tree. This may be digitized or generated synthetically. When the cross-section is synthesized, the number of rings and their thickness and color variation should be parameters of the model. Figure 12.1 (see color section) shows such a synthetic wood texture being applied to a model of a wooden display cabinet. The same model, with different parameters, was used to create the oak effect on the desk in Figure 12.2 (see color section). The wood grain for the legs of the desk was rotated relative to the grain on the desk top.

12.2.2. Fur and Scales

Biological surface texture such as fur, scales and feathers can be approached in one of three ways.

12.2.2.1. Texture Mapping

Provided that the perturbations to the surface shape are small, traditional surface shading methods can be applied to give the appearance of fur, feathers and scales.

The snake in Figure 12.3 (see color section) was created using a combination of a painted texture map and a depth map made by rendering a periodic array of scales. The depth map was used both for bump mapping and to blend the color map with a filler color. This helped to give the scales a distinct almost modeled appearance. For animals such as close-cropped horses and deer their surfaces are smooth, but the effects of hair laying parallel to the skin surface require the use of an anisotropic shading model. The most straightforward of these involves treating the surface as a set of parallel cylinders. The amount of light reflected may either be pre-computed and stored in a pseudo-reflectance map (Miller 1988a) or computed analytically (Poulin and Fournier 1990).

12.2.2.2. Explicit Geometric Modeling

A second approach to rendering fur is to model the hairs as explicit geometry. For fur, a jittered lattice of points in surface parameter space is used to define the positions of the roots of the hairs. The tangent vectors and surface normal define a coordinate frame in terms of which the geometric model can be generated. For hairs a fine cylinder or cone must be used. Because of the very high curvature of the hair surface it is necessary to take explicit steps to prevent aliasing of the shading model. This may be done using the same model as was used for the anisotropic shading in the previous section. Figure 12.4 (see color section) shows a simple surface model with and without hair. Note that the surface underneath was shaded using the anistropic reflectance model. This helped to reduced the contrast between the hair and the body, leading to a fuller looking coat of fur.

12.2.2.3. Volumetric Modeling

One disadvantage of the explicitly geometric model is that real hairs can be very fine which leads to aliasing problems. A way round this problem is to treat fur or hair as an anisotropic bundle of fibers embedded within a given volume. Each volume becomes an anisotropically reflecting atmospheric element. This model is described in Kajiya and Kay (1989), and a similar approach is discussed in Perlin and Hoffert (1989). Unfortunately the volumetric approach requires a large amount of computation. This problem can be overcome to a certain extent by exploiting the parallel nature of the algorithm running on multiprocessor machines.

12.2.2.4. The Future

A difficulty with the volumetric approach arises when making animations. It is hard to work out how to modify the volumes based on collisions with other objects. For explicit geometrical models each hair must be collided with other obstacles and with each other. Successful animations of colliding fur and long hair may have to wait for efficient collision culling algorithms and faster computers.

12.2.3. Snow on Surfaces

The deposition of snow on surfaces is a complex process involving millions of individual flakes. The key to animating the motion of particulate snow through the air is a having a good model of the wind velocity (Sims 1990). However, for snow which has already settled onto surfaces, approximate shaders may be used. In Oppenheimer (1986) an algorithm attributed to Williams uses a pseudo-light source to deposit snow. This snow is then illuminated by other light sources in the scene. This idea was modified by the author to be a more controllable orientation dependent texture. If the dot product between the surface normal and the snow direction (usually straight up) was less than a threshold, then no snow was deposited. If, it was above the threshold, then the difference was used to define a smoothly varying depth. This reached a maximum value when the normal was parallel to the snow direction. The depth produced in this way was used to define a snow layer whose opacity and normal depended on the orientation. To prevent the surface from looking too uniform, the surface normal was perturbed using a fractal noise function before applying the snow effect. Figure 12.5 (see color section) was produced using this technique. The snow on the street-car is reasonably convincing, even though the snow has no real geometrical depth. This technique does not work well for macroscopic snow features such as drifts. These had to be modelled interactively to produce Figure 12.6 (see color section).

12.3. Atmospheric Effects

One important component of natural scenes is the effect of atmospheric scattering off of particles in the space between surfaces. In its simplest formulation this manifests itself as a continuous uniform fog. In its more detailed form it produces the color of a sunset (Klassen 1987) and shows the path of light beams as they fall between leaves in a forest (Max 1986a).

12.3.1. Fog and Layered Fog

It is best to start by considering an infinitesimal element of scattering material such as is shown in Figure 12.7.

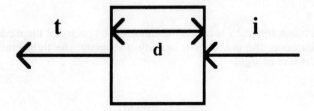

Figure 12.7. An atmospheric element

Incoming light has its intensity scale by a factor t

$$t = e^{-da} \tag{12.3}$$

Where d is the thickness of the element and a is the attenuation constant of the material.

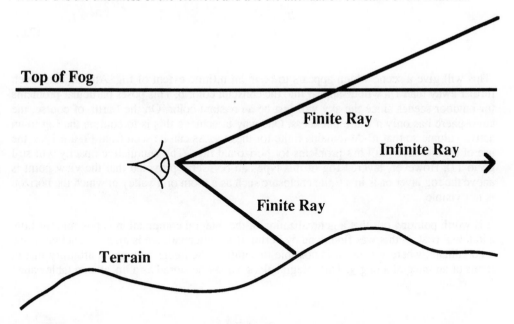

Figure 12.8. Layered fog

For a material of variable attenuation and finite thickness

$$t = e^{-\int a\ dr}$$

(12.4)

The integral of a along the line r is called the cumulative opacity of the medium. For a gas of uniform incandescence, the cumulative opacity also gives the light emitted towards the observer along the line of sight.

$$i = b\ (1 - e^{-\int a\ dr})$$

(12.5)

Where i is the light scattered along the ray and b is the brightness of light emitted from the fog.

When computing the effects of fog there are a number of ways of evaluating the cumulative opacity. The first is to assume that a is constant everywhere. In that case

$$\int_A^B a\ dr = a\ |B\text{-}A|$$

(12.6)

This will give a scene which appears to be in an infinite extent of fog. Any objects much further away than 1/a will disappear into the constant color b. This poses particular problems for outdoor scenes since the sky will just be a constant color. On the Earth, of course, the atmosphere has only a finite thickness. One way to achieve this is to confine the fog to an active volume so that |B-A| remains finite for the sky. As can be seen from Figure 12.8, the use of a finite layer still has problems for horizontal rays. The cumulative opacity will still go to 1.0. However, layered fog of this type can be useful provided that the view point is above the fog layer or is in a finite enclosure such as a room or a valley in which the horizon is not visible.

It is worth pointing out that a generalization of the integral computation is possible for little additional cost — this was first done by Perlin. If the attenuation a is made a function of the y coordinate, where y is up, it is possible to compute the integral along an arbitrary line in terms of an integral along y. This integral along y may be stored as a linear sum table called S

$$S\ (A) = \int_{y=-\infty}^{y=A} a\ dy$$

(12.7)

$$S\ (B) - S\ (A) = \int_A^B a\ dy$$

(12.8)

$$\int_A^B a\, dr = \int_A^B a\, dy\, \frac{d\, r}{dy} = (A\,(B) - S\,(A))\frac{1}{r_y} \qquad (12.9)$$

This formulation allows the use of arbitrary vertical variations of the optical density. Figure 12.9 (see color section) shows the use of layered fog in which the fog density decreases exponentially with altitude. The fog is evident at the surface of the lake but fades away near the peaks of the mountains.

12.3.2. Sky Color

An alternative generalization useful for outdoor scenes is to have a curved atmosphere. If the Earth was really flat and infinite, the Sun's rays would have to travel through an infinite thickness of fog at sunset. Sunsets would be black!

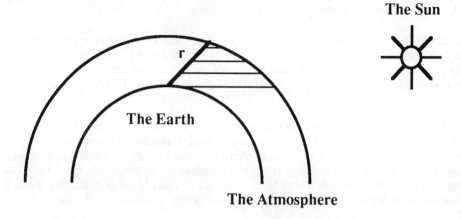

Figure 12.10. Curved atmosphere geometry

So far we have considered the fog as incandescent or at least evenly illuminated. In fact, of course, for terrestrial atmospheres, the light from the sky is scattered sunlight. To compute this effect we need to sample the atmosphere along the line of sight in a way which takes into account the illumination of each part of the atmosphere from the Sun. As shown in Figure 12.10, for each sample along r, a new ray has to be fired towards the Sun. The opacity of this secondary ray attenuates the illumination falling on that portion of the atmosphere. For a constant density shell, the length of the ray through the atmosphere can be used to compute this opacity. Once the amount of illumination has been computed, the amount of that light which is scattered must be determined. In general the scattering depends on the angle between the illumination vector and the view direction. It also depends on the wavelength of the light. Blue light is scattered more readily than green or red light. This topic is covered in great detail in Klassen (1987). In fact, for realistic images, it is necessary to split the atmosphere into a number of such shells each with different optical properties. Figure 12.11 /see color section) shows vertical slices through a sunrise animation which indicates the color changes which take place as the Sun direction vector is changed (Miller 1988b). The "gain" which controlled the displayed brightness of the image was adjusted over time so that the colors of dawn would be visible without washing out for the brighter portion of the sequence. As with real sunrises, the effective brightness varied by at least an order of magnitude as the dawn progressed.

Since each ray computation requires a double integral, such atmospheric calculations can be very expensive. However, the intensity variations are always slowly varying functions of orientation. Because of this, the atmospheric calculations may be computed on a finite grid of angular coordinates and intermediate rays can use interpolated values for the colors. The problem of sampling becomes more acute if the clouds cast shadows on the atmosphere. Then the sampling rate along primary and secondary rays is determined not by the change in atmospheric scattering but by the rate of change of the cloud density with position. The correct treatment of this problem is potentially very expensive. Except for the special case of having the illumination directly over head (Max 1986b), these types of atmospheric shadows have been largely ignored.

12.3.3. Clouds and Smoke

Clouds come in many shapes and sizes. Nearly planar clouds may be approximated by a fractal function being used to modulate the transparency of a plane. The fractal function is usually clipped against a threshold value to control the fraction of clear sky to cloud. The application of this idea to space-filling clouds is illustrated in Figure 12.12.

The dot product between the surface normal $\vec{n}$ and the sight vector $\vec{i}$ times the radius of the sphere is equal to half the line of sight through the cloud d. For a volumetric evaluation, the atmospheric effect would have to be integrated along the line d. To make a convincing-looking cloud, a fractal noise function could be computed whose amplitude is a function of the distance from the center of the sphere. This sort of calculation is expensive since it requires sampling the noise function at a large number of points along the line for each cloud.

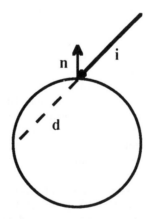

Figure 12.12. Cloud ray geometry

An approximation to this volume integral in Gardner (1984) and Gardner (1985) just samples the noise function on the surface of the sphere (or ellipsoid) and uses the dot product between the sight vector and the surface normal to compute a threshold for the noise function. Because the noise function is a solid texture it has the effect of blending together clouds which intersect. The dot product of the illumination direction with the surface normal is used to approximate the effects of shading. However, because this dot product is discontinuous, it is necessary to blend the intensities of overlapping surfaces together based on their relative depths. An alternative is to have a large number of intersecting ellipsoids with the maximum opacity for any given ellipsoid being kept quite small. This minimizes intersection discontinuities, but it does cost more since the number of noise evaluations increases with the depth complexity of the scene. Figure 12.13 (see color section) shows the use of a large number of such ellipsoids to approximate the appearance of cumulus clouds.

12.4. Water

Water and other fluids provide an interesting challenge for computer animation. Since full volumetric solution of the Navier–Stokes equations is still prohibitively expensive, a number of approximate methods, based on analytic solutions for special case boundary conditions are often used. Also, approximate particle methods may be used.

12.4.1   Analytic Models for Water Waves

Analytic analysis of water wave motion in the ocean has led to number of approximate models (Le Mehaute 1976; Crapper 1984; Stoker 1957). Often a simple periodic wave pattern is analysed to see how the wave velocity changes with wavelength or water depth, and to study how the wave shape evolves. The deep ocean model leads to waves with a velocity which is independent of the depth and is equal to the temporal frequency divided by the spatial frequency. For shallow water waves, the wave velocity is independent of wavelength and is proportional to the square-root of the depth. Both analyses show non-linear effects which change the shape of the wave as well. For the shallow wave case, a wave packet may be followed as it approaches a shore, with the wave velocity being adjusted because of the depth (Peachey 1986; Ts'o and Barsky 1987). Ad hoc models may also be included to change the shape of the waves, leading to highly specialized but successful techniques for making appealing animations (Fournier and Reeves 1986)

12.4.2.   Finite Difference Simulations of Water Waves as Height-Fields

An alternative approach is to use numerical methods to solve the wave equation on two-dimensional grids of samples. The water is considered in terms of vertical columns within which there is a uniform flow. The flow between adjacent columns is computed and the volume is conserved. By expressing the equations of motion in terms of an implicit solver, a rapid stable wave model may be created which allows changing boundary conditions (Kass and Miller 1990). Figure 12.14 (see color section) shows a still created by such a simulation. The water flows round obstacles and has ripples traveling on its surface.

12.4.3. Particle-based Water Models: Globular Dynamics

Particle systems are useful when simulating spray from waterfalls (Sims 1990). However, real liquids have particles which collide together and interact in complex ways. Globular dynamics is a technique for computing the interaction of particles with each other in a way which simulates the physics of fluids and foams (Miller and Pearce 1989). If two particles interact it is necessary that the forces they apply to each other be radial otherwise angular momentum will not be conserved. The forces between them must also be equal and opposite otherwise linear momentum will not be conserved. Given this restriction, the radial profile of the force can be arbitrary. There are two types of forces which may be considered. The radial positional forces cause the particles to repel and attract each other at different distances. The radial damping forces cause the particles to slow down based on their relative velocities. Note that, in this formulation, the forces all go to zero at a finite range.

In fact, the range and intensity of the two terms may be used to create a variety of different behaviors in the material.

(a) Short range damping and short range repulsion leads to particles which collide inelastically but stay separate.

(b) Long range damping and short range repulsion leads to particles which tend to cluster together and flow. The short range repulsion term approximately conserves volume whereas the damping term simulates the effects of viscosity.

(c) If a medium range attraction term is added, the particles tend to stick together. A small amount of attraction leads to foam-like behavior where the material can pile up into structures which are easily deformed. If the attraction term is increased, the particles form regular lattices or "crystals".

Figure 12.15 (see color section) illustrates a vertical jet as it is sprayed up into the air. Initially the top-most particles follow a parabolic trajectory, but then, as they descend they interact with particles pushing their way upwards. A convincing fluid-like motion results.

There are several problems with globular dynamics as a technique. The first is the need to have the number of particles increase proportional to the volume of the fluid. Surface-based technique have a number of samples which is proportional to the 2D surface area of the fluid which is independent of the depth. A second problem is that smooth fluid-like behavior only occurs when the repulsion-force profile for the particles if relatively soft. If it is too sudden and strong a force, the particles behave like golf balls and stack up in crystals rather than flow. However, the soft profile means that the fluid only loosely conserves volume. For an animation, this may not be too much of a disadvantage.

12.5. Conclusions

It is evident from current work in computer graphics, that a large number of natural phenomena may be approximated using computer graphics techniques. When these effects are used in combination with more traditional approaches to surface design approaches, such as in Figure 12.16 (see color section), it is possible to create images which are both pleasing to look at and reasonably realistic.

References

Crapper G (1984) *Introduction to Water Waves*, John Wiley, New York.

Fournier A, Reeves WT (1986) A Simple Model of Ocean Waves, *Proc. SIGGRAPH '86, Computer Graphics*, Vol. 20, No. 4, pp. 75-84.

Gardner GY (1984) Simulation of Natural Scenes Using Textured Quadric Surfaces, *Proc. SIGGRAPH '84, Computer Graphics*, Vol. 18, No. 3, pp. 11-20.

Gardner GY (1985) Visual Simulation of Clouds, *Proc. SIGGRAPH '85, Computer Graphics*, Vol. 19, No. 3, pp. 297-304.

Hall R (1988) *Illumination and Color in Computer Generated Imagery*, Springer-Verlag, Berlin, ISBN 0-387-96774-5.

Kajiya JT, Kay TL (1989) Rendering Fur with Three-Dimensional Textures, *Proc. SIGGRAPH '89, Computer Graphics*, Vol. 23, No. 4, pp. 271-280.

Kass M, Miller GSP (1990) Rapid Stable Fluid Dynamics for Computer Graphics, *Proc. SIGGRAPH '90, Computer Graphics*, Vol. 24, No. 4, pp. 49-58.

Klassen VR (1987) Modelling the Effect of Atmosphere on Light, *ACM Transactions on Graphics*, Vol. 6, No. 3, pp. 215-238.

Le Mehaute (1976) *An Introduction to Hydrodynamics and Water Waves*, Springer-Verlag, New York 1976.

Max N (1986a) Atmospheric Illumination and Shadows, *Proc. SIGGRAPH '86, Computer Graphics*, Vol. 20, No. 4, pp. 117-124.

Max N (1986b) Light Diffusion Through Clouds and Haze, *Computer Vision, Graphics and Image Processing*, Vol. 33, pp. 280-292.

Miller GSP (1988a) From Wire-frames to Furry Animals, *Proceeding of Graphics Interface '88*, Edmonton, Alberta, pp. 138-145.

Miller GSP (1988b) Natural Phenomena animation in SIGGRAPH '88 Electronic Theater.

Miller GSP, Pearce A (1989) Globular Dynamics: A Connected Particle System for Animating Viscous Fluids, *Computers and Graphics*, Vol. 13, No. 3, pp. 305-309.

Oppenheimer P (1986) Real Time Design and Animation of Fractal Plants and Trees, *Proc. SIGGRAPH '86, Computer Graphics*, Vol. 20, No. 4, pp. 55-64.

Peachey DR (1986) Modeling Waves and Surf, *Proc. SIGGRAPH '86, Computer Graphics*, Vol. 20, No. 4, pp. 65-74.

Perlin K (1985) An Image Synthesizer, *Proc. SIGGRAPH'85, Computer Graphics*, Vol.19, No3, pp.287-296.

Perlin K, Hoffert EM (1989) Hypertexture, *Proc. SIGGRAPH '89, Computer Graphics*, Vol. 23, No. 3, pp. 253-262.

Poulin P, Fournier A (1990) A Model for Anisotropic Reflection, *Proc. SIGGRAPH '90, Computer Graphics*, Vol. 24, No. 4, pp. 273-282.

Sims K (1990) Particle Animation and Rendering Using Data Parallel Computation, *Proc. SIGGRAPH '90, Computer Graphics*, Vol. 24, No. 4, pp 405-413.

Stoker J (1957) *Water Waves*, Interscience, New York.

Ts'o P, Barsky B (1987) Modeling and Rendering Waves, *ACM Transactions on Graphics*, Vol. 6, No. 3, pp. 191-214.

13

Techniques for Rendering Filiform Objects

André M. LeBlanc and Russell Turner
Computer Graphics Lab, Swiss Federal Institute of Technology, Lausanne

13.1. Introduction

Filiform structures occur in the natural environment in various forms and embrace a wide variety of phenomena. They are, by definition, very thin threadlike objects that yield, in aggregate form, highly complex and somewhat nebulous volumes such as fur, hair and fibrous material. Larger and more detailed geometry such as grass, plants or tree branches may also exhibit the same filiform structure when seen at a greater distance. The finer geometry recedes as a result of distance and gradually becomes invisible to the eye. The larger structures, however, remain and define the aggregate form of the object. Another important source of filiform phenomena result from dynamic particle motion blurring. The trajectory of small, fast moving particles during a single animation frame is traced to yield a trailing filament.

This chapter divides the filament rendering problem into two camps. The first tries to resolve the problem by sampling the geometry in object space, on a pixel by pixel basis. These are essentially ray-tracing methods. The second approach uses image buffer techniques, which operate on the entire pixel array simultaneously. Here, individual objects are projected onto the pixels and composited, object by object, to arrive at a final picture.

13.2. Sampling geometry

The most obvious, brute-force approach to rendering filiform objects is to model each individual strand as a curved cylinder, and attempt to render them as surfaces. This immediately runs into several serious problems. For most practical scenes, a strand width is quite a bit less than the size of a pixel, resulting in a serious aliasing problem. Furthermore, the sheer number of cylinder primitives, together with the large amount of oversampling necessary to overcome aliasing will overwhelm most raytracing programs.

Therefore, it is not surprising that most successful attempts at rendering filiform objects with raytracing have been achieved by categorically avoiding explicit models of geometry. Instead, they rely on three-dimensional textures to provide the necessary detail and give only an illusion of geometry.

13.2.1. Fur using Raytracing

Miller (1988a, 1988b) rendered a furry caterpillar by raytracing an image made of explicit hairs. Each hair was modeled with triangles arranged in the shape of a pyramid. Oversampling was used to avoid aliasing but apparently no illumination or shadowing were used, only color mapping. Although the number of hairs was relatively small and their thickness large, this technique was nonetheless rather computationally intense.

13.2.2. Fur with Texels

A texel is a type of model intermediate between a surface texture and geometry. It is defined as a three-dimensional array, where each element holds information on density, local orientation of micro-geometry and a lighting model. This information is distributed freely in the array to model how light interacts with highly detailed geometry. Kajiya and Kay (1989) used this technique to render fur on a teddy bear. Texel arrays were modeled and laid out on the surface of the bear.

13.2.2.1. Texel Illumination Model for Hair

Kajiya and Kay (1989) defined an illumination model (Kajiya 1985) that follows directly from the underlying cylindrical nature of a hair strand. Figure 13.1 shows a segment of hair and the important vector quantities used in the model. The unit tangent vector, $\vec{t}$, represents the direction of the hair's axis. The light vector, $\vec{l}$, points in the direction of the light source. The reflection vector, $\vec{r}$, points in the direction of reflected light and is the direction of maximum specular reflection. The eye vector, $\vec{e}$, points in the direction of the viewer. The angles θ and ϕ are the angles from the tangent vector to the light vector and eye vectors respectively.

Diffuse Component

The diffuse component of the reflectance can be obtained by integrating the Lambert cosine law along the illuminated half of the cylinder to yield a simple function of the angle θ:

$$\text{Diffuse Reflectance} = K_D \sin(\theta) \qquad (13.1)$$

where K_D attenuates the reflected intensity as a function of the radius of the cylinder.

This does not, however, take into account self-shadowing, that is, the fact that half of the hair strand is in its own shadow.

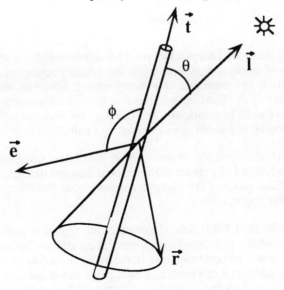

Figure 13.1. Vector quantities

Specular Component

The specular component is derived essentially by taking a Phong specular distribution and rotating it around the hair axis. This is motivated by making a symmetry-based argument. At any section along the length of the hair, there are surface normals pointing in all directions perpendicular to the tangent vector, $\vec{t}$. Therefore, the surface of the hair will reflect light in a cone-shaped 360 degree radial pattern formed by rotating the $\vec{r}$ vector around the hair axis. This cone represents the angles of maximum specular reflection. The Phong specular component is calculated by taking the angle between this cone and the eye vector, $\vec{e}$, which equals $\phi + \theta - \pi$, and using this as the angle for the standard Phong equation:

$$\text{Specular Reflectance} = K_S \cos^n(\phi + \theta - \pi) \tag{13.2}$$

13.2.2.2. Rendering Texels

Texels are rendered using raytracing. A ray, emanating from the eye, intersects a texel array. From this point of intersection, the ray marches through the texel accumulating the reflected intensities from each visited array element. Shadowing is rendered by spawning a second ray towards the light at each element.

13.2.3. Fur with Hypertextures

Perlin and Hoffert (1989) employed volume densities to model soft furlike objects. A volume region is defined in space in which geometry is modeled as pseudo-random density functions. No illumination or shadowing was modeled.

13.3. Image Buffer Techniques

Instead of sampling geometry on a pixel by pixel basis, image buffer techniques approach the rendering problem on an object by object basis. The primary advantage of rendering a scene this way comes from the assurance that every object, however small it may be, will somehow contribute to the final image. There is no risk of undersampling geometry or accidently missing objects. In animations, this can limit the flickering effect caused by small objects that keep poping in and out of a sampling ray's path.

Image buffer techniques resemble, in some sense, the classic special effects photographic process by which individual objects are projected onto film and then composited together at a later stage into a final picture. The computer simply adds flexibility to this process and automates compositing operations.

Porter and Duff (1984; Duff 1985) defined a compositing algebra to combine and blend raster images. This compositing technique, sometimes called alpha-blending (Carpenter 1984), allows raster operations to be performed on a frame buffer according to an alpha channel. The alpha channel is an additional component of each pixel, along with the red, green and blue components, which can be used to control the amount by which an incoming image is blended with the one already present in the frame buffer.

Hidden surface removal via frame buffers is done by storing depth values at each pixel into a z-buffer. These values are compared with incoming pixels to keep the nearest ones and discard the farthest (hidden) ones.

One of the advantages of using alpha-blending and z-buffer techniques is that they are easily implemented in hardware and many advanced frame-buffer architectures incorporate alpha channel and z-buffer bitplanes. These machines support pixel compositing operations and hidden surface removal.

13.3.1. Hair using Z-Buffer

Csuri et al. (1979) rendered fur-like volumes by modeling each hair as a single triangle laid out on a surface. A z-buffer algorithm was used for hidden surface removal. No antialiasing or shadowing was done.

Watanabe and Suenaga (1989) modeled human hairs as connected segments of triangular prisms and were able to render a full head of straight human hair in a reasonably short time using a hardware z-buffer renderer with Gouraud shading. Although the hair model had a realistic number of hairs (more than a million primitives), the illumination model was quite simplistic and apparently no attempt was made to deal with aliasing. As a result, the images have a stiff, wire brush-like appearance.

13.3.2. Grass and Fire using Particle Systems

The term "particle systems" was first used by Reeves (1983) but now encompasses a range of techniques (Reeves and Blau 1985, Sims 1990, Smith 1984). Fundamentally, a particle system is an animation technique based on dimensionless points which represent very small dynamic objects. Since the original purpose of the technique was to animate particles of fire in motion (for a sequence in the film *Star Trek II: The Wrath of Khan*), the points were displaced along their paths of motion during one animation frame to simulate motion blur, yielding thin three-dimensional line segments.

Later, the same technique was used to represent static images with thin filaments, such as grass (Reeves and Blau 1985). As a result, the term "particle" often refers, in fact, to a filament which may have a considerable length.

A particle system is rendered by painting each particle in succession onto the frame buffer. The particle's color contribution is calculated and combined with the pixel's existing color via alpha-blending.

13.3.2.1. Shadow Projection

Using particle systems and a frame buffer, (Reeves and Blau 1985) were able to render an antialiased, natural looking field of grass containing over half a million particles in a reasonable amount of CPU time. The technique, however, has several limitations. In particular, shadowing is limited, using a stochastic model for local self-shadowing and a simple texture map projected onto the grassy field for shadows of external objects.

This consists of projecting a two-dimensional shadow pattern onto an object from the point of view of each light. This method is limited to certain geometrical configurations where the three-dimensional nature of the shadow volume cast by objects is not significant.

13.3.3. Shadow-Buffers and Pixel-Blending

Kajiya and Kay (1989) demonstrated the importance of shadows in rendering realistic looking hair. Hair presents a wide variety of shadow effects due to the more complex geometry and the interaction between the hairless objects (the background scene) and the hair. To render naturalistic hair, shadows must be cast not only from hair onto hair, but also from the hair onto the hairless objects and from the hairless objects onto the hair.

LeBlanc et al. (1991) introduced a hybrid rendering method that enables shadows of hair to be incorporated into any scene. This method makes use of both raytracing and image buffer techniques to generate images in a multi-step pipeline — hairless objects are handled by raytracing and hair is incorporated among the raytraced objects as a post-processing step. In both steps, shadowing is handled with shadow buffers.

13.3.3.1. Shadows with Shadow Buffers

Shadow buffers are created by projecting a scene onto a pixel array from the point of view of the light source (Williams 1978). Only one piece of information, the depth or z value, is stored for each pixel. This results is a two-dimensional array which records the regions of space which are not visible from the light source and therefore in shadow. One shadow buffer is necessary for each light source together with the projection matrix used to create it.

With this information, it is possible to render an image with shadows by taking a point on a surface and transforming it into the shadow buffer's coordinates system. If the projected depth is greater than the depth in the shadow buffer, the pixel is considered to be in shadow for that light source.

Reeves et al. (1987) proposed a technique to produce softer shadows (penumbra), called percentage closer filtering. In this technique, (as in Williams 1978), a point on a surface is transformed to the shadow buffer's coordinates system and its depth is computed. It is then compared with a *region* of depth values in the shadow buffer to yield a value that indicates the percentage of shadowing for that region. This results in shadows with soft edges which resemble penumbra. The degree of softness can be varied to simulate a diffuse light source by enlarging or reducing the area of the sample region.

Rendering Shadows

Rendering hair with shadows requires that shadow buffers of the hairless objects be generated for each light source (Figure 13.2a, see color section). These shadow buffers will handle all shadows coming from the hairless objects.

To cast shadows from the hair onto the scene requires an augmented shadow buffer that also includes hair. This is achieved quickly by using a hardware-based line-drawing algorithm together with z-buffer hidden surface removal. Hair segments are fed to the graphics hardware resulting in a depth-map, as seen from a light source (Figure 13.2b, see color section).

The two shadow buffers are then combined into one. At each pixel, the depth values are compared and the lower value is retained, resulting in a scene-and-hair composite shadow buffer (Figure 13.2c, see color section). The composite scene-and-hair shadow buffer will then be used to determine the shadowing percentages, resulting in shadows cast by all objects in the scene, including hair.

The composite scene-and-hair shadow buffer is then fed into the raytracing renderer, generating a scene with hair shadows but no hair (Figure 13.2d, see color section). As discussed below in section 13.3.3.2, hair with shadows will then be blended into the scene to create a final image with full shadowing (Figure 13.2f, see color section).

Lighting Model with Shadows

Taking the hair intensity equation defined by Kajiya and Kay (1989) (see Section 13.2.2.1), the diffuse and specular components, together with ambient and shadowing components result in the following reflected intensity equation:

$$I = K_A + \sum_i S_i L_i (K_D \sin(\theta) + K_S \cos^n(\phi + \theta - \pi)) \tag{13.3}$$

where I is the total reflected intensity, L_i the intensity of light i, S_i the percentage of shadowing from L_i's composite scene-and-hair shadow buffer and K_A an ambient term.

13.3.3.2. Pixel Blending

A strand of hair, which is basically a long curved cylinder, is represented as a three-dimensional curve (polyline of segments) together with a radius. The complete hairstyle data structure therefore consists of a very large number (often over one million) of three-dimensional line segments together with a scalar thickness value.

The next task is to render the individual hairs into the hairless image (Figure 13.2d, see color section) in a manner such that aliasing artifacts are avoided. In a normal viewing configuration, the thickness of a human hair is much less than half a pixel width and tens or hundreds of hair strands contribute to the intensity of a single pixel. Antialiasing is accomplished using a pixel blending technique which is similar to a method developed for particle system rendering.

The Aliasing Problem
A straightforward solution to the aliasing problem is to treat each pixel as a square and then consider that portion of the hair strand passing through the projection of the pixel. The light intensity contributed by that segment of the hair strand within the boundaries of the pixel projection is considered to be that hair's contribution to the pixel intensity.

Therefore, to correctly render a single pixel, the light intensity contributed by every hair passing through the projection of the pixel must be blended together properly, along with the underlying hairless image, to form the final pixel intensity. This process is called pixel blending.

A hair strand's intensity contribution to the pixel is equal simply to the intensity of the hair, I, times the fractional area of the pixel that the hair occupies. The total color value of the pixel P therefore is:

$$P = F_B B + \sum_i F_j I_j \qquad (13.4)$$

where B is the intensity of the pixel background image, F_B is the fraction of pixel area covered by the background (hairless) image, I_j is the hair intensity of hair j, and F_j is the fraction of pixel area covered by hair j.

Pixel Blending
If the pixel intensity is initialized to the background value, then each hair strand's intensity can be blended into the pixel in back-to-front order in proportion to its projected surface area. The intensity of the pixel P_n after blending in the nth hair strand is therefore:

$$P_0 = B \,,$$

$$P_n = (1 - A_n)P_{n-1} + A_n I_n \qquad (13.5)$$

where B is the background image intensity, I_n is the intensity of the nth hair and A_n is the area of the hair strand's projection.

Rendering Segments
The pixel blending based algorithm requires that, for each pixel, the hair strands are blended in back-to-front order. Also, only visible hair strands should be blended, that is, strands obscured by hairless objects in the background image are not visible and therefore should not be blended.

This requires depth information of each pixel in the hairless image (Figure 13.2e) and the depth of each strand. A common z-buffer hidden surface removal is used to discard hidden hair pixels. The remaining strands' pixels are blended into the image.

Rendering a hair strand in this manner takes advantage of standard antialiased line-rendering algorithms and z-buffer capabilities which have been implemented in hardware in many commercially available graphics hardware systems. It is therefore a relatively fast method for rendering antialised hairs with full shadowing.

References

Carpenter L (1984) The A-buffer, an Antialiased Hidden Surface Method, *Proc. SIGGRAPH '84, Computer Graphics*, Vol.18, No3, pp. 103-108.

Csuri C, Hakathorn R, Parent R, Carlson W, Howard M (1979) Towards an interactive high visual complexity animation system, *Proc. SIGGRAPH '79, Computer Graphics*, Vol.13, No2, 1979, pp. 289-299.

Duff T (1985) Compositing 3-D Rendered Images, *Proc. SIGGRAPH '85, Computer Graphics*, Vol.19, No3, pp. 253-259.

Kajiya JT (1985) Anisotropic Reflection Models, *Proc. SIGGRAPH '85, Computer Graphics*, Vol.19, No3, pp. 15-21.

Kajiya JT, Kay TL (1989) Rendering Fur with Three Dimentional Textures, *Proc. SIGGRAPH '89, Computer Graphics*, Vol.23, No3, pp. 271-280.

LeBlanc A, Turner R, Thalmann D (1991) Rendering Hair using Pixel-Blending and Shadow-Buffers, *Journal of Vizualisation and Computer Animation*, Vol.2, No3.

Miller GSP (1988a) From Wire-Frame to Furry Animals, *Proc. Graphics Interface '88*, pp. 138-146.

Miller GSP (1988b) The Motion Dynamics of Snakes and Worms, *Proc. SIGGRAPH '88, Computer Graphics*, Vol.22, No4, pp. 169-178.

Perlin K, Hoffert E (1989) Hypertexture, *Proc. SIGGRAPH '89, Computer Graphics*, Vol.23, No3, pp. 253-262.

Porter T, Duff T (1984) Compositing Digital Images, *Proc. SIGGRAPH '84, Computer Graphcis*, Vol.18, No3, pp. 253-259.

Reeves WT (1983) Particle Systems - A Technique for Modeling a Class of Fuzzy Objects, *Proc. SIGGRAPH '83, Computer Graphics*, Vol.17, No3, pp. 359-376.

Reeves WT, Blau R (1985) Approximate and Probabilistic Algorithm for Shading and Rendering Structured Particle Systems, *Proc. SIGGRAPH '85, Computer Graphics*, Vol.19, No3, pp. 313-322.

Reeves WT, Salesin DH, Cook RL (1987) Rendering Antialiased Shadows with Depth Maps, *Proc. SIGGRAPH '87, Computer Graphics*, Vol.21, No4, pp. 283-291.

Sims K (1990) Particle Animation and Rendering Using Data Parallel Computation, *Proc. SIGGRAPH '90, Computer Graphics*, Vol.24, No4, pp. 405-413.

Smith AR (1984) Plants, Fractals and Formal Languages, *Proc. SIGGRAPH '84, Computer Graphics*, vol.18, No3, pp. 1-10.

Watanabe Y, Suenaga Y (1989) Drawing Human Hair Using Wisp Model, *Proc. Computer Graphics International '89*, pp. 691-700.

Williams L (1978) Casting Curved Shadows on Curved Surfaces, *Proc. SIGGRAPH '78, Computer Graphics*, Vol.12, No3, pp. 270-274.

14

Fractals And Their Applications

Prem K. Kalra
University of Geneva

Fractals, introduced by Mandelbrot (1977, 1982) have blossomed tremendously in the recent years. Fractal geomtery and its concepts have become significant tools in natural sciences such as physics, chemistry, biology, geology, metereology and material sciences. In addition, fractals are of great interest to graphic designers and filmmakers for their ability to simulate (model) most of the natural phenomenon. Fractal images though arising from simple rules manifest a high degree of visual complexity. Computer graphics has played an important role in the development and growth of fractal geometry as a new discipline, by allowing visual depiction of its varying applications.

14.1. Introduction

Geometric modelling of complex objects is a difficult process. Natural objects such as trees, plants, mountains and clouds constitute an important class of complex objects. The concept of fractals has significant potential for such purposes. The word fractal is derived from the Latin adjective "fractus" which means broken or fragmented. Fractal objects are entities that cannot be represented with Euclidean methods. Thus, a fractal curve cannot be described as one-dimensional geometric entity and a fractal surface cannot be described as a two-dimensional entity. They have fractional dimension, a number that agrees with our intuitive notion of dimension.

Fractals have the property of self-similarity, i.e. they are invariant under change of scale. In other words, when any small portion of fractals is magnified, it produces a fractal similar to the original fractal itself. Therefore, the basic principle of generating fractals involves repetetive application of a specified transformation function to points within a region of space. The amount of details included in the final display of the object depends on the number of iterations performed and the resolution of the display system.

Fractals can be classified into three major types depending upon the process of their generation (Kalra 1988). These are geometric fractals, algebraic fractals and random fractals. In another classification scheme (Barnsley et. al 1988) geometric fractals and algebraic fractals are clubbed into one class called deterministic fractals.

The ensuing sections of this chapter are organised as follows. The next section describes the geometric fractals and their generating techniques. Section 14.3, presents the visually interesting images obtained from the algebraic fractals. Then, random fractals are given. The applications of each type are appropriately illustrated in the corresponding section. Finally, some concluding remarks are included.

14.2. Geometric Fractals

14.2.1. Generating Method

Geometric fractals are generated from a basic geometric shape called the generator. A classical example of a fractal curve generated with a regular generator is shown in Figure 14.1. The construction of the fractal curve starts from a line segment, in the next step, the line segment is replaced by the given generator shown in Figure 14.1. At this stage, the curve has four line segments. These four line segments are further replaced by a proportional copy of the given pattern in the subsequent step. The process of replacing each line segment by the given generator is repeated till the length of each line segment in the resulting fractal curve diminishes to a preselected limiting value. Fractals thus generated exhibit the property of exact or strict self-similarity.

14.2.2. Characteristics of a Generator

A generator can have different geometric shapes. The attributes of a generator can be characterized as

(1) Number of segments
(2) Segment ratio (similarity ratio)
(3) Layout (angles and connectivity of segments)
(4) Fractal dimension

In Figure 14.1, these attributes are illustrated. The fractal dimension which is defined as

$$D = \log(N)/\log(1/r) \qquad (14.1)$$

where, N is the number of segments and r is the similarity ratio, characterizes the shape of the resulting fractal curve. It also indicates the wiggliness of the curve. As D increases from 1 towards 2 the resulting curves progress from "line like" to "plane filling" curves. Several illustrations of geometric fractals using generators of different D are given by Mandelbrot (1982).

14.2.3. Variations in Generating Method

The generating technique adopted may also vary (Kalra 1988). These techniques may involve flipping of segments, considering different traversals for each segment and multiplicity of segments. All these techniques provide a rich class of geomteric fractals to create aesthetic and visually interesting patterns.

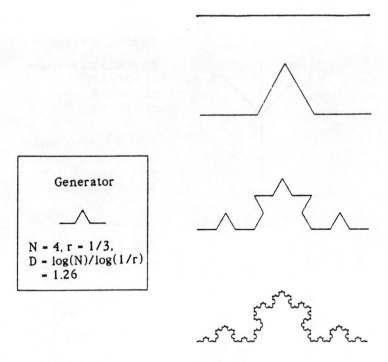

Figure 14.1. Generation of a geometric fractal

14.2.4. Applications

Some of the fractal curves (e.g. von Koch curve) simulate crude models of coastlines. Generation of a tree skeleton in two dimensions is an extension of fractal generation from a given regular pattern or generator. Different shapes of tree skeleton can be obtained by varying different parameters attached to the generator of a tree, namely, number of branches, branch to stem length ratio and branch angles. Figure 14.2, shows such a generator and the steps for the generation of the tree skeleton. Special features such as wind effect can be added by changing the branch angle as the process of generation progresses. Oppenheimer (1986) presented a real time fractal computer model of branching objects. These include simple orderly plants, complex gnarled trees, leaves, vein systems as well as inorganic structures such as river deltas and snowflakes. By manipulating the generic parametres one can modify the geomtery of the object in real time using tree based graphics hardware. Addition of random effects of the environment produces greater diversity and realism. Increasing the number of significant parameters yields more complex and evolved species.

Another application of these geometric fractals includes generating fractal textured objects (Kalra 1988). Here, a geometric texture (roughness) is appended to the basic geometry of the object to obtain the textured (sculptured) object. Figure 14.3 shows an object created by using an interpolating technique (Gujar et. al 1988) of the two end contours. One of the contours is "fractalized" to generate the textured object.

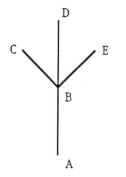

Number of branches = 3

Branch to stem ratios
r1 = BC/AB,
r2 = BD/AB,
r3 = BE/AB,

Branch to stem angles
a1 = ∠ABC,
a2 = ∠ABD,
a3 = ∠ABE,

Tree Generator

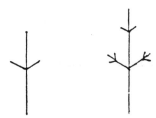

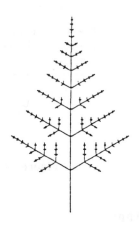

Figure 14.2. Generation of a tree skeleton

Figure 14.3. A fractal textured object

14.3. Algebraic Fractals

This section describes fractals which are obtained from iterations of some algebraic transformation functions. The mathematics of iteration has a long history. However, the striking beauty and complexity of the resulting shapes in the complex plane were not revealed until the recent investigations of Mandelbrot (1982). Norton (1982) has further extended the display of the dynamics of these non-linear transformations in three dimensions.

14.3.1. Function $z \leftarrow z^2 + c$

Mandelbrot considered a self-squared function $f(z) = z^2 + c$, where z and c are complex numbers. The basic principle of generating algebraic fractals is as follows. An initial value of z (say z_0) and of c are chosen. For this value of c, the function is iterated ($z_n \leftarrow z^2_{n-1} + c$) until the value of z_n reaches a preselected limiting value or the number of iterations reaches a maximum allowable value. The number of iterations carried out for this value of c is used to assign a color to the corresponding point in the region. If $c = c_x + ic_y$, then with the range $-2.0 \leq c_x \leq 0.5$ and $-1.25 \leq c_y \leq 1.25$ and $z_0 = (0.0, 0.0)$, the image obtained of the algebraic fractal is shown in Figure 14.4 (see color section). Many experiments selecting the region and the type of iterations (c-plane and z-plane) for the above function can be performed (Kalra 1988). Different divergence tests to assign the color to the pixel give rise to a variation in the resulting image.

14.3.2. Function $z \leftarrow z^\alpha + c$

A generalized Mandelbrot function $f(z) = z^\alpha + c$ was also considered (Kalra 1988), where α may be integer or real, positive or negative. It was observed that there is a direct effect of the value of α on the resulting image. The number of lobe structures arising in the image is given by $\lfloor |\alpha-1| \rfloor$. When a is real, the magnitude of the fractional part of α shows the size of a small lobe structure being generated. Figure 14.5a and 14.5b (see color section) show the algebraic fractals generated from the above function with $\alpha=10$, and $\alpha=-5$ respectively. Further extensions of some experiments and the conjectures made for the resulting shape of the images generated from this function have also been carried out (Nagarjuna et. al 1990).

14.3.3. Other Functions

There have been several other functions considered to generate this class of fractals (Pickover 1990, Jones 1990, Davidoff 1990).

14.3.4. Fractals from Quaternions

Norton (1982) extended the display of these algebraic fractals in three dimensions. He presented fractals generated using the mathematics of quaternions. A quaternion is defined as

$$A = a_0 + \vec{i} a_1 + \vec{j} a_2 + \vec{k} a_3 \qquad (14.2)$$

where $\vec{i}$, $\vec{j}$, $\vec{k}$ (like i in a complex number) are unit vectors in three orthogonal directions perpendicular to the real x-axis. The rules for quaternion multiplications are similar to those for the vector cross product in three dimensions. For generating fractals the variables of the transformation function are represented as quaternions.

14.3.5. Applications

Algebraic fractals are used to display the dynamical systems (Barnsley et al. 1988), which deal with many physical and mathematical processes that evolve in time. Some dynamical systems are predictable (stable) and some are unpredictable (unstable). The regions in the unstable set are known as chaotic set. Fractals make it possible to study, display and access these chaotic sets. They also add an aestheic sense in the study of their behavior.

14.4. Random Fractals

When the genaration of fractals is a random process, random (stochastic) fractals are obtained. Brownian motion in one variable constitute the simplest random fractal. Random fractals exhibit statistical self-similarity. The statistical self-similarity refers to the property in which the magnification of a smaller portion of a fractal results into a fractal, which is seemingly but not exactly similar to the original fractal itself.

14.4.1. Generating Methods

The algorithms to generate random fractals can be presented in different categories (Barnsley et. al 1988). For example, in one category, an approximation of random fractal with some resolution is used as input and the algorithm produces an improved approximation with resolution increased by a certain factor. This process is repeated with output used as new input until the desired resolution is achieved (e.g. mid point displacement methods). In the second category only one approximation of a random fractal is computed namely for the final resolution. Images for different resolutions are possible but require that most of the computations have to be redone, e.g. Fourier filtering method. The third approach may be the approximation of a fractal obtained via iterations. After each step the approximation is somewhat improved, but the spatial resolution does not necessarily increase by a constant factor in each iteration. It is not in the scope of this chapter to describe each category in detail. For more details refer to (Barnsley et al. 1988). These algorithms can easily be extended to higher dimensions (2 and 3). Figure 14.6 illustrates a random fractal curve obtained using mid point displacement method (Carpenter 1980). The process of generation involves determining the mid point of the given line segment. This mid point is displaced by a random amount and it becomes the common end point of the two new fractals subcurves. The process is repeated till the desired level of detail is achieved. Figure 14.7 shows a random landscape generated using the mid point displacement method (Fournier et al. 1982) in two dimensions.

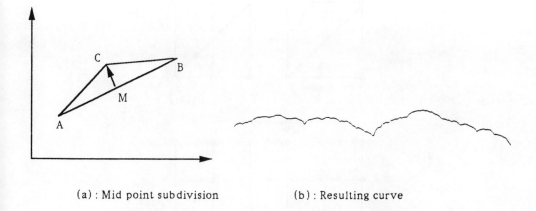

(a) : Mid point subdivision   (b) : Resulting curve

Figure 14.6. Generation of a random fractal curve

Figure 14.7. Fractal landscape

There have been several researches done to approximate the random fractals in two dimensions. Miller (1986) has examined three methods for the generation of fractals based on recursive subdivision. The new approach of subdivision introduced by him does not have the problem of creasing or artifacts. The other existing approaches namely, triangular edge subdivision and dimond square subdivision give rise to the undesirable effects of artifacts. Figure 14.8 shows the schemes of these three subdivisions. The new approach square–square subdivision leads to an interpolant which in the limit is a biquadratic surface.

A method of constrained fractal generation to model realistic terrains is developed by using hybrid of splines and fractals (Szeliski and Terzopoulos 1989).

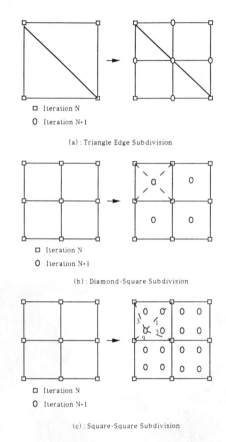

Figure 14.8. Three subdivision methods.

14.4.2. Applications

Random fractals are very suitable to model many of the natural phenomena such as coastlines, mountains, landscapes and clouds. For example, curves of coastlines are obtained using random fractals in one dimension, fractal mountains are obtained by the algorithms in two dimensions and similarly fractal clouds are example of the result of extending the algorithm to three dimensions.

Magnenat-Thalmann et al. (1987) demonstrate the use of mid point subdivision method to model candies (see Figure 14.9, color section). The impact of geometric parameters for controlling the algorithm was also studied and illustrated.

An interesting application of fractals is to characterize the speech waveform (Pickover and Khorasani 1986). The speech waveform is a highly irregular shaped signal which can be treated as a coastline and studied using fractal mathematics. It is believed that the fractal approach provides both a conceptual and an analytical (numerical) tool for better understanding of speech. Fractals are also used to represent music (Barnsley et al. 1988).

14.5. Conclusion

The computer rendering of fractal shapes leaves no doubt of their relevance to nature. Conversely, fractal geometry now plays a central role in the realistic rendering and modelling of natural phenomenon in computer graphics. With fractal geometry, the quest for scientiific understanding and realistic computer graphic imagery can return to the everyday natural world. This chapter demonstrates the potential of fractals for its varying applications in the real world.

Acknowledgement

The author gratefully acknowledges his MSc thesis supervisors Dr.V.C.Bhavsar and Prof.U.G.Gujar for their invaluable guidance during the course of the thesis work. The financial support from NSERC (Canada) is appreciated.

References

Barnsley MF, Devaney RL, Mandelbrot BB, Peitgen H, Saupe D, Voss RF (1988) *The Science of Fractal Images* (Eds Peitgen H and Saupe D), Springer-Verlag, Berlin.

Carpenter LC (1980) Computer Rendering of Fractal Curves and Surfaces *Proc. SIGGRAPH '80, Computer Graphics.*

Davidoff F (1990) Dynamic Fractals, *Computer and Graphics*, vol. 14, no. 1, pp. 135-136.

Fournier A, Fussel D, Carpenter L (1982) Computer Rendering of Stochastic Models, *Comm. of the ACM*, vol. 25, no. 6, pp. 371- 384.

Gujar UG, Bhavsar VC, Datar NN (1988) Interpolation Techniques for 3D Object Generation, *Computer and Graphics*, vol. 12, no. 3.

Jones JD (1990) Three unconventional representation of the Mandelbrot set, *Computer and Graphics*, vol. 14, no. 1, pp. 127-129.

Kalra PK (1988) *Fractals and their Applications*, M.Sc. Thesis, School of Computer Science, University of New Brunswick, Fredericton, Canada.

Magnenat-Thalmann N, Burgess M, Forest L, Thalmann D (1987) A geometric study of parameters for the recursive mid point subdivision, *The Visual Computer*, No3, pp1.45-151

Mandelbrot BB (1977) *Fractals: Form Chance and Dimension*, W.H. Freeman Company, San Francisco, CA.

Mandelbrot BB (1982) *The Fractal Geometry of Nature*, W.H. Freeman Company, San Francisco, CA.

Miller GSP (1986) The Definition and Rendering of Terrain Maps, *Proc. SIGGRAPH '86, Computer Graphics*, vol. 20, no. 3, pp. 39-48.

Nagarjuna V, Gujar UG, Bhavsar VC (1990) Julia Sets of $z^{\cdot\cdot}z^a+c$, *Proc. Computer Graphics International '90*, pp. 133-143.

Norton A (1982) Generation and Display of Geometric Fractals in 3-D, *Proc. SIGGRAPH '82, Computer Graphics*, vol. 16, no. 3, pp. 61-67.

Oppenheimer PE (1986) Real Time Design and Animation of Fractal Plants and Trees, *Proc. SIGGRAPH '86, Computer Graphics*, vol. 20, no. 4, pp. 55-64.

Pickover CA (1990) A note on inverted Mandelbrot sets, *The Visual Computer*, Vol.6, No4.

Pickover CA, Khorasani AI (1986) Fractal Characterization of Speech Waveform Graphics, *Computer and Graphics*, vol. 10, no. 1, pp. 51-61.

Szeliski R, Terzopoloulos D (1989) From Splines to Fractals, *Proc. SIGGRAPH '89, Computer Graphics*, Vol.23, No3.

Figure 12.4. "Oscar's Coat" showing anisotropic shading and fur by Gavin Miller and Jon Hunwick, © Gavin Miller

Figure 12.5. "Queen West Village" showing slope-dependent snow by Gary Mundell, Paul Roy, Andrew Pearce, Patricia Anderson and Gavin Miller, © Alias Research Inc., Toronto, Canada

Figure 12.6. ''Midtown Plaza'' by Semmania Luk Cheung, Mary Lynn Machadu and John Coldrick, Design Vision Christmas Card, © Design Vision, Toronto, Canada

Figure 12.9. ''Lost Horizon'' by Steve Williams and Gavin Miller, © Alias Research Inc., Toronto, Canada

Figure 12.11. ''Sunrise'' by Gavin Miller, © Alias Research Inc., Toronto, Canada

Figure 12.13. "The Heavens" by Gavin Miller, © Alias Research Inc., Toronto, Canada

Figure 12.14. A frame from "Splash Dance" by Michael Kass, Gavin Miller and Ned Greene, © Apple Computer Inc., Cupertino, California

Figure 12.15. A globular dynamic fountain by Gavin Miller, © Apple Computer Inc., Cupertino, California

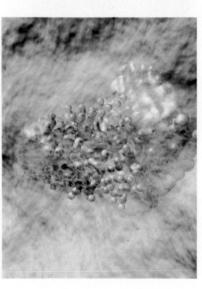

Figure 12.16. "Curling Up by the Fire" by Gavin Miller, Steve Williams, Patricia Anderson, Gary Mundell and Andrew Pearce, © Alias Research Inc., Toronto, Canada

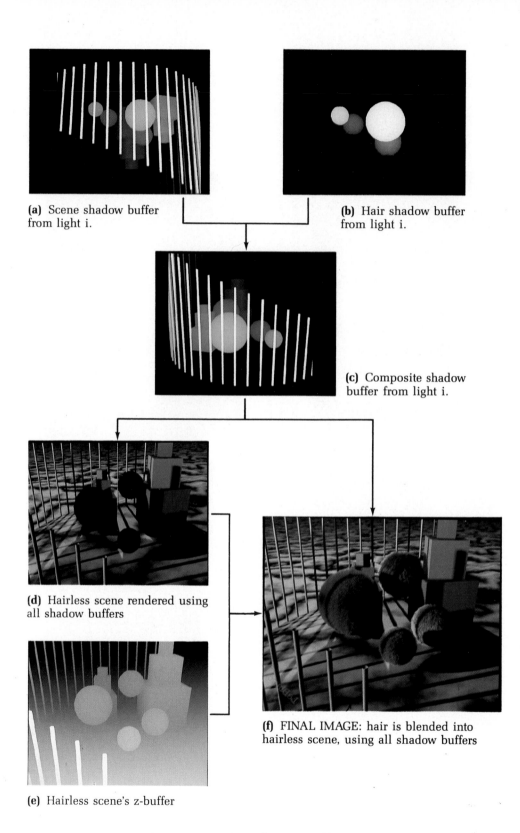

(a) Scene shadow buffer from light i.

(b) Hair shadow buffer from light i.

(c) Composite shadow buffer from light i.

(d) Hairless scene rendered using all shadow buffers

(e) Hairless scene's z-buffer

(f) FINAL IMAGE: hair is blended into hairless scene, using all shadow buffers

Figure 13.2. Hair rendering pipeline

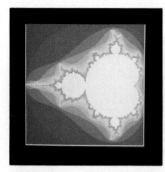
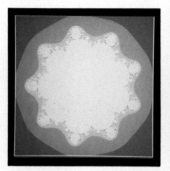
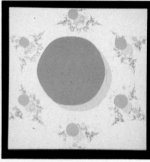

Figure 14.4. Algebraic fractal
from Mandelbrot's function

Figure 14.5 (a) $\alpha = 10$

Figure 14.5 (b) $\alpha = -5$

Figure 14.5. Algebraic fractal from function $z \leftarrow z^\alpha + c$

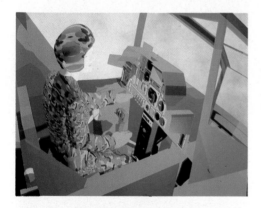

Figure 14.9. Candles obtained by the midpoint subdivision method, © 1987 Nadia
Magnenat Thalmann and Daniel Thalmann

Figure 15.1. Ray-traced Apache helicopter
cockpit with simulated operator, by Pei-Hwa
Ho, Eunyoung Koh, and Jiahe Lu, using *Jack*.
The helicopter cockpit and helmet models
were supplied by Barry Smith of the A3I
project at NASA Ames Research Center. The
human figure is based on a biostereo-
metrically-scanned body supplied by Kathleen
Robinette of Wright-Patterson Air Force Base

Figure 15.2. A room with two contour bodies.
Each has a full 17 segment torso which is
positioned by realistic motions in the
vertebrae. The image was designed and ray-
traced in *Jack* by Dawn Vigliotti and Welton
Becket

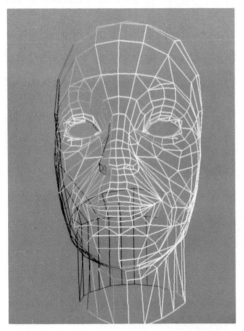

Figure 16.1 Typical face model polygon structure

Figure 16.2. Example face 1

Figure 16.3. Example face 2

Figure 16.4. Example face 3

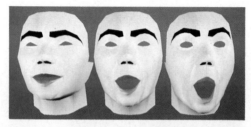

Figure 16.5. Key expression interpolation. The middle face is an interpolation of the left and right key poses

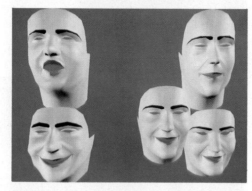

Figure 16.6. Bi-linear conformation interpolation. The center face is an interpolated blend of the four corner faces

Figure 17.1. A frame from the film *Flashback*

Figure 17.4. A frame from the film *Flashback*

Figure 18.2. A motion difficult to achieve without dynamics (Design: Arghyro Paouri)

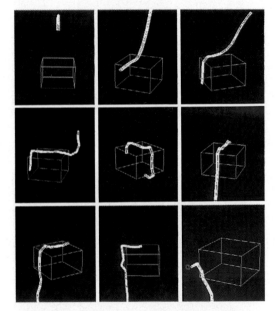

Figure 18.5. A dynamic simulation

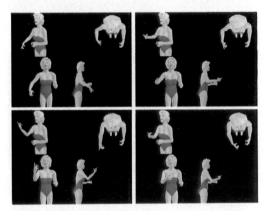

Figure 18.6. Marilyn draws letters

Part 4

Advances in Computer Visualization

15

Human Modeling in Visualization

Norman I. Badler
Computer and Information Science Department, University of Pennsylvania

Visualizing the appearance, capabilities and performance of humans is a challenging task. From modeling realistic or at least reasonable body size and shape, through the control of the highly redundant body linkage, to the simulation of plausible motions, human figures offer numerous computational problems and constraints. A variety of these issues will be examined, focusing on the broad yet vertically-integrated effort at the University of Pennsylvania. Our research has produced a Silicon Graphics Iris 4D workstation-based system, called *Jack*^{TM}, for the definition, manipulation, animation, and human factors performance analysis of simulated human figures. Built on a powerful representation for articulated figures, *Jack* offers the interactive user a simple, intuitive, and yet extremely capable interface into any 3D articulated world. *Jack* incorporates sophisticated yet highly usable algorithms for anthropometric human figure generation, a flexible torso, multiple limb positioning under constraints, view assessment, reach space generation, and strength guided performance simulation of human figures. Of particular importance is a simulation level which allows access to *Jack* by high level task control, an object-oriented knowledge base, task decomposition and natural language instructions. Thus human activities can be visualized from high level task understanding and planning as well as by interactive specification.

15.1. Introduction

The Computer Graphics Research Lab at the University of Pennsylvania has been involved in the research, design, and implementation of computer graphics human figure manipulation software since the late 1970s. The history of this effort is too lengthy to detail here; rather, we wish to describe the current state of our system, called *Jack*.

The *Jack* software is built on Silicon Graphics Iris 4D workstations because those systems have the 3D graphics features that greatly aid the process of interacting with highly articulated figures such as the human body. Of course, graphics capabilities themselves do not make a usable system. Our research has therefore focused on software to make the manipulation of a simulated human figure easy for a rather specific user population: human factors design engineers or ergonomics analysts involved in visualizing and assessing human motor performance, fit, reach, view, and other physical tasks in a workplace environment. The software also happens to be quite usable by others, including graduate students and animators. The point, however, is that program design has tried to take into account a wide variety of physical problem-oriented tasks, rather than just offer a computer graphics and animation tool for the already computer-sophisticated or skilled animator.

This orientation toward *tasks* gives *Jack* its particular flavor. As we are Computer Scientists, we seek computationally general yet efficient solutions to problems. Human factors engineers often analyze a succession of specific tasks or situations. The role we play is transforming the specific needs of the engineer or analyst into the general case so that

- at least some large percentage of situations may be successfully analyzed;
- there is sufficient research required to justify doing the software in the Computer Science environment; and
- conversely, the general problems are difficult enough to expect that a specific problem-oriented approach will be economically or technologically infeasible for a particular human factors engineer.

As we continue to interact with human factors specialists, and particularly our research sponsors, we have come to appreciate the broad range of problems they must address. The challenge to embed a reasonable set of capabilities in an integrated system has provided dramatic incentives to study issues and solutions in 3D interaction methodologies, multiple goal positioning, visual field assessment, and strength guided motion, to name a few. Our Lab effort has involved full-time staff and dozens of students over the past few years. They have worked cooperatively and collaboratively on the common *Jack* framework. It must be noted, however, that the principal architect of the *Jack* system is Cary Phillips. To a great extent the "look and feel" of *Jack* (as well as the name) is due to him.

The remainder of this chapter discusses the major *Jack* features, organized around the topics of body and other geometric object structures, anthropometry, user interface, positioning, animation, analyses, rendering, and external interfaces. The final section briefly outlines some of the relevant work in progress in our Lab.

15.2. Summary of *Jack* Features

Jack is a Silicon Graphics Iris 4D Workstation-based system for the definition, manipulation, animation, and human factors performance analysis of simulated human figures. Built on a powerful representation for articulated figures composed of joints and segments with boundary geometry, *Jack* offers the interactive user a simple, intuitive, and yet extremely powerful interface into any 3D articulated world using only the three-button mouse, keyboard, and pop-up menus. All *Jack* software has been written in *C* at the University of Pennsylvania; it does not depend on any third-party software (or hardware) outside the usual Silicon Graphics Iris utilities. In this section we discuss the major features currently available in *Jack*.

15.2.1. Body and Other Geometric Object Structure

Bodies as well as all other geometric objects, called *figures*, are represented externally to *Jack* in a language (*Peabody*) which describes their attributes and topological connections (Phillips and Badler 1988). Figures consist of segments connected by joints, each with various degrees of freedom and joint limits. Important points on each segment are termed *sites* and are used, for example, to describe the attachment locations of joints or the positions of notable landmarks.

Geometric transformations called *constraints* are used to position figures in the world coordinate reference frame.

The surface geometry associated with a segment has its own local coordinate system and is typically described as a network of polygons called *psurfs*. Geometry and topology editing facilities written by Osman Niazi are supplied in *Jack* though it is not intended to be or substitute for a "real" Computer-Aided Design system. *Jack* is very comfortable obtaining its geometric data from other systems (Section 15.2.8).

15.2.1.1. Default Body Model

The default human figure in *Jack* consists of 39 segments, 38 joints, and 94 degrees of freedom, including a full 17 vertebra spine (Section 15.2.1.8). Normally the hands and feet are only minimally articulated (but see Section 15.2.1.6), though if included add 30 more segments, 30 more joints, and 33 more degrees of freedom.

15.2.1.2. User-Specifiable Topological Structures

The body structure is not built into *Jack*; rather, the default body is there for user convenience. Any topological structure can be defined through *Peabody* and manipulated in *Jack*. In particular, this allows the use of figure models with greater or lesser articulation, as well as mechanisms, robots, insects, and so on. We frequently use a simpler human figure model or even a Puma robot model for testing purposes. Detailed spine, hand and finger models can be substituted for the simpler segments and used in any combination desired.

The joints that connect figure segments typically have up to three rotational degrees of freedom (translational degrees of freedom are allowed but are not used in the human models). Joint centers are described in terms of sites on the connected segments. While real human joints are not so simple, this model suffices for most ergonomic analyses. For a brief discussion of our efforts addressing more flexibility in joint action, see Section 15.3.6.

15.2.1.3. Independent Surface Geometry per Segment

For interactive manipulation, detailed human figure surface geometry is usually unnecessary, however, the *psurfs* associated with each segment may be as simple or complex as desired. The default human model has a rather polyhedral appearance to keep the number of polygons low for graphical display update efficiency. The more accurate figures (the contour bodies, Section 15.2.1.7) may have hundreds of polygons per segment to give a smoother and more rounded appearance. The selections can be mixed from segment to segment: for example, a smoother head model with simple arms.

15.2.1.4. Other Body Models

Since the topology and geometry of figures are completely accessible, building any other existing body in *Peabody* and *psurfs* should be a rather simple matter. Transforming the segment topology is straightforward, and most geometry formats are readily converted into *psurfs*. Perhaps the most effort would be involved in establishing commensurate sites on each segment for the joint connections. For example, we are presently converting the Crew Chief model (Easterly 1990) into a *Jack*-compatible figure.

15.2.1.5. Surface "Clothing"

Clothing a figure is important for ergonomic analyses since clothing often affects mobility and joint limits. *Jack* presently contains three types of clothing:

- A rather simple kind which is simply a color differentiation for various segments (e.g. brown legs and lower torso yield "pants," blue upper torso and arms, a long-sleeved "shirt," etc.);
- A more realistic "thick" clothing, implemented by Eunyoung Koh, which is the actual expansion of the segment geometry (hence its diameter) relative to the segment axis while still preserving the overall shape (see Figure 15.1, color section);
- Additional equipment (such as helmets, tool belts, pockets, air supplies, etc.) attached or worn by simply adding appropriate geometric models to segments.

All three improve graphics appearance. The second and third approach are the more serious since thick clothing and equipment should affect joint limits. We have used iterated motion and collision detection to measure reduction of mobility due to clothing volume. This contextual modification of body capabilities is currently under development (Section 15.3.6). The attachment of loose fitting or draped clothing is another matter entirely and is not addressed here.

15.2.1.6. Hand Model

Jack contains a simple geometric hand model, constructed by Wallace Ching, with fully articulated and joint-limited fingers and thumb. The more interesting feature, however, is an automatic grip. Given a geometric object that is to be grasped, the user can specify one of three types of grips—power, precision, or disk (Iberall 1987)—and *Jack* will move the hand to the object then move the fingers and hand into a reasonable grip position. The actual grip is completed by using real-time collision detection on the object's geometry to determine when finger motion should cease.

15.2.1.7. Biostereometric Contour Bodies

One of the most interesting body databases in *Jack* is derived from biostereometric (photographically) scanned body surface data of 76 subjects. Originally supplied by Kathleen Robinette of the U.S. Air Force Armstrong Aerospace Medical Research Laboratory, the data consist of approximately 6000 data points for each subject, organized by body segment and arranged in parallel slices. Marc Grosso, Jeff Weinberg, and Pei-Hwa Ho determined reasonable joint centers from the segment contours and surface landmark data, converted the segment topology into *Peabody* structures, and tiled the contours into polyhedral meshes (Fuchs et al. 1977).

The major difficulty with the contour data is that it looks very realistic in the standard posture, but immediately develops annoying gaps when the joints are moved. Eunyoung Koh recently remedied this in a general fashion that extends as well to the clothing defined by the segment expansion method. Given two adjacent segment geometries, a procedure generates a curved surface to fill in a plausible solid connection between them depending on the joint angle and the respective tangents to the segments. This procedure fills the "gaps" between the scanned segment geometries and, by extension, the clothing defined over them.

The single torso segment in the original scanned body data was rigid. In Section 15.2.1.8 we describe how we dramatically improved that situation.

15.2.1.8. 17 Segment Flexible Torso with Vertebral Limits

The lack of accurate flexibility in the torso is a notable weakness of most anthropometric models. Even the biostereometric bodies suffered from torso rigidity. Recently, Gary Monheit has constructed a 17 segment vertebral column (from lumbar to thoracic) whose movements are dictated by kinematic limits and some simple parameters (Monheit and Badler 1991). The torso, in turn, is broken into 17 corresponding "fat" slices, one for each vertebra. With this arrangement it is easy to have the contour body bend and "breathe" in a very realistic fashion (Fig. 15.2, color section). Movements of the torso are basically described by lateral, saggital, and axial rotations of the neck. The flexible spine shape is history-dependent, that is, the motion of each vertebra in space is not determined solely by these rotations: other parameters such as motion-resisting joints, and the motion-originating joint affect its actual path.

15.2.1.9. Facial Model

Humans have faces, and *Jack* provides two mechanisms for presenting a face on a human figure.

- A photograph of a [real] face may be texture mapped onto a contour body head. The figure bears a close resemblance to a real person and the resulting image looks reasonable even when rotated. The disadvantages are the rather delicate (for correct) positioning of the texture on the head and the requirement of ray-tracing to see the face. Welton Becket and Dawn Vigliotti have provided this feature.
- A polyhedral model of a generic face may be used on a special head *psurf*. The advantages are that the polygons are displayed directly and, most importantly, the facial features are *animated* (Pelachaud et al. 1991). While not important (perhaps) for human factors work, the expressions certainly enliven finished animations. The original facial data was supplied by Steve Platt (1985) and extensively modified by Catherine Pelachaud, Soetjianto, and Khairol Yussof.

15.2.2 Anthropometry

A body model is one thing; being able to easily make it correspond to human size variation is another. Anthropometric scaling of body models is an important component of *Jack* (Grosso et al. 1989a, 1989b).

15.2.2.1. Segment and Joint Attributes

The human figures used in *Jack* have various attributes associated with them that are used during manipulation and task analysis. The current set includes segment dimensions, joint limits, moment of inertia, mass, center of mass, and joint strength (Grosso et al. 1989a, 1989b). Segment dimensions are used to scale the segment geometry for proper sizing. Joint limits are used to restrict motion. Mass, center of mass and moments of inertia are used during dynamic simulations. The strength data is used for certain reach and lifting tasks.

Raw anthropometric measurements (e.g. for specific landmarks or composite measurements such as "sitting height") can also be associated with an individual in the database.

The strength data may be based on tabular (empirical) data or strength prediction formulae (Wei 1990). Strength parameters may be either scaling (e.g. gender, handedness) or non-scaling (e.g. depending on the population). In any case the user may alter the stored data or formulae to conform to whatever model is desired.

15.2.2.2. Population Percentiles or Individuals

Either population statistics may be used to provide percentile data, or else an actual database of [real] individuals may be used. The former, e.g., is common in US Army analyses, while the latter is often used by NASA for the specific individuals in the astronaut trainee pool.

15.2.2.3. Spreadsheet Interface for Selection, Changes, or Database Query

The interface to the anthropometry database is through *SASS*: the Spreadsheet Anthropometric Scaling System (Grosso et al. 1989b). As part of *Jack* it offers flexible access to all the body attributes and a simple mechanism for changes. Specific body models may be selected or customized as needed. Queries about the contents of the anthropometric database are constructed entirely from pop-up menus without requiring user knowledge of a particular database query language. For example, the query "Find all females under the 25th percentile in stature who have left elbow strength greater than 15 ft-lbs" is constructed by direct menu selection of each field, relation, and value. Individuals satisfying arbitrary requirements may be listed and selected for creation and display. *Peabody* model files are created by *SASS* and made available to *Jack*. Alternatively, one can interactively manipulate the current body in *SASS* while displaying it in *Jack* to rapidly try out the effect of varying the individual, population percentile, gender, joint limits, etc.

15.2.2.4. Concurrent Display of Interactively Selected Dimensions

As noted above, a human figure may be modified by *SASS* while it is being displayed in *Jack*. In fact, the process is much more powerful than just updating a display. In Section 15.2.4.4 we will see that a figure may be subject to arbitrary goals for one or more of its joints. These goals are maintained (subject to joint limits and body integrity) during interactive manipulation. The process also applies to segment attribute changes done interactively in *SASS*: as the segment lengths change, e.g., the body will move to maintain the required position, orientation, or viewing constraints. It is therefore very easy to assess posture and viewing changes (as well as success or failure) across population percentiles or gender.

15.2.2.5. On-Screen Interactive Strength Data Display

Besides the numeric listing of strength data, a graphical display feature is available. Interactive displays of joint torque or end-effector forces may be shown in *Jack* as the user manipulates the figure directly (Wei 1990). Current as well as cumulative maximum forces or torques are displayed as moving bars in a *strength box* whose axes correspond to the joint's degrees of freedom. Individual, gender differentiated, and population percentile (95th, 50th, and 5th) strengths may be compactly and comparatively displayed.

Torques along a joint chain may be shown, too. Given a force on an end-effector, *Jack* can compute the reaction forces generated anywhere else in the body. Since the body is an active mechanism, forces may be resisted in differing amounts by activating different muscle groups. Phil Lee and Susanna Wei have implemented displays that show, given a weight held by an end-effector, the reaction forces (torques) at each joint degree of freedom along a given chain (Wei 1990). In addition, a trace of the "safe" and "unsafe" regions (relative to the current strength model) is left in the display as the end-effector is moved about, producing a direct and real-time visualization of the accessible space.

15.2.2.6. Body Somatotypes

Pei-Hwa Ho has examined the original biostereometric contour body dataset to select specimens covering the approximate midpoint and extremes of body somatotype for each of the 5th, 50th, and 95th percentile males and females: 18 body "styles" in all. This set is integrated into *SASS* with a new attribute for somatotype. The user can select a gender, somatotype, and percentile, causing one of the 18 prototype bodies to be scaled to the individual segment dimensions. The figures retain significant realism in form while providing infinite variability across all shape dimensions.

15.2.2.7. Multiple Figures

Jack allows the manipulation and display of as many figures as desired up to the memory limits of the hardware. There are no restrictions whatsoever on the geometry, topology, or anthropometry used across the several figures.

15.2.3 User Interface

One of the the most attractive features of *Jack* is the natural user interface into the three-dimensional world (Phillips and Badler 1988). A significant part of the interface is offered by the hardware capabilities of the Silicon Graphics Iris 4D workstation platform upon which *Jack* is built. The software, however, makes this hardware power controllable.

15.2.3.1. Three Button Mouse and Keyboard

Jack relies solely on the standard Iris 4D three button mouse and keyboard for interaction. The mouse is used to perform direct manipulation on the 3D scene, e.g. selecting objects by picking their images, translating objects by holding down one or two mouse buttons corresponding to spatial coordinates, etc. The mouse is also actively used to negotiate through the pop-up command menus. The keyboard is used for occasional command entry. The escape and control keys are used as meta-mouse buttons, e.g. to change the button interpretations from translation to rotation, or the affected coordinate frame from global to local.

15.2.3.2. Menu-Driven Commands

The command menus are built from the standard Iris menu library. There is a tradeoff in making all the commands accessed this way: simplicity and an uncluttered screen are advantages, while on the other hand frequently used commands are treated the same as infrequently used ones.

15.2.3.3. Command Completion

To alleviate the menu bottleneck, any *Jack* command may be entered via the keyboard. To save typing, and to act as a simple help system, command completion shows the choices for any partially-entered command.

15.2.3.4. Natural 3D Interactive Interface

The naturalness of the interface arises from the coherence of hand motions with the mouse and the correspondence between mouse cursor motion on the 2D screen, a 3-D cursor (looking like a "jack") in the world, and 3D objects displayed there. In particular, translations and rotations are selected with the mouse buttons (and perhaps a key), and the mouse motion is transformed into an appropriate 3D cursor movement. Rotations display a wheel perpendicular to the selected axis; motion of the mouse cursor about the wheel display invokes a 3D rotation about the actual axis. Any joint limits are respected.

Object selection is done by simply placing the mouse cursor over the desired part. If more than one object lies under the cursor, a button push cycles among the possibilities which are highlighted in turn.

Other motions that are easy to perform in *Jack* include real-time end-effector dragging (Section 15.2.4.5). The position and orientation of the end-effector is controlled by the same mouse and button interpretation method.

15.2.3.5. Multiple Windows

Jack supports multiple independent windows into the current environment. Thus, e.g. one could be a global view, one could be a view from a figure's eye, another could be a view from a certain light source (to see what is being illuminated), etc. The camera and lights are represented as *psurfs* so that they may be positioned and observed just as any other object in the scene. Of course, as the camera is moved in one view, the corresponding camera view window shows the changing image. The same result obtains if a window view is attached to a figure's eye (or hand, etc.).

15.2.3.6. Perspective or Orthographic Views

The view in a window may be either perspective or orthographic. The latter is most useful when dimensions are important. In perspective, the three orthographic projections may be optionally displayed within the same window as wireframe "shadow" images on the imaginary walls and floor. These greatly assist in object and goal positioning.

15.2.3.7. Feature on/off Toggles

There are a number of display features which may be turned on or off at will. These include the orthographic projections, a ground plane, shaded or wireframe mode, background star field, motion traces, and so on.

15.2.3.8. Command Language Files

Any *Jack* scene can be written out as an environment file; when read in it restores the exact situation for continued manipulation. Even more useful is the *Jack command language* or *jcl* file. This is a record of the *Jack* commands issued during a selected portion of an interactive (or program-controlled) session. The *jcl* files may be recursive in the sense that they may contain commands to read and execute other *jcl* files. Such files also provide a command format for external (non-interactive) control of *Jack*, e.g. from an animation procedure.

15.2.4 Positioning

The manipulation power in *Jack* comes from novel real-time articulated figure positioning algorithms. These imbue the jointed figure with "behavioral fidelity"; that is, the ability to respond to varied positioning *goals* as well as to direct joint rotation.

15.2.4.1. Joint Degrees of Freedom

Joint angles may be manipulated directly to position a figure. During rotation, a rotation wheel will appear only for allowed degrees of freedom.

15.2.4.2. Rotations Subject to Joint Limits

During rotation, the displayed wheel will follow the cursor, but the joint will only be allowed to rotate to the joint limits. For two and three degree of freedom joints, the joint limits are tested in the individual rotation directions. This is not totally correct, especially for a complex joint such as the human shoulder, but it suffices for most purposes. Adding more accurate joint limits is possible in the future (Section 15.3.6).

15.2.4.3. End-Effector Position and Orientation Goals

One of the most powerful features of *Jack* is the positioning of a joint by specifying the other end of the kinematic chain (e.g. the shoulder or the waist for a hand movement), and giving the end-effector an arbitrary position or orientation goal (or both) in space. Using a real-time inverse kinematics procedure based on non-linear optimization (with linear constraints) written by Jianmin Zhao, a joint space solution (subject to joint limits) is computed for the intermediate joints along the chain (Phillips et al. 1990; Zhao and Badler, 1989). The solution moves the selected joint (end-effector) to the goal if it is reachable, otherwise it moves as close as feasible given the figure posture, the joint chain, and the joint limits. Any failure distance is reported numerically as well. This movement does not represent how a person would actually move, nor does it attempt to find the "best" or most "natural" position. It merely achieves goals. For better postures, additional goals can be created and maintained (Section 15.2.4.4).

There are several goal types available:

- position (a point in space)
- orientation (e.g., a particular orientation of the proximal segment coordinate space)
- position and orientation (weighted to arbitrate conflicts: e.g. a position may be achievable only by violating the orientation goal or *vice versa*, so the weight determines which to favor)
- aim (a specified direction on the proximal segment should point at the desired point; this is frequently used for eye and camera positioning)
- view (a specified direction; like "aim" except that twist is not allowed so the camera or eye view will not rotate (roll) along its sighting axis)
- line (a position anywhere along the line is acceptable)
- plane (a position anywhere in the plane is acceptable)
- half-space (a position anywhere in the half-space volume is acceptable)

In order to distribute intermediate joint motions more realistically, a stiffness parameter can be set for each joint degree of freedom if desired, or for the chain as a whole. The stiffness forces motion to be favored or resisted more in a degree of freedom, e.g. to encourage torso bending rather than twisting. Over a chain, the stiffness may favor motion at the proximal or at the distal end.

Inverse kinematics executes in "real-time," meaning that most positioning actions are accomplished in time that is not much different than that required by a real person.

15.2.4.4. Multiple Simultaneous Position and Orientation Goals

The goal satisfaction procedure has the additional advantage of operating on multiple simultaneous goals of any of the above types. For example, a figure can be seated by supplying goals for the feet (to stay on the floor), the center hip (to be near and just above the chair seat), the knees (to stay in front of the hips) and the neck (to stay above the waist). Some of these goals may be plane goals (such as for the feet) or half-plane goals (to keep the waist above the seat and in front of the chair back). As usual, joint limits are respected and the best solution (though it may be a local rather than global minimum) satisfying the goals is displayed. If the goals are not entirely satisfiable, some minimum distance solution will be offered. If the results are not acceptable, more goals may be added. This algorithm still runs in real time for modest numbers of goals; it is superlinear convergent with each iteration of complexity of just $O([nm])$ where n is the number of degrees of freedom and m is the number of goals. A sample posture to move the figure's head over the end of a large upright tube, aim the view to see the bottom of the tube, and grasp the tube with two hands at opposite sides while keeping the elbows out in a plane parallel to the tube axis took only 23 seconds to solve on a Personal Iris workstation.

15.2.4.5. Real-time End-Effector Dragging

Since inverse kinematics is available, and since multiple goals may be active, *Jack* allows a joint to be moved interactively by attaching a position or orientation goal to the 3D cursor controlled by the mouse (Phillips et al. 1990). The solution time is actually reduced because the current posture is likely to be close to the solution at the next input position, so the algorithm converges quickly. To avoid waiting for the solution, however, *Jack* updates the joint angles at every graphics window update by taking the solution obtained thus far. As the goal is moved or rotated, the posture changes as quickly as possible and "catches up" with the user whenever there is a significant pause in cursor motion.

15.2.4.6. Rotation Propagation when Joint Limits are Exceeded

A consequence of joint limits and inverse kinematics is apparent "behavioral fidelity" in the manipulated figure. If the wrist is twisted, the rotations propagate along the arm toward the fixed end as joint limits are encountered. Thus the user can freely move the joints about and the remainder of the body will act in a reasonable fashion.

15.2.4.7. Constrain Center of Mass of Entire Figure

Cary Phillips developed an interesting application of the multiple goal solution algorithm by constraining the center of mass of a figure (Phillips and Badler 1991). The center of mass is not a specific joint or point of the body, rather it is a computed quantity. Nonetheless, *Jack* permits it to be a participant in a goal. By constraining the center of mass to lie along a line goal above the figure's support polygon, a *balanced reach* may be effected. The motion is most dramatic when only one foot is constrained to the floor; moving a hand causes the other leg to lift off the floor for counterbalance when it is needed! Another example is the "worm on a fishhook": a linear chain of segments (the worm) is attached at one end to a point in space (the hook) and allowed to dangle below. As the free end of the worm is dragged about, the segments wiggle and contort to maintain the center of mass along a line goal below the hook. In Phillips and Badler (1991) we have used this capability to simply animate subtle weight shifting, single steps, and turning activities. In addition, since the computation of the center of mass will depend on any objects attached to the body (e.g. being held or worn), the motions automatically compensate for the new distribution of weight.

15.2.5   Animation

The manipulations in *Jack* discussed so far are not really "animations" as we have already mentioned. For an animation we expect some coherence and smoothness to the figure's motion; it is not enough to merely animate a numerical search no matter how clever or effective it is. *Jack* incorporates a number of mechanisms to produce human-like motion.

15.2.5.1. Key Parameter Specification and Rational Spline Interpolation

The simplest method of animation is based on the specification of a series of postures and the subsequent interpolation of the joint angles to create a smooth sequence of "in-between" postures. The important postures are called "keys"; the joint angles from key to key are parameterized by time (given for each key) and interpolated to compute values at any other time. A textual interface written by Jean Griffin helps in the creation and editing of the script keys and times. Jianmin Zhao implemented a method of interpolation and motion control using rational spline curves in a fashion similar to that described by Steketee and Badler (1985).

The ability to key on parameters is extended in *Jack* to include constraints and goals. Thus the beginning, duration, and end times of any constraints may be provided. As the interpretation of the constraints proceeds in temporal order, a body posture satisfying the current set of active constraints is produced for each frame time.

While capable of creating effective motion sequences, key parameter approaches put the burden of motion design on the user/animator, requiring skill and patience to define the key postures. There are alternatives, but each with advantages and disadvantages. *Jack* includes a useful selection, as we explain below.

15.2.5.2. Forward Dynamics

One method of creating accurate and realistic motion is to use the physics of forces and torques to drive a figure (e.g. (Armstrong et al. 1987; Wilhelms 1987). The results are physically correct, but the problem is in determining the proper directions, magnitudes, and timings of the forces. Most people (or animators) cannot do that. Moreover, the motions tend to work best on passive figures (when they are under the control of external forces, e.g. falling, dangling, crashing) rather than on active ones (when the person is trying to perform some task, e.g. reaching, lifting, throwing).

For completeness, *Jack* offers motion control by force and torque specification using forward dynamics to compute joint positions and orientations. This procedure is being built by Mike Edwards.

15.2.5.3. Strength Guided Motion

A rather more useful, but more restricted, animation method developed by Phil Lee uses the inherent strength model stored for a human figure as the basis for computing certain types of motion. If the task involves moving a weight rather slowly to some goal position, then a *strength guided motion* algorithm computes a motion path based on the strength model and two additional parameters (Lee et al. 1990). The parameters are the comfort level at which the motion should be performed and the allowed deviation from a straight-line path to the goal. Using a number of strategies based on the available torque at each joint in an arm (plus upper torso) joint chain, the algorithm computes an acceptable posture at every instant (say, 15 times a second) of the action. Strategies include moment reduction, pull back, adding joints, and recoil to bring comfort to acceptable levels. Present limitations are two-dimensional paths, upper body chains, and inverse kinematics incremental positioning rather than a more realistic dynamical rate-control process (Sections 15.3.3 and 15.3.4). A useful range of lifting and reaching motions may be produced already, however, including weight lifting, rising from a chair, pulling the body upwards in a chin-up, and two-person coordinated lifting.

15.2.5.4. External Control

Cary Phillips and Jeff Esakov coded the beginnings of a very powerful animation mechanism in *Jack*. By attaching a joint angle or some other parameter such as arm length or object size to a Unix *socket*, external processes can be used to control their values. The process can reside anywhere on the Ethernet attached to the host workstation, including the host itself. The process can be another user, an autonomous procedure, a physical sensor, or a simulation. Thus a gauge needle's rotation can be controlled by an external simulation, a joint angle could be read from a goniometer on an actual subject, or an object's location could be controlled by another user interacting in the same space, for example (Blanchard et al. 1990).

15.2.6 Analyses

All the *Jack* features are available to compute certain aspects of some of the most commonly performed task analyses.

15.2.6.1. Reach Space

Jack can display a trace of any site; in particular, it can show the path of an end-effector as it is manipulated. The resulting trace gives a good idea of the reachable space as the end-effector is dragged about. Any joint chain can be used due to the general inverse kinematics solution. Other algorithms being studied by Tarek Alameldin can compute the reachable space boundary or volume off-line (Alameldin et al. 1990).

15.2.6.2. Eye View

We have already seen that *Jack* can show the view from any object, in particular, a figure's eye. Besides the normal perspective view, a simplified retinal projection window may be drawn. Objects in front of the eye are mapped into a (radius, angle) polar plot. When features such as foveal or peripheral areas are drawn in the retinal window, the relative visibility of scene features may be assessed. Much of the useful effort in this analysis mode was accomplished by a collaboration between Cary Phillips of our lab, Aries Arditi of The Lighthouse in New York, and Mike Prevost of the NASA Ames A3I project.

15.2.6.3. Translucent View Cones

In addition to the retinal window, translucent view "cones" may be displayed from the eyes of a human figure. With the apex at the eye lens center, the shape of the cones follows any desired polygonal path, e.g. foveal area. By aiming the eyes with an interactive goal, the view cones follow the point of interest, converging or diverging as needed (subject to eye "joint" limits). Since the cones are translucent, workplace objects show though, giving the user a good impression of what can and cannot be seen by the subject.

15.2.6.4. Torque Load and Comfort during Reach

Since the strength guided motion computes the instantaneous (static) joint torques in the current (changing) body posture, this information is available for display. During such actions, moving bar charts can show the level of comfort, physical work, or fatigue.

15.2.6.5. Real-Time Object–Object Collision Detection

In collaboration with the GRASP (General Robotics and Active Sensory Perception) Lab in our department, a real-time collision detection facility was added to *Jack*. For efficiency, only a pair of selected convex objects are checked in real-time. The general problem is very costly (time-consuming) in complex, changing environments. Given that the user is normally in control of the simulated figure's motion, the limitation to checking, say, a lower arm against another object is useful but clearly sub-optimal. As we have mentioned, it is used to accomplish the hand grip in *Jack*.

15.2.6.6. Interactive Body Sizing under Active Constraints

We have already mentioned in Section 15.2.2.4 that changes to bodies made in *SASS* would maintain (as well as possible) any active constraints. Thus testing workplace reaches over any population range is nearly trivial: e.g. constrain the feet or lower body, set the reach goal for the desired end-effector, and alter the percentile field of the appropriate *SASS* spreadsheet display. In another situation, suppose the eye is constrained to the design eye point of a cockpit, the hands and feet are positioned to appropriate goals, and the shoulders and hips are restrained by point goals representing a suitable restraint system. Then running through the percentiles with reach goals for the hands, feet, and hips will show how well or how poorly the population can carry out that task.

15.2.6.7. Hooks to AI-based Simulation System and Knowledge Base

The ultimate analysis tool is a simulation which executes some task and drives the human figure with a set of goals and timings. We are actively working in this area. Jeff Esakov is building a system, called *YAPS*, which is basically an object-oriented discrete event simulator running over a Knowledge Base (Esakov et al. 1989; Esakov and Badler, 1991). Jugal Kalita has constructed verb semantics describing generic methods for achieving certain goals (Kalita and Badler 1990). Presently the lexicon of executable tasks includes computational definitions for *open, close, push, pull, put, place, slide, reach*, and *look-at*, as well as a few spatial prepositions and adverbial modifiers. A temporal planner organizes the goals in a reasonable order (Badler et al. 1988; Esakov and Badler 1991). A human performance rate predictor based on Fitts' Law (if appropriate) (Fitts 1954) is used to postulate reasonable task durations for reach and viewing actions (Esakov et al. 1989). At the highest level, simple natural language task commands are accepted and animated (Kalita and Badler 1990; Badler et al. 1990). The *YAPS* system supports some simple task planning and task interruption capabilities.

The *YAPS* simulation and Knowledge Base are written in CommonLisp. *YAPS* drives *Jack* figures through the UNIX socket interface. At NASA Ames, the *MIDAS* simulator performs a similar function, communicating parameters over the network and driving the *Jack* figure as a helicopter pilot mannequin.

15.2.7. Rendering

Besides the hardware rendering available for polyhedral models on the Iris workstation, the *Jack* system includes a sophisticated ray-tracer written by Welton Becket. Its capabilities include anti-aliasing, textures, specularity, translucency, reflections, shadows, multiple light sources, material properties, and chromatic aberrations. It successfully rendered hundreds of images for a movie containing over 45 000 polygons at an average rate of about four images per 45 minutes an Iris 4D/240.

15.2.8. External Interfaces

Jack can obtain geometric information from several commercial systems, including Wavefront Technologies, SDRC I-DEAS, MultiGen, and BRL-CAD. This list grows as sponsors require *Jack* to handle data from diverse CAD systems.

15.3. Work in Progress

Jack is an evolving system with continual enhancements motivated by our desire to achieve certain graphic and animation goals as well as provide ever more powerful and usable human performance understanding and modeling. The following sections outline some of the enhancements in progress or scheduled for the near future.

15.3.1. Additional Strength Data

The present strength data for the arms must be augmented by similar data for the upper torso. Hand (grip) strength would also be a useful addition. The strength data we use is for isometric exertion and does not necessarily reflect proper values for strength during motion. There are many issues surrounding the validity of strength data. We prefer that the user supply an acceptable strength model simply because ours is probably not very good. *SASS*, however, makes changing the strength prediction functions or adding new tabular empirical data rather straightforward.

15.3.2. Fatigue Model

During strength guided motion, *Jack* can compute a measure of the work or energy expenditure per unit time. This should be expressible as a muscle group load and hence generate some specific strength loss due to fatigue. Phil Lee is incorporating a reasonable fatigue model into *Jack* so that strength changes can dynamically affect movement (or the mere holding) of a weight.

15.3.3. General Force Trajectory

The limits to strength guided motion must be relaxed. We have already extended the algorithm to 3D motions. Somewhat more important is having a satisfactory strength model. The ability of *SASS* to interpolate strength values is critical to success here.

15.3.4. Dynamics Rate-Control during Strength Reach

Strength guided motion uses inverse kinematics to do the incremental positioning of the end-effector. A more accurate model is being developed by Phil Lee and Wallace Ching that uses a dynamics approach to insure that end-effector motion does not exceed realistic and consistent accelerations. There will be interesting interactions between the concurrent needs to reach the goal, sustain coherent muscle group [strength] activity, monitor comfort levels, and manage fatigue.

15.3.5. Walk Procedure

The motions of the figure often appear stilted as it is unable to locomote other than by floating or sliding. We have implemented a walk procedure based on Bruderlin and Calvert's (1989) model. A reach task involving the entire body will then use locomotion to bring the end-effector within a suitable distance of the goal. (A definition of "suitable" must be determined.) Concomitant problems include path planning and collision avoidance if obstacles are present. A preliminary *Jack*-compatible spatial path planner based on the algorithm by Lozano-Perez and Wesley (1979) is available for experiments.

15.3.6. Dependent Joints

The original *Peabody* and *psurf* structure, while robust, must be enhanced to permit groups of joints to work together as a unit. The idea is that these joint dependencies provide for more natural motion and easier control. The 17 segment spine and torso is a good example of the kind of dependency that is required. Other examples include clavicle motion as a function of shoulder position (Otani 1989; Badler et al. 1989) and head motion dictated by eye direction (Sparks 1989). Jianmin Zhao and Cary Phillips are working out the changes in *Jack* needed to incorporate such structures. Incorporating the full spine into the reach without affecting execution performance has just been demonstrated.

Related problems include complex shoulder joint limits based on the shoulder position rather than just the geometrically required three [independent] degrees of freedom. This assumes even greater importance when dealing with the computation of joint limits based on clothing. It may not be possible to pre-compute the limits; rather, they may have to be detected as a certain tolerable level of intersection (collision) between adjacent segments and their attached geometry. In this case, joint motion is determined by segment compressability. (The converse problem is somewhat easier; e.g. see (Gourret et al. 1989; Magnenat-Thalmann and Thalmann 1990; Chadwick et al. 1989) for segment deformation given joint angles. The finite element approach may be viable for our version of the problem as well.)

15.3.7. Anthropometry Updates

We are presently redesigning *SASS*. Changes include a corrected implementation of segment percentiles within a population, more appropriate segment scaling relative to the given population, surface landmark to segment dimension relationships, stature adjustments when certain individual segment dimensions are changed, and global (cross-attribute) effects such as mass changes when sizes are changed.

Additional populations are also being examined for conversion into *SASS* format, especially the recent US Army soldier data.

An attractive idea for training applications is to read the user's own anthropometry from a login file, and use his or her body description as the default scaling for the *Jack* figure. Tasks being performed would then be sympathetic to the user's own capabilities.

15.3.8. Clothing Experiments

We are trying some simplified methods for defining clothing. One "trick" is to represent the garment as an articulated figure with "joints" at various seams. The garment is then brought to the proper shape by applying multiple simultaneous goals to bring the various parts into proper alignment or contact (e.g. [point] buttons to [point] button holes, zippers to line goals, etc.). Additional goals position the garment on the figure by identifying major points of contact (e.g. shoulders, front of chest, elbow, etc.).

15.3.9. Three-Dimensional Input Devices and Virtual Environments

In a previous system we experimented with direct 3D input through a Polhemus 6-degree of freedom digitizer (Badler et al. 1987). We were limited by the rather slow speed of the inverse kinematics algorithm then available to us. Moreover, that algorithm suffered by providing a solution that was too local. With the new inverse kinematics procedure in *Jack* it should be easy to connect a spatial input device to drag the selected end-effector around in direct mimicry of the user's hand motion.

15.3.10. Passive Position Sensing

Since the early 1970s we have tried to understand how a computer could be programmed to observe human activity and describe or at least mimic the motions in a computer graphics model (Badler 1975; O'Rourke and Badler 1980). The ability to control a realistically shaped and behaved human figure with *Jack* opens the possibility of real-time monitoring activities. The inverse kinematics procedures may be robust enough to work from a few two-dimensional (e.g. image plane) joint positions and known anthropometric dimensions to establish 3D locations for all the joints. Thus, given a [real] person performing some task in a remote location and passive monitoring from one or more video cameras, a simulated figure of the same size could be fit in *real-time* to the acquired positions. This real-time automated modeling will permit the indirect and low cost monitoring of EVA or other novel work activities where physical mock-ups are currently the only option. The computer models can be used for task planning, safety testing, task load predictions, and — by making measurements on the simulated model — indirect assessment of physiological states such as fatigue or comfort without direct sensing or verbal communication.

15.3.11. High Level Task Control

Controlling human motion tasks specified by language commands or instructions is a long-term goal of our research. Analysis of the form and content of instructions has begun in collaboration with Computer and Information Science department faculty members Bonnie Webber and Mark Steedman (Badler et al. 1990).

15.3.12. Task Planner

One of the principal issues involved in understanding and executing instructions is the form of the action planner. Classical planning strategies do not seem to suffice for human motion because people are highly redundant mechanisms and use flexible, incremental, and interruptable plan execution. A reactive and incremental planning scheme for executing conditional and temporal instructions is being investigated by Moon Jung. One novel feature is "posture planning" which eases the computational burden at the geometry level while providing high-level "advice" on suitable body positioning strategies.

15.3.13. Task Performance Time Database

The Fitts' Law formulation for task time performance is adequate for very simple reach and view tasks. For more generality the strength model can be referenced to obtain estimates of minimum trajectory times. This approach, however, is limited to knowing the strength model and, moreover, does not adequately compute timings for more complex task units (e.g. inserting a bolt into a hole). Libby Levison is examining several task time databases to see how they might be incorporated into the planner. These databases will be extremely useful for task analyses where nominal time–motion studies for such tasks have been extensively measured.

15.3.14. Language and Speech Interfaces

Once the natural language instructions can be used to generate a plan for execution by the simulated figure in *Jack*, a next step is to try speech input for the same set of understood commands. This work is presently underway in collaboration with Siemens Corporate Research in Munich using their speech understanding system.

15.4. Conclusion

Even though *Jack* is under continual development, it has nonetheless already proved to be a substantial computational tool in analyzing human abilities in physical workplaces. It is being applied to actual problems involving space vehicle inhabitants, helicopter pilots, maintenance technicians, foot soldiers, and tractor drivers. This broad range of applications is precisely the target we intended to reach. The general capabilities embedded in *Jack* attempt to mirror certain aspects of human performance, rather than the specific requirements of the corresponding workplace. There is only one "version" of *Jack*; though its features are sometimes motivated by a particular application, the solutions are shared by all who support the research effort. Of course, there are some general problems we wanted to solve that have contributed much to *Jack* from our own research perspective. We have enough on this queue to keep us busy for a long time.

Acknowledgements

This research is partially supported by Lockheed Engineering and Management Services (NASA Johnson Space Center), NASA Ames Grant NAG-2-426, NASA Goddard through University of Iowa UICR, FMC Corporation, Martin-Marietta Denver Aerospace, Deere and Company, Siemens Research, NSF CISE Grant CDA88-22719, and ARO Grant DAAL03-89-C-0031 including participation by the US Army Human Engineering Laboratory and the US Army Natick Laboratory.

References

Alameldin T, Sobh T, Badler N (1990) An adaptive and efficient system for computing the 3-D reachable workspace, *Proc. IEEE International Conf. on Systems Engineering*, Pittsburgh, PA, IEEE Computer Society Press, Los Alamitos, CA, pp.503-506.

Armstrong W, Green M, Lake R (1987) Near-real-time control of human figure models, *IEEE Computer Graphics and Applications*, Vol. 7, No. 6, pp.52-61.

Badler N (1975) *Temporal scene analysis: Conceptual descriptions of object movements.* PhD dissertation, Department of Computer Science, University of Toronto, 1975. University of Pennsylvania, Computer and Information Science, Technical Report MS-CIS-76-4.

Badler N, Kushner S, Kalita J (1988) *Constraint-based temporal planning*, Technical Report, Dept. of Computer and Information Science, Univ. of Pennsylvania, Philadelphia, PA.

Badler N, Lee P, Phillips C, Otani E (1989) The *Jack* interactive human model, *Concurrent Engineering of Mechanical Systems*, Vol. 1, *Proc. First Annual Symposium on Mechanical Design in a Concurrent Engineering Environment*, University of Iowa, Iowa City, IA, pp.179-198.

Badler N, Manoochehri K, Walters G (1987) Articulated figure positioning by multiple constraints, *IEEE Computer Graphics and Applications*, Vol. 7, No. 6, pp.28-38.

Badler N, Webber B, Kalita J, Esakov J (1990) Animation from instructions, in: Badler N, Barsky B, Zeltzer D (eds.) *Making Them Move: Mechanics, Control, and Animation of Articulated Figures*, Morgan-Kaufmann, San Mateo, CA, pp.51-93.

Blanchard C, Burgess S, Harvill Y, Lanier J, Lasko A, Oberman M, Teitel M (1990) Reality built for two: A virtual reality tool, *Proc. SIGGRAPH '90, Computer Graphics* Vol. 24, No. 2, pp.35-36.

Bruderlin A, Calvert T (1989) Goal-directed, dynamic animation of human walking, *Proc. SIGGRAPH '89, Computer Graphics* Vol. 23, No. 3, pp.233-242.

Chadwick J, Haumann D, Parent R (1989) Layered construction for deformable animated characters, *Proc. SIGGRAPH '89, Computer Graphics*, Vol. 23, No. 3, pp.243-252.

Easterly J (1990) Crew-Chief: A model of a maintenance technician, AFHRL Technical Paper 90-19.

Esakov J, Badler N. (1991) An Architecture for Human Task Animation Control, in: P.A. Fishwick, R.S. Modjeski (eds.) *Knowledge-Based Simulation: Methodology and Applications.*, Springer Verlag, New York, pp.162-199.

Esakov J, Badler N, Jung M (1989) An investigation of language input and performance timing for task animation, *Proc. Graphics Interface '89*, Waterloo, Canada, pp.86-93.

Fitts P (1954) The information capacity of the human motor system in controlling the amplitude of movement, *Journal of Experimental Psychology*, Vol. 47, pp.:381-391.

Fuchs H, Kedem Z, Uselton S (1977) Optimal surface reconstruction from planar contours, *Comm. of the ACM*, Vol. 20, No. 10, pp.693-702.

Gourret J-P, Magnenat-Thalmann N, Thalmann D (1989). Simulation of object and human skin deformations in a grasping task, *Proc. SIGGRAPH '89, Computer Graphics*, Vol. 23, No. 3, pp.21-30.

Grosso M, Quach R, Badler N (1989) Anthropometry for computer animated human figures, in: Magnenat-Thalmann N, Thalmann D (eds.) *State-of-the Art in Computer Animation*, Springer-Verlag, Tokyo, pp.83-96.

Grosso M, Quach R, Otani E, Zhao J, Wei S, Ho P-H, Lu J, Badler N (1989) *Anthropometry for computer graphics human figures*, Technical Report, MS-CIS-89-71, Dept. of Computer and Information Science, University of Pennsylvania, Philadelphia, PA.

Iberall T (1987) The nature of human prehension: Three dextrous hands in one, *IEEE Conference on Robotics and Automation*, pp.396-401.

Kalita J, Badler N (1990) A Semantic analysis of a Class of Action Verbs Based on Physical Primitives, *Proc. 12th Annual Meeting of the Cognitive Science Society*, Lawrence Erlbaum Associates, Hillsdale, NJ, 1990, pp.412-419.

Kalita, J.K., and N.I. Badler, A Semantic Analysis of

Lee P, Wei S, Zhao J, Badler N (1990) Strength guided motion, *Proc. SIGGRAPH '90, Computer Graphics*, Vol. 24, No. 4, pp.253-262.

Lozano-Perez T, Wesley M (1979) An algorithm for planning collision-free paths among polyhedral obstacles, *Comm. of the ACM*, Vol. 22, No. 10, pp.560-570.

Magnenat-Thalmann N, Thalmann D (1990) Human body deformations using joint-dependent local operators and finite-element theory, in: Badler N, Barsky B, Zeltzer D (eds.) *Making Them Move: Mechanics, Control, and Animation of Articulated Figures*, Morgan-Kaufmann, San Mateo, CA, pp.243-262.

Monheit G, Badler N (1991) A kinematic model of the human spine and torso, *IEEE Computer Graphics and Applications*, Vol. 11, No. 2.

O'Rourke J, Badler N (1980) Model-based image analysis of human motion using constraint propagation, *IEEE Trans. PAMI*, Vol. 2, No. 6, pp.522-536.

Otani E (1989) *Software tools for dynamic and kinematic modeling of human motion*, Master's thesis, Department of Mechanical Engineering, University of Pennsylvania, Technical Report, MS-CIS-89-43, Philadelphia, PA.

Pelachaud C, Badler N, Steedman M (1991) Issues in facial animation, in: Magnenat Thalmann N, Thalmann D (eds.): *Computer Animation '91*, Springer-Verlag, Tokyo, pp.13-28.

Phillips C, Badler N (1988) Jack: A toolkit for manipulating articulated figures, *ACM/SIGGRAPH Symposium on User Interface Software*, Banff, Canada, pp.221-229.

Phillips C, Badler, N. (1991) *Interactive behaviors for bipedal articulated figures*, Technical Report MS-CIS-91-03, Department of Computer and Information Science, University of Pennsylvania, Philadelphia, PA.

Phillips C, Zhao J, Badler N (1990) Interactive real-time articulated figure manipulation using multiple kinematic constraints, *Proc. SIGGRAPH '90, Computer Graphics* Vol. 24, No. 2, pp.245-250.

Platt S (1985) *A structural model of the human face*, PhD Dissertation, Department of Computer and Information Science, University of Pennsylvania.

Sparks D (1989) The neural control of orienting eye and head movements, *Proc. of the Dahlem Conference on Motor Control*, Berlin.

Steketee S, Badler N (1985) Parametric keyframe interpolation incorporating kinetic adjustment and phrasing control, *Proc. SIGGRAPH '85, Computer Graphics* Vol. 19, No. 3, pp.255-262.

Wei S (1990) *Human strength database and multidimensional data display*, PhD Dissertation, Department of Computer and Information Science, University of Pennsylvania, Philadelphia, PA.

Wilhelms J (1987) Using dynamic analysis for realistic animation of articulated bodies, *IEEE Computer Graphics and Applications*, Vol. 7, No. 6, pp.12-27.

Zhao J, Badler N (1989) *Real time inverse kinematics with joint limits and spatial constraints*, Technical Report MS-CIS-89-09, Department of Computer and Information Science, University of Pennsylvania, Philadelphia, PA.

16

Techniques for Facial Animation

Frederic I. Parke
New York Institute of Technology

16.1. Introduction

In recent years there has been considerable interest in computer based 3D character animation. A part of this is a renewed interest in the development of facial animation techniques. The initial efforts to represent and animate faces using computers go back almost 20 years (Chernoff 1971; Parke 1972; Gillenson 1974).

Faces are interesting and challenging because of our everyday familiarity with faces and facial expression as a major channel of communication between people. In our interactions with people, we rely heavily on our evaluation of facial expressions. We are able to detect very subtle differences and changes in facial expression. Understanding facial expression is one of the earliest skills we learn as children. We can easily recognize many specific faces from a vast universe of essentially similar faces.

Facial representation and facial animation share the same set of issues as other representation and animation activities; modeling, motion control, and image rendering. A major difference for faces is our criteria for judging the success of our efforts. We tend to be very critical of attempts at facial representation and animation. The quest for realism runs headlong into the fact that a "realistic" face which is just a little wrong, receives strong critical reaction from most viewers.

A few applications for facial animation, such as visualizing the results of planned surgery, require realistic physically correct facial models. However, many animation applications only require that the faces be believable in a given story telling context and that the audience establish an emotional relationship with the characters portrayed. Caricatures and purposeful facial exaggeration (Brennan 1982) are often more acceptable than attempts at realism.

Facial modeling is concerned with developing geometric descriptions or procedures for representing faces. Facial modeling addresses the issues of facial conformation, realism, likeness, expressiveness, and animatability. Facial motion control is concerned with the techniques and algorithms for specifying and controlling facial motions into and between expressions and conformations. Facial image sequences depend on the use of high quality image rendering techniques. Fortunately a rich and diverse body of rendering techniques exists. In our discussions here, we assume that the rendering software needed to create the desired images is readily available.

16.2. Facial Modeling

The detailed anatomy of the head and face is a complex assembly of bones, cartilage, muscles, nerves, blood vessels, glands, fatty tissue, connective tissue, skin, and hair (Fried 1976; Warfel 1973; Friedman 1950). To date, no facial animation models which represent this complete detailed anatomy have been reported.

In most representations, the visible surfaces of the face are modeled as networks of connected polygons as is shown in Figure 16.1 (see color section). The goal of the various animation techniques is to control the polygon vertices, over time, such that the rendered facial surfaces have the desired shapes in each frame of the animated sequence. A few implementations such as Waite (1989) and Nahas et al. (1988) have used curved surface modeling techniques rather than polygon modeling techniques. However, the goal of specifying and controlling surface shape remains the same.

There is a strong temptation to model the face with left/right symmetry. This simplifies both the surface definition and control aspects of facial models. However, faces are not really symmetric. Structural and expression asymmetries are an important characteristic of real faces. Much facial "personality" is a result of these asymmetries.

16.2.1. Data Sources

All face models rely on 3D surface data. This data may be obtained by measuring the surfaces of real faces or facial sculptures or by interactively "sculpting" the desired data. Surface measurement can be done using 3D digitizers, photogrammetric techniques, or laser scanning techniques.

The digitizing approach requires physically positioning a 3D "locator" at each surface point to be measured. This process requires a significant amount of time. Since real faces tend to move and change shape over time, the digitizer method works best with face sculptures which do not change shape during the measuring process. The digitizer used may be based on mechanical, acoustic, or electromagnetic properties. The Polhemus electromagnetically based digitizer is probably the most widely used hardware for this purpose.

Photogrammetric and laser scanning techniques allow direct digitization of real faces. The photogrammetric approach "freezes" facial expressions photographically. Multiple photographs of the face are taken simultaneously from different points of view. From these multiple 2D views, the desired 3D data points can be computed (Parke 1974).

Laser scanning techniques, such as those developed by Cyberware, can digitize both sculptures and real faces. This process produces a very large regular mesh of data values in a cylindrical coordinate system. Post processing of this data is often required to extract data matching the facial topology used by the model. This processing may include data "thinning", filtering, and interpolation. In some scanning systems, the process may also capture surface color information in addition to 3D surface position data.

Interactive surface editors provide an alternative to measuring faces. This approach allows the modeler to create and modify surfaces by interactively manipulating vertex positions or control points. This is analogous to "sculpting" the desired surfaces. Stereo display techniques, which present slightly different views to each eye, may be used for true 3D perception of the surface shapes as they are being created or modified.

16.2.2. Topology Issues

What underlying geometric structure should be used for the facial surface? The possibilities include a regular polygonal mesh, an arbitrary polygon network, a single bi-cubic surface, an assemblage of bi-cubic surfaces, or a hybrid of these. Whichever structure is used, it must allow surface shape changes as needed for the various face conformations and expressions.

Providing useful surface shape control is crucial to successful facial animation. Polygonal networks and meshes require direct control of all vertex positions. Each vertex position must be explicitly specified. Bi-cubic surface control (Bartels et al. 1987) is more indirect, requiring only that surface control points be explicitly specified.

The density of surface defining information should be distributed corresponding to surface curvature. Areas of high surface curvature need a high density of defining information, areas of lower curvature need less defining information. In general, higher density is needed in those areas which require subtle surface control such as the eyes and the mouth; the major expressive areas of the face.

16.2.3. Complete Heads

Many face models only deal with the expressive facial "mask" as shown in Figures 16.5 and 16.6 (see color section). The face should be viewed as an integrated part of a complete head. A complete model includes the back of the head, the neck, hair, facial hair, ears, eyeballs, and the inside of the mouth including the teeth, gums, and tongue. The ability to specify the conformations of the ears, teeth, hair, and hair style is important in representing faces of specific people or characters.

Ears are very individual and are important in capturing and representing likeness. They are also difficult to model. Ears have complex surfaces requiring a large number of polygons or complex bi-cubic surfaces with many control points.

Hair has been and continues to be a challenge to the face modeler. Polygon or bi-cubic surfaces are not very good representations for hair. The facial images in Figures 16.2, 16.3, and 16.4 (see color section) represent hair with a large number of polygons and a very large number of vectors. For these images, the hair polygons and vectors were computed procedurally using random perturbation of the polygons and vectors. Particle system techniques (Reeves 1983) have been used with limited success. Ideally, the hair should behave dynamically in response to head and air motions.

Detailed, dynamic eyes are very important to successful expression animation. Eye tracking motions and even pupil dilation changes add realism to the animation. Details of iris coloration and light reflections from the eyeballs add "life" to the face.

Integrating the face, head and neck into the rest of the body is an important aspect of 3D character animation. In reality, the head is connected with the rest of the body through the complex muscle and bone structures of the neck. The dynamics of head and neck motions are discussed in Peterson and Richmond (1988).

16.3. Animation Control

For any animation model, the question of control interfaces or "control handles" for the animator is very important. The goal for faces is to provide a wide range of natural and intuitive expression and conformation control.

The development of facial animation may be viewed as two independent activities; the development of control parameterizations and the development of implementation techniques. The control mechanisms that have been used in facial animation are reviewed below. These control schemes may be viewed as control parameterizations. Animation then becomes the process of specifying and controlling parameter set values as functions of time.

From the animators point of view, the interesting questions are: (1) what are the parameters, (2) are the parameters adequate and appropriate, and (3) how are these parameters manipulated. The animator is not usually interested in the implementation algorithms or implementation details but only in the animation functionality provided.

From the implementors point of view the interesting questions are: (1) what parameters should be provided, (2) what user interface to the the parameters should be provided, and (3) what techniques should be used to actually implement the facial animation system.

Most of the work in recent years has concentrated on the latter of these, on specific implementation techniques. Relatively little work has been done on establishing optimal control functionality and control interfaces. The functionality provided by each implementation has been primarily influenced by the characteristics of the particular implementation technique rather than attempting to fulfil a well understood set of functionality and interface goals. Questions concerning useful, optimal, and "complete" control parameterizations remain mostly unanswered. The development of complete low level parameterizations will also enable the development of higher levels of control abstraction.

There are two major categories of control parameters; expression parameters and conformation parameters. The most often addressed of these is concerned with changes of facial expression. Conformation control is used to specify a particular individual face from the universe of possible faces. In the ideal case these two categories of control are orthogonal. Conformation should be independent of expression and expression independent of conformation.

16.4. Review of Facial Animation Techniques

16.4.1. Key Expression Interpolation

Among the earliest and still most widely used schemes for implementing and controlling facial animation is the use of key expression poses and interpolation. Parke (1972) first demonstrated the use of this approach to produce viable facial animation. The basic idea and the control parameterization are very simple; and also limited. The idea is to collect, by some means, geometric data describing the face in at least two different expression poses. Then a single control parameter, an interpolation coefficient, is used as a function of time to change the face from one expression into the other. Figure 16.5 (see color section) illustrates this approach. Two key expression poses are shown on the left and the right of the image. The middle image is an interpolation of the key poses.

This approach can be expanded in several ways. More than two expression poses may be used. If for example, four expressions are available then two interpolation coefficients or parameters may be used to generate an expression which is a bi-linear blend of the four key poses. If eight key expressions are available then three interpolation parameters may be used to generate a tri-linear expression blend. Four interpolation parameters and 16 key expressions allow blending in a four-dimensional interpolation space. Higher dimensionalities are also possible but are probably not useful to the animator.

Another way of exploiting multiple expression poses is to allow pair-wise selection of the key poses to be interpolated. This involves three parameters; the starting pose, the ending pose, and the interpolation value.

Again, if many expression poses are available, they could be selected four at a time and used as the basis for bi-linear expression blending. Or even selected eight at a time as the basis for tri-linear blending. The possible variations on these schemes seem quite open ended. However, their usefulness is not established.

These approaches are certainly not limited to linear interpolation. The vast array of parametric curve, surface, and volume techniques (Bartles et al. 1987) can also be used as the basis for generating expression blends of key poses. The key pose vertices would provide the geometric control points required by these techniques.

A useful extension to the expression pose interpolation approach is to subdivide the face into a number of regions. Independent interpolation parameters are then used for each region. This extends the control parameter space in an intuitive way. An example of this approach, first presented by Kleiser (1989), is to divide the face into an upper region and a lower region. The upper region is used primarily for emotional expression while the lower region is used primarily for speech expression. This allows some orthogonality between emotion and speech control. Special care must be exercised along the boundaries between the interpolation regions.

It should be pointed out that the use of key poses and interpolation is not limited just to expression animation. If poses for several different individuals are used, then animation of the face from one individual conformation into another is possible. Figure 16.6 (see color section) illustrates bi-linear interpolation of four different individual faces. The central face is a blend of the four corner faces.

The key pose interpolation schemes outlined above have limitations. First, the range of expression control is directly related to the number and disparity of expression poses available. An expression which falls outside the bounds of the key pose set is unattainable except perhaps by extrapolation, an inherently risky approach. In all but the simplest cases, providing intuitive, orthogonal control parameters to the animator is difficult. Also, each of the key poses requires an explicit geometric data collection or generation effort. For a large set of poses, this is a daunting task. If different individual faces, as well as various expression poses, are to be included then the number of key pose data sets required may become very large.

16.4.2. Ad-Hoc Parameterizations

Motivated by the difficulties associated with key pose interpolation, Parke (1974, 1982) developed ad-hoc parameterized models. The desire was to create an encapsulated model which would generate a very wide range of faces based on a limited set of input parameter values. The goal was a model which allowed control of both facial expression and facial conformation. As stated above, the challenge is to determine a "good" set of control parameters and then to implement a model that uses these parameters to generate the desired range of faces. The ideal model would allow any possible face with any possible expressions to be specified by selecting the appropriate parameter value set. The ad-hoc models created to date are certainly less than ideal, but do allow a wide range of expressions for a fairly wide range of facial conformations. Example faces generated with this approach are shown in Figures 16.2, 16.3, and 16.4 (see color section).

The ad-hoc models have developed with little theoretical basis and without careful attention to facial anatomy. They have been experimentally derived to represent the visible surface features of the face based on observation and a general knowledge of the underlying structures. For the ad-hoc models developed to date, the parameter sets are fairly primitive and low level. The approach has been to apply operations such as rotation, scaling, positional offsets, and interpolation in combination to regions of the face. The control parameters provided include:

Expression	Conformation
eyelid opening	jaw width
eyebrow arch	forehead shape
eyebrow separation	nose length and width
jaw rotation	cheek shape
mouth width	chin shape
mouth expression	neck shape
upper lip position	eye size and separation
mouth corner position	face region proportions
eyes "look at"	overall face proportions

About ten expression parameters allow the animator to specify and control a wide range of facial expression. As implemented, about 20 parameters are used to control a limited range of facial conformation. Conformation parameterization is more open ended and less understood than expression parameterization.

16.4.3. Muscle Action Models

Several models have been developed which are based on simplified models of facial bone structure, muscles, connective tissue, and skin. These models provide the ability to manipulate facial expression based primarily on simulating the characteristics of the facial muscles.

Platt and Badler (1981) developed a partial face model in which the vertices of the face surface (the skin) were interconnected elastically and also connected to the underlying bone structures by muscles modeled with elastic properties and contraction forces. The face expression was manipulated by applying forces to the elastically connected skin mesh via the underlying muscles. The muscle actions used were patterned after the Facial Action Coding System (FACS) described below. A detailed look at the properties of human skin is presented in Pieper (1989).

16.4.4. The Facial Action Coding System

A widely used scheme for describing facial expressions was developed by Ekman and Friesen (1977). Although not intended for use in computer animation, this descriptive scheme has been used as the basis for expression control in a number of facial animation models. This system describes the most basic facial muscle actions and their effect on facial expression. Ekman developed this system as a means of describing or encoding all possible facial expressions. It includes all muscle actions which can be independently controlled. Examples of the 46 Facial Action Coding units are listed below.

Action Unit	Muscular Basis
Lip Corner Puller	Zygomatic Major
Lower Lip Depressor	Depressor Labii
Lip Tightener	Orbicularis Oris
Chin Raiser	Mentalis
Upper Eyelid Raiser	Levator Palpebrae Superioris
Dimpler	Buccinnator
Wink	Orbicularis Oculi

16.4.5. Additional Muscle Models

Waters (1987, 1989) developed a face model which includes two types of muscles; linear muscles that pull, and sphincter muscles that squeeze. Like Platt and Badler, he used a simple spring and mass model for the skin and muscles. However, his muscles have vector properties which are independent of the underlying bone structure. This makes the muscle model independent of specific face topology. Each muscle has a zone of influence. The influence of a particular muscle is reduced as a function of radial distance from the muscle vector point. Waters also used control parameters based on FACS.

Magnenat-Thalmann et al. (1988) developed another muscle based model in which the control parameters are "Abstract Muscle Action" (AMA) procedures. These AMA procedures are similar to but not the same as the FACS action units. A partial list of the 30 AMA procedures is given below.

Vertical_Jaw Close_Upper_Lip
Right_Eyelid Close_Lower_Lip
Left_Eyelid Compressed_Lip
Right_Zygomatic Move_Right_Eyebrow
Left_Zygomatic Move_Left_Eyebrow

These AMA procedures are not independent, so ordering of the actions is important. This model allows facial control by manipulating the parameter values at the low-level AMA procedures and also at a higher "expressions" level. "Expressions" are formed by controlling AMA procedures in groups. Two types of expression level control were developed; emotions and phonemes.

Extensions to the Waters model have recently been reported (Terzopoulos and Waters 1990). The same FACS based control parameterization is retained but the facial tissues are now modeled using a three layer deformable lattice structure. The three layers correspond to the skin, the subcutaneous fatty tissue, and the muscles. The bottom surface of the muscle layer is attached to the underlying bone.

16.4.6. "Performance" Driven Animation

Several authors have reported facial animation control techniques that rely on information derived from human performances. An early example of this is a technique used in making the short animated film "Tony De Peltrie." Bergeron and Lachapelle (1985) reported on the use of expression mapping or expression slaving. A human face was photographically digitized for a large number of expressions. A technique was then developed to map from the normal human face to the very exaggerated "Tony" caricature face. The human face shape change in the various digitized expressions was mapped to the caricature face. In this way a library of character expressions was developed and used to control the animation.

Parke at NYIT used more traditional rotoscoping techniques in conjunction with a parameterized facial model to animate the "hostess" character in the "3DV" animation. Video of a live action performance was manually analyzed on a frame by frame basis to determine key frame parameter values. These key parameter values were then smoothly interpolated to control the final facial animation to match the spoken soundtrack.

At the SIGGRAPH 88 film show, deGraf and Wahrman demonstrated a real time facial animation system. This system (deGraf 1989) used a high performance graphics workstation to display a parameterized face controlled in real time. The real time control was achieved using special purpose interactive input devices called "waldos." The waldo is an multi-axis electromechanical device that allowed a "puppeteer" to control a number of facial parameters simultaneously in real time.

Recently Terzopoulos and Waters (1990) reported on the development of automated techniques for estimating face muscle contraction parameters from video sequences. They report that these muscle contraction parameters can be used to drive a facial animation model or as input to further analysis such as automatic expression recognition.

Williams (1990) has also reported on techniques to automatically track information from video performances and to use that information to control facial animation. In his system, a number a fiducial points on the surface of a real face are automatically tracked. The locations of these points are used to control a texture map based technique which generates quite realistic facial animation.

16.5. Speech Synchronization

Speech synchronized animation is important in the context of this discussion for two reasons. First, any facial animation system should certainly support speech animation. Second, as we shall see, speech animation control is often a good example of second level parameterized control. Speech animation is often controlled using a higher level parameterization built on top of a lower level basic parameterization. The approach of building more abstract, higher level parameterizations on top of lower level, more detailed parameterizations can be very powerful.

The second level parameterization used in speech animation is usually in terms of speech phonemes. A fairly small number of phonemes are needed to produce convincing speech animation. These required phonemes may be specified in terms of the lower level basic parameters. The high level control is then defined in terms of phoneme transitions which are in turn transformed into the lower level parameter transitions.

It is important that the speech parameterization be orthogonal to the emotional parameters. The same words may be spoken with a number of different emotional overlays. A phrase may be said with joy, with sadness, with anger, or even with no emotion at all.

The second level phoneme parameterization approach has been used by Bergeron and Lachapelle (1985), Lewis and Parke (1987), Hill et al. (1988), Magnenat-Thalmann et al. (1988) and Wyvill (1989). Parke (1974) produced the first speech animation using only basic low level parameters.

Speech animation points to a deficiency in most facial models. Few models include the interior of the mouth. High quality speech animation requires that at least the most visible part of the tongue and the more visible teeth be included. Control of the tongue should be included in the low level parameter set and reflected in the higher level phoneme parameterization.

Efforts to automate the production of speech animation have been reported by Hill et al. (1988) and Lewis and Parke (1987). These two approaches are quite different. The approach reported by Hill was to start with text for the desired speech. This text is then transformed into a phoneme sequence which is in turn used to control speech generation algorithms or hardware and to control a parameterized facial model. The generated synthetic speech and the facial image sequence are merged to form the final speech animation.

In the approach reported by Lewis, the desired speech is spoken and recorded. This recording is then digitally sampled and algorithmically analyzed to produce a timed sequence of pauses and phonemes. This timed sequence is then used to control a facial animation model using a second level phoneme parameterization. The generated facial image sequence is merged with the original spoken soundtrack to form the final speech animation.

16.6. Ideal Facial Animation Models

The ideal model and control interface is one which allows the animator to "easily" specify any individual face with any speech and/or expression sequence. This is in fact the definition of a "universal" parameterization; one which enables all possible individual faces and which enables all possible expressions and expression transitions. No implemented facial model to date is even close to being universal. The FACS system seems the best current basis for expression parameterization, but is probably not ideal from the animators viewpoint. Moreover, none of the existing facial animation systems appears to implement the complete set of FACS action units.

As was outlined above, most of the implementations have focused on expression control. Only the early work by Parke (1974, 1982) included control of conformation as part of the parameterization. The available bases for conformation parameterizations are much more tenuous. Sources of conformation information include anatomy, physical anthropology, and the art disciplines concerned with human representation. Principles from sculpture and portraiture (Hogarth 1981) may be useful and the notions of distortion and exaggeration from conventional animation play a role.

Input and guidance from animators is certainly needed in the development of good, useful models. The focus should probably be on developing powerful control parameter sets that are motivated by the needs of the facial animator and NOT based on the characteristics of a particular implementation scheme.

16.6.1. Quality of Models

Assuming that truly universal models are not possible, at least in the near term, what are the metrics for judging the quality of a facial model? Attributes such as image quality, realism, range of control, parameter complexity, and intuitive natural interfaces immediately come to mind. Certainly an important measure is the range of possible faces and expressions that can be specified. How much of the universe of faces and facial expression is covered by the parameterization? Judgement in this aspect is somewhat application dependent. For example, if the application only requires animation of one specific character then conformation control is not a big issue.

The number and complexity of parameters and intuitive natural interfaces are directly related attributes. The number of parameters provided and the overall complexity of the parameterization should be just sufficient. Unnecessary parameters or parameter complexity should be avoided. Ease of use will be strongly coupled to how natural and intuitive are the parameters and the interface to the parameters.

Subtlety and orthogonality are also measures of parameterization quality. Control of subtle variations in expression and conformation is a measure of model quality. Independence of the parameters is also an issue. A change in one parameter value should have a minimal and predictable interaction with other parameters. Changes in one parameter should not require reworking other parameter values. This is particularly true for the interactions between expression and conformation parameters and between speech and expression parameters.

Another measure of an effective parameterization is its capability to serve as the basis for higher levels of control abstraction. As in the case of speech animation, the construction of control parameters at higher levels of abstraction, built on top of the basic parameterization should be possible.

16.7. Future Directions

A major focus of future efforts should be on the development of powerful models with the effective general parameterizations discussed above. The availability of such models would greatly facilitate development of very capable character animation systems. It would also support the developments outlined below.

16.7.1. Behavior Driven Systems

An area of much current interest in the computer animation community is the development of animation techniques that operate at the behavior level. At this level, the animator/director expresses the desired actions in terms of high level behaviors rather than in detailed low level motions. This work has concentrated on high level activities such as legged locomotion and grasping objects. The underlying detailed control parameters for these activities are very well defined and understood.

The ability of the animator to specify facial actions in terms of high level behaviors is certainly desired. The availability of complete, well defined low level control parameterizations for the face would greatly facilitate the development of behavior level facial animation capabilities.

16.7.2. Story Driven Animation

Takashima et al. (1987) outline the development of a story driven animation system. This is an example of animation control at a very high level of abstraction. Their system was limited to simple childrens stories. However, it did demonstrate a useful framework for such systems. Their framework is based on three major activities; story understanding, stage direction, and action generation. One can envision future story driven systems which would include facial animation. Story understanding and stage direction are largely knowledge based AI activities. Behavior driven facial animation systems as discussed above would be a part of the action generation activity.

16.8. Summary

The basic concepts of facial modeling and motion control have been introduced and number of specific facial animation implementations have been reviewed. Each of these incorporates a surface modeling scheme and an associated animation control scheme. In most cases, the control paradigm for each model is intimately related to its implementation technique. Control for facial animation may be viewed as a parameterization issue. Parameterization development and implementation development may be decoupled. Control research should focus on developing high quality general parameterizations and interfaces while implementation research should focus on developing optimum techniques for generating faces and facial expressions based on these parameterizations.

Developing truly "universal" face models appears very difficult and may not be possible. However work to date indicates that the development of useful, broadly applicable models is feasible and very worthwhile. Development of powerful low level animation models and control schemes will support the development of higher level, more abstract levels of control including behavior driven and story driven animation.

References

Bartels R, Beatty J, Barsky B (1987) *An Introduction to Splines for use in Computer Graphics and Geometric Modeling*, Morgan Kaufmann, Los Altos CA

Bergeron P, Lachapelle P (1985) Techniques for Animating Characters, *SIGGRAPH '85 Tutorial Notes: Advanced Computer Graphics Animation*, No2, pp.61-79

Brennan SE (1982) *Caricature Generator*, M.S. Thesis, MIT, Cambridge MA

Chernoff H, (1971) *The Use of Faces to Represent Points in N- Dimensional Space Graphically*, Technical Report 71, Project NR-042-993, Office of Naval Research

deGraf B, (1989) Notes on Facial Animation, *SIGGRAPH '89 Tutorial Notes: State of the Art in Facial Animation*, No22, pp.10-11

Ekman P, Friesen WV (1977) *Manual for the Facial Action Coding System*, Consulting Psychologists Press, Palo Alto CA

Fried LA (1976) *Anatomy of the Head, Neck, Face, and Jaws*, Lea & Febiger, Philadelphia

Friedman SM (1970) *Visual Anatomy: Volume One, Head and Neck*, Harper & Row, New York

Gillenson, ML (1974) *The Interactive Generation of Facial Images on a CRT Using a Heuristic Strategy*, Ph.D. Dissertation, Ohio State University, Columbus, OH.

Hill DR, Pearce A, Wyvill B (1988) Animating Speech: An Automated Approach Using Speech Synthesis by Rules, *The Visual Computer*, Vol.3, No5, pp.277-289

Hogarth B (1981) *Drawing the Human Head*, Watson-Guptill Publications, New York

Kleiser J, (1989) A Fast, Efficient, Accurate Way to Represent the Human Face, *SIGGRAPH '89 Tutorial Notes: State of the Art in Facial Animation*, No22, pp.37-40

Lewis JP, Parke FI (1987) Automated Lipsynch and Speech Synthesis for Character Animation, *Proc. CHI+CG '87*, Toronto, pp.143- 147

Magnenat-Thalmann N, Primeau E, Thalmann D (1988) Abstract Muscle Action Procedures for Human Face Animation, *The Visual Computer*, Vol.3, No5, pp.290-297.

Nahas M, Huitric H, Saintourens M (1988) Animation of a B-spline Figure, *The Visual Computer*, Vol.3, No5, pp.272-276

Parke FI (1972) Computer Generated Animation of Faces, *Proc. ACM Nat'l Conf.*, 1:451-457 also M.S. Thesis, Technical Report UTEC-Csc-72-120, University of Utah, Salt Lake City, UT.

Parke FI (1974) *A Parametric Model for Human Faces*, Ph.D. Dissertation, Technical Report UTEC-CSc-75-047, University of Utah, Salt Lake City, UT.

Parke FI (1982) Parameterized Models for Facial Animation, *IEEE Computer Graphics and Applications*, Vol.2, No9, pp.61-68

Peterson BW, Richmond FJ (1988) *Control of Head Movement*, Oxford University Press, Oxford

Pieper S (1989) *More than Skin Deep: Physical Modeling of Facial Tissue*, M. S. Thesis, MIT Media Lab, Cambridge MA

Platt SM, Badler NI (1981) Animating Facial Expressions, *Proc. SIGGRAPH '81, Computer Graphics*, Vol.15, No3, pp.245-252

Reeves WT (1983) Particles Systems, *Proc. SIGGRAPH '83, Computer Graphics*, Vol.17, No3, pp.359- 376

Takashima Y, Shimazu H, Tomono M (1987) Story Driven Animation, *Proc. CHI+GI'87* Conf, Toronto, pp.149-153

Terzopoulos D, Waters K (1990) Physically Based Facial Modeling, Analysis, and Animation, *Journal of Visualization and Computer Animation*, Vol.1, No2, pp.73-80

Waite C (1989) *The Facial Action Control Editor, Face: A Parametric Facial Expression Editor for Computer Generated Animation*, M. S. Thesis, MIT, Cambridge MA

Warfel JH (1973) *The Head, Neck and Trunk*, Lea & Febiger, Philadelphia, PA.

Waters K (1987) A Muscle Model for Animating Three-Dimensional Facial Expression, *Proc. SIGGRAPH '87, Computer Graphics*, Vol.21, No3, pp.17-24

Waters K (1989) Modeling 3D Facial Expressions, *SIGGRAPH '89 Tutorial Notes: State of the Art in Facial Animation*, No22, pp.127- 160

Williams L (1990) Performance Driven Facial Animation, *Proc. SIGGRAPH '90, Computer Graphics*, Vol.24, No3, pp.235-242

Wyvill B (1989) Expression Control Using Synthetic Speech, *SIGGRAPH '89 Tutorial Notes: State of the Art in Facial Animation*, No22, pp.163-175.

17

Techniques for Cloth Animation

Nadia Magnenat Thalmann and Ying Yang
MIRALab, University of Geneva

This chapter surveys techniques and methods for the modeling and animation of cloth. Two kinds of approach are discussed: the geometric and the physical. We also compare two important physics-based cloth models, and propose some basic requirements in the design of a cloth animation system. The problems of processing collision and self-collision processing are also discussed.

17.1. A Survey of Cloth Animation Techniques

17.1.1. Introduction

In recent years *Cloth Animation* has become an important subject in computer animation, and many efforts have been made in this field. Cloth animation includes not only the modelling of garment on the human body, but also such things as flags, curtains, tablecloths and stage screens.

Cloth animation has wide practical implications, it can be applied in many areas, such as computer cartoon films, TV advertisements and engineering simulations, but perhaps the most interesting one is in fashion design. Cloth animation will involve the three-dimensional design of the garment, dressing the mannequins and the animated depiction of the dress being worn on the computer screen. It will change the traditional process of garment design in two dimensions, and let people know what their garments will be like and how they will look when they are worn, before they are actually manufactured. A fashion for design tool cloth animation will not only allow the visualization of the fashion being designed, but also reduce the design time and cost. We believe that in near future this kind of modern fashion design tool will come into being.

Cloth animation may be separated into two problems:

(1) cloth animation without considering collisions; shape and deformations due to gravity and wind

(2) cloth collisions with the synthetic actor and collisions of clothes with themselves

Methods of animating cloth are strongly related to techniques for representing soft objects and flexible surfaces.

There are two main kinds of flexible models.

(1) Models based on the geometric properties of the objects.

(2) Models based on the physical properties of the object.

17.1.2. Geometric Methods

In the geometric approach, the shape of flexible objects is entirely described by mathematical functions. It is not very realistic and cannot create complicated deformable clothes, but it is fast. The geometric approach is suitable for representing single pieces of the objects or clothes with simple shapes, which are easily computed, but geometric flexible models have not incorporated concepts of quantities varying with time, and are weak in representing physical properties of cloth such as elasticity, anisotropy, and viscoelasticity. For these reasons, synthetic results are generally somewhat natural.

Weil (1986) presents a solution for the following specific problem: the location of a piece of cloth in three dimensions is fixed at chosen constraint points. The piece of cloth is to be represented with all its folds as it hangs from these constraint points. The cloth is assumed to be rectangular and is represented by a grid. There are two steps in the method.

(1) Approximation to the surface within the convex hull of the constraint points

> This step consists of tracing curves from every constraint point to each of the other constraint points. Weil used the equation of the curve from the two end points and the length of the thread hanging between them. This curve is called the **catenary** and is of the form:

$$y = A + B \cosh \left(\frac{x\text{-}b}{a}\right) \tag{17.1}$$

> As constraint points are connected by tracing catenaries between them, the grid points which lie along the lines between the constraint points can be positioned and triangles are created. This series of triangles can then be used for the approximation of the surface. Each triangle is repeatedly subdivided until all grid points in its interior have been positioned.

(2) Iterative relaxation process
> This relaxation of points is iterated over the surface until the maximum displacement of the points during one pass falls below a predetermined tolerance.

In their work as an interactive garment design system, Hinds and McCartney (1990) represent a trade mannequin with bi-cubic B-spline function, then create a number of three-dimensional surface panels with surfaces offset from the body by varying amounts determined by the designer. Finally they use a geometrically weighted offset method to combine these surface panels together, so that garment is formed. To incorporate such features as drape and fold embellishments into the surface description, they make use of sinusoidal function.

Magnenat-Thalmann et al. (1988) present algorithms for computing hand deformations and animation methods for depicting hands grasping objects. The method used for body deformations in the film *Rendez-vous à Montréal* (Magnenat-Thalmann and Thalmann 1987) is also a geometric approach but does not work for loosely fitting clothes.

Kunii and Gotoda (1990) used singularity theory to provide modeling primitives for garments and their wrinkles.

17.1.3. Physical Methods

Physics-based approaches describe the shape of flexible objects mainly through the use of differential equations. They incorporate the physical properties of the objects, such as mass, stiffness, and damping factor, and use elasticity theory and mechanics to establish the differential equations. This approach is widely applied in various flexible models. These can realistically describe the deformations of the objects and clothes. The results of animation using a physical approach thus tend to be more realistic and satisfactory than geometrically-based methods.

Platt and Barr (1988) show how to use mathematical constraint methods based on physics and optimization theory to create controlled, realistic animation of flexible models. Gourret et al. (1989) develop a finite element method for simulating deformations of objects and the hand of a synthetic character during a grasping task. Moore and Wilhelms (1988) present two collision detection algorithms, describe the modeling of collisions of arbitrary bodies using springs, and present an analytical collision response algorithm for articulated rigid bodies that conserves linear and angular momentum. Terzopoulos et al. (1987) employ elasticity theory to construct differential equations that model the behavior of non-rigid curves, surfaces and solids as a function of time. Lafleur et al. (1991) discuss the problem of detecting collisions of very flexible objects like cloth with almost rigid bodies like human bodies, and use a very thin force field around the obstacle surface to avoid collision. Aono focuses on a physics-based non-rigid object model for the behavior of cloth, and its simulation with given forces and boundary conditions. More deeply and fully than other works, Aono (1990) takes account of inhomogeneity, anisotropy, and viscoelasticity of cloth in his flexible cloth models. These works concentrate mainly on elasticity theory, kinetics and physics. In the work of Aono, we find a good flexible model for cloth animation, which includes intuitive parameters such as Young's modules, Poisson's ratio, and Lame's constant, so it is very easy to control the difference among cloth objects with distinct fibre characteristics. In addition, since the model incorporate inhomogeneity, global and local anisotropy, and viscoelasticity of cloth in a unified framework, they can be applied to a great variety of cloth objects.

From the above description, we can see that the research on soft objects and flexible surfaces are maturing, their algorithms are getting increasingly complex and the results more realistic. Research in this field has wide and deep implications.

17.1.4. Comparison between two Physically-Based Cloth Models

17.1.4.1. Two Models

Two different approaches to the physically-based surface models of clothes may be compared.

In the first model (Terzopoulos et al. 1987), the equation governing the motion of a deformable surface model is based on the variational principle of mechanics in Lagrange's form as follows:$\|(G-G^0)\|\vec{\epsilon}$

$$\frac{\partial}{\partial t}\left(\mu\frac{\partial\vec{r}}{\partial t}\right) + \gamma\frac{\partial\vec{r}}{\partial t} + \frac{\delta\vec{\epsilon}(\vec{r})}{\delta r} = \vec{f}(\vec{r},t) \tag{17.2}$$

where $\vec{r}(\vec{a},t)$ is the position of the particle a at time t, $\vec{a} = [\alpha_1,\alpha_2]$ are the intrinsic material coordinates of the point in a surface Ω, $\mu(\vec{a})$ is the mass density of the body at $\vec{a}$, $\gamma(\vec{a})$ is the damping density and $\vec{f}(\vec{r},t)$ is the net externally applied force, $\vec{\epsilon}(\vec{r})$ is the net instantaneous potential energy of the elastic deformation of the surface.

A reasonable strain energy for a elastic deformable surface in space is:

$$\vec{\epsilon}(\vec{r}) = \int_{\Omega}\|(G-G^0)\|_{\alpha}^2 + \|(B-B^0)\|_{\beta}^2 \, d\alpha_1 d\alpha_2 \tag{17.3}$$

where $\|.\|_{\alpha}$ and $\|.\|_{\beta}$ are weighted matrix norms, and

$$G_{ij}(\vec{r}(\vec{a})) = \frac{\partial\vec{r}}{\partial\alpha_i} \cdot \frac{\partial\vec{r}}{\partial\alpha_j} \qquad\qquad B_{ij}(\vec{r}(\vec{a})) = \vec{n} \cdot \frac{\partial^2\vec{r}}{\partial\alpha_i\partial\alpha_j} \tag{17.4}$$

where $\vec{n} = [n_1,n_2,n_3]$ is the unit surface normal at point $\vec{a}$, G_{ij} is the metric tensor or the first fundamental form, B_{ij} is the curvature tensor or the second fundamental form, while the superscript ^{0} denotes the correspondingly fundamental forms associated with the natural shapes of a surface.

Using a weighted matrix norm to obtain the following simplified deformable energy for a surface:

$$\vec{\epsilon}(\vec{r}) = \int_{\Omega}\sum_{i,j=1}^{2}(\eta_{ij}(G_{ij}-G^0_{ij})^2 + \xi_{ij}(B_{ij} - B^0_{ij})^2) \, d\alpha_1 d\alpha_2 \tag{17.5}$$

where $\eta_{ij}(\vec{a})$ and $\xi_{ij}(\vec{a})$ are weighting functions. η_{ij} controlling the shrinking or growing deformation of the surface , as η_{ij} is increased , the material's resistance to such deformation increases. Similarly ξ_{ij} controls the flattening or curving deformation of the surface, as ξ_{ij} is increased, the material becomes more resistant to such deformation.

With standard finite difference approximation methods and numerical integration over time, we obtain a semi-implicit integration procedure. This procedure therefore evolves the dynamic solution from given initial conditions by solving a time sequence of static equilibrium problems for the instantaneous configurations $\vec{r}_{t+\Delta t}$. The sparse linear system can be solved with the Gauss–Seidel method. An example from the film *Flashback* is shown in Figure 17.1 (see color Section).

The second model (Aono 1990) is based on elasticity theory and the following assumptions.

(1) The cloth is homogeneous, isotropic and linearly elastic in its initial state.

(2) The cloth is in equilibrium at any time under given applied forces, according to D'Alembert's principle.

(3) The cloth is a perfect thin surface, and never expands or contracts along the surface normal.

The equilibrium equation of motion in a Cartesian coordinate system corresponding to assumption 2 becomes

$$\frac{\partial \tau_{ix}}{\partial x} + \frac{\partial \tau_{iy}}{\partial y} + \frac{\partial \tau_{iz}}{\partial z} + f_i = \rho \frac{\partial^2}{\partial t^2} u_i + c_i \frac{\partial}{\partial t} u_i \tag{17.6}$$

where τ_{ij} (i,j = x,y,z) is the stress, f_i is an applied force along the i-axis direction (i =x,y,z), c_i is a damping coefficient, u_i (assuming $u = u_x$, $v = u_y$, $w = u_z$) is a displacement, and ρ is the density of the cloth. By eliminating τ_{ij} from the relations between stress τ_{ij} and strain ε_{ij}, and strain–displacement relation:

$$\varepsilon_{ij} = \frac{1}{2} \left(\frac{\partial u_i}{\partial x_i} + \frac{\partial u_j}{\partial x_i} \right) \tag{17.7}$$

then consider the third assumption:

$$\frac{\partial u}{\partial z} = \frac{\partial v}{\partial z} = \frac{\partial w}{\partial z} = 0 \tag{17.8}$$

the equation of motion for the cloth model is obtained:

$$G \nabla^2_{x,y} u_i + (\lambda + G)\frac{\partial}{\partial x_i} e_{x,y} + f_i = \rho \frac{\partial^2}{\partial t^2} u_i + c_i \frac{\partial}{\partial t} u_i \tag{17.9}$$

where G is the modulus of rigidity, λ is the Lame's constant and

$$\nabla^2_{x,y} = \frac{\partial^2}{\partial x^2} + \frac{\partial^2}{\partial y^2} \tag{17.10}$$

$$e_{x,y} = \frac{\partial u}{\partial x} + \frac{\partial v}{\partial y} \tag{17.11}$$

By discretizing the equation (17.9) with the finite difference method, we obtain formulae allowing the direct calculation of the position of each node on the cloth for the time sequence $0, \delta t, 2\delta t, 3\delta t, ...$

Aono's cloth model can also take account of the inhomogeneity, anisotropy and viscoelasticity of a cloth (see (Aono 1990) for more detail).

17.1.4.2. Comparison

Both models are based on mechanics and elasticity theory and have the potential of producing realistic and natural animation sequences, but they have different advantages and disadvantages.

Terzopoulos' cloth model is based on the variational principle in Lagrange's form, it incorporates the deformation process in a differential equation based on energy conservation, and focuses mainly on the controllability of deformable shapes by parameters derived from differential geometric consideration. It has the following characteristics.

- It is a parametric surface model. Thus it can be conveniently applied in various two dimensional parametrically discretized domains. It has a time parameter so the animation is easily effected.

- Its stiffness and elastic energy are controlled by the metric weighting factor η_{ij} and the curvature weighting factor ξ_{ij}, These parameters are not compatible with those employed in structural analysis, such as Young's modulus, Poisson's ratio, Lame's constant, and the rigidity modulus. As a result, it is not easy to incorporate the behaviors of cloth objects with different fibre characteristics by adjusting η_{ij} and ξ_{ij}.

- The discretized system of the model is implicit and not always stable. It is not always clear how to choose proper parameters to keep the system stable. Procedures for solving the system are time-consuming.

Aono's cloth model is based on the equilibrium equation of elasticity theory and D'Alembert's principle. It has following characteristics:

- It includes physical parameters in material and fibre engineering, such as Young's modulus, Poisson's ratio and Lame's constant, so it is controllable intuitively and easily so as to incorporate the behaviors of cloth objects with different fibre characteristics.

- It can be enhanced by taking account of the anisotropy and viscoelasticity of the cloth material.

- The discretized system of the model is explicit and stable. No energy matrix like that in Terzopoulos' model needs to be calculated in this system. Solving the system is thus faster than in Terzopoulos' model.
- The main limitation of the model is that it has been established in a three dimensional coordinate system and cannot be applied to two-dimensional parametrically domain.

17.1.4.3. Discussion and Suggestion

Through the comparison of Terzopoulos' and Aono's model , we conclude that the latter is a good flexible model for cloth animation, but it is not a parametric surface model, so that its use is limited. It also emerges in this comparison that both models can only be applied to rectangularly discretized domains. Generally, however, clothes consist of various polygons seamed together. Can a new cloth model be defined so as to overcomes this limitation ?

This may be possible by defining the original equilibrium equation of Aono's model over a two dimensional parametric domain and by selecting the nodes of the discretization so as to define the polygonal cloth panel.

17.1.5. Collision Methods

In cloth animation, such as a flag or a skirt flattering in the wind, collisions occur between different parts of the cloth and between the cloth and other objects, such as a human body. The elastic surface model divides the cloth into many small parts, each part constrained by the adjacent parts or external forces. When collision involves a part, extra constraints should be imposed on that part to prevent the cloth from intersecting itself or other objects.

Moore and Wilhelms (1988) introduce collision detection algorithms and collision response algorithms for articulated rigid bodies that conserve linear and angular momentum. As we have already mentioned, Von Herzen et al. (1990) propose numerical algorithms to detect geometric collisions between pairs of time-dependent parametric surfaces.

17.2 Development Strategy for Cloth Animation

17.2.1. Requirements

After investigating the various existing approaches to cloth animation, it seems clear that to achieve realistic results, a cloth animation system should satisfy the following requirements:

(1) There should be a physically based cloth surface model which can accurately take into account the physical properties of cloth, and within which cloth panels can be easily defined and joined together.

(2) There should be a general interactive interface for cloth definition, which can conveniently create and adjust the original geometric cloth surface into various shapes and sizes in two and three dimensions.

(3) There should be a good implementation interface for carrying out the cloth animation and for adjusting the geometric parameters of the cloth, its physical properties, and its physical environment.

The physically based cloth surface model is of prime importance. This should take into account such physical properties as mass, stiffness, damping factors, inhomogeneity, anisotropy and viscoelasticity. The model should be deformable under external forces and its own internal elastic energy, should detect collisions of the cloth with itself and with external objects, and should be able to create constraint forces when collisions occur. With this model, diverse kinds of clothing can be created and animated by defining and adjusting the geometric sizes, the physical properties of cloth and the external forces applied to it.

The geometric parameters of clothes include the edge numbers, sizes, vertices etc. The physical parameters include mass, damping factors, stretch factors, curvature factors, Young's modulus, Poisson's ratio and Lame's constant. The parameters of external physical environment include boundary conditions at the clothes' edges, gravity, the directions, and magnitudes of external forces and the origins of wind forces. The cloth panels should be seamed together to achieve at least C0 continuity, in some seams C1 continuity can be reached where the elastic energy is continuous.

17.2.2. A Stepwise Methodology for Cloth Animation

Cloth animation is a recent area and should be developed in steps of increasing difficulty. Because of the complexity of treating clothing on human bodies in motion under external conditions, we have adopted a four-step approach. For each step, we consider a certain number of factors:

- fixed points or contact points
- external forces (e.g. wind)
- properties of the cloth (integrity, shape, flexibility, elasticity)
- collisions and interactions with obstacles (e.g. human body)
- self-collisions (collision of cloth with itself)

17.2.2.1. First step: flag simulation

This is a very simple case because there are only few contact points (links between the flag and the flagpole). Collisions with the flagpole and self-collisions may be neglected, without sacrificing much realism.

17.2.2.2. Second step: skirt animation

This is much more complex: it should take into account collisions with the legs and the pelvis. We have simulated this kind of motion in our film *Flashback* (scene with Marilyn Monroe on a subway vent).

17.2.2.3. Third step: complex clothes

For clothes like shirts or jackets, the factors to be considered are not so easily enumerated. For a flag, no human body was involved; skirt animation could be considered largely independent of the human body. But for a shirt, the shape is directly dependent on body and motion; the starting shape is modified by a collision detection algorithm taking into account gravity and wind. This requires a generalization of the collision algorithm. This is still an intermediate step, because the cloth shape will be defined in an artificial way. The shirt will be shaped as it was on a mannequin and not folded or on a hanger. In fact, it will be necessary to consider this starting shape as basically conforming to the human body, in order to apply the collision algorithm.

17.2.2.4. Fourth step: general case

Having to start with clothes shaped as if they are on a mannequin is an important restriction on the designer. The objective is a scene where a synthetic actor opens a cupboard, takes out a folded shirt, unfolds it and puts it on. This involves a complete change in the shape of the cloth. Our current methodology of collision processing is not applicable as is. It will be necessary to take into account collisions when the shirt is put on and when it is on the body in motion.

17.3. Flashback: Animation of a Skirt

17.3.1. Introduction

To comply with above requirements, we are developing a new cloth animation system. We have already developed a preliminary version (Lafleur et al. 1991) corresponding to the second step of our stepwise methodology (see 17.2.2). The elastic cloth surface model is based on the one introduced by Terzopoulos et al. (see Section 17.1.4). It has been extended to polygonal regions. A collision detection and processing algorithm has been introduced.

17.3.2. Collision Detection and Constraint Force

In our collision detection and prevention method, a very thin force field around the obstacle surface is created to avoid collisions. The force field is divided into contiguous non-overlapped cells which completely surround the cloth surface or object surface. First, the intersections between the cloth point and the cells are calculated. As soon as a point enters into a cell, a repulsive reaction force is applied to the cloth point. The direction and the magnitude of this force depend on the velocities, the normals and distance between the point and the surface.

The intersection between a cloth point and a triangle facet of cloth or object is calculated by solving the following equation:

$$P = P_0 + N_0 \cdot w + ((P_1 - P_0) + (N_1 - N_0) \cdot w) \cdot u + ((P_2 - P_0) + (N_2 - N_0) \cdot w) \cdot v \quad (17.12)$$

with $0 \le u < 1$ $0 \le v < 1$ $u + v \le 1$ $-w_{max} \le w \le w_{max}$

where P is the cloth point, P_0, P_1, P_2 the three triangle vertices of facet and N_0, N_1, N_2, the normals at vertices respectively, where the parametric variables u, v and w define the cell volume and w_{max} is half the length of the smallest edge of the triangle of vertices P_0, P_1, P_2.

The repulsion is simulated by temporarily adding a spring between P and a point P_t on the triangle surface. From u and v, the position P_t, the velocity V_t and the normal N_t can be computed:

$$P_t = P_0 + (P_1-P_0) \cdot u + (P_2-P_0) \cdot v \tag{17.13}$$

$$V_t = V_0 + (V_1-V_0) \cdot u + (V_2-V_0) \cdot v \tag{17.14}$$

$$N_t = \text{sign}(w) \cdot (N_0 + (N_1-N_0) \cdot u + (N_2-N_0) \cdot v) \tag{17.15}$$

Then the repulsion force is calculated as:

$$F_{repulsion} = K_1 \left\{ \exp \left[K_2 \left(\frac{w_{max} - |w|}{w_{max}} \right) - 1 \right] + K_3 \cdot ((V_t-V) \cdot N_t) \right\} \cdot N_t \tag{17.15}$$

where the first term on the right hand side depends on the distance between the points P and P_t, the second depends on the relative velocity of P relatively to P_t and K_1, K_2 and K_3 are constants.

17.3.3. How was the Skirt Animation Carried out?

First step: cloth creation

To produce a synthetic actor with animated clothes, we consider a decomposition of the actor into sections, each section to be dressed separately. On selected sections, a cloth is positioned, endowed with a rectangular discretized grid. This requires the specification of body curves where the cloth must be fixed (e.g. waist, shoulders). These curves are generated by a modeller, positioned in a section then numbered. For example, for Marilyn's skirt, we use a closed curve composed of equidistant points (waist). The figure is obtained by cutting Marilyn's body at the waist level and filtering the resulting curve to obtain equidistant points. The skirt was a simple conic shape with given length and angle.

Second step: simulation process without collisions and parameter adjustement

Simulation may be performed using standard parameter values. First simulations may produce a rather elastic skirt. Parameters should then be adjusted to correct this. These parameters are geometric and dynamic.

Geometric parameters determine cloth dimensions and shape. Even with as simple a shape as a skirt or a scarf, results are rather realistic.

Dynamic parameters have an impact on motion. Generally, most parameters are fixed during skirt creation and are not modified during the animation. However, nothing prevents us from varying them in order to refine the motion and obtain more realistic results. These dynamic parameters may be classified into two categories: internal and external. Internal parameters drive local forces in the cloth like stretching and curvature. External parameters are forces acting on the cloth such as gravity and wind effect. Table 17.1 presents the parameters involved in a simulation.

1 internal dynamic parameters - horizontal, vertical ranges for the finite differences - inertia mass (acceleration) - damping factor (velocity) - coefficient of resistance to lengthening, controlling stretching between neighboring points - coefficient of resistance coefficients to folding or creasing, controlling curvature
2 external forces - wind characterized by its origin and its force - air viscosity - gravity
3 relaxation parameters - maximal number of iterations in one relaxation - time interval between relaxations - maximal error for stopping a relaxation

Table 17.1. Simulation parameters

The most useful parameters for modifying the appearance of the motion are the density, the damping factor, resistance coefficients, the wind and the time interval.

Simulation is an iterative process which is rather slow. Once all parameters have been adjusted, the animator "leaves the system run". A simulation is a sequence of states over time. The process for finding a new equilibrium between each change of state is called *a relaxation process*. This process is itself iterative. The number of iterations necessary for the convergence depends on all parameters and particularly on the time interval between relaxations. The less elasticity is decreased (coefficient increasing) the more the system is unstable and tends to diverge, which necessitates a reduction of the time interval. The goal is to find the largest interval which avoids divergence and produces a satisfactory animation. It should be noted that the simulation speed depends linearly on the number of points in the skirt.

Third step : collision detection

Once correct values have been found, a new skirt is created based on these values. Then collision detection is enabled. As the algorithm speed depends on the number of obstacle polygons, it is prudent to take into account only polygons which are likely to intersect the cloth. For the example of Marilyn's skirt, only the pelvis and the legs are considered (Figure 17.2).

The algorithm is more efficient when the obstacles are fixed and there is no processing of self-collisions. Thus initial trials consider the skirt as falling on a fixed body.

The collision detection process is almost automatic. The animator has only to provide to the system the list of obstacles and indicate whether they are moving or not. For a walking synthetic actor, moving legs are of course considered as a moving obstacle. A number of parameters have been planned in order to modify the behavior of the collision detection method: shield depth, shield force and damping factor.

Figure 17.2. Skirt animation (only collisions with the pelvis and the legs are considered)

Fourth step : complete simulation

Finally, obstacles may be moved between each state. It should be however noted that excessively large variations in position cannot be detected or may make the system diverge. Figures 17.3 and 17.4 (see color section) show us two images from the film *Flashback*.

Figure 17.3. A scene from the film *Flashback*

17.4. A New Interactive Interface for Cloth Design

We are now developing a new cloth animation system based on 3D interactive devices. In this system, a 3D interactive cloth definition interface will be established, so that we can easily create a garment on an actor's body and define other cloth items such as flags, curtains, stage screens and tablecloths.

Our methodology is based on the ball and mouse metaphor (LeBlanc et al. 1991) already used for designing shapes of synthetic actors (Paouri et al. 1991). Using a spaceball we rotate and zoom on the human body or other objects and, using the mouse, we first identify key points on the human body or on the objects, and then create cloth panels passing each of these points, finally we seam these panels together to form the garment or cloth things, such as skirts, T-shirts and pants. For fashion design, the 3D cloth panels should be transformed into 2D polygonal panels in order to produce cutting patterns. With the elastic surface model the 2D panels can be put on the human body and deformed to 3D panels by applying external forces, and seamed by using local constraints.

With the 3D interactive cloth definition interface we can conveniently design and create various kinds of clothes. We can also set the physical parameters of the clothes with respect to their texture and materials.

The implementation of the cloth animation proceeds in four steps:

(1) Designing and creating of cloth panels geometrically and defining their physical parameters.
(2) Putting the cloth panels on the human body or objects and seaming them together.
(3) Animating cloth with the movement of human body or other objects in the external physical environment.
(4) Modifying the parameters of the cloth and the physical environment in order to adjust the cloth animation system.

Acknowledgements

The research is partly supported by the Fonds National Suisse de la Recherche Scientifique, le Fonds National Suisse de la Recherche Scientifique, le fonds FCAR du Québec and the Natural Sciences and Engineering Research of Canada. The author would like to thank Professor Davis Sankoff from the University of Montreal for his useful comments and suggestions in reviewing the text.

References

Aono M (1990) A Wrinkle propagation Model for Cloth, *Proc. Computer Graphics International '90*, Springer-Verlag, Tokyo, pp.96-115
Gourret JP, Magnenat Thalmann N, Thalmann D (1989) Simulation of Object and Human Skin Deformation in a Grasping Task, *Proc. SIGGRAPH '89, Computer Graphics*, Vol.23, No.3, pp.21-30

Hinds BK, McCartney J, Interactive garment design, *The Visual Computer* (1990) 6, pp.53-61

Kunii TL, Gotoda H (1990) Modeling and Animation of Garment Wrinkle Formation Processes, *Proc. Computer Animation'90*, Springer, Tokyo, pp.131-147

Lafleur B, Magnenat Thalmann N, Thalmann D, Cloth Animation with Self-Collision Detection, in: Kunii TL (ed.) *Modeling in Computer Graphics*, Springer-Verlag, Tokyo

LeBlanc A, Kalra P, Magnenat-Thalmann N, Thalmann D (1991), Sculpting With the "Ball & Mouse" Metaphor, *Proc. Graphics Interface '91*, Calgary, to appear

Magnenat-Thalmann N, Laperriere R, Thalmann D (1988) Joint-Dependent Local Deformation for Hand Animation and Object Grasping, *Proc. Graphics Interface '88*, pp.26-33

Magnenat-Thalmann N, Thalmann D (1987) The Direction of Synthetic Actors in the Film Rendez-vous à Montréal, *IEEE Computer Graphics and Applications*, Vol. 7, No 12, pp.9-19

Moore M, Wihelms J (1988) Collision Detection and Response for Computer Animation, *Proc. SIGGRAPH'88, Computer Graphics*, Vol.22, No.4, pp.289-298

Paouri A, Magnenat Thalmann N, Thalmann D (1991) Creating Realistic Three-Dimensional Human Shape Characters for Computer-Generated Films, *Proc. Computer Animation '91*, Springer-Verlag, Tokyo

Platt JC, Barr AH (1988) Constraint Methods for Flexible Models, *Proc. SIGGRAPH'88, Computer Graphics*, Vol.23, No.3, pp.21-30

Terzopoulos D, Platt J, Barr A, Fleischer K (1987) Elastically Deformable Models, *Proc. SIGGRAPH'87, Computer Graphics*, Vol. 21, No.4, pp.205-214

Von Herzen B, Barr AH, Zatz HR (1990) Geometric Collisions for Time-Dependent Parametric Surfaces, *Proc. SIGGRAPH'90, Computer Graphics*, Vol.24, No.4, pp.39-46

Weil J (1986) The Synthesis of Cloth Objects, *Proc. SIGGRAPH '86, Computer Graphics*, Vol.20, No.4, pp.49-54

18

Dynamic Simulation as a Tool for Three-dimensional Animation

Daniel Thalmann
*Computer Graphics Lab, Swiss Federal Institute of Technology,
Lausanne*

18.1. The Movie Approach as opposed to the Physics Approach

There are two ways of considering three-dimensional computer animation (Magnenat Thalmann and Thalmann 1990) and its evolution: the movie approach and the physics approach. The first approach corresponds to an extension of traditional animation methods by the use of the computer. The second approach corresponds to simulation methods based on laws of physics, especially laws of mechanics. The purpose is not the same: traditional methods allow us to create three-dimensional characters with exaggerated movements while simulation methods are used to try to model a human behavior accurately.

For example, consider the bouncing ball example as described by Lasseter (1987). The motion is improved by introducing squash and stretch. When an object is squashed flat and stretches out drastically, it gives the sense that the object is made out of a soft, pliable material. This is a well known trick used by many traditional animators. It does not produce a realistic simulation, but it gives an impression to the viewer. A bouncing ball motion may be also completely simulated by computer using laws of mechanics such as Newton's laws and quantum conservation. Deformations may be calculated by using complex methods like finite element theory (Gourret et al. 1989). No approach is better than the other; it is like comparing a painting and a photograph. Both are representations of a particular world. If we consider character animation, it is easier to create emotions using a keyframe approach than using mechnical laws. Emotional aspects could very well be simulated using a more formal approach, they would require emotion models be incorporated in a physics-based animation system.

In this chapter, we will emphasize the simulation approach and show its advantages in the context of creating simple and complex animations.

18.2. Kinematic Simulations

Animating articulated limbs by interpolating key joint angles corresponds to forward kinematics. For generating goal-directed movements such as moving the hand to grasp an object, it is necessary to compute kinematics. Figure 18.1 shows the principles of forward and inverse kinematics.

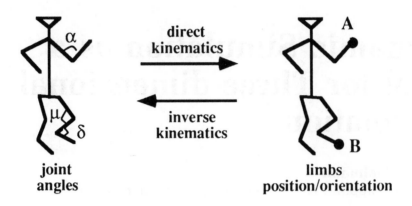

Figure 18.1. Forward and inverse kinematics

18.3. Dynamic Simulations

Kinematic-based systems are generally intuitive and lack dynamic integrity. The animation does not seem to respond to basic physical facts like gravity or inertia. Only modeling of objects that move under the influence of forces and torques can be realistic. For example, the motion in Figure 18.2 (see color section) is difficult to achieve without dynamics). Forces and torques cause linear and angular accelerations. The motion is obtained by the dynamic equations of motion. These equations are established using the forces, the torques, the constraints and the mass properties of objects.

A typical example is the motion of an articulated figure which is governed by forces and torques applied to limbs. These forces and torques may be of various kinds:

- torques coming from parent and child links,
- forces at the hinges,
- external effects such as contact with objects or arm-twisting.

There are three advantages of introducing dynamics into animation control:

- reality of natural phenomena is better rendered,
- dynamics frees the animator from having to describe the motion in terms of the physical properties of the solid objects,

- bodies can react automatically to internal and external environmental constraints: fields, collisions, forces and torques.

There are also serious disadvantages.

Typically, a hierarchy is built first, then internal parameters are set until the desired effect is obtained. This is a severe limitation, because it means that systems are hard for the animator to control. Parameters (e.g. forces or torques) are sometimes very difficult to adjust, because they are not intuitive. For a car, it is easy to choose the parameters of a spring or of a shock absorber, it is more difficult to adjust those used to simulate the equivalent forces and torques produced by muscle contractions and tensions in an animated figure. The animator does not think in terms of forces or torques to apply to a limb or the body in order to perform a motion.

Another problem is the amount of CPU time required to solve the motion equations of a complex articulated body using numerical methods. This considerably reduces the possibility of interaction of the user with the system. Only very short sequences may be produced, because of the lack of complete specification for complex motions and because of the CPU time required for certain methods.

Moreover, although dynamics-based motions are more realistic, they are too regular, because they do not take into account the personality of the characters. It is unrealistic to think that only the physical characteristics of two people carrying out the same actions make these characters different for any observer. Behavior and personality of the human beings are also an essential cause of the observable differences. Several ideas for gracefulness and style in motion control are proposed by Cohen (1989).

Methods based on parameter adjustment are the most popular approach to dynamics-based animation and correspond to *non-constraint methods*. They will be discussed in more detail in Section 18.4. There is an alternative: the *constraint-based methods*: the animator states in terms of constraints the properties the model is supposed to have, without needing to adjust parameters to give it those properties. Four kinds of constraints are discussed in Section 18.5: *kinematic constraints*, *dynamic constraints*, *energy constraints* and *spacetime constraints*.

In dynamic-based simulation, there are also two problems to be considered: the *forward dynamics* problem and the *inverse-dynamics* problem (see Figure 18.3). The forward dynamics problem consists of finding the trajectories of some point (e.g. an end effector in an articulated figure) with regard to the forces and torques that cause the motion. The inverse-dynamics problem is much more useful and may be stated as follows: determine the forces and torques required to produce a prescribed motion in a system. For an articulated figure, it is possible to compute the time sequence of joint torques required to achieve the desired time sequence of positions, velocities and accelerations using various methods.

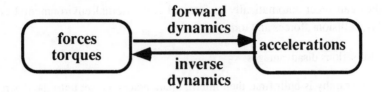

Figure 18.3. Forward and inverse dynamics

18.4. Non-Constraint-Based Methods

Non-constraint methods have been mainly used for the animation of articulated figures. There are a number of equivalent formulations which use various motion equations:

- the Newton–Euler formulation
- the Lagrange formulation
- the Gibbs–Appell formulation
- the D'Alembert formulation

These formulations are popular in robotics and more details about the equations and their use in computer animation may be found in Thalmann (1990)

18.4.1. The Newton–Euler Formulation

The Newton–Euler formulation is based on the laws governing the dynamics of rigid bodies. The procedure in this formulation is to first write the equations which define the angular and linear velocities and accelerations of each link and then write the equations which relate the forces and torques exerted on successive links while under this motion. The vector force $\vec{F}$ is given by the Newton's second law (Equation 18.1) and the total vector torque $\vec{N}$ by Euler's equation (Equation 18.2).

$$\vec{F} = m_i \, \ddot{\vec{r}_i} \tag{18.1}$$

$$\vec{N} = J_i \, \vec{\omega}_i + \vec{\omega}_i \times (J_i . \vec{\omega}_i) \tag{18.2}$$

Newton–Euler's methods were first developed with respect to the fixed, inertial coordinate system (Stepanenko and Vukobratovicz 1976; Vokobratovicz 1978). Then methods were derived with respect to the local coordinate system.

18.4.2. The Lagrange Formulation

The equations of motion for robots (Magnenat Thalmann and Thalmann 1988) can be derived through the application of the Lagrange's equations of motion for non conservative systems:

$$\frac{d}{dt}\left(\frac{\partial L}{\partial \dot{q}_i}\right) - \frac{\partial L}{\partial q_i} = \phi_i \tag{18.3}$$

where $L =$ Lagrangian $= T - V$
           $T =$ kinetic energy
           $V =$ potential energy
           $q_i =$ generalized joint coordinate representing the internal coordinate of the i-th joint

           $\dot{q}_i =$ first time derivative of q_i

           $\phi_i =$ generalized force applied to the i-th link; this generalized force can be thought of as the force (for sliding joints) or torque (for revolute joints) active at this joint.

Uicker (1965) and Kahn (1969) use the 4x4 rotation/translation matrices introduced by Denavit and Hartenberg (1955) (see Thalmann 1990). Once the kinetic and potential energy is expressed in terms of these matrices and their derivatives, the Lagrange equation is easily applied and the generalized forces ϕ_i may be found. Unfortunately, the process of evaluation is very time consuming, because it is proportional to the fourth power of the number of links.

Major steps in the Lagrange method are as follows:

(1) select suitable coordinates to define the system,
(2) write the constraint relations between coordinates,
(3) write the expressions corresponding to the kinetic and potential energies,
(4) use Lagrange's equation for defining the differential equations,
(5) get enough equations in order to find all accelerations,
(6) write the expressions of the applied force for each coordinate.

Vasilonikolidakis and Clapworthy (1991a) present the application of inverse Lagrangian dynamics for the purpose of animating articulated bodies. The method is reformulated to calculate the ground reaction forces that apply to the body.

18.4.3. The Gibbs–Appell Formulation

For a body with n degrees of freedom, matrix formulation of the Gibbs–Appell equations are as follows:

$$M^{-1}(\vec{q} \cdot \vec{V}) = \vec{\ddot{c}} \tag{18.4}$$

$\overrightarrow{q}$ is the generalized force at each degree of freedom: M is an n x n inertial matrix and $\overrightarrow{V}$ a n-length vector dependent on the configuration of the masses and their velocity relative to each

other. If $\overrightarrow{q}$, M and $\overrightarrow{V}$ are known, the equations can be solved for the generalized accelerations

$\overset{..}{\overrightarrow{c}}$ (n-length vector of the local angular or linear acceleration at each degree of freedom). This corresponds to the inverse-dynamics problem.

18.4.4. The D'Alembert Formulation

The *D'Alembert's principle of virtual work* states that if a system is in dynamic equilibrium and the bodies are allowed to move a small amount (virtual displacement) then the sum of the work of applied forces, the work of internal forces will be equal and opposite to the work of changes in momentum.

Isaacs and Cohen (1987) use the D'Alembert formulation in their DYNAMO system (see 18.5.1). In the case study, described in Section 18.8.2, the synthetic actress Marilyn draws letters, the motion calculation is also based on the Principle of Virtual Work.

18.4.5. Matrix and Recursive Formulations

Two dynamic formulations are possible:

(1) A set of simultaneous equations are formed and solved for the accelerations; this is the matrix formulation; it implies a matrix inversion and the formulation typically yields $O(n^3)$ or $O(n^4)$ complexity.

(2) A recursive relationship propagating

18.4.5.1. Matrix Formulations

Wilhelms and Barsky (1985) use the Gibbs–Appel formulation for her animation system Deva; however the method is abandoned (Wilhelms 1990), because the matrices generated are not sparse and the cost of solving for accelerations is prohibively expensive (cost of $O(n^4)$). Isaacs and Cohen (1987) also use a matrix formulation in their method of constraint simulation (see Section 18.5.1).

18.4.5.2. Recursive Formulations

Orin et al. (1979) propose that the forces and the torques be referred to the link's internal coordinate system. Armstrong (1979) and Luh et al. (1980) calculate the angular and linear velocities in link coordinates as well. Armstrong uses coordinate systems located at the joints: Luh et al. employs coordinate systems located at the link centers of mass. Armstrong (1979) presents a method based on the hypothetical existence of a linear recursive relationship between the motion of and forces applied to one link, and the motion of and forces applied to its neighbors. A set of recursion coefficients is defined for each link and the coefficients for one link may be calculated in terms of those of one its neighbors. The accelerations are then derived from the coefficients. The method is only applicable to spherical joints, but its computational complexity is only O(n), where n is the number of links. Based on this theory, Armstrong et al. (1987) designed a near real-time dynamics algorithm and implemented it in a prototype animation system. To reduce the amount of computer time required, Armstrong et al. (1987) make some simplifying assumptions about the structure of the figure and can produce a near real-time dynamics algorithm. They use frames which move with the links and an inertial frame considered fixed and non-rotating. The transformation from one frame to another is done by multiplying a column vector on the left by a 3x3 orthogonal matrix. Armstrong et al. introduce a last equation relating the acceleration at the proximal hinge of a son link s of link i to the linear and angular accelerations at the proximal hinge of i.

Hollerbach (1980) proposes a recursive formulation of the Lagrangian dynamics in three parts:

(1) backward recursion of the velocities and accelerations working from the base of the manipulator to the end link,

(2) forward recursion of the generalized forces working from the end link to the base of the manipulator,

(3) use of 3x3 rotation matrices instead of 4x4 rotation–translation matrices and homogeneous coordinates.

18.5. Constraint-based Methods

18.5.1. Kinematic Constraints

Isaacs and Cohen (1988) discuss a method of constraint simulation based on a matrix formulation. Joints are configures as kinematic constraints, and either accelerations or forces can be specified for the links. They describe a system called DYNAMO that performs dynamic simulation on linked figures. Three means for achieving control have been defined:

1) kinematic constraints permitting traditional keyframe animation systems to be embedded within a dynamic analysis

2) behavior functions allowing the figure to react to its surroundings

3) inverse dynamics for determining the forces required to perform a specified motion.

The dynamic system is treated as an explicit time series analysis with predictor corrector methods maintaining accuracy and efficiency in the solution. Behavior functions determine, at each moment, forces acting on a linkage and/or specific motion which is to occur.

In a new paper (Isaacs and Cohen 1988) about mixed methods for complex kinemtic constraints in dynamic figure animation, they propose an integration of direct and inverse kinematics specifications within a mixed method of forward and inverse dynamics simulation.

18.5.2. Energy Constraints

More generally, an approach to imposing and solving geometric constraints on parameterized models was introduced by Witkin et al. (1987). Constraints are expressed as energy functions, and the energy gradient followed through the model's parameter space.

Witkin et al. propose the following list of geometric constraints which may be cast in the form of energy functions:

- attachment to a fixed point: a point on a surface is attached to a specific point on space.

- surface-to-surface attachment: points on two surfaces must coincide, their tangent planes at those points must also coincide and the surfaces should not interpenetrate.

- floating attachment: a point on an object is attached to some point on a second object; the point of contact may slide freely on the second object

- slider constraint: a point on an object is restricted to lie on a line in space

- collision: collision constraints may be imposed without calculating surface intersections; an implicit function is used; it is zero everywhere on the object's surface, negative inside and positive outside.

It is also possible to impose constraints directly on model parameters.

18.5.3. Dynamic Constraints

Using dynamic constraints, Barzel and Barr (1988) build objects by specifying geometric constraints; the models assemble themselves as the elements move to satisfy the constraints. Their modeling system consists of:

- instantiating primitive bodies (sphere, torii, rods etc.) with geometrical characteristics, density, rotational inertia tensor

- external applied forces: gravity, springs, damping forces given by specific parameters like damping coefficients or spring constants

- geometric constraints of various types:

    . point-to-nail constraint: a point in the body is fixed to a specified location; the body may swivel or swing about the constrained point.

. point-to-point constraint: this is the joint between two bodies which may move about it, but the two constrained points should stay in contact

. point-to-path constraint: a point on an object should follow an arbitrary path

. orientation constraint: objects are rotated in order to be aligned

. point-to-line constraint: a point on an object is restricted to lie on a given line

. sphere-to-sphere constraint: two spheres are required to touch, but they may slide along each other

Attachment to a point and slider constraints like described in Section 18.5.2 are also proposed.

Once a model is built, it is held together by constraint forces. Constraint forces are calculated to apply to the bodies such that they behave in accordance with user-specified geometric constraints; the computation of these forces is the typical inverse dynamics problem, which consists of two parts: (1) finding forces to meet a constraint, and (2) finding forces to maintain a constraint.

Platt and Barr (1988) extend dynamic constraints to flexible models. They introduce two new types of constraints:

- reaction constraints: they can force a point to follow a path, or to lie on the outside of a polygonal model. They cancel forces that violate the constraint. Reaction constraints are applicable to constraining elastic models on a point-by-point basis.

- optimization constraints: two types exist:

    1) penalty method where an extra energy that penalizes incorrect behavior is added to the physical system

    2) augmented Lagrange constraints method which is a constrained optimization method that adds differential equations that compute Lagrange multipliers of the physical system.

18.5.4. Spacetime Constraints

Witkin and Kass (1988) propose a new method, called Spacetime Constraints, for creating character animation. The requirements contained in the description, together with Newton's laws, comprise a problem of constrained optimization. The solution to this problem is a physically valid motion satisfying the constraints.

In this new approach, the character motion is created automatically by specifying:

. *what* the character has to be
. *how* the motion should be performed
. what the character's *physical structure* is
. what physical *resources* are available to the character to accomplish the motion

The problem to solve is a problem of constrained optimization. The solution is a physically valid motion satisfying the *what* constraints and optimizing the *how* criteria. The spacetime constraint approach conforms to principles of traditional animation as anticipation or suqash-and-stretch.

18.6. Collisions and Responses to the Environment

An important advantage to the use of dynamic simulation is the processing of interactions between bodies. The interaction may be first identified then a response may be generated. The most common example of interaction with the environment is the collision. Analytical methods for calculating the forces between colliding rigid bodies have been presented. Moore and Wilhelms (1988) modeled simultaneous collisions as a slightly staggered series of single collisions and used non-analytical methods to deal with bodies in resting contact. Hahn (1988) prevented bodies in resting contact as a series of frequently occuring collisions. Baraff (1989) presented an analytical method for finding forces between contacting polyhedral bodies, based on linear programming techniques. The solution algorithm used is heuristic. A method for finding simultaneous impulsive forces between colliding polyhedral bodies is described. Baraff (1990) also proposed a formulation of the contact forces between curved surfaces that are completely unconstrained in their tangential movement. A collision detection algorithm exploiting the geometric coherence between successive time steps of the simulation is explained. Von Herzen et al. (1990) developed a collision algorithm for time-dependent parametric surfaces.

Terzopoulos et al. (1987) and Platt and Barr (1988) proposed to surround the surfaces of deformable models by a self-repulsive collision force, this is a *penalty* method. Lafleur et al. (1991) addresses the problem of detecting collisions of very flexible objects, such as clothes with almost rigid bodies, such as human bodies. In their method, collision avoidance also consists of creating a very thin force field around the obstacle surface to avoid collisions. This force field acts like a shield rejecting the points. The volume is divided into small contiguous non-overlapped cells which completely surround the surface. As soon as a point enters into a cell, a repulsive force is applied. The direction and the magnitude of this force are dependent on the velocities, the normals and the distance between the point and the surface. More details may be found in Chapter 17.

Hahn (1988) describes the simulation of the dynamic interaction among rigid bodies taking into account various physical characteristics such as elasticity, friction, mass and moment of inertia to produce rolling and sliding contacts. Terzopoulos and Fleischer (1988) propose dynamic models for simulating inelastic behaviors: viscoelasticity, plasticity and fracture.

18.7. Dynamic Simulation of Animal Locomotion and Human Walking

For many years there has been a great interest in natural gait simulation. Zeltzer (1982) describes the use of finite state control to simulate human walking. Girard and Maciejewski (1985) use inverse kinematics to interactively define gaits for legged animals. Boulic et al. (1990) describe a global human walking model with kinematic personification. The model is built from experimental data based on a wide range of normalized velocities. It is based on a simple kinematic approach designed to keep the intrinsic dynamic characteristics of the experimental model. Figure 18.4 shows an example.

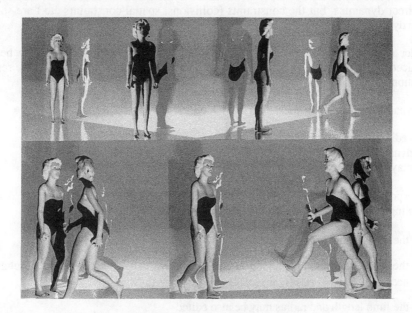

Figure 18.4. A walking model

Although Girard's model (Girard 1987) also incorporates some dynamic elements for adding realsim, it is not a truly dynamic approach. Also Bruderlin and Calvert (1989) propose a hybrid approach to the human locomotion which combines goal-oriented and dynamic motion control. Knowledge about a locomotion cycle is incorporated into a hierarchical control process. Decomposition of the locomotion determines forces and torques that drive the dynamic model of the legs by numerical approximation techniques. Rather than relying on a general dynamic model, the equations of motion of the legs are tailored to locomotion and analytically constrained to allow for only a specific range of movements.

McKenna and Zeltzer (1990) describe an efficient forward dynamic simulation algorithm for articulated figures which has a computational complexity linear in the number of joints. The simulation is capable of generating gait patterns and walking phenomena observed in nature. Vasilonikolidakis and Clapworthy (1991b) propose a method based on inverse Lagrangian dynamics for animating human walking. The issue of ground reaction forces is addressed and solved using a reformulation of the Lagrangian algorithm.

Miller (1988) describe a dynamic simulation of the motion of legless figures like snakes and worms. Animals are modeled as mass–spring systems. Muscle contractions are simulated by animating the spring tensions. Miller (1991) also describes an interactive dynamic-based system which controls the dynamic and time-dependent aspects of simulation.

18.8. Case Studies

18.8.1. An Example of a Program of Dynamic Simulation: Dynamik

Dynamik use both direct dynamics and inverse dynamics. The basic simulation algorithm uses direct dynamics, but the constraints (collisions, spatial constraints etc.) are solved by inverse dynamics.

In order to make the simulations more realistic, the concept of friction has been also introduced. Only one kind of friction is taken into account: the friction due to the resistance to rotation at the joints. Friction due to air is ignored.

The Dynamik system is composed of:

(1) an editor of dynamic bodies
(2) a dynamic simulator
(3) a playback system

The purpose of the editor is to build articulated bodies and to specify dynamic data. Data concerning a selected limb may be interactively changed.

- the mass of the limb may be modified

- the mass center is initialized at the geometric center, but it could be changed if necessary

- the limb length and radius may be also edited

There are also specific data for the joints:

- a friction factor may be entered; it is applied to each rotation axis and corresponds to an energy loss

- joint angles may be modified to change the limb orientation

- angle limits for the current joint relative to each rotation axis

- relative and absolute positions

Dynamic controls should be introduced to define motions to be applied to the articulated bodies. These controls consist of constraint activations. Available constraints include: external forces, external torques, "wind" forces, collisions against planes or parallelepipeds, limb connections, positioning in 3-space and rotational motions.

The dynamic simulator computes the complete simulation according to user parameters such as time range simulation, gravity and display options.

The playback system plays, in real-time, the simulation calculated by the dynamic simulator. An example of simulation produced by the system is shown in Figure 18.5 (see color section).

18.8.2. Marilyn Draws Letters

Consider the problem of writing letters on a blackboard. To simulate the writing of a letter, the hand trajectory may be introduced as a kinematic constraint. But how can we control the dynamic behavior of the whole arm and the realism of its motion ? When we write, it is not the hand trajectory which controls the arm motion but the arm muscles which move the hand. A dynamic approach is much more realistic. For this reason, we have produced (Arnaldi et al. 1989) a dynamics-based animation sequence consisting of Marilyn's arm, where the hand reaches a point from a rest position and then successively draws letters O and M from this point. Figure 18.6 (see color section) shows an example.

To produce this sequence, we used a mechanical approach which treats open and closed chains indifferently . It is based on the principle of virtual work (Hégron et al. 1988) associated with Lagrange's multipliers. It can be expressed as letting the Lagrangian parameters of one multibody system (positional and rotational parameters of each object) be submitted to holonomic constraints (joint between two objects) and non holonomic constraints (e.g. wheel which is rolling without sliding on the ground).

By application of the principle of virtual work, computations are performed in a symbolic way to produce the equations of motion. The next step in the animation process is to solve this set of equations numerically for each frame. To do this a simple Newton–Raphson algorithm is used with the jacobian matrix symbolically computed.

Consider again our example of Marilyn: her arm is a four link chain: clavicle, upper arm, lower arm, hand. Each link is modeled as a cylinder to simplify computation of mechanical properties. One type of joint is used to build the arm: ball and socket. To render muscle actions, we add, for each degree of freedom, a spring, a damper and a torque. For realistic mechanical modeling, we can use a non linear spring and a viscous damper to represent passive viscoelastic characteristics of muscles (Winter 1979). Thrusts are added to ensure that motion lies within human capabilities (some degrees of freedom of the ball and socket are restricted, such as in the elbow joint).

Let us now describe the different steps of the arm motion. First, from an initial position, the hand reaches a point on a plane (step 1). Second, from this point the hand draws the letter on the plane (step 2).

As mentioned in the previous sections, it is very difficult to find the different torques to apply to each degree of freedom of the arm to ensure that the hand describes the right trajectory. The inverse problem has to be solved: we know explicitly all the points on the reference trajectory, and, without applying any torque explicitly the hand has to respect this trajectory.

One solution is to create a new joint between a point on the hand and the trajectory. Let X_h be the point on the hand and X_t the point on the trajectory (this point moves with time), the constraint expression f is now:

$$f_t = X_h - X_t \qquad (18.5)$$

To solve the motion equation with respect to this constraint, a penalization scheme is used. The joint is computed as a spring between the hand and the trajectory. This is a static solution because at a time step X_t is specified and the constraint f_t is met.

A second solution consists of applying automatic control theory as used in robotics. No specification of an explicit trajectory is now necessary. We will only specify the constraint to be met as:

$$f = X_h - X_g \qquad (18.6)$$

where X_g represents the goal.

We require this constraint to be met not immediately, but to evolve through time in accordance with a specified damped oscillation differential equation. The introduction of critical damping is here of special interest in controlling the motion of X_h as shown by Barzel and Barr (1988).

Acknowledgements

The author would like to thank Arghyro Paouri for the design of images. The Dynamik system has been implemented by Rejean Gagné from the University of Montreal. The dynamic Marilyn's hand animation has been performed in cooperation with Gerard Hégron and Bruno Arnaldi from IRISA, University of Rennes. The research was partly supported by "le Fonds National Suisse pour la Recherche Scientifique", Natural Sciences and Engineering Council of Canada and the FCAR foundation.

References

Armstrong WW (1979) Recursive Solution to the Equations of Motion of an N-Link Manipulator, *Proc. 5th World Congress Theory Mach.Mechanisms*, Vol.2, pp.1343-1346
Armstrong WW, Green M, Lake R (1987) Near Real-Time Control of Human Figure Models, *IEEE Computer Graphics and Applications*, Vol. 7, No 6, pp.28-38.
Arnaldi B, Dumont G, Hégron G, Magnenat-Thalmann N, Thalmann D (1989) Animation Control with Dynamics, in: Magnenat-Thalmann N, Thalmann D (eds) *State-of-the-Art in Computer Animation*, Springer, Tokyo, pp.113-124.
Baraff D (1989) Analytical Methods for Dynamic Simulation of Non-Penetrating Rigid Bodies, *Proc. SIGGRAPH '89, Computer Graphics*, Vol. 23, No3, pp.223-232.
Baraff D (1990) Curved Surfaces and Coherence for Non-Penetrating Rigid Body Simulation, *Proc. SIGGRAPH '90, Computer Graphics*, Vol. 24, No4, pp.19-28.

Barzel R, Barr AH (1988) A Modeling System Based on Dynamic Constraints, *Proc. SIGGRAPH '88, Computer Graphics*, Vol. 22, No4, pp.179-188.

Boulic R, Magnenat-Thalmann N, Thalmann D (1990b) A Global Human Walking Model with real time Kinematic Personification, *The Visual Computer*, Vol.6, No6, pp.344-358.

Bruderlin A, Calvert TW (1989) Goal-Directed Dynamic Simulation of Human Walking, *Proc. SIGGRAPH '89, Computer Graphics*, Vol. 23, No3, pp.233-242.

Cohen MF (1989) Gracefulness and Style in Motion Control, *Proc. Mechanics, Control and Animation of Articulated Figures*, MIT, Boston.

Denavit J, Hartenberg RS (1955) A Kinematic Notation for Lower Pair Mechanisms Based on Matrices, *J.Appl.Mech.*, Vol.22, pp.215-221.

Girard M (1987) Interactive Design of 3D Computer-Animated Legged Animal Motion, *IEEE Computer Graphics and Applications*, Vol. 7, No 6, pp.39-51.

Girard M, Maciejewski AA (1985) Computational Modeling for the Computer animation of Legged Figures, *Proc. SIGGRAPH '85, Computer Graphics*, Vol.19, No3, pp.263-270.

Gourret JP, Magnenat Thalmann N, Thalmann D (1989) Simulation of Object and Human Skin Deformation in Grasping Task, *Proc. SIGGRAPH '89, Computer Graphics*, Vol.23, No.3, pp.21-30.

Hahn JK (1988) Realistic Animation of Rigid Bodies, *Proc. SIGGRAPH '88, Computer Graphics*, Vol. 22, No 4, pp.299-308.

Hégron G, Arnaldi B, Dumont G (1988) Toward General Animation Control, in: Magnenat-Thalmann N, Thalmann D (eds) *New Trends in Computer Graphics*, Springer, Heidelberg, pp.54-63.

Hollerbach JM (1980) A Recursive Lagrangian Formulation of Manipulator Dynamics and a Comparative Study of Dynamics Formulation Complexity, *IEEE Trans. on Systems, Man, and Cybernetics*, Vol. SMC-10, No11, pp.730-736.

Isaacs PM, Cohen MF (1987) Controlling Dynamic Simulation with Kinematic Constraints, Behavior Functions and Inverse Dynamics, *Proc. SIGGRAPH'87, Computer Graphics*, Vol. 21, No4, pp.215-224.

Isaacs PM, Cohen MF (1988) Mixed Methods for Complex Kinematic Constraints in Dynamic Figure Animation, *The Visual Computer*, Vol. 4, No6, pp.296-305.

Kahn ME (1969) *The Near-Minimum-Time Control of Open-Loop Articulated Kinematic Chains*, Stanford Artificial Intelligence project, AIM-106.

Lafleur B, Magnenat Thalmann N, Thalmann D, Cloth Animation with Self-Collision Detection, in: Kunii TL (ed.) *Modeling in Computer Graphics*, Springer-Verlag, Tokyo

Lasseter J (1987) Principles of Traditional Animation Applied to 3D Computer Animation, *Proc. SIGGRAPH '87, Computer Graphics*, Vol. 21, No4, pp.35-44.

Luh JYS, Walker MW, Paul RPC (1980) On-line Computational Scheme for Mechanical Manipulators, *Journal of Dynamic Systems, Measurement and Control*, Vol.102, pp.103-110.

Magnenat-Thalmann N, Thalmann D (1988) Mechanics and Robotics for Animating Synthetic Actors, *SIGGRAPH '88 Course Notes on Synthetic Actors: The Impact of Artificial Intelligence and Robotics on Animation*, ACM, pp.85-98.

Magnenat-Thalmann N, Thalmann D (1990) *Computer Animation: Theory and Practice*, 2nd edition, Springer-Verlag, Tokyo.

McKenna M, Zeltzer D (1990) Dynamic Simulation of Autonomous Legged Locomotion, *Proc. SIGGRAPH '90, Computer Graphics*, Vol. 24, No 4, pp.29-38.

Miller G (1988) The Motion Dynamics of Snakes and Worms, *Proc. SIGGRAPH '88, Computer Graphics*, Vol. 22, No4, pp.169-173.

Miller G (1991) MacBounce: A Dynamics-Based Modeler for Character Animation, *Proc. Computer Animation '91*, Springer-Verlag, Tokyo.

Moore M, Wihelms J (1988) Collision Detection and Response for Computer Animation, *Proc. SIGGRAPH'88, Computer Graphics*, Vol.22, No.4, pp.289-298.

Orin D, McGhee R, Vukobratovic M, Hartoch G (1979) Kinematic and Kinetic Analysis of Open-Chain Linkages Utilizing Newton-Euler methods, *Mathematical Biosciences*, Vol.31, pp.107-130.

Platt JC, Barr AH (1988) Constraint Method for Flexible Models, *Proc. SIGGRAPH '88, Computer Graphics*, Vol. 22, No4, pp.279-288.

Stepanenko Y and Vukobratovic M (1976) Dynamics of Articulated Open Chain Active Mechanisms, *Mathematical Biosciences*, Vol.28, pp.137-170.

Thalmann D (1990) Robotics Methods for Task-level and Behavioral Animation, in: Thalmann D (ed) *Scientific Visualization and Graphics Simulation*, John Wiley, Chichester, UK, pp.129-147.

Terzopoulos D, Platt JC, Barr AH, Fleischer K (1987) Elastically Deformable Models, *Proc.SIGGRAPH'87, Computer Graphics*, Vol. 21, No 4, pp.205-214.

Terzopoulos D, Fleischer K (1988) Deformable Models, *The Visual Computer*, Vol.4, No6, pp.306-331.

Uicker JJ (1965) *On the Dynamic Analysis of Spatial Linkages Using 4x4 Matrices*, Ph.D Dissertation, Northwestern University, Evanston, IL.

Vasilonikolidakis N, Clapworthy GJ (1991a) Inverse Lagrangian Dynamics for Animating Articulated Models, *Journal of Visualization and Computer Animation*, Vol.2, No3.

Vasilonikolidakis N, Clapworthy GJ (1991b) Design of Realistic Gaits for the Purpose of Animation, *Proc. Computer Animation '91*, Springer-Verlag, Tokyo.

Von Herzen B, Barr AH, Zatz HR (1990) Geometric Collisions for Time-Dependent Parametric Surfaces, *Proc. SIGGRAPH '90, Computer Graphics*, Vol. 24, No4, pp.39-48

Vukobratovic M (1978) Computer method for Dynamic Model Construction of Active Articulated Mechanisms using Kinetostatic Approach, *Journal of Mechanism and Machine Theory*, Vol.13, pp.19-39.

Wilhelms J (1990) Dynamic Experiences, in: Badler NI, Barsky BA, Zeltzer D (ed) *Making Them Move*, Morgan Kaufmann, San Mateo, CA, pp.265-279.

Wilhelms J, Barsky BA (1985) Using Dynamic Analysis to Animate Articulated Bodies such as Humans and Robots, in: Magnenat-Thalmann N, Thalmann D (eds) *Computer-generated Images*, Springer, Tokyo, pp.209-229.

Winter DA (1979) *Biomechanics of Human Movement*, Wiley Interscience, Chichester, UK.

Witkin A, Fleischer K, Barr AH (1987) Energy Constraints on Parameterized Models, *Proc. SIGGRAPH '87, Computer Graphics*, Vol.21, No4, pp.225-232.

Witkin A, Kass M (1988) Spacetime Constraints, *Proc. SIGGRAPH '88, Computer Graphics*, Vol.22, No4, pp.159-168.

Zeltzer (1982) Motor Control Techniques for Figure Animation, *IEEE Computer Graphics and Applications*, Vol. 2, No9, pp.53-59.

19

Deformable Models: Formulations and Applications

Demetri Terzopoulos
University of Toronto and Schlumberger LSC

19.1. Introduction

Methods for describing shape and motion are of central concern to computer graphics modeling. Geometry has proven useful for modeling stationary objects whose shapes do not change over time. Computer animation, however, has recently been able to achieve astonishing realism by exploiting concepts from physics. In physically-based animation, numerical procedures compute the motions of models in simulated physical worlds in accordance with Newtonian mechanics, and images are synthesized by graphically rendering the model's state variables over time. Model behavior can be controlled through physical parameters, forces, constraints, obstacles, heat, and other environmental influences. Actuators, such as simulated muscles, may also be incorporated into the models to create self animating objects. Users can vividly "experience" the virtual reality created in the machine when physically-based models are simulated at interactive rates on parallel computers with associated hardware to support real-time graphical visualization and human-computer interaction. For a general discussion of the physically-based modeling paradigm see (Terzopoulos et al. 1989).

This chapter reviews physically-based techniques for modeling nonrigid shape and motion. *Deformable models* (Terzopoulos and Fleischer 1988b) are a class of free-form curve, surface, and solid modeling primitives founded on principles that govern the dynamics of nonrigid bodies. They were designed primarily to facilitate the creation of highly realistic computer animations. To this end, deformable models idealize broad regimes of material response under diverse environmental conditions. The models are capable of a wide variety of natural behaviors, including elasticity, viscoelasticity, plasticity, fracture, conductive heat transfer, thermoplasticity, melting, and fluid-like behavior in the molten state. Their physical parameters describe qualitatively familiar behaviors, such as stretchability, flexibility, resiliency, fragility, conductivity, viscosity, etc.

Deformable models are appropriate in computer graphics applications, where the concern for convenience and tractability motivates mathematical abstraction and computational expediency. Although computationally more demanding than most free-form geometric primitives, deformable models are in many ways superior. Most importantly, since deformable models are fundamentally dynamic, their governing equations provide a unified description of nonrigid shapes and their typically complex motions through space.

The remainder of this chapter surveys the author's research on deformable models and glimpses at related work by other researchers. First, several deformable model formulations are briefly reviewed. Then, three deformable model application areas are discussed: graphics modeling and animation, computer vision, and data approximation and analysis.

19.2. Deformable Model Formulations

Deformable models are based on the (variational) principles of continuum mechanics. These laws are usually expressed in the form of dynamic differential equations. Realistic deformable model animations are created by formulating such equations of motion in various different ways and simulating them using standard numerical algorithms. This section describes several formulations, including elastic, hybrid, parameterized, inelastic, thermoelastic, and stochastic deformable models.

Elastic models (Terzopoulos et al. 1987) simulate nonlinear elastic materials. They incorporate deformation energies that are invariant with respect to rigid-body motions, which impart no deformation, and grow monotonically with the magnitude of the deformation. The energy functionals are expressed as integral measures of the instantaneous deformation of a model away from its prescribed reference shape. The deformation is quantified in a convenient way using the fundamental forms of differential geometry (metrics, curvatures, etc.). Lagrange equations of motion balance the resulting elastic forces against inertial forces due to the mass distribution of the model, frictional damping forces, and externally applied forces. The formulation works well in practice for models whose shapes are moderately to highly deformable.

Hybrid models (Terzopoulos and Witkin 1988) involve deformable and rigid dynamics operating in concert. The hybrid formulation yields well-conditioned discrete equations for complicated deformable shapes, particularly as the rigidity of models is increased beyond the stability limits of the elastic model formulation. We decompose deformations into a reference component, which may represent an arbitrary free-form shape, and a displacement component allowing deformations away from this reference shape. The former evolves according to rigid-body dynamics, while equations of nonrigid motion based on linear elasticity govern the latter. The set of dynamic equations governing hybrid models includes coupling effects between rigid-body modes and deformational degrees of freedom.

Parameterized models (Terzopoulos and Metaxas 1991) extend the capabilities of hybrid models by incorporating the global shape variables of parameterized geometric primitives and parameterized deformations. In principle, this formulation allows us to create deformable versions of the parameterized solid primitives employed in graphics and CAD, such as spheres, cylinders, etc. The evolution of the various degrees of freedom of the model is dictated by a set of coupled differential equations which generalize the hybrid model equations described above. These equations include terms that govern the evolution of the global variables which have been inherited from the solid primitive as well the evolution of the local shape variables inherited from elastically deformable splines. The equations of motion also include inertial terms which couple the rigid-body, global deformational, and local deformational degrees of freedom of the model.

Inelastic models (Terzopoulos and Fleischer 1988a) are a powerful model-building medium. Unlike elastic models, which immediately regain their natural, undeformed shapes as soon as all external forces are removed, inelastic models simulate the mechanical behaviors commonly associated with high polymer solids such as modeling clay or silicone putty. Consequently, inelastic models serve as a sort of freely sculptable "computational plasticine." Free-form shapes may be created by interactively applying simulated forces on the inelastic model to stretch it, squash it, mold it, and so forth. Inelastic models tractably simulate three canonical inelastic behaviors---viscoelasticity, plasticity, and fracture. These behaviors may be incorporated into any of the elastic models described above by introducing internal processes which dynamically control resiliency and fragility as a function of deformation.

Thermoelastic models (Terzopoulos et al. 1991) are nonrigid primitives capable of heat conduction, thermoelasticity, melting, and fluid-like behavior in the molten state. They are most easily formulated as discrete physical models involving the interactions of particles with mass, nonlinear springs, and interparticle attraction/repulsion forces. Thermoelastic models feature nonrigid dynamics governed by Lagrangian equations of motion and conductive heat transfer governed by the heat equation for nonhomogeneous, nonisotropic media. In its solid state, the discretized model is composed of thermoelastic elements interconnecting particles arranged in a lattice. The stiffness of a thermoelastic element decreases as its temperature increases, and the unit fuses when its temperature exceeds the melting point. The molten state of the model involves a multibody molecular dynamics simulation in which "fluid" particles, broken free from the lattice, interact through pairwise long-range attraction forces and short-range repulsion forces.

Stochastic models (Szeliski and Terzopoulos 1989) combine deterministic deformable behaviors with random processes. This leads to the marriage of two well-known modeling techniques---splines and fractals. On the one hand, spline shapes are easily constrained and suitable for modeling smooth, man-made objects like teapots while, on the other hand, fractals, though difficult to constrain, are suitable for synthesizing the various irregular shapes found in nature, such as mountainous terrain. Constrained fractals are a class of deformable models that combine these seemingly opposed features by exploiting a remarkable relationship between fractals and generalized energy-minimizing splines which may be derived through Fourier analysis. Constrained fractals are generated by a stochastic relaxation algorithm which "bombards" a spline subject to shape constraints with modulated white noise, letting the spline diffuse the noise into the desired fractal spectrum as it settles into equilibrium.

19.3. Deformable Model Applications

The previous section presented deformable model formulations which complement one another in several ways. Together, they provide an arsenal of widely applicable tools and techniques. This section discusses the application of the arsenal to some difficult problems in computer graphics, computer vision, and data analysis.

19.3.1. Computer Graphics Modeling

Deformable models offer a broad range of nonrigid behaviors that can be exploited to create complex static or dynamic computer graphics objects. We will review applications to realistic object modeling and animation, interactive virtual worlds, and human facial animation, followed by a quick look at related work by other researchers.

19.3.1.1. Realistic Modeling and Animation of Nonrigid Objects

Graphics and animation with deformable models has been demonstrated in a series of publications (Terzopoulos et al. 1987; Terzopoulos and Fleischer 1988a,b; Terzopoulos and Witkin 1988; Terzopoulos et al. 1991). We have applied the elastic model formulation with obstacle constraints to model stretchy shrink-wrap and heavy balls resting on spongy solids. We have animated various cloth objects including wind-blown flags, flying carpets dropping over obstacles, and draped clothing. Using fracture processes in inelastic models, we have animated nets tearing as they are pulled over obstacles and cloth tearing violently as a result of shearing forces. We have animated thermoelastic models in a simulated physical world populated by hot constraint surfaces. A thermoelastic solid is dropped into a "funnel," which is then heated to first soften the solid, then to melt it so that it dribbles onto a hot floor below. In another demonstration, a "plasticine" bust of Victor Hugo was created by using the inelastic model formulation. The natural shape of the bust was derived from 3D data acquired by scanning a statuette of the famous author with a laser range sensor. The model was then deformed plastically by applying simulated forces with an articulated geometric model of a robot hand, pinching Hugo's cheek, pulling, and releasing to show a final deformation.

Cooking with Kurt (Fleischer et al. 1987) is a more elaborate animation that intimately combines live and synthetic images. It demonstrates that animating physically-based models in a simulated physical environment is a powerful alternative to the common practice of creating animation by key-framing and spline in-betweening. The action begins with live video of Kurt Fleischer walking into his kitchen and placing several large vegetables (squashes and an eggplant) on a cutting board. The vegetables "come to life" in what appears to be the physical kitchen table environment. They bounce, slide, roll, tumble, and collide with one another and with the table-top, cutting board, and back wall. The vegetables were modeled using the hybrid deformable model formulation (Terzopoulos and Witkin 1988). Physically-based vision techniques (see Section 19.3.2) played a key role in the reconstruction of the 3D reference shapes of the models from a single 2D video frame. The deformable models were animated by numerically simulating their discrete equations of motion given the forces at work---gravity, "rocket thruster" driving forces, "servo control" forces for balancing and following choreographed paths, and interaction forces arising from friction and collision among the deformable models and surfaces in the simulated physical environment.

19.3.1.2. Interactive Deformable Models in Virtual Worlds

Several experimental 2D and 3D virtual worlds have been implemented which incorporate elastic and inelastic models (Terzopoulos and Fleischer 1988a,b; Waters and Terzopoulos 1990a). The user can interact with these models by applying simulated forces through interactive devices, including a standard 2D mouse, a Polhemus 3SPACE device, a DataGlove, and a SpaceBall. An important theme of this work is to exploit the fact that inelastic deformable models emulate many of the behaviors that make natural modeling compounds useful for sculpting complex shapes. In the not too distant future we will be able to assimilate many of the natural conveniences of this traditional art into state-of-the-art geometrically-based design systems. In the physical/geometric CAD/CAM/CAE system of the future, users aided by stereoscopic and haptic input-output devices will be able to carve "computational plasticine" and apply simulated forces to it to create free-form shapes interactively with the same fluency that children create shapes using real plasticine, or that experienced designers sculpt automobile bodies out of clay.

19.3.1.3. Facial Modeling and Animation

The expressive power of the human face makes it an attractive but elusive target for computer graphics modelers and animators. One of the hardest challenges has been to develop computational models of the face capable of synthesizing the various nuances of facial motion quickly and convincingly. There is a prevalent need for such models, not just for the animation of synthetic human characters, but also for a variety of other applications ranging from low bandwidth teleconferencing to plastic surgery.

The purely geometric nature of prior face models limits their realism because it ignores the fact that the human face is an elaborate biomechanical system. Terzopoulos and Waters (1990b) have developed a 3D dynamic face model which can be simulated and rendered on a high-end graphics workstation to synthesize real-time animated facial images. An important innovation is the use of an anatomically-based facial muscle process to control a physically-based deformable model of human facial tissue---a spring-mass lattice with nonlinear elastic properties (Waters and Terzopoulos 1990b). The face model is generic inasmuch as its structure is independent of specific facial geometries. Polygonal facial representations are generated through photogrammetry of stereo facial images or through nonuniform meshing of detailed facial topographies provided by laser range sensors (Terzopoulos and Waters 1991). The tissue and muscle models are then associated with the accurate 3D facial geometry.

Compared to what is achievable with reasonable effort using earlier geometric models of the face, superior realism results from the use of deformable models to emulate complex facial tissue deformations in response to muscle activity. The actions of the muscle actuators embedded in the physically-based face model may be coordinated and controlled using a facial action coding system to produce meaningful expressions.

19.3.1.4. Other Work

We conclude this section by briefly mentioning other efforts aimed at the physically-based modeling of nonrigid objects for computer graphics. The following list is by no means exhaustive.

Platt (1988 1989) has proposed several physically-based constraint methods for controlling deformable model animations. Several authors have explored the modeling and animation of cloth using elastic surface models (Feynman 1986; Lundin 1987; Haumann 1987; Kunii and Gotoda 1990). A simple, discrete deformable surface is the tension net proposed by Platt and Badler (1981) as a simple tissue model in their facial animation work. A more sophisticated model of facial tissue was proposed by Pieper (1989). Gourret et al. (1989) have developed an elastic finite element model of the deformable tissue in human hands which interacts realistically with deformable objects during grasping. Miller (1988) has incorporated muscle actuators into discrete deformable models to synthesize self-locomoting snakes and worms. He has also implemented dynamic particle systems for modeling fluids and powders (Miller and Pearce 1989). These models involve pairwise interparticle forces similar to those used in our thermoelastic models, as does a thermal particle technique developed by Tonnesen (1991) for modeling deformable solids that can melt into fluids when heated and resolidify when cooled. Sims (1990) describes the massively parallel implementation of dynamic particle systems for the simpler case where there are no interparticle forces. The dynamic system that Kass and Miller (1990) employ to model the surfaces of pools of water may be interpreted as an elastically deformable surface with some additional constraints. A restricted class of deformable models, affine models, is formulated by Witkin and Welch (1990). Pentland and Williams (1989) apply polynomial deformations to volumetric models. Chadwick et al. (1990) apply deformations to objects using the dynamics of a spring-mass lattice whose mass points serve as the control vertices of a free-form polynomial deformation. Celniker (1991) explores deformable curve and surface models as an interactive medium for free-form shape design with applications to CAD/CAM.

19.3.2. Computer Vision Modeling

Computer vision is the inverse problem to computer graphics. Whereas graphics involves image synthesis from object models, vision is concerned in part with image analysis to reconstruct models of imaged objects. As we have already stated, the equations of motion which govern the behavior of deformable models make them responsive to externally applied forces. Hence, a powerful approach to solving the reconstruction problems of computer vision is to immerse deformable models in ambient force fields computed from image data and simulate the equations of motion through time. The force fields are designed to mold deformable models into shapes that are consistent with imaged objects of interest. When objects move in the world, their images and, consequently, the force fields derived from them evolve over time. If the force fields are generated appropriately, they move deformable models nonrigidly to track the imaged objects, maintaining consistency with their shapes and motions.

19.3.2.1. Curve and 3D Models

Snakes (Kass et al. 1987) are planar deformable contour models that behave like simulated stretchy, springy wire. Snakes provide a simple and accurate means of interactively localizing and tracking edges and other curvilinear features of interest in natural grey-level images. We embed snakes in image force fields designed to attract them towards bright or dark regions, towards high contrast edges, or other salient image features. As the snake settles down into a local energy minimum, its internal strain energy allows it to complete continuous contours over poorly defined features. Snakes are useful for interactively segmenting objects of interest from background in cluttered images. They are effective motion trackers in image sequences. For example, we have applied them to track the nonrigid motion of people's lips as they are talking and to extract the movements of other important facial features from images (see Section 19.3.2.2).

Deformable cylinders (Terzopoulos et al. 1988) are a class of models capable of recovering the shapes and motions of free-form, flexible, quasi-axisymmetric objects from images. We construct a deformable cylinder by wrapping a deformable surface into a tube and passing a deformable spine through the center of the tube. The two components are coupled together with forces that encourage the tube to be as symmetric as possible around the spine. Deformable cylinders are able to reconstruct the 3D shapes of natural objects from their images, and to track their nonrigid motions in space. We have successfully exploited their reconstruction capabilities in the "Cooking with Kurt" animation to create geometrically accurate 3D animate vegetable models from a single video frame showing real vegetables (see Section 19.3.1.1) (Terzopoulos and Witkin 1988).

Deformable superquadrics (Terzopoulos and Metaxas 1991) are an instance of the parametrically deformable model formulation described in Section 19.2. The models incorporate the global shape parameters of a conventional superellipsoid with the local degrees of freedom of a spline. In vision applications, the model's global deformational degrees of freedom capture gross shape features from visual data, while the local deformation parameters reconstruct the details of complex shapes. We have implemented a system for applying hard and soft constraints to deformable superquadrics (Metaxas and Terzopoulos 1991). This is a complex task for dynamic models that can deform both locally and globally, but it is necessary for assembling multibody models for use in vision and computer animation. In a constrained system like an articulated human figure, one knows at the outset how the parts of the composite model should fit together. The difficulty is in choosing values of the various parameters to achieve the desired effect. The constraint satisfaction procedure automatically computes the translational, rotational, and deformational variables of deformable superquadric models to assemble articulated objects.

19.3.2.2. Facial Image Analysis

Quick, robust facial image analysis is desirable for numerous applications. For example, low bandwidth teleconferencing requires the real-time extraction of facial control parameters from live video at the transmission site and the reconstruction of a dynamic facsimile of the subject's face at a remote receiver. The physically-based facial model (see Section 19.3.1.3) suggests that a good foundation for facial image analysis is the anatomy of the face, especially the arrangements and actions of the primary facial muscles. Our first step has been to consider the problem of estimating dynamic facial muscle contractions from video sequences of expressive human faces (Terzopoulos and Waters 1990b,c). The challenge is to extract facial features and track their nonrigid motions in the image plane. We use snakes (see section 19.3.2.1) to estimate the position of the head and to track the nonrigid motions of the eyebrows, nasal furrows, mouth, and jaw in the image plane. Using the snake-derived measurements, we can estimate dynamic facial muscle contractions. These estimates make appropriate control parameters for resynthesizing facial expressions through our face model. The estimation procedure can form the basis of a performance driven facial animation technique which reproduces the facial expressions of an actor from video input.

19.3.3. Data Interpolation, Approximation, and Interpretation

Another important application area for deformable models is in data analysis. Examples are the fitting of surfaces to gridded and scattered data, adaptive sampling and reconstruction, and geophysical and biomedical data interpretation.

19.3.3.1. Fitting Surfaces to Scattered Data

Deformable models are applicable to the multivariate approximation of functions from large quantities of scattered data (noisy samples of an unknown function and its derivatives), a problem of significant practical importance in various engineering fields (Terzopoulos 1986, 1988). Surface fitting may be stated mathematically as a variational problem which has an intuitive physical interpretation. The elastic energy of a deformable surface model plays the role of a (regularization) constraint which requires the fitted surface to vary smoothly. Springs connected from the data points to the surface impart forces which deflect the surface from its nominally planar state. The surface attains an equilibrium, fitted shape consistent with the scattered height or slope data. The stiffness of each spring is proportional to the accuracy of the associated data point. The fitting of *piecewise continuous* surfaces to scattered data is a much more difficult issue. It is addressed by interpreting the physical parameters of the deformable surface model---locally variable rigidity and tension---as local continuity control parameter functions. Detection of discontinuities amounts to identifying the deformable model's distributed continuity parameters from the input data (Terzopoulos 1988).

Local discretization of the surface fitting problem in the multivariate domain is achieved using finite elements. The resulting large, sparse system of quasilinear algebraic equations presents severe computational difficulties, since it can have dimensionality 10^4--10^6 or greater in practice; however, multigrid methods offer efficient iterative solutions.

19.3.3.2. Stochastic Surface Modeling

The multigrid approach leads to a fast way of computing the constrained fractal formulation described in Section 19.2. The stochastic relaxation algorithm eventually achieves equilibrium, but the convergence can be unacceptable slow in practice. To accelerate convergence, we use course-to-fine relaxation on a multigrid pyramid. Equilibrium is first attained on a course grid and it serves as an initial condition for relaxation on the next finer grid. Aside from computer vision, the deterministic and stochastic surface fitting algorithms have been applied to problems in digital cartography. For example, we have applied constrained fractals to reconstruct and synthesize realistic terrain models from sparse elevation data (Szeliski and Terzopoulos 1989).

19.3.3.3. Adaptive Sampling and Reconstruction

The confluence of discrete deformable models with ideas from numerical grid generation has led to the development of adaptive mesh models that nonuniformly sample and reconstruct input data (Terzopoulos and Vasilescu 1991). Adaptive meshes are assembled from nodal masses connected by adjustable springs. Acting as mobile sampling sites, the nodes observe interesting properties of input data, such as gradients and curvatures. The springs automatically adjust their stiffnesses based on the locally sampled information in order to concentrate nodes near rapid shape variations. Thus, an adaptive mesh optimally distributes the available degrees of freedom in accordance with the local complexity of the input data. We have applied adaptive meshes to image compression and reconstruction. Another important application area is automatic geometric mesh generation from densely sampled data acquired by scanning objects with range sensors. A recent example of this is the construction of nonuniform facial meshes from range images of faces (Terzopoulos and Waters 1991).

19.3.3.4. Geophysical Applications

Physically-based deformable modeling techniques and fast surface and volume rendering have been incorporated into an interactive environment aimed at facilitating the visualization and interpretation of multidimensional geophysical data, such as seismic surveys. A general problem of interest is the modeling and visualization of 3D stratified structures. A first step has been to apply snakes to the 2D problem of localizing "horizons" in seismic data slices and tracking them over subsequent slices to trace out 3D subsurfaces (Waters and Terzopoulos 1990a). The deterministic and stochastic deformable surface approximation techniques mentioned above are of general interest in addressing the 3D problem directly (Terzopoulos and Waters 1990a). We have also developed a 3D stratified model that combines geometric and physically-based deformation and promises to be useful for representing a wide variety of layered geological structures. The model represents free-form geometric deformations in terms of tensor product splines, which the user may modify by displacing points of a 3D control mesh. The user may also produce physically-based deformations by applying simulated forces to the model. We have included elastic deformations simulated by a layered assembly of hexahedral, isoparametric finite elements with adjustable elastic properties. The results to date demonstrate the potential power of deformable models in geophysical modeling and interpretation.

19.3.3.5. Biomedical Application

Deformable models offer promise new techniques for modeling the complex free-form shapes of many biological structures and the shape deformations that such structures undergo over time. For example, to study the relationship between nerve cell morphology and function, neuroscientists need accurate three-dimensional models of nerve cells that facilitate detailed anatomical measurement and the identification of internal substructures. Serial transmission electron microscopy has been a source of such models since the mid 1960s, but model reconstruction and analysis remains incredibly time consuming. Deformable models offer a more efficient approach to reconstructing and visualizing 3D nerve cell models from serial microscopy. Carlbom et al. (1991) describe a prototype interactive system that promises to significantly reduce the time required to build such models. The key ingredients of the system are a digital "blink comparator" for section registration, snake models (see Section 3.2.1) for semi-automated cell segmentation, and voxel-based techniques for 3D reconstruction and visualization of complex cell volumes with internal structures. By exploiting interactive deformable models it may be possible to reduce the effort required to reconstruct and analyze a complete dendrite from a few months to a few days. Applications of deformable models to other biomedical problems such as the reconstruction of dynamic 3D models of the heart from computer tomography data of the chest are currently underway.

19.4. Conclusion

This chapter has surveyed the author's research on deformable models, a class of physically-based primitives that have been developed for the modeling and animation of nonrigid computer graphics objects. Curve, surface, and solid deformable models are governed by the mechanical principles of continuous bodies whose shapes can change over time. These primitives are capable of a variety of behaviors, including elasticity, viscoelasticity, plasticity, fracture, conductive heat transfer, thermoplasticity, melting, and fluid-like behavior in the molten state. Several formulations of deformable models have been reviewed and three application areas have been investigated---graphics modeling and animation, computer vision, and data analysis.

Deformable models have been applied extensively to the synthesis of realistic images and animations of nonrigid objects from simple flags to complex expressive faces. Simulating deformable models in virtual worlds at interactive rates suggests interesting new scenarios for physically-based shape design. The usefulness of physically-based deformable modeling techniques has also been demonstrated in computer vision, the "inverse graphics" problem of reconstructing shape models from naturally acquired images. Deformable models and associated physically-based graphics and vision techniques are poised to revolutionize the analysis and visualization of complex multidimensional data sets, including biomedical and geophysical volume data.

Acknowledgements

The author is a fellow of the Canadian Institute for Advanced Research. The research surveyed in this chapter has benefited from contributions by Ingrid Carlbom, Kurt Fleischer, Michael Kass, Dimitri Metaxas, John Platt, Richard Szeliski, Manuela Vasilescu, Keith Waters, and Andrew Witkin, and from discussions with many others. Carl Feynman generously assisted with massively parallel implementations on the CM-2. The support of Schlumberger Corporation and the Natural Sciences and Engineering Research Council of Canada is gratefully acknowledged.

References

Carlbom I, Terzopoulos D, Harris KM, (1991) Reconstructing and Visualizing Models of Neuronal Dendrites, *Proc. Computer Graphics International* (CGI'91), Cambridge, MA, June.

Celniker G (1991) Deformable Curve and Surface Finite Elements for Free-form Shape Design, *Proc. SIGGRAPH '91, Computer Graphics*, Vol.25.

Chadwick JE, Haumann, D.R, Parent, R.E (1989) Layered Construction for Animated Deformable Characters, *Proc. SIGGRAPH '89, Computer Graphics*, Vol.23, No3, pp.243-252.

Feynman CR (1986) *Modeling the Appearance of Cloth*, MSc Thesis, Dept. of Electrical Engineering and Computer Science, MIT, Cambridge, MA.

Fleischer K, Witkin A, Kass M, Terzopoulos, D (1987) Cooking with Kurt, in *ACM SIGGRAPH Video Review*, Issue 36: SIGGRAPH '87 Film and Video Show.

Gourret JP, Magnenat Thalmann N, Thalmann D (1989) Simulation of Object and Human Skin Deformations in a Grasping Task, *Proc. SIGGRAPH '89, Computer Graphics*, Vol.23, No3, pp.21-30.

Haumann D (1987) Modeling the Physical Behavior of Flexible Objects, in: Barr A et al. (eds) *Topics in Physically-Based Modeling*, ACM SIGGRAPH '87 Course Notes, Vol. 17.

Kass M, Miller G (1990) Rapid, Stable Fluid Dynamics for Computer Graphics, *Proc. SIGGRAPH '90, Computer Graphics*, Vol.24, No4, pp.49-57,.

Kass M, Witkin A, Terzopoulos D (1987) Snakes: Active Contour Models, *International Journal of Computer Vision*, Vol.1, No4, pp.321-331.

Kunii TL, Gotoda H (1990) Singularity Theoretical Modeling and Animation of Garment Wrinkle Formation Processes, *The Visual Computer*, 6(6), pp.326-336.

Lundin D (1987) Ruminations of a Model Maker, *IEEE Computer Graphics and Applications*, Vol.7, No5, pp.3-5.

Metaxas D, Terzopoulos D (1991) Constrained Deformable Superquadrics and Nonrigid Motion Tracking, *Proc. Computer Vision and Pattern Recognition Conference* (CVPR-91), Maui, HI, June.

Miller G (1988) The Motion Dynamics of Snakes and Worms, *Proc. SIGGRAPH '89, Computer Graphics*, Vol.22, No4, pp.169-178.

Miller G, Pearce A (1989) Globular Dynamics: A Connected Particle System for Animating Viscous Fluids, in: Barr A et al. (eds) *Topics in Physically-Based Modeling*, ACM SIGGRAPH '87 Course Notes Vol. 30.

Pentland A, Williams J (1989) Good vibrations: Modal Dynamics for Graphics and Animation, *Proc. SIGGRAPH '89, Computer Graphics*, Vol.23, No3, pp.215-222.

Pieper S (1989) *More than Skin Deep: Physical Modeling of Facial Tissue*, MSc Thesis, Media Laboratory, MIT, Cambridge, MA.

Platt J (1989) *Constraint Methods for Neural Networks and Computer Graphics*, PhD Thesis, Dept. of Computer Science, California Institute of Technology, Pasadena, CA (Caltech-CS-TR-89-07).

Platt J, Barr A (1988) Constraint Methods for Flexible Models, *Proc. SIGGRAPH '88, Computer Graphics*, Vol.22, No4, pp.279-288.

Platt SM, Badler NI (1981) Animating Facial Expressions, *Proc. SIGGRAPH '81, Computer Graphics*, Vol.15, No3, pp.245-252.

Sims K (1990) Particle Animation and Rendering using Data Parallel Computation, *Proc. SIGGRAPH '90, Computer Graphics*, Vol.24, No4, pp.405-413.

Szeliski R, Terzopoulos D (1989) From Splines to Fractals, *Proc. SIGGRAPH '89, Computer Graphics*, Vol.23, No3, pp.51-60.

Terzopoulos, D (1986) Regularization of Inverse Visual Problems Involving Discontinuities, *IEEE Transactions on Pattern Analysis and Machine Intelligence*, Vol.8, No4, 413-424.

Terzopoulos, D (1988) The Computation of Visible-Surface Representations, *IEEE Transactions on Pattern Analysis and Machine Intelligence*, Vol.10, No4, pp.417-438.

Terzopoulos, D, Fleischer, K (1988a) Modeling Inelastic Deformation: Viscoelasticity, Plasticity, Fracture, *Proc. SIGGRAPH '88, Computer Graphics*, Vol.22, No4, pp.269-278.

Terzopoulos D, Fleischer K (1988b) Deformable Models, *The Visual Computer*, Vol.4, No6, pp.306-331.

Terzopoulos D, Metaxas D (1991) Dynamic Models with Local and Global Deformations: Deformable superquadrics, *IEEE Transactions on Pattern Analysis and Machine Intelligence*.

Terzopoulos D, Vasilescu M (1991) Sampling and Reconstruction with Adaptive Meshes, *Proc. Computer Vision and Pattern Recognition Conference* (CVPR-91), Maui, HI, June.

Terzopoulos D, Waters K (1990a) An Algorithm for Reconstructing Faulted Subsurfaces from Scattered Data, *Proc. Schlumberger Software Conference* (SSC'90), Austin, TX, March, pp.2.245-2.250.

Terzopoulos D, Waters K (1990b) Physically-Based Facial Modeling, Analysis, and Animation, *The Journal of Visualization and Computer Animation*, Vol.1, No2, pp.73-80.

Terzopoulos D, Waters K (1990c) Analysis of Dynamic Facial Images using Physical and Anatomical Models, *Proc. Third International Conf. on Computer Vision* (ICCV'90) Osaka, Japan, December, pp.727-732.

Terzopoulos D, Waters K (1991) Techniques for Realistic Facial Modeling and Animation, *Proc. Computer Animation '91*, Springer-Verlag, Tokyo, pp.59-74.

Terzopoulos D, Witkin A (1988) Physically-based Models with Rigid and Deformable Components, *IEEE Computer Graphics and Applications*, Vol.8, No6, pp.41-51.

Terzopoulos D, Platt J, Fleischer K (1991) Heating and Melting Deformable Models, *The Journal of Visualization and Computer Animation*, Vol.2, No2, (see, also, Proc. Graphics Interface '89).

Terzopoulos D, Witkin A, Kass M (1988) Constraints on Deformable Models: Recovering 3D Shape and Nonrigid Motion, *Artificial Intelligence*, Vol.36, No1, pp.91-123.

Terzopoulos D, Platt J, Barr A, Fleischer K (1987) Elastically Deformable Models, *Proc. SIGGRAPH '87, Computer Graphics*, Vol.21, No4, 1987, pp.205-214.

Terzopoulos D, Platt J, Barr A, Zeltzer D, Witkin A, Blinn J (1989) Physically-Based Modeling: Past Present and Future, *SIGGRAPH '89 Panel Proc., Computer Graphics*, Vol.23, No5, pp.191-209.

Tonnesen D (1991) Modeling Liquids and Solids using Thermal Particles, *Proc. Graphics Interface'91*, Calgary, AL, June.

Waters K, Terzopoulos D (1990a) Interactive Visualization and Interpretation of 3D Geophysical Data on a Graphics Superworkstation, *Proc. Schlumberger Software Conference* (SSC'90), Austin, TX, pp.2.329-2.334.

Waters K, Terzopoulos D (1990b) A Physical Model of Facial Tissue and Muscle Articulation, *Proc. First Conf. on Visualization in Biomedical Computing* (VBC'90), Atlanta, GA, pp.77-82.

Witkin A, Welch W (1990) Fast Animation and Control of Nonrigid Structures, *Proc. SIGGRAPH '90, Computer Graphics*, Vol.24, No3, pp.243-252.